Performance and the
Middle English Romance

Studies in Medieval Romance

ISSN 1479–9308

General Editor
Corinne Saunders

Editorial Board
Roger Dalrymple   Rhiannon Purdie   Robert Allen Rouse

This series aims to provide a forum for critical studies of the medieval romance, a genre which plays a crucial role in literary history, clearly reveals medieval secular concerns, and raises complex questions regarding social structures, human relationships, and the psyche. Its scope extends from the early Middle Ages into the Renaissance period, and although its main focus is on English literature, comparative studies are welcomed.

Proposals or queries should be sent in the first instance to one of the addresses given below; all submissions will receive prompt and informed consideration.

Professor Corinne Saunders, Department of English,
University of Durham, Durham, DH1 3AY

Boydell & Brewer Limited, PO Box 9, Woodbridge, Suffolk, IP12 3DF

Previously published volumes in the series are listed at the back of this book.

Performance and the Middle English Romance

Linda Marie Zaerr

D. S. BREWER

First published 2012
D. S. Brewer, Cambridge

ISBN 978 1 84384 323 8

D. S. Brewer is an imprint of Boydell & Brewer Ltd
PO Box 9, Woodbridge, Suffolk, IP12 3DF, UK
and of Boydell & Brewer Inc.
668 Mount Hope Ave, Rochester, NY 14620–2731, USA
website: www.boydellandbrewer.com

A CIP catalogue record for this book is available
from the British Library

The publisher has no responsibility for the continued existence or accuracy
of URLs for external or third-party internet websites referred to in this book,
and does not guarantee that any content on such websites is,
or will remain, accurate or appropriate.

Papers used by Boydell & Brewer Ltd are natural, recyclable products
made from wood grown in sustainable forests

Designed and typeset in Adobe Minion Pro by
David Roberts, Pershore, Worcestershire

Printed and bound by
CPI Group (UK) Ltd, Croydon, CR0 4YY

Contents

Musical Examples

To my Family

Acknowledgements

I AM deeply grateful that this book emerged, not in dreary isolation, but from a community so vibrant and inspiring that the meticulous assembling, sorting, thinking, and writing were a delight.

Two colleagues have been crucial in the development of this book. Míceál Vaughan generously read the entire manuscript and responded with a balanced perspective that guided me in reframing the terms of the discussion. Timothy McGee read the chapters most directly engaged with music and provided both detailed suggestions and several overall observations that contributed to making the book more useful. Moreover, he provided a fiddle of his own construction, a beautiful instrument which allowed me to broaden my experiments and compare Jerome of Moravia's tunings on three different fiddles of varying construction. Nicole Clifton, Maria Dobozy, and James Wade also read chapters, and all of them offered insightful comments that reached beyond the chapters they read. Evelyn Birge Vitz, who has worked together with me for many years, encouraged me in the initial stages of my proposal. I am fortunate to have such colleagues; they make this profession a joy.

I am also indebted to my performance companions, especially my sister Laura Zaerr, a skilled and sensitive harpist who creates symbiotic performances in heartfelt partnership. Fiddle player Shira Kammen converted me to the medieval fiddle, and she continues to inspire me with her playing and delightful collaboration. I have also benefited from working in long-term partnership with Joseph Baldassarre, Aage Nielsen, Corey McKnight, Gail Vaughan, Thomas Talboy, and Dwayne Blackaller. I have learned much from them of the varying ways text and music can interact.

The family I grew up in prepared me to encounter medieval romance. My father told me stories, my mother read them to me, my sister and I created them together, and my brother broadened our world. Our feasts resounded with songs and instrumental music from 'Bile Them Cabbages Down, Boys' to the 'Trout' Quintet. All of my original family continue to be involved with my work, and I am particularly grateful to my mother, Lois Marie Zaerr, for setting the musical examples for this book.

This book would not have been possible without the support of my husband Mark Jost, who keeps me grounded and provides sensible responses my work in preparation; and my nine-year-old daughter Laura, who dwells with me among stories and songs and improvises in Dorian mode.

Many others have offered help and encouragement. Boydell & Brewer editor Caroline Palmer provided sound suggestions from a broad base of publishing experience, the anonymous reader responded with insightful suggestions and welcome encouragement, and music editor David Roberts offered timely advice on the musical examples. My students have been a continual source of inspiration and fresh perspectives, as have the members of the Medieval Society, especially Lee Ann Turner, who shares many of the same experiences, and Amy Brueggemann, who helped with the index. Boise State University has supported me throughout, and the Department of English, in particular, has been gracious in taking over responsibilities while I immersed myself in this project. Finally I thank the kind and generous librarians I have encountered over so many years in my pursuit of romance manuscripts and books with uncut pages, and especially the interlibrary loan office at my university for their creative acquisition of obscure works.

Abbreviations

ANTS	Anglo-Norman Text Society
BEC	*Bibliothèque de l'École des chartes*
BL	British Library
BN	Bibliothèque nationale
CUL	Cambridge University Library
EETS ES	Early English Text Society Extra Series
EETS OS	Early English Text Society Original Series
METS	Middle English Text Series
PMLA	*Publications of the Modern Language Association*
REED	*Records of Early English Drama*
SATF	Société des Anciens Texts Français
TEAMS	The Consortium for the Teaching of the Middle Ages

Where references to romance titles and line numbers would interrupt the flow of the text, citations are placed in endnotes.

Introduction

> Menstrelles that walken fer and wyde,
> Her and ther in every a syde,
> In mony a dyverse londe,
> Sholde, at her bygynnyng,
> Speke of that ryghtwes kyng
> That made both see and sonde.
> Who-so wylle a stounde dwelle,
> Of mykyll myrght y may you telle,
> And mornyng ther a-monge;
> Of a lady fayr and fre,
> Her name was called Emare,
> As I here synge in songe.
>
> (Emare, lines 13–24)[1]

(Minstrels, who walk far and wide, here and there in every direction, in many different lands; these minstrels should begin [as I have] by speaking of that righteous king who made both sea and sand. If you will linger a while, I may tell you of great mirth mingled with mourning, of a fair and gracious lady called Emaré, as I here sing in song [*or* as I hear sung in song].)

T HE Middle English romances create a performance context for themselves, and the use of modern historical performance can provide a tool to explore and inform theories that have until now been based largely on examination of texts. Much has been done in the last three decades to understand the manuscript tradition of English medieval romances more fully and to acknowledge its textuality; however, the minstrel tradition of the romances, because it is more elusive, has been largely ignored. Yet evidence does exist that offers a realistic and grounded understanding of minstrel performance of narrative. The object of this book is to integrate current textual, musicological, and cultural scholarship with a performer's perspective on how English minstrels performed romances with music, and to explore how that musical dimension illuminates some of the extant romances. This work has direct implications for the study of the prosody of Middle English romances. It also affects studies of transmission and reception, and should contribute to the discussion of characteristics of the popular romance.

---

[1] Passages from the Middle English romances are quoted from the editions listed in the Bibliography.

The Middle English Romance – 'Sum Farand Thinge Eftir Fode'

The Middle English romances are notorious for their diversity, encompassing accounts of historical battles and stories of beneficent lions and werewolves; alliterative long lines, couplets, tail-rhyme stanzas, and prose; stories with strong religious perspectives, and stories with strong chivalric perspectives; tales of love and tales of war. Some patterns can be traced among the romances, many of which are based on Continental or Insular French sources. They often present a world unbound by mundane time and place, often tinged with the exotic. The characters are almost always drawn from the nobility and marked by idealism, and the plots most commonly have happy endings. Often an individual hero or heroine is faced with a set of challenges or a task.

The romances have been subdivided in a variety of ways. The touchstone for all study of the subject, the *Romances* volume of *A Manual of the Writings in Middle English, 1050–1500*, classifies the material according to subject.[2] Dieter Mehl in his influential reassessment of the genre divides the texts according to length, with an additional category for 'homiletic romances'.[3] Metre has frequently been used to distinguish among couplet, alliterative, and tail-rhyme romances, leading to such focused studies as Rhiannon Purdie's discussion of tail-rhyme as a uniquely English form.[4] The diversity in approaches to the Middle English romance rivals the diversity of the works themselves.[5]

Yet the genre resists definition and categorization, and most recent discussions have moved toward a fluid understanding of the romances. Ad Putter suggests that 'we should think of them as forming a complex network of relationships and similarities, not as a set that can be defined on the basis of specific properties common to each of its members.'[6] A similar flexibility is implied in Yin Liu's notion, drawn from cognitive linguistics, of a 'prototype genre', in which the category of romance 'is defined not by its boundary but by its best examples (its prototypes)'.[7] In her discussion of romance, Helen Cooper observes, 'The romance genre – any genre, indeed – is best thought of as a lineage or a family of texts rather than a series of incarnations or clones of a single Platonic Idea.'[8]

[2] J. Burke Severs, ed., *A Manual of the Writings in Middle English, 1050–1500*, 1: *Romances* (New Haven, CT: Connecticut Academy of Arts and Sciences, 1967).

[3] Dieter Mehl, *The Middle English Romances of the Thirteenth and Fourteenth Centuries* (London: Routledge & Kegan Paul, 1968).

[4] Rhiannon Purdie, *Anglicising Romance: Tail-Rhyme and Genre in Medieval English Literature* (Cambridge: D. S. Brewer, 2008).

[5] For a discussion of earlier critical reception of the Middle English romance, see Joanne A. Rice, *Middle English Romance: An Annotated Bibliography, 1955–1985* (New York and London: Garland Publishing, 1987), pp. xviii–xxiii.

[6] Ad Putter and Jane Gilbert, eds, *The Spirit of Medieval English Popular Romance* (Harlow: Pearson Education, 2000), p. 2.

[7] Yin Liu, 'Middle English Romance as Prototype Genre', *The Chaucer Review* 40.4 (2006): 335–53, at p. 338.

[8] Helen Cooper, *The English Romance in Time: Transforming Motifs from Geoffrey of Monmouth to the Death of Shakespeare* (Oxford: Oxford University Press, 2004), p. 8.

If we extend the notion of a 'network of relationships' further, we should include not just the verbal texts that survive in our manuscripts, but also the irrecoverable instances of such texts performed with music by minstrels, stories that may intersect and overlap with the literary artefacts in a number of ways but which are not available to us for direct analysis. No textual record of such performances is possible, so we should not look for one or be surprised not to find one. Performances are ephemeral – and fundamentally unique.

This broader notion of romance is supported by the term itself, derived from the Old French *romanz*, the language of the people; by extension romances are stories available to the 'lewede' as well as the learned, whether courtly, bourgeois, or other. The romances are not written for scholars, though they may be quite sophisticated and demand perspicacity in their audiences.[9]

The beginning of the fourteenth-century *Richard Coer de Lyon* applies this concept in an English context. The original stories are created in French, but many people do not understand French. The 'lewede' (who do not know French and may not be able to read) still want to hear noble tales, stories (such as this one) about knights from England (told in the language of the people of England):

> Ffele romaunses men maken newe,
> Off goode knyghtes, stronge and trewe;
> Off here dedys men rede romaunce,
> Bothe in Engeland and in Ffraunce:
> Off Rowelond, and off Olyver,
> And off every Doseper;
> Off Alisaundre, and Charlemayn;
> Off kyng Arthour, and off Gawayn,
> How they were knyghtes goode and curteys;
> Off Turpyn, and of Oger Daneys;
> Off Troye men rede in ryme,
> What werre ther was in olde tyme;
> Off Ector, and off Achylles,
> What folk they slowe in that pres.
> In Frenssche bookys this rym is wrought,
> Lewede men ne know it nought –
> Lewede men cune Ffrensch non,
> Among an hondryd unnethis on –;
> Nevertheles, with glad chere,
> Ffele off hem that wolde here
> Noble jestes, I undyrstonde,
> Off doughty knyghtes off Yngelonde.
>
> (lines 7–28)

---

[9] The question of audience has formed the basis of numerous studies. Two recent collections of essays on popular romance in medieval England address topics relating to this issue in terms of specific texts: Putter and Gilbert, *Spirit of Medieval English Popular Romance*; and Nicola McDonald, ed., *Pulp Fictions of Medieval England: Essays in Popular Romance* (Manchester: Manchester University Press, 2004).

(People create many new romances about good knights, who are strong and true. Both in England and France people read about their deeds in romances: about Roland and Oliver and all the paladins; about Alexander and Charlemagne; about King Arthur and Gawain, how they were good and courteous knights; about Turpin and the Danish Oger. People read about Troy in rhyme and about the war that happened there long ago, about Hector and Achilles and the people they slew in the press of battle. This rhyming verse is written down in French books. Uneducated people do not understand it; scarcely one among a hundred knows French. Nevertheless, I recognize that many of them are eager to hear noble gestes about doughty knights of England.)

The idea of romance is here reinscribed in terms that make sense even for mono-lingual speakers of Middle English, preserving the awareness of an audience who wants entertainment rather than something they have to work to understand. Similarly, in *Partonope of Blois* we are told that the unlearned can benefit from hearing stories, either sung or told in ordinary language:

> To the lewed also, parde,
> Is goode sum-tyme for to here.
> For by herynge he may lere
> Thynge that fryste he ne knewe;
> And to soche folke olde thynge ys new,
> Whanne hyt ys in gestes songe,
> Or els in prose tolde wyth tonge.
>
> (lines 21–7)

(It is good, by God, for an unlearned person sometimes to hear [stories], for by hearing he may learn something that he did not know before, and to such people an old thing is new when it is sung in a *geste* or else told with the tongue in ordinary language.)

We do not have access to the romances *as* they were performed in the thirteenth through fifteenth centuries, and we never will. It is vital, however, not to discount the existence of minstrel versions simply because we cannot see them. We have historical evidence that romances were performed and evidence of a familial relationship between those performed tales and the written versions we know. We can, furthermore, learn much about the nature of the lost performances by looking at their textual relatives.

As Derek Pearsall has acutely pointed out, tracing a historical morphology of romance involves 'the assembling and reconciliation of evidence as to date, dialect, manuscript provenance, metrical form, exact class of audience, type of source, type of story and range of art', a task complicated 'by the ambiguous or disputed nature of much of this evidence'.[10] His adjuration to sort out the details

---

[10] Derek Persall, 'The Development of the Middle English Romance', *Mediaeval Studies* 27 (1965): 91–116, at pp. 95–6.

has been admirably followed, as evidenced by numerous solid tools for studying manuscripts containing Middle English romances,[11] facsimiles of romance manuscripts,[12] analyses of particular manuscript collections,[13] treatments of specific romances,[14] and discussions of contexts for romance.[15]

Yet in a study of romance performance, these textual features and alliances, while still important, take on a more ancillary function. A performance may be influenced by a text much removed in time and place, and similarly performances may inspire textual modifications, though not necessarily in terms that would be classified as 'transmission'. For example, a scribe, remembering a performance, may be motivated to adjust a text in subtle or indirect ways. In an attempt to find information about performance of narrative in medieval England, the romance texts are useful as a body of material that limns a minstrel tradition (whether reliably or not), and as a group of texts that presents similar subject matter to what minstrels inferentially performed, including verse forms minstrels most likely employed.

Since there is a family of Middle English romance texts, it would prove helpful to include all the members we know. Despite the generic complexity and the tendency of the romances themselves to include unexpected items, there is surprising agreement among lists of romances. Severs, Mehl, and Rice diverge in very few entries, and they have provided the foundation for most subsequent treatments. Consequently, I have formulated a list of eighty-three verse romances to consider in this book. I do not consider the works of Chaucer, Gower, and Lydgate because they draw on romance conventions to achieve something other than romance. Similarly I have excluded the prose romances on the grounds that they are too far removed from musical performance. The verse romances

---

[11] See, for example, Gisela Guddat-Figge's essential *Catalogue of Manuscripts Containing Middle English Romances*, Münchener Universitätschriften 4 (Munich: Wilhelm Fink, 1976); and Murray J. Evans, *Rereading Middle English Romance: Manuscript Layout, Decoration, and the Rhetoric of Composite Structure* (Montreal: McGill-Queen's University Press, 1995).

[12] Notably Derek Pearsall and I. C. Cunningham's facsimile edition of *The Auchinleck Manuscript: National Library of Scotland Advocates' MS. 19.2.1* (London: Scolar Press, 1977); and D. S. Brewer and A. E. B. Owen's facsimile edition of *The Thornton Manuscript (Lincoln Cathedral MS.91)* (London: Scolar Press, 1975). The National Library of Scotland has also produced a digital facsimile of the Auchinleck Manuscript at <http://auchinleck.nls.uk/> (7 June 2011).

[13] A few examples include John J. Thompson, *Robert Thornton and the London Thornton Manuscript: British Library MS 31042* (Cambridge: D. S. Brewer, 1987); Lynne Blanchfield, "The Romances in MS Ashmole 61: An Idiosyncratic Scribe', in *Romance in Medieval England*, ed. Maldwyn Mills, Jennifer Fellows, and Carol M. Meale (Cambridge: D. S. Brewer, 1991), pp. 65–88; and Ralph Hanna, 'Reconsidering the Auchinleck Manuscript', in *New Directions in Later Medieval Manuscript Studies: Essays from the 1998 Harvard Conference*, ed. Derek Pearsall (Woodbridge: York Medieval Press, 2000), pp. 91–102.

[14] Most recently, see Jennifer Fellows and Ivana Djordjevic, eds, *Sir Bevis of Hampton in Literary Tradition* (Woodbridge: D. S. Brewer, 2008); and Alison Wiggins and Rosalind Field, *Guy of Warwick: Icon and Ancestor* (Woodbridge: D. S. Brewer, 2007).

[15] See Rhiannon Purdie and Michael Cichon, eds, *Medieval Romance, Medieval Contexts* (Woodbridge: D. S. Brewer, 2011).

themselves, looked at as a whole, provide useful information in the study of minstrel performance.

The Minstrels and the Critics

Minstrels rank with dragons and enchantresses in the realm of Middle English romance. They have taken on an almost mythical status in discussions, to the extent that those who believe in minstrel presentation of romance are termed 'romantic'.[16] Although most scholars now acknowledge that minstrels 'helped to define, legitimate, and even romanticize'[17] romance performance, there is still no unified collection of documents relating to that study, and the meticulous care in gathering and collating detailed information and working out a comprehensive understanding of complex relationships that has been applied to other branches of scholarship on romance, has not yet been applied in this area.

The origin of this neglect goes back to the early days of scholarly interest in medieval romance in England, when, in 1765, Thomas Percy published his popular *Reliques of Ancient English Poetry*, expressing a kind of horrified fascination with minstrels, who 'seem to have been the genuine successors of the ancient Bards, who united the arts of Poetry and Music, and sung verses to the harp, of their own composing'.[18] He surmised:

> tho' some of them only recited the compositions of others, many of them still composed songs themselves, and all of them could probably invent a few stanzas on occasion. I have no doubt but most of the old heroic ballads in this collection were produced by this order of men. For altho' some of the larger metrical romances might come from the pens of the monks or others, yet the smaller narratives were probably composed by the Minstrels who sung them.[19]

He saw the minstrel as a 'privileged character'[20] in medieval society, though by the time of Elizabeth I, they 'had lost much of their dignity, and were sinking into contempt and neglect'.[21]

Joseph Ritson, in his anthology of *Ancient Songs from the Time of Henry the Third to the Revolution*, positioned himself in direct opposition to Percy, pointing out that entertainment in Norman courts would have been in French, and therefore could not represent a continuous English tradition.[22] He characterized minstrels

---

[16] See Putter and Gilbert, *Spirit of Medieval English Popular Romance*; and George Shuffelton, 'Is There a Minstrel in the House?: Domestic Entertainment in Late Medieval England', *Philological Quarterly* 87.1–2 (2008): 51–76.

[17] Shuffelton, 'Domestic Entertainment', p. 70.

[18] 'An Essay on the Ancient Minstrels', in Thomas Percy, *Reliques of Ancient English Poetry*, 3 vols (Dublin: P. Wilson and E. Watts, 1766), vol. 1, pp. xi–xx, at p. xi.

[19] Percy, *Reliques*, vol. 1, p. xii.

[20] Percy, *Reliques*, vol. 1, p. xiii.

[21] Percy, *Reliques*, vol. 1, p. xv.

[22] 'Observations on the Ancient Minstrels', in Joseph Ritson, *Ancient Songs from the Time of Henry the Third to the Revolution* (London: J. Johnson, 1790), vol. 1, pp. i–xxvi, at p. ii.

as 'twanging and scraping',[23] and connected John of Gaunt's minstrel court with 'the most shocking and brutal barbarity'.[24] He concluded that '[t]he art of printing was fatal to the Minstrels who sung; people begun [*sic*] to read, and, unfortunately for the Minstrels, their compositions would not bear reading'. Unlike ballads, which 'were smooth and regular' and 'united to a simple but pleasing melody', the minstrel songs 'were without tune, and could not be performed, even by themselves, without the twang of a harp, or the scrape of a fiddle'.[25]

Despite numerous inaccuracies in Ritson's material, heirs of his debunking argument for a degraded historical minstrel came to be associated with more rigorous scholarship, and heirs of Percy's exuberant delight in a native minstrel tradition became linked with unwillingness to examine beyond surface appearances.

The two figures shared a preference for the values of their own era, and united in regarding medieval romances as containing 'all the monstrous extravagances of wild imagination, unguided by judgment and uncorrected by art'.[26] Ritson went further in stating that we have nothing more than 'a few rude ballads', and '[n]ot a single piece is extant in which an English Minstrel speaks of himself'.[27] It is intriguing to find that a significant part of his case against artistic integrity in the medieval minstrel rested on the assertion that the term 'minstrel' in English 'implied an instrumental performer, and generally a fidler, or such like base musician'.[28] His phrasing goes beyond the obvious observation that words must be articulated in romance performance; a singer, for Ritson, is morally superior to a mere instrumentalist, and a harper is superior to a fiddler.[29]

This initial controversy set the terms for subsequent discussion of romance, and that conversation was lodged in a dispute about performance. For example, E. K. Chambers, like Percy, argued that minstrels went underground after the Norman Conquest, 'and that they pursue a more or less subterranean career until the fourteenth century brings the English tongue to its own again'.[30] He addressed the cultural gulf between the English and Anglo-Norman traditions by suggesting, first, that the 'native English Gleemen were eclipsed at courts by the Taillefers and Raheres of the invading host', though they continued often as a 'mouthpiece of popular discontent'; and, second, that they 'learnt to mingle with their Anglo-Norman *confrères*: they borrowed the themes of Continental minstrelsy, translating *roman*, *fabliau* and *chanson* into the metres and dialects of the vernacular.'[31]

---

[23] Ritson, *Ancient Songs*, p. vi.

[24] Ritson, *Ancient Songs*, p. ix.

[25] Ritson, *Ancient Songs*, p. xvii.

[26] 'On the Ancient Metrical Romances', in Percy, *Reliques*, vol. 3, pp. i–xxiv, at p. ii.

[27] Ritson, *Ancient Songs*, p. xii.

[28] Ritson, *Ancient Songs*, p. xiii.

[29] Ritson, in fact, refutes one of Percy's minstrel examples by asserting that 'women never sung to the harp', *Ancient Songs*, p. viii.

[30] E. K. Chambers, *The Mediaeval Stage*, 2 vols (Oxford: Clarendon Press, 1903), vol. 1, p. 43.

[31] Chambers, *Mediaeval Stage*, pp. 75–6.

On the other side of the controversy, Richard Leighton Greene's influential discussion of the term 'minstrel' explicitly followed Ritson in linking minstrels with instrumental performance to the exclusion of any song, citing in support a few illustrative documents, and observing that only certain instruments are suited to song accompaniment, and minstrels tend to be identified by their instrument.[32] He also noted that 'the musicians' or minstrels' gallery was located at the opposite end of the hall from the high table on floor or dais, and therefore at a distance quite suitable for instrumental music during dinner but ill-adapted to song'.[33]

Both these arguments, and many others ranging on both sides of the controversy, relied heavily on an arrangement of carefully selected documents and literary references. It is not my purpose to provide a comprehensive overview of the debate;[34] instead, I want to look at a few of the more recent developments.

For a few decades, minstrels became an alarming topic. In this climate, Andrew Taylor's pivotal article (1992) made a cogent case for a 'complex and frequently hostile relation between the writer and the performer'.[35] He cemented earlier arguments that the Middle English romances 'are a transitional literature; written for readers, they deliberately evoke an oral heritage'.[36] He went on to grapple realistically with the performance challenges implied by the documents and literary descriptions of minstrel performance, concluding:

> Given these difficulties we must expect that the medieval English *gestour* would have been accustomed to modify his works drastically from one night to another. He could not be bound by a fixed text, even if the text were conveniently divided into shorter units. He needed to adapt the list of heroes to appeal to local sympathies, curtail tedious episodes and omit inappropriate ones, and expand the narrative when his audience gave him ear. Rarely would he have been able to perform a poem of more than a few hundred lines in its entirety. Whatever the *gestours* were reciting, therefore, they cannot, as a general rule, have been reciting the romances, or at least if they were, they must have been in the habit of doing outrageous violence to their texts.[37]

Ironically, this argument, which seems on the surface to dismiss minstrels as irrelevant in relation to the Middle English romance, actually points the way to a more grounded understanding of medieval performance by freeing minstrels

---

[32] Richard Leighton Greene, *The Early English Carols*, 2nd edn (Oxford: Clarendon Press, 1977), pp. cxxv–cxxvi.

[33] Greene, *Early English Carols*, p. cxxxvi.

[34] For a summary of the controversy, see Nancy Mason Bradbury, *Writing Aloud: Storytelling in Late Medieval England* (Urbana: University of Illinois Press, 1998), pp. 1–21; and Mark Amodio, ed., *Oral Poetics in Middle English Poetry* (New York: Garland Publishing, 1994), pp. 1–28.

[35] Andrew Taylor, 'Fragmentation, Corruption, and Minstrel Narration: The Question of the Middle English Romances', *The Yearbook of English Studies* 22 (1992): 38–62, at p. 39.

[36] Taylor, 'Fragmentation', p. 54.

[37] Taylor, 'Fragmentation', p. 58.

from the literal texts extant today. His model helps explain such clerical contempt for minstrels as we find in Robert Mannyng's regret that minstrels don't perform *Sir Tristrem* as Thomas wrote it,[38] and the dissociation of the *Speculum Vitae* (and a number of romances themselves) from the 'vayne carpynge' of 'mynstraylles and iestours'.[39] We see also in the *Piers Plowman* C-text why feast entertainment might not always have been carefully documented by scholars. Here *gestes* and harp and fiddle and other instruments are all grouped with farting:

> Y can nat tabre ne trompy ne telle fayre gestes,
> Farten ne fythelen at festes, ne harpe,
> Jape ne jogele ne genteliche pipe,
> Ne nother sayle ne sautrien ne syngen with the geterne.
> (*Passus* XV, lines 205–8)[40]

(I cannot play the tabor nor the trumpet, nor tell fair *gestes*, fart, nor fiddle at feasts, nor harp, joke nor juggle nor nobly pipe, nor dance, nor psaltery, nor sing with the gittern.)

Clearly, popular performance in late medieval England, as today, was not always highly regarded. A range of musical ability and genre seems evident, and narrative is consistently associated with instruments. As Taylor describes it, minstrel performance was capable of expressing a wide range of artistic integrity and sophistication, and that freedom from textual constraint explains why it was sometimes greeted with suspicion by those who loved books.

Over the centuries, both sides of the minstrel controversy have been tempered into something very like agreement. Ad Putter, after a lucid summary of the debate, effectively reconciles the two perspectives: 'Romances passed easily from the hands of readers to the memories of minstrels or listeners, and from the oral recitations of minstrels or amateurs back into the writings of scribes.'[41] Since most critics today acknowledge a place for minstrel performance of narrative, it is surprising how little substantive work has been done in this area.

In his condensed discussion of Continental narrative music, John Stevens observed, 'To my knowledge no new evidence has turned up and no new

---

[38] Robert Mannyng complains that *Sir Tristrem* would be the best *geste* ever if only people said it the way Thomas made it: 'That may thou here in sir Tristrem,/ ouer gestes it has be steem/ ouer alle that is or was,/ if men it sayd as made Thomas.' (lines 97–100). (Robert Mannyng of Brunne, *The Chronicle*, ed. Idelle Sullens, Medieval and Renaissance Texts and Studies 153 [Binghamton, NY: Center for Medieval and Early Renaissance Studies, 1996].)

[39] Ralph Hanna, ed., *Speculum vitae: A Reading Edition*, 2 vols, EETS 331, 332 (Oxford: Oxford University Press, 2008), lines 36 and 39.

[40] References to *Piers Plowman* are from George Kane, ed., *Piers Plowman: The A Version* (London: Athlone Press/Berkeley: University of California Press, 1988); and George Russell and George Kane, eds, *Piers Plowman: The C Version* (Berkeley: University of California Press, 1997). In the A-text, too, Gluttony contributes to the musical performance at the inn by blowing 'the rounde ryvet at the riggebones ende' (the round horn at the end of the backbone, line 190) and then staggers off 'lik a glemans bicche' (like a gleeman's dog, line 194).

[41] Putter and Gilbert, *Spirit of Medieval English Popular Romance*, p. 13.

hypotheses have been proposed over the last fifteen years.'[42] Since that 2000 article, new evidence for performance that incorporates a musical dimension has emerged in such studies as Carol Symes, *A Common Stage*,[43] and Evelyn Birge Vitz, *et al.*, *Performing Medieval Narrative*.[44] Though growing awareness of a diverse and pervasive performance tradition has also characterized study of Middle English narrative, the paucity of evidence about music has discouraged serious consideration of musical elements in Middle English romance performance. Yet there is evidence of ongoing musical performance of narrative into the sixteenth century in England.[45] Scrutinizing the musical dimension of the romances can illuminate their characteristics more fully and provide a more rounded understanding of the performance context that has been demonstrated to be so crucial.

Historical documents relating to narrative performance with music have not been assembled in a coherent and comprehensive form. John Southworth's book *The English Medieval Minstrel*,[46] brings together useful material and perspectives, though it has been somewhat discredited for its inaccuracies and scanty coverage.[47] A number of excellent studies focus on a particular venue or situation.[48] A few articles address the musical dimension of romance, notably Karl Reichl's well-reasoned discussion of melodic possibilities for extant romances and parallels in Turkic epic poetry performance.[49] The *Records of Early English Drama* series is invaluable for its documentation of a range of performances, but its focus on drama makes it an unwieldy tool for the study of musical performance of narrative.

The textual branches of the Middle English romance family have been studied with increasing clarity, and the practice of reading aloud has been researched and

[42] John Stevens, 'Reflections on the Music of Medieval Narrative Poetry', in *The Oral Epic: Performance and Music*, ed. Karl Reichl, Intercultural Music Studies 12 (Berlin: Verlag für Wissenschaft und Bildung, 2000), pp. 233–48, at p. 246.

[43] Carol Symes, *A Common Stage: Theater and Public Life in Medieval Arras* (Ithaca, NY: Cornell University Press, 2007).

[44] Evelyn Birge Vitz, Nancy Freeman Regalado, and Marilyn Lawrence, eds, *Performing Medieval Narrative* (Cambridge: D. S. Brewer, 2005).

[45] See Michael Chesnutt, 'Minstrel Poetry in an English Manuscript of the Sixteenth Century: Richard Sheale and MS. Ashmole 48', in *The Entertainer in Medieval and Traditional Culture: A Symposium*, ed. Flemming G. Andersen, Thomas Pettitt and Reinhold Schröder (Odense: Odense University Press, 1997), pp. 73–100.

[46] John Southworth, *The English Medieval Minstrel* (Woodbridge: Boydell Press, 1989).

[47] Richard Rastall and Andrew Taylor are currently collaborating on a history of minstrels which promises to provide much fuller and more interdisciplinary coverage.

[48] See, for example, Constance Bullock-Davies, *Menestrellorum Multitudo: Minstrels at a Royal Feast* (Cardiff: University of Wales Press, 1978); Constance Bullock-Davies, *Register of Royal and Baronial Minstrels, 1272–1327* (Woodbridge: Boydell Press, 1986); Richard Rastall, 'The Minstrel Court in Medieval England', *Proceedings of the Leeds Philosophical and Literary Society* 18.1 (1982): 96–105; and Richard Rastall, 'The Minstrels of the English Royal Households, 25 Edward I–1 Henry VIII: An Inventory', *Royal Musical Association Research Chronicle* 4 (1967): 1–41.

[49] Karl Reichl, 'Comparative Notes on the Performance of Middle English Popular Romance', *Western Folklore* 62.1 (2003): 63–81.

explicated.[50] Curiously, although the realities of minstrel performance of romance have not been seriously addressed, evidence of orality in the romances has been considered in some detail.

'This Song I Herde Sing' – Orality in a Broader Cultural Context

In 1982, William A. Quinn and Audley S. Hall, drawing on the oral-formulaic theory developed by Parry and Lord,[51] presented a detailed study of oral improvisation in early Middle English romance,[52] and this led to a number of related studies. Many of the early discussions looked for evidence of improvised composition in the romances. It became apparent, however, that this approach was not fully applicable to the romances because written composition was so fundamentally involved. Turning in another direction, Murray McGillivray found evidence of memorial transmission in the variants of some of the romances.[53] Paul Zumthor also incorporated written dimensions into the study of orality with his concept of *mouvance*, assessing the amplitude of variation among texts.[54] He gave impetus to a recognition of text as a written manifestation of a speech act, and established the significance of physical presence and of gesture in performance of a text.[55] Exploring minstrel performance of the Middle English romances in similar terms, Michael Chesnutt responded to the heterogeneity of the material by proposing 'a structural and stylistic continuum within which each text must be placed according to its degree of conformity with the norms of oral composition.'[56]

In the 1990s two important compilations of essays, *Vox intexta: Orality and Textuality in the Middle Ages* (ed. Doane and Pasterack)[57] and *Oral Tradition in the*

[50] A cogent discussion of the topic is presented in Joyce Coleman, *Public Reading and the Reading Public in Late Medieval England and France* (Cambridge: Cambridge University Press, 1996).

[51] Albert Lord, *The Singer of Tales* (Cambridge, MA: Harvard University Press, 1960); and Milman Parry, *The Making of Homeric Verse. The Collected Papers of Milman Parry*, ed. Adam Parry (Oxford: Clarendon Press, 1982).

[52] William A. Quinn and Audley S. Hall, *Jongleur: A Modified Theory of Oral Improvisation and its Effects on the Performance and Transmission of Middle English Romance* (Washington, DC: University Press of America, 1982).

[53] Murray McGillivray, *Memorization in the Transmission of the Middle English Romances* (New York: Garland Publishing, 1990).

[54] Paul Zumthor, 'Intertextualité et mouvance', *Littérature* 41 (1981): 8–16, at p. 16, concludes that 'une typologie des textes serait concevable, qui les classerait en vertu de la plus ou moins grande amplitude de leur mouvance' (a typology of texts would be conceivable in which they were classified according to the greater or lesser amplitude of their *mouvance*).

[55] Paul Zumthor, 'Les Traditions poétiques', in *Jeux de mémoire: Aspects de la mnémotechnie médiévale*, ed. Bruno Roy and Paul Zumthor (Montréal: Les Presses de l'Université de Montréal, 1985), pp. 11–21; and 'Body and Performance', in *Materialities of Communication*, ed. Hans Ulrich Gumbrecht and K. Ludwig Pfeiffer, trans. William Whobrey (Stanford, CA: Stanford University Press, 1994), pp. 217–26.

[56] Michael Chesnutt, 'Minstrel Reciters and the Enigma of the Middle English Romance', *Culture and History* 2 (1987): 48–67, at p. 64.

[57] Alger Nicolaus Doane and Carol Braun Pasternack, eds., *Vox intexta: Orality and Textuality in the Middle Ages* (Madison: University of Wisconsin Press, 1991).

Middle Ages (ed. Nicolaisen),[58] further clarified the various ways oral dimensions may be reflected in medieval texts. Tim William Machan, in particular, provides a model that is helpful in considering the relationship between the minstrel tradition and the extant English romance manuscripts, suggesting 'that a variety of the conscious alterations effected by scribes as they "copied" texts are similar to the changes made by oral poets as they re-create songs – that a model of improvisation can describe the performance qualities of both oral poets and scribes'.[59]

No one model explains all the evidence; it is clear that in England, as in mainland Europe, narrative took many forms and interacted with considerable fluidity. We find evidence of remembered performance taking written form, and of written text transformed into performance. Narrative manuscripts provide hints of composition and considerable evidence of improvisation, whether scribal or other.

In understanding the shifting blend of orality and textuality in the Middle English romances, it is vital to remember that the romances participate in a broader cultural context. Helen Cooper observes that romances share features with history, ballad, allegory, *chanson de geste*, and saint's life,[60] but the continuities extend also to genres we associate more confidently with performance. The stanza structure and expression of performance context in English drama is often identical to romance. These lines from the Towneley play of the Prophets could easily inhabit a romance:

> As God of heven has gyffyn me wit,
> Shall I now syng you a fytt
> With my mynstrelsy.
> Loke ye do it well in wrytt,
> And theron a knot knytt,
> For it is prophecy.
>
> Myrth I make till all men
> With my harp and fyngers ten,
> And warn theym that thay glad;
>
> (lines 103–11)[61]

(As God of Heaven has given me understanding, I will now sing you a fytt [a section of a narrative poem] with my minstrelsy. Make sure you write it down well and add a conclusion, for it is prophecy. I make mirth for all people with my harp and my ten fingers and encourage them to rejoice.)

Here, as in some of the romances, a narrative song accompanied by the harp is presented as the source for a written story which, in turn, is presented orally.

---

[58] W. F. H. Nicolaisen, ed., *Oral Tradition in the Middle Ages*, Medieval and Renaissance Texts and Studies 112 (Binghamton, NY: Medieval and Renaissance Texts and Studies, 1995).

[59] Tim William Machan, 'Editing, Orality, and Late Middle English Texts', in *Vox intexta*, ed. Doane and Pasternack, pp. 229–45, at p. 237.

[60] Cooper, *English Romance in Time*, p. 10.

[61] *The Towneley Plays*, ed. Martin Stevens and A. C. Cawley, 2 vols, EETS ss 13, 14 (Oxford: Oxford University Press, 1994).

Although David is certainly a figure from the past, the actor presenting that character is not. It would be difficult to argue that the performance model presented in this unambiguously dramatic work is either imaginary or outdated. It is, of course, possible, that an actor could pretend to play the harp and simply speak the lines. It is more probable, however, that he would sing the lines while playing the harp, as he claims to do in the text. This passage, then, provides evidence from the late fifteenth century of a performer singing tail-rhyme stanzas with instrumental accompaniment.

This instance is even more compelling when we realize that the documents associated with drama show extensive evidence of musical performance where no musical notation survives. A few songs for specific plays from the fifteenth-century cycle plays have been preserved, and there are many references to songs in the texts themselves, but JoAnna Dutka observes:

> The external evidence of account books and other documents recording the expenses incurred by the play-producing craft guilds demonstrates clearly … that far more music was used in the plays than the texts actually indicate. This body of information reveals payments for songs, musicians, and instruments not mentioned in the texts.[62]

In fact, the evidence of historical documents may challenge our assumption that the plays were uniformly spoken, rather than sung.

English songs, themselves, show evidence of orality and textuality strikingly similar to the romances, and many poems that are clearly songs do not include notated music. Andrew Hughes observes:

> Of the features in the manuscripts that lead us to the belief that extemporization was the normal method of performance, and oral 'copying' the normal method of transmission, the most noteworthy is the frequency of variants differentiating the 'same' melody transmitted in numerous sources.[63]

Sometimes songs move far in the direction of narrative, as the late-fourteenth-century English lullaby 'Als I lay on Yoolis Night', which consists of sixteen stanzas in ballad metre narrating a dream vision.[64] Only one of the four manuscripts of this song includes a musical setting, and this manuscript was for some time in the possession of a 'joculator',[65] a term associated with narrative performance in

---

[62] JoAnna Dutka, *Music in the English Mystery Plays* (Kalamazoo, MI: Medieval Institute, 1980), p. 2. This book includes the extant songs preserved in the fifteenth-century English cycle plays.

[63] Andrew Hughes, *Style and Symbol: Medieval Music, 800–1453* (Ottawa: Institute of Mediaeval Music, 1989), p. 517.

[64] E. J. Dobson and F. Ll. Harrison, eds, *Medieval English Songs* (London: Faber & Faber, 1979), p. 275.

[65] Dobson and Harrison, *Medieval English Songs*, p. 23, quote this entry from the fly-leaf (their translation): 'Iste liber constat / constat [*struck through*] magistro Johanni [M … Joc]ulator emptor erat sibi a magistro Thoma Turke quondam vicario perpetuo de Biere nunc autem apud Henton in domo Cartusiensi monachus. ¶ et dedit mihi vt supra se [*struck through*] decimo die mensis decembris anno domini millesimo ccccxviij Dominus secum Amen' (this book belongs to Master John [Morton. A *joc*]ulator [entertainer] bought it for himself from Master Thomas Turke formerly

English documents, in this case 'doubtless the harper William Hennynges whose name is written on the recto of the penultimate fly-leaf'.[66] Ten of the sixteen verses consist of a song Mary sings to the infant Jesus narrating the events that have befallen her. This account is nested in another narrative in which the speaker tells his own story. He sings of falling asleep on Christmas Eve and seeing Mary try to rock her child to sleep without a lullaby. When the baby protests, she sings him her story, and the speaker concludes with words evocative of romance beginnings and endings, 'this song I herde sing'. The four manuscript versions of the song present varying quantities of text, and the combination of the text and melody introduces some complications possibly resulting from improvisational elements.[67] The 'joculator' may not have distinguished as sharply as we do between a song such as this and narratives more closely allied to the romances.

'Musicality' may be evident in the romance manuscripts as well as orality and textuality; musical tradition, too, may have left a residue. By acknowledging that the Middle English romances overlap with genres that engage actively with music at a fundamental level, we can approach the romances from a more balanced perspective.

Historical Performance

This book was impelled by performance, over thirty years of performing the Middle English romances, solo and in a number of groups and for many different types of audience. Yet the findings in this book are not based on those performances; rather, these conclusions are grounded in research motivated by the demands of historical performance. Some of the information in this book would be very difficult to derive without a physical fiddle to experiment with, but all of it could be sifted from the relevant documents. Performance cannot substitute for research, cannot provide new information unavailable in the written evidence; performance can, however, suggest possible explanations for evidence, indicate connections that might otherwise remain obscure, map out directions for research that have been ignored, demonstrate universal realities of performance, and insist on interdisciplinary awareness where we are tempted to compartmentalize.

In a recent solo performance, I played the fiddle while singing *The Tournament of Tottenham* from memory, differentiating characters with my voice, facial expressions, and body position. Earlier, at the 2009 Congress on Medieval Studies at Kalamazoo, I performed the same vocal and instrumental music with a troupe of a dozen or so actors, who mimed the story with boisterous energy; in that performance the focus of attention was not on me, but on the actors, and instead of gesturing, I dodged combatants. Many times I have presented a fairly acrobatic spoken performance of the same text with my sister, harpist Laura Zaerr; and in

---

perpetual vicar of Bere [Regis] but now a monk of the Charterhouse at Hinton. And he [the *joculator*] gave it to me, as above-named, on 10 December 1418. The Lord be with him, Amen).

[66] Dobson and Harrison, *Medieval English Songs*, p. 25.

[67] Dobson and Harrison, *Medieval English Songs*, p. 310.

the 1990s, I did a number of similar performances with lutenist Joseph Baldassarre. In 1993, I organized a dramatic performance in which a narrator read the text; the direct discourse, however, was recited (from memory) by the actors; during section breaks and combat, I played the fiddle in a small group of instrumentalists.

These varied instances are instructive. A single performer, interacting with the same text, sometimes sings while playing, sometimes speaks while miming, and sometimes plays intermittently while others produce the text.[68] These modern documented performances interplay intriguingly with the 1432–3 record of payment to players (*lusoribus*) for a performance at Rougemont Castle of 'la Tornment de Totyngham'.[69] We do not know if this performance incorporated some relative of the narrative poem extant today, but it could have. The modern performances show the ease with which a narrative poem can be produced dramatically, the flexibility of a single performer's role, and the varying degrees to which music can be involved in narrative performance.

Still, none of these instances reconstitutes a medieval performance. Even if it were irrefutably certain that my fiddle was constructed exactly as a particular fiddle in late medieval England, reproducing types of wood and instrument and bow construction, even to the precise variation in string gauge and bow curvature; even if we had unambiguous records of what words were produced and what notes sounded at a particular feast at St Swithin's, Winchester, in 1374; even if my technique meticulously followed instrumental and vocal practices employed by the minstrel who played that fiddle at that moment in time and quarter acre of space (with the third string just a touch flat); even so, I could not produce a replica of that performance. I am not that performer, and my audience is not her audience. Our perspectives about religion, about women, about politics, are very different. Our relationships within the performance community, our roles as guest or host or employee or relative, our ages and physical condition, are very different. Our expectations of performance, our shared allusions, our sense of what is comic or deeply moving, are very different. We do not speak the same language they did. Even the weather is different: at that medieval performance the audience may have been seriously distracted by chilly, damp feet in an unusual cold snap.[70]

---

[68] For a video of the solo narration of *The Tournament of Tottenham* with self-accompaniment on the fiddle, see Linda Marie Zaerr, *Music and Medieval Narrative* (Provo, UT: Chaucer Studio, 1911); for an audio recording of the poem with gothic harp, see Linda Marie Zaerr and Laura Zaerr, *Sentimental and Humorous Romances* (Provo, UT: Chaucer Studio, 2007); for an audio recording with medieval lute, see Linda Marie Zaerr and Joseph A. Baldassarre, *Three Medieval Romances* (Boise, ID: Silver Quill, 1992).

[69] William G. Cooke, '*The Tournament of Tottenham*: An Alliterative Poem and an Exeter Performance', *Records of Early English Drama* 11.2 (1986): 2–3. For further discussion of this text see Chapter 5.

[70] Daniel Leech-Wilkinson, *The Modern Invention of Medieval Music: Scholarship, Ideology, Performance* (Cambridge: Cambridge University Press, 2002), p. 9, extends this uncertainty into the present: 'That there can be no objective knowledge of music, either through a historical or an analytical approach, seems clear. Interpretation conscious of its cultural position seems at the moment (though this may change) to be the best that can be hoped for when we try to understand music, whether in the present or the past.'

Any number of historical documents scrupulously detailing who sang or played what material on what instruments for how long, complete with textual and musical notation, could not help us find our way to that medieval performance experience: the infinitely variable tone of voice and dynamic volume, the complex interactions between the rhythms of poetry and the rhythms of music, the movements and gestures of varying amplitude and velocity, the ephemeral facial expressions, the complex, often intuitive, communication among performers and between performers and audience, and the degree to which the audience is engaged in the performance.[71]

But in point of fact, we have no notated music for narrative in medieval England, no texts unambiguously designated for memorized performance, and less than a half dozen clearly documented instances of musical narrative performance. The expectation of finding such records is unrealistic in the light of the model for minstrel performance suggested by Andrew Taylor. Even in our record-hungry culture, analogous documents of live performance are difficult to track down.[72] Live performances are fleeting, and there is no purpose in preserving documents of what occurs; it matters only to the people present, and they, participating in the event directly, do not need documentation. This modern negligence in record keeping practices corroborates recent scholarship: the dearth of unambiguous records of musical narrative performance does not necessarily mean there were no such performances. As I will demonstrate in the following chapters, the evidence of performance we might reasonably expect does, in fact, exist.

Similarly, my experience with terminology bears some consideration. What am

---

[71] For discussion of some aspects of the distance between written documents and performance, see Paul Zumthor, 'The Vocalization of the Text: The Medieval "Poetic Effect"', *Viator* 19 (1988): 273–82; and John Miles Foley, *The Singer of Tales in Performance* (Bloomington: Indiana University Press, 1995).

[72] For example, my vita (constructed according to my university's guidelines) makes some unambiguous references to romance performance, but there is no mention that I play the fiddle. Other performers or ensembles are listed, but the specific role of each performer is not. It is clear that music was involved in some events, but not how I was involved, where I sang, where I presented narration, or on which occasions I exclusively played the fiddle. Furthermore, the vita lists only major performances. A fairly complete catalog of performances could be dredged out of my calendars, but they are listed there by date, time, and venue, with contact telephone numbers. There are scattered records of payment in offices, but, even in our record-ridden culture, I wonder how often they specify exactly what I did. Sometimes there are printed programmes, and they provide detailed information both about the performers and about the material presented; I have quite a few of these crumbling in folders somewhere in my basement. I even have 'minstrel books', from which I have memorized narrative texts. These have been mostly shabby folded papers, long lost or discarded. The only one I still possess is a little notebook into which I copied *The Weddynge of Sir Gawen and Dame Ragnell* in pencil from Bodleian Library, MS Rawl. C. 86. I refer to it from time to time to refresh my memory, but it will not make it out of the next decade.

Recordings, like manuscripts, are far more permanent. The jacket material (nicely protected in plastic) states exactly what occurs on each track, who plays or sings or speaks, and how long it takes (to the nearest second). Sometimes the entire text is included in printed form, and, in the case of the Chaucer Studio recordings of Middle English romances, the recordings are linked with editions produced by TEAMS. Even if the written blurbs were lost, extensive credits appear at the beginning and end of video productions.

I? I have been called a 'performer scholar' (which makes no mention of either fiddle or narrative); a 'fiddle player' or 'musician' (which does not include narrative performance); and 'Linda Marie Zaerr from Boise State University' (which, like 'the Earl of Devon's Minstrel', says nothing of what I perform). My status is similarly elusive. Like most medieval minstrels, I am not a famous performer, and as such I am not shielded from scattered performances for children's birthdays or grocery stores.[73] The primary source of my income does not derive from performance, though my patron gladly accepts performance in lieu of other service, and most of my performance partners are professional musicians. I am often called a 'semi-professional musician'. Would a scholar studying our era classify me as a professional or an amateur? Andrew Taylor notes a common assumption that 'only a minstrel would be likely to memorize a romance in its entirety';[74] I have memorized several. George Shuffelton suggests the possibility that the scribe of MS Harley 2253 might have combined 'the roles of notary, priest, and entertainer',[75] and Thomas Harper at Durham was primarily a carpenter.[76] Who knows how many other household servants or clerics may have worked seriously to develop performance skills?[77] Are they truly 'amateurs'?

Faced with a bewildering array of terms to describe performers, scholars are moving away from the rigid categories earlier proposed toward a recognition that the terms are fluid.[78] For purposes of this study, I will use the term 'minstrel' to refer to anyone seriously engaged in a performance of music or memorized text. While I do not exclude the possibility of reading aloud, I doubt that a minstrel would use it as primary mode. While reading aloud clearly requires skill and training and can be accomplished with varying effect,[79] the task is much less demanding than performing memorized or improvised material. If you do not need a minstrel, why pay one? I have chosen the term 'minstrel' because this is the

---

[73] 'Thei we nought welcom no be, / Yete we mot proferi forth our gle' (*Sir Orfeo*, lines 33–4).

[74] Taylor, 'Fragmentation', p. 43.

[75] Shuffelton, 'Domestic Entertainment', p. 69. Bullock-Davies, *Menestrellorum Multitudo*, p. 25, notes that a number of the people listed as minstrels on the list she discusses 'were serving in the household in other capacities and received court wages for duties far removed from singing songs, playing a musical instrument or acting in plays.'

[76] Richard Rastall, 'Minstrelsy, Church and Clergy in Medieval England', *Proceedings of the Royal Musical Association* 97 (1970–1): 83–98, at p. 91.

[77] Helen Marsh Jeffries, 'Job Descriptions, Nepotism, and Part-Time Work: The Minstrels and Trumpeters of the Court of Edward IV of England (1461–83)', *Plainsong and Medieval Music* 12.2 (2003): 165–77, at p. 166, notes: 'Study of Edward IV's instrumentalists reveals information about working practices that can illuminate our view not only of them, but also of the whole royal household. The anachronistic concept of "full-time" work for instrumentalists, and probably other functionaries as well, may have to be abandoned.'

[78] For instance, Chesnutt, 'Minstrel Reciters', pp. 50–1, points to a range of Middle English terms used for minstrel reciters: '*disour, gestour, rymour, segger, gleyman, jogelour,* or *bourdiour*', demonstrating that the term 'minstrel' does not exclusively designate an instrumentalist.

[79] In high school, I competed at speech tournaments in the categories of 'Humorous Interp' and 'Serious Interp', terms used for reading aloud; reading aloud was still at that time considered a skill worth cultivating and requiring training.

term most commonly used in the Middle English romances themselves, and it is used flexibly, including the other, more specific, categories of performer.[80]

The term 'performance' has attracted considerable attention in the last two decades. We have moved from seeing texts as texts, to imagining texts in performance, to seeing texts as performances in themselves and performances as texts. There is a value in each of these approaches, but none is anything like the experience of playing the medieval fiddle and singing for a group of actual people. In this book, then, I use the term 'performance' exclusively for events at which a person or persons physically produce music and/or words to entertain another person or persons.

But for this to occur, the performer has to make certain definite choices for each performance. A performance can take only one form; it cannot exist amid a range of imagined possibilities. This is where 'historical performance' can serve a more specific purpose. For twenty-one years I struggled to find a way to play a fiddle while reciting a Middle English romance from memory. It wasn't easy. I kept trying ideas I thought should work, but ultimately I could not maintain any approach effectively for more than five minutes. The fiddle always seemed a hindrance, for all my valiant demonstrations. I came very close to writing this book about why it was unlikely that a minstrel would play the fiddle, or any other instrument, with a Middle English romance. But then I found a way to do it, a way in keeping with what we know of medieval instruments and texts. At the very least, historical performance can demonstrate one way in which a minstrel might have played a fiddle to enhance Middle English narrative verse and found in the fiddle a tool to aid memory.

Bruce Haynes points to the value of working with replicas of instruments that are as accurate as possible:

> Instruments can be seen in terms of Darwinian adaptation. They are constantly changing in small ways to make it easier for musicians to perform the music currently in fashion. There is immense pressure on instruments to be as well-adapted as possible to the music of their time. Instrument makers are very receptive to the demands of players, and these demands are the immediate cause of mutations.[81]

By working with instruments that are faithful replicas to the extent of our knowledge, without making intentional changes or 'compromises to modern taste',[82] we may approach the style of the music of that era. I have been working with four different fiddles, embodying very different ways of interpreting what we know of fiddles in late medieval England. I have experimented with tunings following what we know of medieval tuning systems. I have examined a wide range of extant

---

[80] Abigail Ann Young, 'Minstrels and Minstrelsy: Household Retainers or Instrumentalists?' *Records of Early English Drama* 20.1 (1995): 11–17, notes that in Anglo-Latin the term '*ministrallus*' does not necessarily refer to an entertainer, but may be a more generic term for a household functionary.

[81] Bruce Haynes, *The End of Early Music: A Period Performer's History of Music for the Twenty-First Century* (Oxford: Oxford University Press, 2007), p. 151.

[82] Haynes, *End of Early Music*, p. 161.

melodies. I have explored alternative expectations of timbre. I have pursued rhythmic possibilities for music and a wide variety of Middle English verse forms. Intriguingly, I found it possible to draw certain conclusions with reasonable certainty. However they were constructed or tuned, the fiddles invite certain approaches to playing and discourage others or render them impossible. All of the verse forms common in Middle English romance can be easily performed with the fiddle using a single way of thinking about instrumental accompaniment.

Allowing music into the Middle English romances transforms the possibilities, adding layers of potential complexity. Where textual versions of some romances have been described as simplistic or repetitive, musical performance suggests they may be incomplete, missing an indispensible musical component. Similarly metrical irregularities may be relics of sophisticated rhythmic variation. And, of course, the whimsical, self-reflexive quality in so many of the romances takes on living warmth in performance. We do not possess performance versions of the romances, but their textual relatives may provide some clues through judicious application of modern performance.

Historical performance can demonstrate realities of performance common to any era; it can demonstrate that an approach is feasible, and it may sometimes (though not in every case) indicate when an approach is unlikely; when constructed around available historical, musicological, and textual evidence, it can even suggest some concrete possibilities for what medieval performance may have been like.[83] It is thus possible to limit the possibilities, to remove musical performance of romance from the realm of abstract speculation or theoretical discussion. Modern performance can thus be used both as an interpretive strategy concomitant with textual criticism and as a tool for delineating what is possible or reasonable in performance and what forms musical performance might have taken.

Overview

This book moves from the broad context of European narrative to the evidence surrounding minstrel performance in England to analysis of the elements of narrative performance. Chapter 1 explores Continental traditions, which provide a context and palette of tools for studying Middle English romance performance. Metaperformance dimensions in European romance texts create congruence between the performer and the protagonist; they also capture an image of minstrel performance. In this image, gender appears to play a less important role than we might have imagined. But internal references can be perplexing and potentially misleading, as when 1,500 minstrels perform simultaneously at a feast.

Terminology surrounding performance is notoriously elusive, but the verbs describing performance often mention instruments, emphasizing the musical dimension of narrative performance. The same melodies inform our performance

---

[83] Video clips of some performance possibilities based on available evidence may be viewed at https://english.boisestate.edu/lindamariezaerr/videoclips/.

models of both *chanson de geste* and *roman*, and in both cases the evidence is indirect. The absence of notated melodies, however, is a valuable clue to narrative performance, and the evidence we need to construct a topography of performance may be very different from what we might expect. We know how fiddles could be tuned; we have documentation of performance contexts; we have narrative texts with definite characteristics which interact with performance in specific ways; we have performance theory, which indicates universal characteristics; we have indirect melodic evidence from contemporary sources; and we have detailed evidence of the aesthetic and technique of variation and ornamentation. It is in the context of this evidence that we approach the Middle English romance.

Chapter 2 explores minstrel performance of narrative in late medieval England as it is documented in historical sources and as it is portrayed in the Middle English verse romances. As on the Continent, historical evidence for performance in England provides an incomplete picture. Some records explicitly link musical instruments with story performance, and these documents reinforce the Continental evidence that little if any distinction was made between narrative and drama. A record of payment to two fiddle players for performing *Gray Steel*, together with two romance versions of the story and a notated melody from the seventeenth century, suggest specific performance options. The pairing of performers may have been a widespread practice; we see pairs of minstrels in dozens of payment records, and this configuration suggests the possibility of collaborative romance performance, though most narrative performance was probably undertaken by a single performer.

The Middle English verse romances, taken as a whole, provide further clarification. Appendix A provides systematic documentation of references to minstrels in eighty-three romances. This catalogue, to the extent it can be verified by historical records, reveals a remarkably realistic description of minstrel activity: rewards to minstrels and their presence in a wide range of contexts. Furthermore, the references do not, as is commonly supposed, glamorize the figure of the minstrel. When protagonists take on minstrel functions, their performance is consistently linked with love, and it is only in this context that minstrelsy may be glamorized. The romances make a consistent distinction between *romaunces* in books and the performed *gestes* made from them by minstrels. Since the romance vision of minstrels is reliable as far as we know, we may reasonably give credence to what the romances indicate in areas not addressed in the records. The romances frequently refer to minstrels singing or telling stories, sometimes with a musical instrument, sometimes setting this practice side by side with reading romances. Like the manuscript evidence, the minstrel references generally suggest a non-performer's perspective, but they assume a shared cultural experience rather than a nostalgic evocation of the past. Minstrels are sometimes linked with heralds, both historically and in the romances, and one of the functions of minstrels is carrying news and upholding the fame of their patrons, a function that appears to blend with their storytelling function.

All of this suggests an approach to narrative that must be highly flexible, and may be very different from what we have imagined: narrative that can combine with instruments, can be spoken or sung in verse or prose, and can involve many performers or just one. Exploring the musical instruments associated with story-telling can provide more information about how people may have thought of narrative in medieval England. From this point, the book moves to a detailed practical consideration of how minstrels might reasonably have performed narrative.

Both in historical documents and in literary descriptions of performance, chordophones, stringed instruments, are the class of musical instruments most commonly associated with narrative performance. Chapter 3 traces a range of reasonable instrumental options, touching briefly on the lute, but focusing on historical documents and romance references to the harp and the fiddle, the two instruments most compelling linked with romance performance. While the harp is a strong contender for romance accompaniment, it is too versatile to reveal much about performance, and information about the instrument is complicated by symbolic associations. The fiddle is also consistently associated with narrative both in mainland Europe and in Britain, and its structure and tuning limit how the instrument could have been used in accompaniment. The fiddle, therefore, serves well as a test case for how a solo performer may have used an instrument in narrative performance.

The chapter includes a summation of the evidence provided in Appendix B, which is a detailed analysis of evidence relating to the fiddle in late-thirteenth-century France, from which considerable evidence about the tuning and use of the instrument survives. This analysis is structured around application of Jerome of Moravia's three tuning systems to narrative performance, working from the premise that any approach to the medieval fiddle must be robust enough to accommodate the wide variety in size and construction. While each tuning offers a distinct advantage, all three are characterized by a shifting landscape of drones and fleeting application of any improvisational technique. The fiddle thus carries in its structure the principle of variation. Transforming repetition of a simple melody into a complex array of diverse effects, the fiddle and the voice, each intro-ducing variation, combine to create a tremendous range of expressive potential.

The principles of fiddle accompaniment can be extended to the harp and the lute, though they must be adapted to the differences in sound production. All three instruments are characterized by strong and weak sound events, similar to the stressed and unstressed syllables in Middle English verse. Instrumental accompaniment, then, creates patterns of accent that must interact in some way with verse. Study of possible interactions between instrumental music and verse thus has a profound impact on our understanding of metre.

Drawing on music theory, Chapter 4 addresses metre in terms of the intimate medieval connection between verse and music. In the manuscripts of Middle English romances, scribes consistently transform rhythms, creating rhythmic variation that might seem to make a musical setting implausible. Yet French and Latin monophonic songs provide many instances of a melody accommo-dating a varying number of syllables or shifting patterns of stressed syllables. In the English song 'Edi beo thu', too, we find 'corruptions' in both the text and the music similar to those in the Middle English romance manuscripts. Romances in four-stress couplets can be comfortably set to this thirteenth-century polyphonic song, and the varying syllables are easily accommodated. The second melodic line in the song suggests one way an instrument might be used. A fiddler can play this line following a non-synchronous approach to accompaniment. That is to say, the instrument can enhance comprehension of the lexically important stressed syllables by offsetting changes in bow direction so they do not coincide.

Awareness of three types of accent justifies the approach. Phenomenal accents in a text establish a pattern of regularly occurring metrical accents, and simultaneously they establish a higher level pattern of structural accents. An instrument can be used then to reinforce either metrical accents (the stressed syllables) or structural accents (in this case, line beginnings, which often occur on unstressed syllables). Earlier evidence of music linked to phrasing in narrative appears in the musical neumes in manuscripts of Latin hexameter epics.

This introduces the question of how metrical accents are spaced in time, and monophonic song cannot help since there is such controversy regarding rhythmic interpretation. Modern theory indicates that while we perceive metrical accents occurring at equal intervals of time, measurement indicates otherwise. This is particularly helpful in understanding alliterative verse; we do not have to cram wildly varying syllables into even units of time; the alliteration will ensure that time units are perceived as equal. A wave–particle duality model describes our reception of phenomenal rhythms in time: a verse line structure is like a series of ocean waves, endlessly varying in size, shape, and velocity; and a metrical structure is like a series of discreet points we perceive as evenly spaced. We recognize the wave structure in a still-spectator mode, remembering features from the past and relating them into a structural shape; and we count along with the particle series in active-listening mode. We can experience both modes simultaneously or shift from one to another. The concept of recurrence suggests that either pattern may be disrupted, followed by a satisfying return to pattern. The tail-rhyme stanza, in fact, appears to be grounded in recurrence.

A few illustrations from tail-rhyme romance manuscripts demonstrate how these principles can explain some scribal transformations. In a passage from *Sir Cleges* we see an example of recurrence: the tail-rhyme stanza structure, having been established, is suspended while the metrical beat is anomalously maintained; then in the following stanza structural regularity is restored while the pattern of metrical disruption is resumed. A somewhat different application of the principle occurs in the transition from tail-rhyme stanzas to couplets in *Bevis of Hampton*. Here the scribe prepares for the metrical shift by training listeners to accept a range of metrical possibilities, shifting either the number of stresses or the rhyme structure while maintaining the other. At no point do all the rhythmic patterns shift at once. A passage from *The Weddynge of Sir Gawen and Dame Ragnell* provides the most extensive illustration of improvisational thinking drawing on simultaneous rhythmic structures. In this passage, even as the lines break free of the highly flexible tail-rhyme stanza structure, they continue to establish and vary rhythmic structures, engaging both metre and rhyme in creating overlapping fragmentary patterns, often imposing mutually exclusive designs by truncating and offsetting those designs.

So fluid are these realizations of verse design that instrumental accompaniment cannot linger in a frame of evenly spaced bow changes but must become far more dynamic. While this can incorporate the more straightforward modes of accompaniment discussed above, it is much more flexible and varied, more in tune with the aesthetic of variation evident throughout medieval discussions of both verse and music. There are obvious difficulties in notation. The most useful approach is a visible marking of the stanza structure, setting apart the shorter tail-lines, and this is exactly the graphic indication of tail-rhyme structure we see in a number of manuscripts. One of the most intriguing results of this exploration is an awareness of how metrical irregularities in the text provide potential for flexibility and rhythmic sophistication in performance.

Having addressed what we know about metre and the instruments involved with English narrative, we now move to vocal delivery – how the voice might have produced poetry either alone or engaged with instrumental accompaniment. Chapter 5 begins with a reconsideration of historical performance, demonstrating in specific terms how performance experiments can summon together wide ranging information about instruments, vocal delivery, texts, melodies, and rhythms, finding connections that might otherwise be overlooked. This is followed by a model for self-accompanied performance of the Middle English romance with the fiddle, embodying and extending some of the theoretical constructions suggested by John Stevens, Michael Chesnutt, and Karl Reichl.

We should envision a simple melody, embellished improvisationally, that can accommodate the rhythms created by the stressed and unstressed syllables in Middle English verse. This narration is optionally accompanied by an instrument, also characterized by improvised variation, interacting with the narration both at the level of rhythm (metrical articulation and broader structural patterns) and at the level of pitch relations, moving between consonance and dissonance. The melodies cannot be bound in a metrical grid work. Melodies may provide a structure of accents that generally aligns with the romance texts, but they cannot insist upon even spacing of those accents. The romance text will thus create natural variation in a simple melody. The rhythm is dictated by the text, and it sometimes has a duple feel and sometimes a triple feel, and sometimes something more complex.

Drawing on this model, we can reasonably apply actual melodies to Middle English verse romances, on the principle that the *gestes* performed by minstrels would have been similar enough to the extant romances to justify the experiment. In the process of applying melodies, we find more narrative melodies than have been previously noticed, and more justification than we might have expected for applying those melodies.

Beginning with unrhymed alliterative long lines, the chapter demonstrates that both psalm-tones and the one extant *chanson de geste* melody introduce a persistent melodic divide in each line that violates the Middle English tendency for the full line to function as a syntactic unit. The late-thirteenth-century melody for *Der jungere Titurel* offers a solution. Like many English romances, this narrative is an adaptation of a French romance into a stress-based Germanic language. The melody suggests a way of treating alliterative long lines, a pattern of open and closed melodies, not necessarily in strict alternation, with the caesuras marked by one pattern of ornamentation and the line endings by another. This approach addresses the challenges of this metre: the undifferentiated lines, the variable number of syllables (and even stresses) in each line, and the requirement that some lines move through the caesura without a pause.

Moving to the tail-rhyme romance, we discover a contrafactum, a melody from another text, in the thirteenth-century French reverdie 'Volez vous que je vous chant', which shares both a stanza form and a literary trope with *Sir Launfal*. This melody is well suited to the most commonly occurring English tail-rhyme stanza form. Some stanza forms, however, cannot be accommodated by a contrafactum, yet it is possible to construct a melodic framework by drawing on typical patterns of medieval song. While fabrication of a melody within the parameters established for narrative accompaniment cannot reconstruct a medieval performance version, it can demonstrate how a melody can interact with a complex stanza structure. Experimentation with *The Tournament of Tottenham* reveals how a melody highlights aspects of the text, but also how the text transforms the melody.

Romances in couplets are the most easily linked with a melody, and it is here that we have an extant melody assigned to a specific romance, *Gray Steel* (also known as *Eger and Grime*). Although this melody survives in a seventeenth-century version, it contains information about how narrative could have engaged with instrumental accompaniment; the melody fits the fiddle tunings so precisely that varied accompaniment can be produced with little effort, even by an inexperienced musician. The structure of the melody may also indicate a way of thinking about line endings and a way of distinguishing tail-lines by means of an offset accent in a melodic phrase.

Together, these possibilities compellingly narrow and specify the options for how *gestes* in some way related to the Middle English romances could have been performed by minstrels. If we take seriously the possibility that the English romance tradition interacted with a tradition of musical minstrel performance, the consequences for our understanding of the romances may be profound.

Chapter 6 begins with a reminder that the identifying feature of minstrelsy is the bond between minstrel and audience. It touches briefly on some of the problems of modern expectations of performance, in particular our assumption that a recording can accurately represent a live performance. The discussion then revisits historical performance, this time drawing on illustrations from this study to analyse valid ways historical performance can participate in the conversation surrounding the Middle English romance, and articulating reasons why that voice should be heard.

The study of medieval romance is incomplete if we leave out awareness of possible musical performance. If we acknowledge the evidence that the Middle English romances were strongly engaged with a tradition of musical performance, then it is incumbent on us to approach those musical dimensions with the same careful scrutiny that has been afforded to study of the manuscripts. The evidence is very different, but there is enough there to allow us to move beyond generalities. We have narrative melodies from mainland Europe; songs from England; contemporary discussions of rhythm, ornamentation, and the processes of composition and performance; evidence about instrument construction and tuning; and variations among the romance manuscripts considered in the context of musical performance. Piecing these elements together, we can derive a reasonable model of minstrel performance of Middle English *gestes*. A simple melody, continually varied by both voice and instrument, transforms a text within simultaneous and sometimes unaligned rhythmic structures, developing patterns and then breaking them and returning to them. Both text and melody are flexible, responsive to the story itself.

Elements in Middle English romances that may seem simplistic or repetitive, may in fact be incomplete, missing an integral musical dimension. Metrical irregularities may be relics of sophisticated rhythmic variation that make sense only with music. Even romances that may never have been performed may be closely related to performed versions. The romances inhabit a world so filled with music that its absence is the hallmark of grief and isolation.

1

Continental Traditions of Narrative Performance

THE Middle English romances do not stand in isolation; they participate in a shared entertainment tradition with French and Germanic works, both Insular and Continental. This broader European context illuminates references to music and minstrels in England, filling in gaps, clarifying distinctions, and rectifying interpretations. English terminology surrounding performers and performance follows patterns evident throughout Europe; the flexible descriptions of performers, the lack of distinction between drama and narrative, and the ubiquitous involvement of music in the culture indicate ways of conceiving of performance very different from our own. Within this understanding, the involvement of music in narrative and the defining participation of musical instruments in narrative performance may impel us to reinterpret records of minstrel activity in England.

Continental narrative texts themselves are a key source of information. Internal descriptions of minstrels, while potentially misleading, articulate a tradition of minstrel identification with protagonists, and they provide clear evidence of attitudes to performers and the role gender may have played in minstrel performance. Historical documents can corroborate where these references accurately describe the historical realities of minstrel performance of narrative, realities which may extend to England.

Metaperformance Dimensions of Romance – Harping about Harping

Tristan's identity as a minstrel is thematically central in Gottfried von Strassburg's early-thirteenth-century Middle High German poem. As a boy, Tristan modestly admits to an international education in instrumental music:

> mich lêrten Parmenîen
> videln und symphonîen.
> harpfen unde rotten
> daz lêrten mich Galotten,
> zwêne meister Gâloise.
> mich lêrten Britûnoise,
> die wâren ûz der stat von Lût,
> rehte lîren und sambjût.
>
> (lines 3675–82)[1]

---

[1] All references to the text of *Tristan* are from Gottfried von Strassburg, *Tristan*, ed. Rüdiger Krohn, 3 vols (Stuttgart: Reclam, 1980). Translations are from Gottfried von Strassburg, *Tristan*, trans. A. T. Hatto (Harmondsworth: Penguin, 1960).

(Parmenians taught me the fiddle and organistrum, Welshmen the harp and rote – they were two masters from Wales; Bretons from the town of Lut grounded me in the lyre and also in the sambuca.)

These are all stringed instruments, and the catalogue is expanded when, disguised as a minstrel in Ireland, he claims he can play 'liren unde gigen, / harpfen unde rotten' (lyre, fiddle, harp and crowd, lines 7564–65).[2] Yet, except for a demonstration of horn playing that is clearly part of his hunting expertise (lines 3210–22), the only instrument we actually see Tristan play is the harp.

As a fourteen-year-old boy in King Mark's court, in a detailed and technically specific passage, Tristan establishes his skill as a musician by singing and playing a harp he borrows from a minstrel. Later, in a minstrel disguise, he ingratiates himself into Isolde's household with his harp playing. Again disguised as a minstrel, he wins Isolde back from the rote-playing Gandin by playing the harp and singing. At various other points in the story, we see him engaged in harp playing.

In performance by a harper, these passages acquire a metaperformance dimension. That is, the text describes a performance analogous to the vehicle by which the text is being communicated. A musician harps the story of a musician harping. Through the shared action of playing the harp and the shared identity as minstrel, the performer takes on the role of Tristan. The story becomes suddenly more compelling when the protagonist is embodied in the performer, and the boundaries between Arthurian romance and the everyday world are blurred, underscoring associations of love and music, and deepening ironies of deception.

But would the romance have that transformative power in the hands of a fiddler, or would the obvious disjunction between playing the fiddle and playing the harp create a distracting contrast between the character minstrel (a harper) and the performer minstrel (a fiddler)? This question cannot be answered completely, but it is a question we must ask if we take the possibility of minstrel performance seriously. Certainly medieval audiences did not expect the degree of verisimilitude that today's audiences demand of film and theatre, but they may have appreciated moments of congruence. Today, while actors must closely resemble the characters they represent, storytellers are not expected to look like the characters they describe; but the medieval world did not always distinguish, as we do, between narrative and drama. Carol Symes, in her discussion of *Courtois d'Arras*, points to the flexible character of that text, demonstrating that such mutability is typical:

> It [*Courtois d'Arras*] is one of a great many pieces performed during the thirteenth century in Arras and elsewhere, couched in a variety of forms but sharing many of the same functions, audiences, and enactors. This is why all of its scribes have juxtaposed it with an assortment of related entertainments,

[2] A survey of instruments referred to in this romance is provided by Ian F. Finlay, 'Musical Instruments in Gotfrid von Strassburg's "Tristan und Isolde"', *Galpin Society Journal* 5 (1952): 39–43.

and why one of them called it a 'lay' – a ballad, a short story in verse. Like all such pieces, it could be adapted for one or more performers.[3]

Perhaps entertainment on the continuum between drama and narrative was presented with less verisimilitude than our modern theatrical productions but more than our storytelling tradition (which today is largely confined to an audience of children).

There is no reason Gottfried's *Tristan* might not have been performed on occasion by two minstrels (as the two minstrels in the *Roman de Silence* perform the 'lai Mabon', line 2766)[4] or even more, but individual minstrel performance of medieval romance appears to have been most common,[5] and a solo performer would find it easier to travel with one instrument (a harp *or* a fiddle) than two. So the problem of the unaligned instrumentalist remains.

Perhaps audiences would have found enough conjunction in any instrumentally accompanied performance of a romance about an instrumentalist to derive a satisfying pleasure in the dissolution of narrative boundaries. There is another possibility, though. The hero-harpist is a pattern which Christopher Page traces back to the fifth-century Latin *Historia Apollonii Regis Tyri*, and we find it developed in the twelfth-century French *Roman de Horn* and other French romances.[6] In Thomas's version of the Gandin episode, however, Gandin plays the harp and Tristan plays the rote, a string instrument which can be either bowed (like the fiddle) or plucked (like the harp). There may be theoretical and intertextual reasons why a harp or a fiddle might be assigned to a given character,[7] but one very practical possibility might be to strengthen a performer's association with that character. A harp-playing minstrel might well prefer to describe a hero consistently playing a harp, possibly changing the text to accomplish that effect.

In the French romance tradition, the most direct source for the English tradition, heroes disguised as minstrels play either the fiddle or the harp, the two instruments most associated with romance performance.[8] As a guide to actual practice, internal references to minstrel performance must be considered with care, yet

---

[3] Symes, *Common Stage*, pp. 72–3.

[4] References and translations of the *Roman de Silence* are from Heldris de Cornuälle, *Silence: A Thirteenth-Century French Romance*, ed. and trans. Sarah Roche-Mahdi (East Lansing, MI: Colleagues Press, 1992).

[5] See Christopher Page, *Voices and Instruments of the Middle Ages: Instrumental Practice and Songs in France, 1100–1300* (London: Dent, 1987), p. 136.

[6] Page, *Voices and Instruments*, pp. 103–7.

[7] Jennifer Looper, 'L'épisode de la Harpe et de la Rote dans la légende de Tristan: Étude sur le symbolisme de deux instruments de musique', *Cahiers de civilisation médiévale* 38.4 (1995): 345–52, discusses Gottfried's change in terms of attitudes to the rote in Germany. Regional symbolic associations with specific instruments may affect textual choices, and such associations would also align with the instruments typically used by minstrels in the region.

[8] For an intriguing discussion of minstrel disguise, see Marilyn Lawrence, 'Minstrel Disguise in Medieval French Narrative: Identity, Performance, Authorship' (PhD diss., New York University, 2001).

they should not be disregarded. The descriptions of protagonist minstrels together with passages about professional minstrels create a remarkably vivid representation of a minstrel's life and the problems he or she might realistically face. But the internal minstrel references validate minstrel performance in another way when we imagine them performed; they draw attention to the skill of a performer in singing and playing an instrument by describing a similar performance in glowing terms.

We find both effects in the *Roman de la Violette*, where Gerart, tired and wet from his travels, is commanded to perform. He asks to eat and warm up first, but the traitor Lisiart insists he play at once. Gerart's complaint surely reflects a situation historical minstrels would have encountered:

> 'Hé! Las! Fait-il, je vieng molt tempre,
> Quant ma viele m'estuet traire!
> Or puis-jou bien por voir retraire
> Que jongleres mal mestier a;
> Que quant plus froit et mesaise a,
> Tant le semont-on plus souvent
> De chanter et s'eir au vent.'
>
> (lines 1392–98)[9]

('Alas!' he said, 'I have just been thoroughly soaked [*possible pun:* tuned] when I try to take up my fiddle. Now I can easily see that jongleurs have a miserable profession. When we are most cold and uncomfortable, then frequently someone calls on us to sing and be heard in a draught.')

There is a whimsical self-referential quality to this passage in performance; audiences should be aware how difficult it is to perform when you are cold and wet and hungry. Gerart hints that he is not trained as a minstrel, yet, because he is functioning in that role, what follows provides a clear description of a minstrel singing a *chanson de geste* while playing the fiddle:

> 'Faire m'estuet, quant l'ai empris,
> Chou dont je ne sui mie apris:
> Chanter et vïeler ensamble
> Lors commencha, si com moi samble,
> Con chil qui molt estoit senés,
> Un ver de Guillaume au court nes,
> A clere vois et a douch son.
>
> (lines 1399–1405)

('Since I have undertaken it, I must do that which I am not at all taught to do: sing and play the fiddle at the same time.' Then, as it seems to me, he began to both sing and fiddle a *laisse* from [the *chanson de geste*] of Guillaume au

---

[9] This passage is from D. L. Buffum, ed., *Le Roman de la Violette ou de Gerart de Nevers* (Paris: SATF, 1928); the translation is mine.

court nez, like one who was well-skilled in such matters, with a clear voice and a sweet sound.)[10]

Such a passage, immediately followed by an entire *laisse* of the *chanson de geste*, would effectively remind its listeners of the 'clere vois' and 'douch son' they are currently experiencing, stimulating appreciation of the performer.

Yet the romance texts, even as they invite a blurring of minstrel and protagonist, consistently distinguish between professional minstrels and noblemen in disguise as minstrels. An intriguing illustration is the twelfth-century Provençal story of *Daurel et Beton*,[11] in which the noble Beton is brought up by the jongleur Daurel. Beton becomes an outstanding fiddler, and ultimately reveals his nobility by his singing and fiddle playing, but that revelation is possible because he never becomes a genuine jongleur.

Early in the story, Duke Bove gives Daurel the castle of Monclar as a hereditary fief, yet even as he gains wealth and prestige, Daurel remains a jongleur. When Bove is treacherously killed, Daurel rescues Bove's son Beton and flees with him by ship, entertaining him along the way with a song about the events that have befallen them. The subject of this performance by a professional minstrel is more than coincidentally congruent with the subject of the text itself, which is initially described as a 'remarkable song' ('rica canso', line 1).[12] In fact, several times within the story Daurel presents a musical performance of the events of the story.

When they arrive in Babylon, Daurel performs at court, and the Emir offers him wealth and land, but he refuses it, asking instead that Beton be raised at court. The Emir is certain that Beton is too refined be the son of a jongleur, and they decide to test whether he is of noble birth by offering him money to perform for the princess. If he accepts the money, he is the son of the jongleur; if not, he is noble. The distinction is not one of skill, but of perspective. Beton refuses the payment, thus revealing his nobility.

But the romance complicates this explicit sharp distinction. The genuine jongleur Daurel, too, has already refused phenomenal wealth in order to assist Beton. In many ways Daurel and Beton are set parallel. When they go together to exact revenge on Bove's murderer Guy, they take up their fiddles in the guise of a jongleur ('Prendo lor vieulas a guiza de joglar', line 1933). Here the jongleur role is a disguise for both, and they perform together; Beton plays, while Daurel sings a song of Guy's treachery. But when Guy tries to throw a knife at Daurel, Beton casts away his fiddle and his disguise, and cuts off Guy's right arm, thus simultaneously avenging his father and putting aside his identity as a jongleur.

---

[10] Both the text and the translation of this passage are from Page, *Voices and Instruments*, p. 189, which provides a compelling argument for this arrangement of the text.

[11] References to this text are from A. S. Kimmel, ed., *A Critical Edition of the Old Provençal Epic Daurel et Beton* (Chapel Hill: University of North Carolina Press, 1971); the translations are mine. This story is thought to be related to the early-thirteenth-century Anglo-Norman *Boeve de Haumtone*, which is a probable source for the Middle English romance *Bevis of Hampton*.

[12] Silvère Menegaldo, *Le Jongleur dans la littérature narrative des XIIe et XIIIe siècles: du personnage au masque* (Paris: Honoré Champion, 2005), discusses some of the ways the minstrel figure within the story may relate to the author of the text, who may himself be a minstrel, p. 18.

In this differentiation we see an important attitude to performers and performance. Any congruence between jongleur and protagonist preserves the difference in class. A hero is never actually a minstrel; he only maintains the appearance of one. For a nobleman, music is genuine expression of feeling, while for a jongleur it is something to be sold.[13]

Heroine Minstrels and the Role of Gender in Performance

Yet in the francophone tradition, noble protagonists disguised as minstrels are not always men, and it is here that expectations about female performers may be revealed. The early-thirteenth-century *Galeran de Bretagne* blends the minstrel motif into *Lai le Fresne*.[14] In this story, Galeran teaches Fresne a *lai* he has composed. In a detailed passage, she learns the song from him by listening carefully while he sings so that she can determine how to place her fingers on the harp ('celle l'escoute, / Qu'en la harpe ses doiz i boute', lines 2297–8).[15] She thus takes a purely vocal song and adds instrumental accompaniment.[16] This song becomes a pledge between them, a treasure she receives which he vows to share with no other.

Later, when Galeran is about to marry another woman, Fresne arrives disguised as a minstrel, carrying a harp around her neck supported by a cushion. She does not at first play the *lai* Galeran has taught her, but a new song of her own composition, and her music silences all the other minstrels:

> Puis chante quant elle est on my:
> 'Je voiz aux noces mon amy:
> Plus dolente de moy n'y va!'
> Ceste note premiers trova
> Fresne, qui de chanter se peine.
> Les doiz en la harpe pourmaine;
> Si va herpant tant doulcement
> Que li menestrel erraument
> Mettent leurs instruments arriere,
> Car tous leurs sons et leur maniere
> Vallent vers la harpe aussi peu
> Com vers vïelle voix de leu;

---

[13] See Linda Marie Zaerr, 'Songs of Love and Love of Songs: Music and Magic in Medieval Romance', in *Words of Love and Love of Words in the Middle Ages and the Renaissance*, ed. Albrecht Classen (Tempe: Arizona Center for Medieval and Renaissance Studies, 2008), pp. 291–317.

[14] *Galeran de Bretagne* may derive from a different version of the story presented in Marie de France's *Lais*.

[15] References to this text are from Jean Renart, *Galeran de Bretagne: roman du XIIIe siècle*, ed. Lucien Foulet (Paris: Honoré Champion, 1975); the translations are mine.

[16] In the 'hero-harpist' pattern described by Christopher Page, the hero often teaches the heroine to play the harp, and the female role in that motif may be expanded in some romances. Here, although Galeran teaches Fresne a particular song, her musicianship is independent of him, and that is the case in most romances.

S'en sont esbahy touz ensemble.

(lines 6975–87)

(When she was in the midst [of the hall], she sang, 'I saw my beloved at the wedding. Never has there been anyone sadder than I!' Fresne first created this melody, which she took pains to sing. Her fingers linger on the harp, and she harps so sweetly that the minstrels immediately put their instruments behind them, for all their melodies and their technique were worth as little compared to the harp as the howling of a wolf is compared to a fiddle. The entire company [of minstrels] was put to shame.)

No one at the wedding feast is surprised to see a female minstrel; they are astounded at the genuineness of her performance, unaware that her initial song is a lament over her own situation. What sets her apart among the minstrels is her true identity as a noblewoman, and as such she has a very different relationship to music.

Like the other 'chevaliers', Galeran is overwhelmed by her music, but he does not recognize her until she plays the *lai* he has taught her:

> Par un doulx lay le desconforte;
> Les autres laiz, celuy a pris
> Que Galeren li a apris.
> El dit ne mesprent n'en la note:
> De Galeren le Breton note.
> Si l'escoutent toutes et tuit;
> Des moz n'entent nulz le deduit
> Fors que dui; mais li chans est doulx,
> Si les fait entendre a li tous.

(lines 6996–7004)

(She saddens him with a sweet *lai*. [She left aside] the other *lais*, and undertook the one that Galeran had taught her. She performs and does not mangle the song, the melody from Galeren le Breton. Thus they listen to her, each and every one. The delight of the words only two understand, but the song is so sweet that it compels them all to listen to her.)

Fresne achieves reunion with her beloved through music, but that musical connection does not extend to her mother. Fresne's mother Gente sings several songs for Fresne, and Fresne repeats them on the harp, following the same process by which she had learned the *lai* from Galeran, yet Gente identifies her daughter, not by her music, but by the fabric of her dress. Ironically, clothing does not communicate to Galeran; although Fresne wears a clasp Galeran has given her, he fails to identify her by that clasp. Music is the currency of exchange the lovers recognize, and the power of the *lai* to identify Fresne remains private between the lovers. In the English romance tradition, too, as we will see, music is strongly associated with love when it is performed by protagonist musicians.

The tales and music the minstrels sang centred around the nobility. It is not surprising, then, to find that within that fiction noble performers take ownership of the repertory, whether those performers are men or women. The difference in the protagonist's gender apparently does not perturb the class distinction between professional minstrel and member of the nobility that we saw in *Daurel et Beton*.

Fresne is not unique as a thirteenth-century heroine disguised as a minstrel. The *Roman de Silence* presents a female protagonist living as a boy who runs away with minstrels and learns to play both harp and fiddle, though her performance is fraught with ambiguity when her listeners rejoice to hear Silence. In contrast, an actual song is presented in the heroine's voice in *Aucassin et Nicolete*.[17] When her father tries to marry her to a pagan nobleman, Nicolete buys a fiddle and learns to play it. She disguises herself as a jongleur and returns to Provence, where she makes her way back to her beloved Aucassin. She takes up her fiddle and bow, and sings to him the story of their love, thus bringing about their reunion.

This passage evidently draws on a princess fiddler trope we see hinted at in a number of works, but the pattern is most fully developed in one of the three thirteenth-century Continental versions of *Bueve de Hantone*. This romance is particularly relevant to the English romance tradition since it is a close relative of *Bevis of Hampton*. Like Nicolete, Josianne disguises herself as a minstrel and sails across the sea in search of a beloved who is strangely inert. Both Josianne and Nicolete find their beloved in a liminal place, part way up the stairs or returning from a hunt. Each plays the fiddle while singing her story in third person, asserting that she knows nothing of her beloved, and the song is quoted in the text of the poem. In this trope, then, we see a female minstrel singing narrative while playing the fiddle. In both of these romances, the fiddle-playing princess is of Sarrasin origin, though integrated into European culture; and it may be significant that all of the female characters who play the fiddle in English romances are also non-European. We are reminded of the presence of Muslim performers in Western European courts. Lyn Tarte Ramey notes that 'Muslim slave women taken in the siege of Barbastro (Spain) in 1064 were reported by both Muslim and Christian chroniclers to have been exceptional entertainers, and these women were dispersed throughout the courts of Western Europe.'[18] The romance trope may originate in this performance tradition. At the same time, the development of the pattern also suggests a contemporary practice of narrative sung by a woman who accompanies herself on the fiddle.

Although the narrative song itself is more detailed in *Aucassin et Nicolete*, the life of a female minstrel is recounted so vividly in *Bueve*, with such clear expectation of shared assumptions, that some elements seem clearly grounded in current culture. Although Nicolete disguises herself as a male jongleur, Josianne remains a woman in her minstrel disguise; and, just as Beton is consistently recognized as a nobleman, Josianne maintains her status as a lady even when she is living as

---

[17] References to this text are from Mario Roque, ed., *Aucassin et Nicolette* (Paris: Honoré Champion, 1982). See example B.1 for Nicolete's song.

[18] Lynn Tarte Ramey, 'Minstrels and Other Itinerant Performers as Travelers', in *Trade, Travel, and Exploration in the Middle Ages: An Encyclopedia*, ed. John Block Friedman, Kristen Mossler Figg, et al. (New York: Garland Publishing, 2000), pp. 401–2, at p. 401.

a minstrel.[19] At the same time, she functions realistically as a *jougleresse*. We see lovely Josianne travelling together with old Soibaut with his grizzled beard, and patrons speculating whether they are married (line 12154). She plays the fiddle and sings, and he plays the harp, and they compose new songs together (line 12049). As any other stringed instrument players, they fuss over tuning (lines 11965, 12047, 12070), and we see them shuffling with their instruments from their lodging to court, to the city square, to court, and back to their lodging. They go to a tavern together to gather news (lines 11967–94), and they engage in realistic conversation with other musicians and with patrons. Marketing is important; they position themselves carefully to catch the attention of potential patrons.

Most significantly for our study of narrative performance, we see them perform a wide range of material, sometimes together and sometimes individually. At court, they perform together for the lady:

> Lors commencha Josïenne a chanter,
> Notes et lais moult bien a vïeler,
> Li vius Soybaus commencha a harper,
> Bien se commenchent lor son a acorder.
>
> (lines 12087–90)[20]

(Then Josian began to sing, skillfully vielling melodies and *lais*. Old Soibaut began to harp. Their music went together well.)

Later, as Bueve comes home from hunting, Josianne catches his attention by singing a decasyllabic *chanson de geste* while playing the fiddle:[21]

> Si com li rois va la dame aprochant,
> Qu'il pot entendre et ses mots et son chant,
> Lors s'envoisa et chanta hautemant:
> 'Or entendés, chevalier et serjant,
> Bonne canchon et bonne vertu grant
> De Josïenne, qui le cors ot vaillant,
> Qui escapee est Yvorin de Monbranc,
> Ki de Buevon ne set ne tant ne quant,
> Od soi a Thierri, fil Soybaut le sachant.'
> …
> Se li a dit hautement, en oiant:
> 'Venés a court en ce palais plus grant,
> Jou wel öir vous et vostre estrumant.'
>
> (lines 12108–16, 12122–4)

---

[19] Josianne is consistently referred to as dame (e.g. lines 12105 and 12155) even in her minstrel disguise.

[20] References to this text are from Albert Stimming, ed., *Der festländische Bueve de Hantone*, vol. 3 (Dresden: M. Niemeyer, 1914–20); the translations are mine.

[21] The few lines quoted here could represent either a condensation of the *chanson de geste* or the fragment she would have had time to offer. Soibaut mentions more episodes when he suggests the scheme (lines 12050–53).

(Just as the king drew near the lady so he could hear her words and her song, just then she made music and sang loudly: 'Now listen, knight and soldier, to a good song about the great valour of Josianne, who has an excellent figure, and who escaped Yvor of Monbrant. She knows nothing at all about Bueve, who has Terry with him, the son of Soibaut the wise. ... And he [Bueve] said loudly, while listening, 'Come to court in the great palace. I would like to hear you and your instrument.')

Back at court, Josian fiddles a variety of 'little songs' on topics with narrative connections, and Soibaut joins in with his harp:

> Trait sa vïele si commenche son chant,
> Notes et lais et sonnés va chantant
> Et canchonnetes d'Isseut et de Tristant,
> De Menelant et de Troies le grant
> Et de Paris, le fort roy combatant,
> Qui li toli sa moillier la vaillant,
> De Tidorel vait un lai vïelant,
> Et Soybaus harpe, qui le poil ot ferrant,
> Moult se vont bien lor notes acordant;
>
> (lines 12177–85)

(She took up her fiddle and began her song, singing melodies and *lais* and tunes and little songs about Iseult and Tristan; of Menelaus, the strong warring king, and about great Troy and Paris, who had abducted his worthy wife; she vielled a *lai* of Tidorel, and gray-skinned Soibaut harped. Their notes went together very well.)

This list of song topics is similar to the lists of narrative topics encountered in Middle English romances, and the songs are performed by a man and woman together, a combination we will find sometimes repeated in payment records in England.

The image of the female minstrel in romance does not end with the fifteenth century. In the late-fourteenth or early-fifteenth-century prose romance *Ysaÿe le Triste*, for example, Marthe performs a varied repertoire, including narrative presented in many ways, sometimes self-accompanied on the harp, and sometimes her stories are interpolated into the text.[22]

These passages create a compelling image of female minstrels solidly integrated into the performance community, performing the whole range of minstrel repertory, and this representation is historically supported. There are a number of archival records of professional female minstrels in the thirteenth-century. The household accounts of Louis IX in 1239 record a payment to 'Melanz

---

[22] Marilyn Lawrence, 'Oral Performance in *Ysaÿe le Triste*', in *Performing Medieval Narrative*, ed. Evelyn Birge Vitz, Nancy Freeman Regalado, and Marilyn Lawrence (Cambridge: D. S. Brewer, 2005), pp. 89–102, offers a valuable discussion of Marthe, including an appendix detailing elements of each performance. The romance is available in André Giacchetti, ed., *Roman arthurien du Moyen Age tardif*, Publications de l'Université de Rouen 142 (Rouen, Université de Rouen, 1989).

cantatrix,[23] and in 1276 the '*vieleresse*' Alison received payment from the Count of Flanders.[24] A tax book of 1297 lists a '*jugleresse*' named Beitriz d'Arraz and a '*salterionnesse*' named Eudeline.[25] An early thirteenth-century document of the Carité de Notre Dame des Ardents, the earliest documented organization of musicians, refers to its members as '*li confrere. & les consereurs*' (the guild brothers and sisters),[26] and the 1321 Paris corporation of minstrels includes an equal number of women as men and consistently sets the terms *jougleresses* and *menestrelles* beside *jougleurs* and *menestreurs*.[27]

Given the number of female protagonists who are musicians in one capacity or another in a romance, it is reasonable to imagine the convergence of story content and story delivery in performance by a female minstrel. A female minstrel could present a heroine disguised as a minstrel with considerable verisimilitude. But these narratives could not have been performed by women in every case. While there are uncontested records of professional female minstrels in the late Middle Ages, there were clearly more male minstrels. Initially it might seem incongruous for a male minstrel to perform in detail an account of a female musician playing an instrument while singing, but it is important to remember that male minstrels regularly represented female characters convincingly. Medieval audiences commonly saw women played by men in dramatic performances, and, as Evelyn Birge Vitz,[28] Carol Symes,[29] and others have pointed out, the modern distinction between drama and narrative was not as distinct in the Middle Ages.

Maria Dobozy has further demonstrated that the words and melody of a performance were only a part of the overall effect, reminding us that 'the complex set of components that produce a performance consists of the audience, the performer using voice, gesture and the entire body, also the time and location of the performance, the media used (text, melody, instruments), costuming and possibly properties.'[30] Drawing on performance theory, she develops a model of flexible use of a wide range of elements:

> A good performer thus transported the audience to a new reality, a new present. This new present is located in the audience's reaction to the entire performance and not in the words and melody alone. In other words,

---

[23] Yvonne Rokseth, 'Les Femmes musiciennes du XIIe au XIVe siècle', *Romania* 61 (1935): 464–80, at p. 473.

[24] Maria V. Coldwell, '*Jougleresses* and *Trobairitz*: Secular Musicians in Medieval France', in *Women Making Music: The Western Art Tradition, 1150–1950*, ed. Jane Bowers and Judith Tick (Urbana: University of Illinois Press, 1986), pp. 39–61, at p. 46.

[25] Coldwell, '*Jougleresses* and *Trobairitz*', p. 46.

[26] Quoted in Symes, *Common Stage*, p. 100.

[27] B. Bernhard, 'Recherches sur l'histoire de la corporation des ménétriers ou joueurs d'instruments de la ville de Paris', *BEC* 3 (1841–2): 377–404, at p. 387.

[28] Evelyn Birge Vitz, *Orality and Performance in Early French Romance* (Cambridge: D. S. Brewer, 1999).

[29] Symes, *Common Stage*.

[30] Maria Dobozy, *Re-Membering the Present: The Medieval German Poet-Minstrel in Cultural Context* (Turnhout: Brepols, 2005), p. 9.

performance strategies for presenting each song, epic, or romance were repeatedly adapted to produce the greatest aesthetic impression.[31]

Textual denotation is only one resource in live performance. By ascribing to protagonists, whether male or female, the ability to sing a story while playing an instrument, minstrels, whether *jougleurs* or *jougleresses*, remake those characters in their own image. Thus any passage describing either a hero or a heroine disguised as a minstrel simplifies a minstrel's job of rendering that character vividly. In narratives inhabited by protagonist minstrels, both the acceptance of *jougleresses* as commonplace, and the similar terms by which male and female noble musicians are distinguished from professionals, corroborate the hypothesis that the gender of a minstrel matters much less than we might expect.[32]

Minstrels and Minstrel Performance

To this point, I have not specified who the minstrels were, who their audiences were, the context of performance, or the nature of minstrel performance. I am using the term 'minstrel' to refer to professional performers, those whose livelihood is at least partially dependent on their performance, as opposed to noble amateurs such as the troubadour Pons de Capdoill or Bertran II, Count of Forcalquier.[33] More specific terms such as *jongleur* or *vieleresse* are substituted where they are supplied in a text under discussion, but the term 'minstrel' is intentionally left broad enough to include tumblers, dancers, animal trainers, and actors, as well as instrumentalists and singers, because there is strong evidence that the categories of performance were not as discreet as we might expect. L. M. Wright, for example, makes a strong case that the term *jongleur* tends to describe a storytelling 'singer-fiddler', but he concludes that the terms *jongleur* and *menestrel*, when used in their general senses, were 'more or less synonymous'.[34] Archival records throughout medieval Europe reveal a range of types of minstrel, varying in skill and prestige (much as today the concert master of the Chicago Philharmonic might be more highly regarded than a garage band drummer playing in a local bar). While terms used to describe performers may suggest patterns, it is not helpful at this point to define limits.

Similarly the audience for minstrel performance is not specified here because it is difficult to determine with certainty, even for a specific work performed by a particular minstrel. A romance text may clearly indicate a court audience, but that

---

[31] Dobozy, *Re-Membering the Present*, p. 298.

[32] The appropriateness of musical skill to both genders apparently extends to the nobility even when they are not disguised as minstrels. Silence reasons that *joglerie* is an art he can practice either as a nobleman or as a noblewoman (*Silence*, lines 2836–72).

[33] Page, *Voices and Instruments*, p. 7.

[34] L. M. Wright, 'More on the Meanings of Jongleur and Menestrel', *Romance Studies: A Journal of the University of Wales* 17 (1990): 7–19, at p. 18. Menegaldo, *Le Jongleur*, pp. 15–16, while finding distinctions among performers in the records, does not locate those differences in the the terms *jogleor* and *menestrel*.

audience would include servants as well as courtiers. Further, a minstrel might try out his material at a monastery or in a marketplace.[35] We do not have enough information to limit the audience or performance context.

What we can consider, though, is the nature of minstrel performance, and more specifically how minstrels might have performed narrative. Narrative texts themselves, while frequently presenting specific and believable representations of minstrels, sometimes incorporate bewildering features. The late-thirteenth-century Provençal *Roman de Flamenca* describes a feast at which more than 1,500 minstrels perform (line 508). After the meal, the feasters are given cushions and fans, and the minstrels stand up and perform:

> Apres si levon li juglar;
> cascus se volc faire auzir.
> Adonc auziras retentir
> cordas de manta tempradura.
> Qui saup novella violadura,
> ni canzo ni descort ni lais,
> al plus que poc avan si trais.
> L'uns viola<.l> lais del Cabrefoil,
> e l'autre cel de Tintagoil;
> l'us cantet cel dels Fins Amanz,
> e l'autre cel que fes Ivans.
> L'us menet arpa, l'autre viula;
> l'us flaütella, l'autre siula;
> l'us mena giga, l'autre rota;
> l'us diz los motz e l'autre.ls nota;
> l'us estiva, l'autre flestella;
> l'us musa, l'autre caramella;
> l'us mandura et l'autr'acorda
> lo sauteri ab manicorda;
> l'us fai lo juec dels bavastelz,
> l'autre jugava de coutelz;
> l'us vai per sol e l'autre tomba,
> l'autre balet ab sa retomba;
> l'us passet sercle, l'autre sail;
> neguns a son mestier non fail.
>
> (lines 596–620)[36]

(Then the minstrels stood up;
each one wanted to be heard.
Then you would have heard resound

---

[35] My own experience performing medieval romances and music in a grocery store called Waremart (with a loudspeaker heralding fresh bread in aisle 5), and in a cowboy bar called the Ranch Club, lead me to conclude that performers do not always limit themselves to expected venues.

[36] The text and translation are from E. D. Blodgett, ed. and trans., *The Romance of Flamenca* (New York: Garland Publishing, 1995).

strings of various pitches.
Whoever knew a new piece for the viol [fiddle],
a song, a descort, or lay,
he pressed forward as much as he could.
One played the lay of the Honeysuckle,
another the one of Tintagel;
one sang of the Noble Lovers,
and another which Yvain composed.
One played the harp; another the viol;
another, the flute; another, a fife;
one played a rebeck; another, a rote;
one sang the words; another played notes;
one, the sackbut; another, the fife;
one, the bagpipe; another, the reed-pipe;
one the mandora and another attuned
the psaltery with the monocord;
one performed with marionettes,
another juggled knives;
some did gymnastics and tumbling tricks;
another danced with his cup;
one held the hoop; another leapt through it;
everyone performed his art perfectly.)

Clearly there is no attempt at a unified performance, and the resultant cacophony of simultaneous individual or small ensemble renditions is horrifying to imagine. Passages such as this led Andrew Taylor to conclude that minstrel performance of narrative would have been short and fragmentary.[37] While Joseph Duggan suggests that jongleurs at a feast might have been distributed among the guests,[38] it is hard to imagine enough acoustic separation for any focused attention. Christopher Page argues compellingly that such passages reflect a romance preoccupation with 'the flamboyance and luxury of aristocratic life', representing all the kinds of entertainment a participant might have experienced during the entire course of the event.[39]

There are archival records of payments to large numbers of minstrels at specific feasts. At the 1290 marriage of Princess Margaret to John of Brabant 426 minstrels received payment,[40] and at a 1306 Pentecost feast in London 169 minstrels are specifically listed, with a reference to payment to be divided among 'the other minstrels of the company'.[41] These records are frustrating in the information

[37] Andrew Taylor, 'Was there a *Song of Roland*?', *Speculum* 76 (2001): 28–65.

[38] Joseph Duggan, 'Oral Performance of Romance in Medieval France', in *Continuations: Essays on Medieval French Literature and Language in Honor of John L. Grigsby*, ed. Norris J. Lacy and Gloria Torrini-Roblin (Birmingham, AL: Summa Publications, 1989), pp. 51–61, at p. 57.

[39] Page, *Voices and Instruments*, p. 161.

[40] Taylor, 'Was there a *Song of Roland*?', pp. 58–9.

[41] Bullock-Davies, *Menestrellorum Multitudo*, p. 7.

they fail to supply. While it is difficult to imagine any audience tolerating noisy simultaneous independent performances, it is equally difficult to imagine how they might have spaced these performances over time or through numerous rooms.

Perhaps at lavish feasts entertainers engaged in brief, extravagant spectacles, fragments of *chanson de geste* or romance, as Taylor suggests, competing with one another for prominence. It is possible that the audience members would ask the minstrels to be silent so they might hear one particular musician more clearly.[42] But there might easily be other, calmer events, meals on a less grand scale with only one or two entertainers (and many of the romances and payment documents describe such meals), or possibly impromptu entertainments in gardens or chambers (again, internal references and documents support this possibility). On these occasions, significant portions of longer texts might easily have been performed.

Medieval terminology relating to performance is notoriously elusive. The difference between singing and speaking is ambiguous,[43] and words describing literary or musical genres or forms elude the boundaries they claim to define. A catalogue of all the precarious terminology relevant to this study would serve little purpose. Instead, let us examine one term used several times in the *Flamenca* passage, the term *lai*. This term serves well to illustrate why scholars have been reluctant to discuss performance practice with any certainty, yet it is vital for us to understand the range of its medieval uses since a number of the works we classify as 'romances' are sometimes called '*lais*' or associated in some way with the term *lai*.

The *Flamenca* catalogue of feast entertainment lists three types of piece that might be performed with the fiddle: *canzo*, *descort*, and *lais*. A *canzo* is a courtly lyric such as many of the troubadour songs (though *Daurel et Beton* describes itself as a 'canso'). A *descort* is a more problematic notion, probably suggesting some discordance, and it is sometimes used synonymously with *lai*.[44] The term *lai* seems to be characterized in this passage by a list of four specific *lais* self-accompanied on the fiddle: *Cabrefoil*, *Tintagoil*, *Fins Amanz*, and *Ivans*.

---

[42] The Duke of Burgundy in *Silence* asks the two professional minstrels to be quiet because he and the company want to hear Silence more clearly (lines 3237–42), and, as seen above, the stunning performance of Fresne in *Galeran de Bretagne* shames the other minstrels into silence (lines 6983–7).

[43] John Stevens, in his pivotal study *Words and Music in the Middle Ages: Song, Narrative, Dance and Drama, 1050–1350* (Cambridge: Cambridge University Press, 1986), p. 200, observes: 'Can one be sure, for instance, that the distinction between *canter* and *conter* in French is as straightforward as it seems? It seems that in medieval German, at least, the terms *singen* and *sagen* may point to the difference between song and what might better be called chanting or intoning. This is the same distinction as can sometimes be made in Latin between *modulatio* (song-like melody) and *pronuntiatio* (the formal utterance of 'chant'), between *concentus* and *accentus*.'

[44] Stevens, *Words and Music*, p. 142, suggests, 'The *discordia* may be the effect produced by the perpetual change of the form of the strophe; it is a defining feature of the *lai* as it is of the sequence, and this is possibly why the word was chosen to denote certain *lais*.'

In the field of literature, this representation of the *lai* as narrative seems straightforward. Douglas Kelly discusses the term as follows:

> *Lay* is a term used rather loosely to designate a number of real and hypothetical texts in medieval literature. In the twelfth century the authors of narrative lays refer to compositions in music played on the harp, viol, and other instruments by Breton and British musicians; they also refer to presumed actual events – 'adventures' – the memory of which the lays keep alive. It is not clear whether such adventures were told to the accompaniment of music or whether the lays served to explain the adventures the music recalled, as in program music. In any case, the story was turned into verse narrative in French lays.[45]

While suggesting that in general *lais* differ from romances only in their shorter length, he points out that *Ille et Galeron*, over 6,000 lines long, refers to itself as a *lai*.[46] This narrative conception of the *lai* is strengthened when we realize that two of the four *lais* listed in the *Flamenca* passage conveniently align with Marie de France's late-twelfth-century *lais*. *Cabrefoil* is clearly related to *Chievrefoil*, and *Fins Amanz* could easily be an alternate title for *Deus amanz*. In her Prologue, Marie describes her composition of the *lais* as derived from a performance tradition and possibly intended to continue within a more literate, rhymed performance tradition:

> Des lais pensai, k'oïz aveie.
> Ne dutai pas, bien le saveie,
> Ke pur remambrance les firent
> Des aventures k'il oïrent
> Cil ki primes les comencierent
> E ki avant les enveierent.
> Plusurs en ai oï conter,
> Nes voil laissier ne oblier.
> Rimé en ai e fait ditié,
> Soventes fiez en ai veillié!
>
> (lines 33–42)[47]

> (Then I thought of the *lais* I'd heard.
> I did not doubt, indeed I knew well,
> that those who first began them
> and sent them forth
> composed them in order to preserve
> adventures they had heard.

---

[45] Douglas Kelly, *Medieval French Romance* (New York: Twayne Publishers, 1993), p. 10.

[46] Kelly, *Medieval French Romance*, pp. 12–13.

[47] References to Marie de France's *Lais* are from *Les Lais de Marie de France*, ed. Jean Rychner (Paris: Honoré Champion, 1983). Translations are from *The Lais of Marie de France*, trans. Robert Hanning and Joan Ferrante (Durham, NC: Labyrinth Press, 1982).

I have heard many told;
and I don't want to neglect or forget them.
To put them into word [or song] and rhyme
I've often stayed awake.)

The concept of *lai* here is clearly a narrative genre, however it may be transmitted.

But in the field of musicology, the term *lai* is understood very differently, where the primary meaning is a complex lyrical form. In a lengthy discussion of the term, John Stevens further divides the lyrical *lais* into 'Arthurian *lais*', which are typically short strophes inserted into lengthy French prose romances,[48] and 'independent *lais*', which do not exist in a story context and are typically not narrative in character (although their Latin counterparts are sometimes diegetic).[49] The 'independent *lai*' is the form most commonly referred to by musicologists, described by Christopher Page as a form 'of most ambitious design, in which each subdivision of the text had its own metrical form and musical setting.'[50] From a musicological standpoint, then, it would be reasonable to argue that the four *lais* listed in *Flamenca* are lyrical songs about the characters listed or from their point of view rather than narratives, especially since lyrical *lais* titled 'Chievrefueil' and 'Les deux amanz' also survive.[51]

The passage from *Flamenca* cannot resolve the ambiguity about the medieval *lai*, and the etymology does not help us make a determination. The word appears to derive either from 'the Welsh *Llais* or the Gaelic *Laio(dh)*, meaning a musical sound or song, *Laidh* meaning a poem'.[52] Furthermore, the melody of one of the lines of the *Lai des Amants*, which is clearly lyrical rather than narrative, is almost identical with the second line of the *Aucassin et Nicolette* melody, which is incontrovertibly narrative.[53] Even more puzzling is the use, in one of the four manuscripts, of the term *lai* to describe *Courtois d'Arras*, a work which most modern scholars classify as dramatic.[54]

Perhaps our modern insistence in distinguishing between a complex lyrical form, a simpler lyrical form, and a narrative/dramatic form distorts a commonality manifest in the medieval use of the term. A medieval minstrel or audience

---

[48] These lyric insertions are insightfully discussed by Maureen Boulton, *The Song in the Story: Lyric Insertions in French Narrative Fiction, 1200–1400* (Philadelphia: University of Pennsylvania Press, 1993).

[49] Stevens, *Words and Music*, pp. 140–55.

[50] Page, *Voices and Instruments*, p. 93.

[51] Gilbert Reaney, 'Concerning the Origins of the Medieval Lai', *Music & Letters* 39.4 (1958): 343–46, at p. 344.

[52] Reaney, 'Concerning the Origins', p. 343.

[53] Stevens, *Words and Music*, p. 227. Ardis Butterfield, *Poetry and Music in Medieval France: From Jean Renart to Guillaume de Machaut* (Cambridge: Cambridge University Press, 2002), pp. 2–3, observes: 'Our modern determination to see the poetic as somehow divorced from the musical is constantly confounded in this period. Finding the terms to describe the fluctuations and subtleties of their relationship is not easy. A common language often divides musicologists and literary scholars.'

[54] See Symes, *Common Stage*, pp. 71–73.

might think of *lai* more flexibly, perhaps as we think of the noun *musical*, which can refer to a play that is spoken with songs inserted (such as *The Sound of Music*) or a play that is almost entirely sung (such as *The Phantom of the Opera*). Here (as in the medieval usage of *lai*) the term can refer to lyric insertions or a complete story. Further, we might distinguish 'Andrew Lloyd Webber musicals' in something like the way medieval thinkers might have considered 'Breton *lais*', having certain characteristics that separate them from other similar works.

This brief survey of medieval applications of the term *lai* indicates the futility of looking to generic nouns for clarification of minstrel performance. We can more usefully explore minstrel activity by looking at the verbs used for performance. In the *Flamenca* passage quoted above, the minstrels 'vielle' (*viola*) their *lais*, and in *Galeran de Bretagne* Fresne 'va herpant'. The *Roman de la Violette* specifies that Gerart 'chanter et vïeler ensamble', and Beton similarly 'canta e vihola' (line 1505) for the princess. In fact, minstrel performance is frequently referred to in terms of the instrument being played, and in many cases this seems more important than the generic characteristics of the material. Christopher Page has assembled extensive evidence indicating that medieval minstrels 'passed a great deal of their professional lives telling stories', and that these tales were often sung with instruments.[55]

Records of Music for Narrative

Given that terms for instruments are often used to describe narrative performance, a likely place to begin studying minstrel story performance would seem to be the narrative melodies. A distinction is sometimes drawn between Middle English narrative, for which no music survives, and Continental narrative, for which some notated music does survive. When we look at the Continental melodies associated with narrative, however, we encounter complications. It is generally acknowledged that the *chanson de geste* was sung, and of all the French literature surviving in writing it is most linked with oral culture, but no notated melody for a full *chanson de geste* survives.

Johannes de Grocheio, writing in Paris around 1300, includes a description of narrative song in his discussion of Parisian musical practice. One of the three types of *cantus* he enumerates is the *cantus gestualis*:

> Cantum vero gestualem dicimus in quo gesta heroum et antiquorum patrum opera recitantur, sicuti vita et martyria sanctorum et proelia et adversitates quas antiqui viri pro fide et veritati passi sunt, sicuti vita beati Stephani protomartyris et historia regis Karoli.[56]

---

[55] Page, *Voices and Instruments*, p. 19.

[56] Christopher Page, 'Johannes de Grocheio on Secular Music: A Corrected Text and a New Translation', *Plainsong and Medieval Music* 2.1 (1993): 17–41, at pp. 22–3. All quotations and translations of de Grocheio's text are from this edition. In the same passage, de Grocheio goes on to describe the appropriate audience for this type of song. Unlike the other five categories of *cantus* and *cantilena*, designated for noble or young audiences or participants, this type of music

(We call that kind of *cantus* a *chanson de geste* in which the deeds of heroes and the works of ancient fathers are recounted, such as the life and martyrdom of saints and the battles and adversities which the men of ancient times suffered for the sake of faith and truth, such as the life of St Stephen, the first martyr, and the story of King Charlemagne.)

He goes on to specify the characteristics of the genre, the only narrative song he discusses:

Versus autem in cantu gestuali [est] qui ex pluribus versiculis efficitur et in eadem consonantia dictaminis cadunt; In aliquo tamen cantu clauditur per versiculum [both MSS: versum] ab aliis consonantia discordantem, sicut in gesta quae dicitur de Girardo de Viana. Numerus autem versuum in cantu gestuali non est determinatus sed secundum copiam materiae et voluntatem compositoris ampliatur. Idem etiam cantus debet in omnibus versiculis [both MSS: versibus] reiterari.[57]

(The verse in a *chanson de geste* is that which is constituted from many versicles which fall together with the same accord of verbal sound; in some *chansons de geste* the verse ends with a versicle which does not accord in verbal sound with the others, as in the *geste* which is called 'Concerning Girard de Vienne'. The number of verses in a *chanson de geste* is not fixed and may be extended according to the abundance of the raw material and the wish of the one who makes the song. The same melody must be repeated in every versicle.)

Here is clear verification that a single melody is repeated for each line of a *chanson de geste*, and that in some cases the last line of a *laisse* would have a different melody. De Grocheio even articulates how to compose songs, specifying that the text is prepared first, and then an appropriate melody is applied.[58] What emerges from de Grocheio's discussion is a clear practice of composing a poetic text and then applying an appropriate melody. In the case of the *chanson de geste*, the melody is a single line, with possibly a second line of melody applied to the last line of text in each *laisse*. Since the narrative text is lengthy and the melody minute and added later, it is not surprising that such melodies were not notated in manuscripts.

John Stevens identifies three extant *laisse*-type melodies, none of which is

---

is appropriate for the elderly and for workers and people who are neither high nor low: 'Cantus autem iste debet antiquis et civibus laborantibus et mediocribus ministrari dum requiescunt ab opere consueto, ut auditis miseriis et calamitatibus aliorum suas facilius sustineant et quilibet opus suum alacrius aggrediatur. Et ideo iste cantus valet ad conservationem totius civitatis.' (This kind of music should be laid on for the elderly, for working citizens and for those of middle station when they rest from their usual toil, so that, having heard the miseries and calamities of others, they may more easily bear their own and so that anyone may undertake his own labour with more alacrity. Therefore this kind of *cantus* has the power to preserve the whole city.)

[57] Page, 'Johannes de Grocheio', pp. 27–8.

[58] Page, 'Johannes de Grocheio', p. 29.

preserved in a *chanson de geste* manuscript.[59] Into Adam de la Halle's octosyllabic *Jeu de Robin et Marion* (*c.* 1282) is inserted one decasyllabic line (concluding with an additional weak syllable) parodying a *chanson de geste*. Gautiers brags that he can sing *gestes* very well ('Je sai trop bien canter de geste'). When Baudons asks to hear him, he sings one line in vulgar parody: 'Audigier, dist Raimberge, bouse vous di' ('Audigier', said Raimberge, 'I say, "Shit on you!"'). Robins exclaims that he is an 'ors menestreus' (filthy minstrel).[60] Gautiers' '*geste*' melody is syllabic, the weak seventh syllable repeating the pitch of the sixth syllable. This characteristic suggests that lines of varying syllables might have been accommodated by simple repetition of a pitch.

A second melody, this time textless, appears at the end of a brief epic poem of just one *laisse* about the Battle of Annezin. John Stevens proposes three possible applications for this music,[61] but none offers an illuminating connection between text and music.

The third extant *laisse*-type melody is preserved in *Aucassin et Nicolete*, which describes itself as a *cantefable*, a song-story.[62] In the unique manuscript, Paris Bibliothèque Nationale français 2168, prose sections alternate with assonating *laisses*, for each of which the same melody, with minor variations, is notated.[63] Two melodic phrases are written above each of the first two lines of each *laisse*, and a third is inscribed above the last line, which is composed of only five syllables. Although de Grocheio describes a single melody applied to every line of text, it is possible to conceive how one line of ten to twelve syllables might have been extended to fourteen syllables, two lines of an *Aucassin et Nicolete laisse*. In this light, the melody for *Aucassin et Nicolete* fits de Grocheio's description admirably.

While *Aucassin et Nicolete* is often cited as evidence of a *chanson de geste* type of melody, since the verse segments are composed in assonating *laisses*, the lines of these *laisses* are short like the octosyllabic couplets of romance.[64] This work, often described as *sui generis*, thus exhibits characteristics of both the *chanson de geste* and the *roman*. The melody, while it may indicate characteristics of music

---

[59] Stevens, *Words and Music*, pp. 224–6.

[60] Adam de la Halle, *Le Jeu de Robin et Marion*, ed. and trans. Shira I. Schwam-Baird (New York: Garland Publishing, 1994), lines 725–31.

[61] First, it may represent an instrumental postlude, such as the *modi* alluded to by de Grocheio. After so short a poem, this application may have been more appropriate than after longer narratives. Alternatively, the melody could be 'a rounding-off or refrain line', according with de Grocheio's suggestion that the ending line could have a different sound from the others. The third possibility suggests that the music could be applied to the text above, but the poem is in lines of twelve syllables, while the melody consists of seven note groups. It would be difficult to adapt the melody without breaking the ligatures.

[62] Section 41, line 24.

[63] See example 4.3.

[64] Each line normally contains seven syllables, except the last line of each *laisse*, which has five. Octosyllabic couplets can be sung to this melody with very minor adjustments, and the manuscript itself adapts the melody to accommodate eight syllables at one point.

associated with the *chanson de geste*, cannot easily be applied to poetry typical of that genre, which is generally decasyllabic with a caesura.

This blurring of the distinction between epic and romance is also found between the German tradition of the *Epos*, generally Teutonic long-line strophic poems, and the *höfische Versroman*, typically written in shorter lines imitating the French romances.[65] Ewald Jammers has assembled a number of melodies he classes as 'Epische Formeln und Strophen'. He observes that in Germany the strophic melodies generally developed into quatrains such as the epic *Jungeres Hildebrandslied*.[66] Yet the *Titurelmelodie* (*Der jüngere Titurel*), which is identifiably a romance, is dependent on the canzone form and elaborates and extends the lines of the quatrain strophic form.[67] He further points to connections between the German narrative tradition and French lyric tradition, suggesting that the earliest form of strophic melody was probably a couplet-length strophe with an upward movement in the first line and an answering downward pattern in the second, a form also found in the French lyrical *lai*.[68]

We find, then, in the German tradition, a number of narrative melodies, and these strongly support the miscibility of medieval melodic forms. This will be important later in considering the English tradition, since we find in Germany both notated narrative melodies and Germanic translations of French romances which share a number of features with the English romances.

In France, the source of the romance tradition, in contrast with Germany, there is no extant melody for a *roman*. While at first this may seem to strengthen the case that the romances are a literary form, Evelyn Birge Vitz's argument that the octosyllabic couplet is a pre-literary form grounded in French oral culture[69] is strengthened when we realize that the evidence for musical performance of *roman* is no more scant than the evidence for performance of *chanson de geste*, and the body of melodies referred in scholarship is identical for both genres.[70] All hints of melodic performance of either *chanson de geste* or *roman* are thus indirect. In contrast with what has been assumed, the francophone romance tradition shares with the Middle English tradition a lack of extant melodies.

Archival records imply professional performance of narrative with the fiddle or the harp;[71] internal evidence in romances implies such a tradition, both in phrases addressed to a listening audience and in persistent metaperformance elements that not only create a vivid image of minstrel activity, but gain impact in minstrel performance by bringing to life musicians in the story; yet there is almost

---

[65] Stevens, *Words and Music*, p. 215.

[66] Ewald Jammers, *Ausgewälte Melodien des Minnesangs* (Tübingen: Max Niemeyer Verlag, 1963), p. 76.

[67] Jammers, *Ausgewälte Melodien*, p. 77.

[68] Jammers, *Ausgewälte Melodien*, p. 76.

[69] Vitz, *Orality and Performance*, pp. 3–25.

[70] In this discussion, I am discounting the lyrical insertions into romances, since these are not structurally part of the narrative.

[71] See especially Page, *Voices and Instruments*; and Dobozy, *Re-Membering the Present*.

no record of notated music. It is tempting to conclude either that the texts that survive were not performed with music or that it is pointless to speculate about what sung narrative performance might have been like.

Uncertainty and speculation, however, are structural elements in all medieval musicology; even with notated music, there are always some uncertainties about rhythm, pitch, tempo, instrumentation, or other features, and our thinking always occurs within our own cultural context. As Daniel Leech-Wilkinson observes, 'The discipline itself (in common with other research subjects) maintains a group psychology that shapes, through the interplay of professional expectations and rewards, the way questions are framed, investigated and answered.'[72]

Yet there is considerable evidence about performance if we are willing to rethink what constitutes evidence and how it might be used, and if we are willing to live with an incomplete understanding of minstrel performance, one in which we can be relatively certain of some features, but less sure of others. We do not have enough informational wool to weave a flat and complete tapestry portraying the medieval minstrel, but we may have enough strands to link together a three-dimensional reticulated topography of romance performance.

We know much about how fiddles could be tuned; we know many contexts for performance; we have the texts themselves, texts with definite formal characteristics which facilitate some performance approaches and are demonstrably impractical with others; we have performance theory, which can illuminate principles that apply to all performances; we have indirect melodic evidence from a variety of sources; and ironically our best piece of evidence may well be the absence of notated music for a genre which indicates in every way that it was once performed with music.

What we should look for, then, is an approach to musical performance that would render notated music superfluous. From Germany we find a tradition of *Töne*, melodies in a variety of forms which can be applied to a range of texts in that form. In some cases these melodies allow considerable metrical variation in the texts, variation similar to what we find in many of the Middle English romance texts but not in the French tradition. Because these *Töne* would be widely known, there would be no need to notate the melody.

The practice of using *contrafacta*, melodies taken from one context and applied to words in another context, was ubiquitous in medieval Europe, so it is not surprising to find references to stock melodies outside Germany. The troubadour Guiraut del Luc refers to a *sirventes* written 'el son Beves d'Antona', to the tune of *Bevis of Hampton*.[73] The term *sirventes* normally refers to a strophic lyric form, so the melody mentioned could refer to a strophic narrative, but the confluence of form so pervasive in medieval culture makes it possible this could be a version of the melody used for the *laisse*-based Anglo-Norman *Boeve*, thought to be the source for the Middle English *Bevis of Hampton*. Because this story, in many of its forms, shares a fiddle-playing-heroine motif with *Aucassin et Nicolete*, which

---

[72] Leech-Wilkinson, *Modern Invention of Medieval Music*, p. 215.

[73] Stevens, *Words and Music*, p. 223.

contains a notated melody, it is reasonable to expect that the 'son Beves d'Antona' may share characteristics with the *Aucassin et Nicolete* melody.

When we examine the melodies that do survive for longer narratives (not lyric insertions), we consistently find simplicity and repetition. The melodic structure tends to exhibit a narrow range and basically syllabic text setting. The melodies do not always have a stable tonal centre, a characteristic we will consider later, but their basic architecture involves simple patterns with repetition. Ironically, it has been the very simplicity of the melodies that has led to scornful dismissal of an era more willing to endure repetition. In his 1970 edition of *Aucassin et Nicolete*, F. W. Bourdillon observed:

> The music to the verse sections is very simple. What strikes our ears most, if we attempt to sing even a single section through, is the exceeding monotony; and as every one of the sections is noted to be sung to the same air, one would think this must have become almost unbearable. Such repetition is now only tolerated in our religious services; and the monotony of a Gregorian chant, pleasurable in some ears, helps us to understand to some extent how an audience could not only endure but find pleasure in the long-drawn-out drone of these verses.[74]

However, in defiance of this perspective, we find, throughout Europe, that treatises on both rhetoric and music placed value on strategic variation. A medieval singer would not simply repeat the melody again and again. In the decades since Bourdillon's edition, musicologists have developed increasingly precise understanding of the nature and phenomenal extent of improvisatory variation.[75]

Timothy McGee has assembled and discussed in detail a wide range of medieval treatises on singing.[76] He demonstrates that:

> Ornamentation was both the duty and privilege of every composer and soloist; it was the way in which a composer approached his art and the performer executed what was given; it was embodied in the vocal style of the period and undoubtedly in the instrumental style as well.[77]

The ornaments he documents transform the simple narrative melodies, and the very plainness of the melodic material renders it adaptable to the continually varying text. Scholars have observed that medieval melodies often seem unresponsive to the texts set to them. For narrative, this must certainly be true, since each melody must interact with a wide range of textual material. Yet, while

---

[74] F. W. Bourdillon, ed. *Aucassin et Nicolete* (Manchester: Manchester University Press, 1970), pp. xxvi–xxvii.

[75] For an illustration of instrumental variations a vielle player might apply to *Aucassin et Nicolete*, see Appendix B.

[76] Timothy J. McGee, *The Sound of Medieval Song: Ornamentation and Vocal Style according to the Treatises* (Oxford: Clarendon Press, 1998). His compilation of essays on improvisation, Timothy J. McGee, ed., *Improvisation in the Arts* (Kalamazoo, MI: Medieval Institute, 2003) adds other dimensions to the potential for variation.

[77] McGee, *Sound of Medieval Song*, p. 4.

narrative melody in some modern cultures is often remarked on for 'the neutrality and seeming monotony of performance',[78] medieval performance demands variation. In improvisation at the level of ornamentation, medieval narrative melodies can respond to the texts they inhabit. Guido d'Arezzo adjures singers:

> Item ut rerum eventus sic cantionis imitetur effectus, ut in tristibus rebus graves sint neumae, in tranquillis iocundae, in prosperis exultantes et reliqua.

> (Likewise, let the affect of the song express what is going on in the text, so that for sad things grave neumes are used, for serene ones they are delightful, and for auspicious texts exultant, and so forth.)[79]

This advice echoes and reinforces rhetorical treatises, such as Geoffrey of Vinsauf's *Poetria nova*, which advises speakers:

> Vox quaedam sit imago rei; res sicut habet se,
> Sic vocem recitator habe. Videamus in uno.
>   (lines 2039–40)[80]

> (Let the voice be, as it were, a reflection of the subject. As the nature of your subject is, so let your voice be when you rehearse it: let us recognize them as one.)

In fact, treatises on rhetoric, like the treatises on music, are largely taken up with principles of variation, and Geoffrey of Vinsauf, too, describes a number of 'ornaments'.[81] Our modern sharp differentiation between text and music seems artificial in a medieval context, where advice regarding both is discussed in terms of improvisatory performance.

Paul Bracken has constructed a performance model for the *Chanson de Roland* based on melodic patterns that survive in the indirect sources. While the specific approach he develops applies more directly to *chanson de geste* than *roman*, some of his inferences are relevant to both, since his pool of information does not derive from a clearly delineated genre, but rather a broad body of interrelated material. He suggests, 'the written versions of these "recitation formula" type melodies often show evidence that they were varied slightly, rather than endlessly reiterated, and

---

[78] Reichl, 'Comparative Notes', p. 72.

[79] The text and translation are from McGee, *Sound of Medieval Song*, p. 169.

[80] Quotations from Geoffrey of Vinsauf's works are from Edmond Faral, ed., *Les Arts poétiques du XIIe et du XIIIe siècle: recherches et documents sur la technique littéraire du moyen age* (Paris: Honoré Champion, 1962); translations of the *Poetria nova* are from *Poetria nova of Geoffrey of Vinsauf*, trans. Margaret F. Nims (Toronto: Pontifical Institute of Mediaeval Studies, 1967).

[81] For example, in the *Documentum de modo et arte dictandi et versificandi*, p. 284, he observes, 'videre possumus quod clausula rudis quibusdam ornatibus informetur et quod sententia facilis verborum difficultatibus aggravatur.' (We can ... see that a simple statement may be developed with a few simple ornaments and that a facile meaning may be enlarged by more ornate language); the translation is from Geoffrey of Vinsauf, *Documentum de modo et arte dictandi et versificandi*, trans. Roger P. Parr (Milwaukee, WI: Marquette University Press, 1968). Geoffrey posits a number of modes of 'ornata facilitas' and 'ornata difficultas'.

sometimes adapted to variations in the syllabic quantity of the poetic line.'[82] He calls for a loud, clear vocal technique with some ornamentation for emphasis and possible use of facial expression and gesture. While he acknowledges that there is strong evidence for self-accompaniment with a fiddle, he states that the instrumentation 'is a small matter in comparison to the textual and notational evidence reflecting the prevailing vocal aesthetic, for the voice, the poem and its form were almost certainly the most important aspects of such performances.'[83] He concludes that 'even if instrumental accompaniment was used, it was probably minimal, light in texture and certainly subordinated to the dramatic narration of the voice, otherwise these vocal refinements would be inaudible.'[84]

To discount the importance of the instrument, however, is to discount the terms in which minstrel performance is consistently described within the narrative tradition. A minstrel 'fiddles' or 'harps' his material. Certainly instrumental accompaniment must be 'minimal' and 'light', and it must enhance the voice rather than distracting from it, yet the use of an instrument still has a powerful impact in performance, and what the instrument does must be specifically one thing or another. It cannot simply play; it must play something. The subject of much of this book will be how the fiddle might have been used in a memorized performance of romance in England, why an instrument would have been a desired component, and what impact it may have had.

But to try to understand England in isolation from the Continent, and particularly from France, would result in grievous distortion. Nigel Wilkins has persuasively demonstrated the high degree to which England and France shared a common musical and literary culture in the late Middle Ages.[85] Indeed, throughout Europe, we find endless evidence of intertextuality, both chronologically and geographically, and minstrel records abound in travel between England and the Continent.[86] While it is possible to isolate a region, discussing the performance situation at a particular period of time, it is not possible fully to understand the influences on the texts and music performed or the extent and manner these performances may have influenced other regions. In fact, medieval Europe seems to be an ever shifting community, with eddies of isolation, but general currents that affect most members of the community, though often in different ways and at different times.

It seems reasonable, then, while not assuming Continental evidence must apply to the situation in England, not to exclude the possibility of its influence

---

[82] Paul Bracken, '*Halt sunt li Pui*: Toward a Performance of the *Chanson de Roland*', *Nottingham Medieval Studies* 47 (2003): 73–106, at p. 104.

[83] Bracken, '*Halt sunt li Pui*', p. 102.

[84] Bracken, '*Halt sunt li Pui*', p. 103.

[85] Nigel Wilkins, 'Music and Poetry at Court: England and France in the Late Middle Ages', in *English Court Culture in the Later Middle Ages*, ed. V. J. Scattergood and J. W. Sherborne (London: Duckworth, 1983), pp. 183–204.

[86] For example, Craig Wright, *Music at the Court of Burgundy, 1364–1419: A Documentary History*, Musicological Studies 28 (Henryville, PA: Institute of Medieval Music, 1979), documents numerous sojourns of English minstrels in Burgundy and of Burgundian minstrels in England.

even when positive evidence is scant. Where there is continuity in a textual tradition between France and England, we may consider the possibility of some continuity in the instrumental tradition.[87] Where features of narrative melodies are consistent between France and Germany, we may consider incorporating those features in an English model.

In approaching the narrative performance situation in England, we may draw on a wide range of information from the Continent. We can identify aesthetics of performance that extend throughout Europe, such as the high value placed on variation within a frequently inextricable musical and textual culture. We can recognize characteristics among melodies associated with narrative. We have information about instruments used for accompaniment and their tuning. We know much about minstrels from historical, iconographic, and internal textual evidence. We have German translations of French romances, translations that share some features with the English romances and for which there is some musicological evidence. Perhaps most important, we know that within the earlier Continental romance tradition, a tradition for which there is strong evidence for musical performance, melodies were almost never notated. It is within this context, particularly as it can be illuminated by modern performance, that we begin our consideration of minstrel performance of the Middle English romance.

---

[87] The interconnectedness of cultural tradition is even more evident when we remember that France and England were not distinct nations through most of the time we are discussing.

2

The English Minstrel in History and Romance

FOUR categories of evidence survive concerning minstrels in late medieval England: historical documents, visual images and artefacts, notated music, and references in literary works, primarily the romances. No category provides as much information as we might wish, and all are susceptible to misinterpretation. Iconography is most useful in delineating musical instruments, which we will leave for future chapters. Similarly, detailed discussion of music manuscripts will be meaningful only after an understanding of narrative performance has been developed. This leaves two categories to consider. Historical documents and literary depictions, taken together, establish a complex and plausible model for minstrel performance of narrative. The evidence is indirect, very much what we should expect for ephemeral performance. Yet clues do exist that have not yet been explored. When we step back from generic boundaries between narrative and drama, and put aside distinctions between actors, storytellers, and musicians, the traces of narrative performance become clearer.

We find evidence of a flexible storytelling tradition in which the same tales were read in books as *romaunces* and told by minstrels as *gestes* or *lays*. Minstrels operated in a wide range of venues, and their performance responded to diverse needs; both stories and music would have necessarily undergone radical transformation as a minstrel moved from competitive *mirth* at a noisy feast, to solo boredom aversion on a long journey, to narration with a colleague in a king's chamber. Similarly, the relationship between minstrels and their patrons may not have been as uniform as we have imagined; in addition to performing for patrons, minstrels may sometimes have collaborated with them or taught them.

As a first step in developing a schema for minstrel performance, we will look in detail at one intersection of historical records, extant literary documents, and a narrative melody. While it has been generally assumed that no melody exists for the Middle English romances,[1] that is not strictly true, as we shall see. In addition to providing clear evidence of instrumentally accompanied sung performance of a Middle English romance, this assembly of information documents the practice of two-person partnerships in narrative presentation, and it provides grounds for understanding why narrative performance records have gone unrecognized and a means of bringing to light some missing pieces.

---

[1] For example, Reichl, 'Comparative Notes', p. 66, states, 'From medieval England no melodies for narratives in Middle English have been preserved.'

The Fiddlers who Sang 'Gray Steel'

On 19 April 1497 the twenty-four-year-old King James IV of Scotland paid nine shillings to 'tua fithelaris that sang Graysteil to the King'.[2] This is one of the few historical records that explicitly describe sung narrative with instrumental accompaniment in late medieval Britain.

The tale of *Gray Steel*, called *Eger and Grime* today, survives in two versions, one, referred to by its editorial history as Huntington-Laing, represents three extant late-seventeenth- and early-eighteenth-century print editions; and the other is found in the seventeenth-century Percy Folio.[3] Both renderings of the tale are thought to derive from a fifteenth-century version, and, though primarily in four-stress couplets, the poem shows some evidence of an earlier tail-rhyme form.[4] The story was so popular in the sixteenth and seventeenth centuries that Gray Steel became a nickname for dashing disrupters of order;[5] there are references to a number of sixteenth- and early-seventeenth-century editions,[6] and several ballads appear to be partially based on *Eger and Grime*.[7] The tale was linked with other popular medieval romances that survive in manuscript form, notably *Bevis of Hampton* and *Guy of Warwick*,[8] tales which show up in a high proportion of medieval story lists.[9]

A remarkable feature of this romance is the survival of an actual melody for 'Gray Steel'. In 1839 George Farquhar Graham transcribed a number of pages in lute tablature 'from the Lute-Book of Sir Robert Gordon of Straloch in Aberdeenshire, dated 1627–29'.[10] The original manuscript was lost a few years later, but Graham's transcription, including 'Gray Steel', still exists. The melodic structure of the song is *ABABCBCB*, a form we would associate with a stanzaic poem. Yet a 1686 satirical poem on the Marquis of Argyle 'is to be sung according to old *Gray Steel*', and this poem, like the extant versions of *Eger and Grime*, is in four-stress

---

[2] Thomas Dickson, et al., ed. *Compota Thesauriorum Regum Scotorum*, 13 vols (Edinburgh: HM General Register House/Her Majesty's Stationery Office, 1877–1978), vol. 1, pp. 329–30.

[3] The extant print editions are *The History of Sir Eger, Sir Grahame, and Sir Gray-Steel* (Glasgow: Robert Sanders, 1669 and Glasgow?, 1687) and *The History of Sir Eger, Sir Grahame, and Sir Gray-Steel Newly Corrected and Amended* (Edinburgh?, 1711). The Percy Folio is BL Add. MS 27879.

[4] James Ralston Caldwell, ed., *Eger and Grime*, Harvard Studies in Comparative Literature 9 (Cambridge: Harvard University Press, 1933), pp. 42–3.

[5] Caldwell, ed., *Eger and Grime*, pp. 6–9.

[6] Caldwell, ed., *Eger and Grime*, pp. 10–12.

[7] David C. Fowler, *A Literary History of the Popular Ballad* (Durham, NC: Duke University Press, 1968), pp. 142–3.

[8] In 1549 *The Complaynt of Scotlande* mentioned 'syr egeir and syr gryme' just before *Bevis of Southampton* as a story told by shepherds; and in 1630 John Taylor listed as 'Inke and Paper-murthering fictions' and 'lyes' 'Amadis de Gaule, Huon, Sir Egre, Beuis, Guy, the Mirrour of Knighthood, the seuen Champions, Chinon, Sir Dagonet, Triamore, Monsieur Mallegrindo, Knight of the Frozen Ile' (Caldwell, ed., *Eger and Grime*, pp. 10–11).

[9] Both *Bevis of Hampton* and *Guy of Warwick* appear in four of the six medieval lists examined in Liu, 'Middle English Romance as Prototype Genre', p. 342.

[10] National Library of Scotland Advocates' MS 5.2.18.

couplets.[11] It is easy to sing the seventeenth-century satirical poem and either version of *Eger and Grime* to the lute-book melody, though I find it most effective to view the melodic pairs *AB* and *CB* as a palette rather than a rigid sequence, an approach I will discuss later.

We have no assurance that the melody notated for the lute is the same as the setting for the satirical poem nearly sixty years later, yet this seems likely, since the author of the poem assumes the 'old' tune is well enough known that there is no need to notate it. This reference confirms the Continental practice of using stock melodies associated with narrative. We are reminded of Guiraut del Luc's *sirventes* written to the tune of 'Beves d'Antona', but in this case a melody survives.

Of course, we have even less assurance that the melody sung by the two fiddle players in 1497 is the same as the lute melody notated over a hundred years later, yet some relationship seems likely in the light of the melodic characteristics I will discuss in Chapter 6. Similarly, the fiddlers probably did not sing either of the two texts of *Eger and Grime* we possess today, but there is a good chance that what they produced bore some familial connection with the versions we know.

The performance itself may have taken a number of forms. It is possible that one performer played the fiddle while the other sang, possibly switching on occasion; or both may have played while one sang, or both may have played while both sang, or they may have taken turns,[12] or they may have put aside their instruments for this piece and acted it out.

Although we cannot be certain of the performance configuration, the pairing of performers is suggestive. While the Huntington-Laing rendition of *Eger and Grime* is more coherently organized and fully developed, David Fowler has argued that the Percy Folio presents episode pairings that may reflect a performance perspective.[13] In fact, the framework of the story (in whatever form it may have taken) centres on two knights' parallel encounters with an invincible knight and a lovely lady in an other world context. The structure invites a dialogue approach, and a heavily dramatized version would be natural for two minstrels.

The presence of two performers here serves as a reminder that, as illustrated by *Courtois d'Arras*, medieval texts do not distinguish sharply between narrative and drama.[14] Terminology for performers similarly urges us to accept a more flexible notion of story presentation. John Wasson notes that in medieval England the term *histrio*, which we would normally translate as *actor* from Classical Latin, is

---

[11] *An Brief Explanation of the Life, or a Prophicy of the Death of the Marquess of Argyle, with Diverse Others Therupon* (Edinburgh, 1686).

[12] John Purser, 'Graysteil', in *Stewart Style, 1513–1542: Essays on the Court of James V*, ed. Janet Hadley Williams (East Linton: Tuckwell Press, 1996), pp. 142–52, at p. 146, suggests that the length of the poem would put too much strain on a single singer's voice, but the 'twa fithelaris' could have taken turns singing.

[13] Fowler, *Literary History of the Popular Ballad*, pp. 143–6. Although Fowler observes that this pairing is a later development, it could equally well characterize an earlier performed version.

[14] Nancy van Deusen, *The Harp and the Soul: Essays in Medieval Music* (Lewiston, NY: Edwin Mellen Press,1989), p. 75, points out, 'Medieval writers are basically silent on the subject of "drama". Even an attempt to formulate a word to describe and substantiate it is missing.'

'a generic term, synonymous with *ministrallus* and *mimus*, which often refers to a musician'.[15] In the mid-fourteenth century in Italy, Alberico da Rosciate describes a tradition in which two actors sing *gesta*, and this practice may have extended more broadly:

> Unde postea apparuerunt comedi idest socij, qui pariter recitabant comedias, idest magnalia que occurebant, unus cantando alter succinendo et respondendo. Et isti comedi adhuc sunt in usu nostro et apparent maxime in partibus Lombardie aliqui cantatores qui magnorum dominorum in rithmis cantant gesta, unus proponendo, alius respondendo.[16]

> (Then comic actors appeared, that is, colleagues who together recited comedies, that is, [stories] of the great things that occurred, the first actor singing, the second answering and responding to the first. And these actors are in our tradition and appear mostly in parts of Lombardy where there are [also] some singers who sing the deeds of great lords in rhyme, the first declaring and the second answering.)

Two-person partnerships are practical. Travel is safer and more enjoyable for two people than for one, and performances can be far more flexible, drawing on histrionic, vocal and instrumental abilities. The range of textures and possibilities when the skills of two performers are combined is far greater than the range of an individual. At the same time, each individual is likely to be more highly paid in a two-person partnership than in a larger group.[17]

Richard Rastall points to evidence for pairing of instrumentalists, especially trumpets and bowed strings, in medieval Britain,[18] and similar pairing may apply to other types of performers. Account books for Durham Priory, for example, record between 1333 and 1377 seven payments 'duobus histrionibus', two 'duobus ministrallis', and one to 'two players'. In addition, payments are noted to two trumpeters, to a trumpeter and a minstrel, to two different pairs of named harpers (in each case one harper is blind), to a blind French entertainer with his small nephew ('Et cuidam ystrioni caeco franco cum uno puero fratre suo'), and to a man playing a lute while his wife sings ('In uno viro ludenti in uno loyt et uxori eius cantanti').[19]

---

[15] John M. Wasson, ed. *REED: Devon* (Toronto: University of Toronto Press, 1986), p. 543.

[16] Quoted in Timothy J. McGee, *The Ceremonial Musicians of Late Medieval Florence* (Bloomington: Indiana University Press, 2009), p. 257, trans. p. 78.

[17] I have taken part in three long-term duos and one year-long partnership with two actors. Sometimes the groupings overlap. Throughout my career I have performed with my sister, who plays the gothic harp, and she has on occasion joined with other musical partners. Additional musicians join in from time to time. This modern set of performance configurations is based on geographical, employment, and family relationships similar to those existing in the Middle Ages, and it may help explain the phrasing in some medieval accounts listing pairs or small groups among individuals.

[18] Richard Rastall, 'Some English Consort-Groupings of the Late Middle Ages', *Music & Letters* 55.2 (1974): 179–202, at pp. 186–7 and 197–9.

[19] Chambers, *Mediaeval Stage*, vol. 2, pp. 240–4.

The records for April surrounding the 1497 payment to 'tua fithelaris' in the accounts of the Lord High Treasurer of Scotland provide an illuminating context. The day before, the king commanded ten shillings be paid to 'ana man and ane woman that sang to the King'. Again we have a pairing, but with different information. This time we know the gender of the performers and that they sang, but not what they sang or if they also played instruments. We do not know why they received one shilling more than the fiddlers. A few days earlier, payment was made to 'Johne harpar witht the ane hand', which could refer to a harper named John or a man named John Harper.[20] Whatever service he provided for entertainment, he received nine shillings.

A general pattern of nine or ten shillings seems fairly standard for a performance, whether by one or two people, and for other services as well. Within the same week, nine shillings were also paid to 'the gardinare of Linlithquo', to 'ane cheld that brocht apillis to the King fra the prouest of Dunbertane', and to 'the lorymare that wirkis in the Castel of Striuelin'. Thome Barkar and Johne Lam each received thirteen shillings four pence for their week's wages. The records of payments to performers mingle comfortably with payments for other sorts of labour, and the rate of pay seems comparable.

Sometimes entertainment and other services mingle. Just four days after the payment to the two fiddlers, we find another record of payment for narrative performance. On 23 April, eighteen shillings were given to 'Widderspune the fowlar, and for fowlis and tales telling'.[21] The sum of eighteen shillings is suggestive since Widderspune's service is itemized: it seems reasonable to infer he received nine shillings for the birds he brought and nine shillings for his storytelling. 'Widderspune, that brocht wild fowlis to the King' is also listed less than a month earlier in the midst of a list of minstrels paid at Easter on 28 March.[22] Without the later reference to 'tales telling', it would be difficult to understand Widderspune's inclusion in this list, and these two references together illustrate how easily narrative references can be irrecoverably occluded. We can have no idea what sort of tales Widderspune told or how he told them. Perhaps, like the charismatic mason 'captin Cox' less than seventy years later, he had a wide range of romances and other tales and songs 'all at hiz fingers endz'.[23]

[20] If Johne Harpar were a musician, it is easy to imagine his repertoire would have included *Gray Steel*. With its severed hand motif, the story would turn the inconvenience of playing with one hand into an advantage, a point of similarity between the performer and the character Gray Steel, who loses a hand, which is then passed about as a token of his destruction.

[21] *Compota Thesauriorum*, vol. 1, p. 330.

[22] *Compota Thesauriorum*, vol. 1, p. 326.

[23] R. W. Ingram, ed., *REED: Coventry* (Toronto: University of Toronto Press, 1981), p. 273–4. Robert Lanham's letter dated 1575 describes Captain Cox and lists in his repertoire stories we would class in several different genres: 'And fyrst captin Cox, an od man I promiz yoo: by profession a Mason, and that right skilfull, very cunning in fens, and hardy as Gawin, for hiz tonsword hangs at his tablz eend: great ouersight hath he in matters of storie: For az for king Arthurz book, Huon of Burdeaus, The foour suns of Aymon, Beuys of Hampton, The squyre of lo degree, The knight of courtesy, and the Lady Faguell, Frederik of Gene, Syr Eglamoour, Sir Tryamoour, Syr Lamwell, Syr Isenbras, Syr Gawyn, Olyuer of the Castl, Lucres and Eurialus, Virgil's life, The castl of Ladiez. The wido

The cluster of records within a two-week time frame shows considerable variety in entertainment, and it is easy to see how narrative performance might go unmentioned at the time or unrecognized today in payment records. Just over a decade later, in January 1508, the same document, the accounts of the Lord High Treasurer of Scotland, lists a payment of five shillings 'to Gray Steill, lutar', and just below that another five shillings 'to ane jestour'.[24] Did a performance of *Gray Steel* occur, or was Gray Steill the name of the lute player? If *Gray Steel* was performed, did the lute player perform it as a solo or in conjunction with the 'jestour' (on the principle that *gestours* might perform *gestes*)? The two payments together make up ten shillings, the standard fee for entertainment a decade earlier.

Historical Records of Narrative Performance in Late Medieval England

The records surrounding the 'tua fithelaris' reference do not provide all the information we would like, but at least there are some hints. But where are the earlier records? All of the historical records most commonly cited as instances of narrative performance come from Thomas Warton's *History of English Poetry*.[25] Warton notes:

> Seventy shillings were expended on minstrels, who accompanied their songs with the harp, at the feast of the installation of Ralph abbot of Saint Augustin's at Canterbury, in the year 1309. At this magnificent solemnity 6,000 guests were present in and about the hall of the abbey.[26]

He assumes the minstrels were singing 'romantic stories', but we can be certain only that they sang and played the harp (or some related instrument); this is not an explicit reference to sung narrative with instruments. Six thousand guests may be an exaggeration, but if even a tenth that number were present, it is hard to imagine minstrels providing more than a pleasant background sound or small pools of entertainment which may or may not have involved storytelling.

Warton goes on to quote a lucid record of a sung narrative performance that took place in 1338, 'when Adam de Orleton, bishop of Winchester, visited his cathedral priory of Saint Swithin in that city'. The record details the name of the performer, the subjects of two of his songs, and the location of the performance. This is the only such record I know of for fourteenth-century England:

> Edyth, The King & the Tanner. Frier Rous, Howleglas, Gargantua, Robinhood, Adambel, Clim of the clough & William of cloudesley, The Churl & the Burd, The seauen wise Masters, The wife lapt in a Morels skin, The sak full of nuez. The seargeaunt that became a Fryar, Skogan, Collyn cloout. The Fryar & the boy, Elynor Rumming, and the Nutbrooun maid, with many moe / than I rehearz heere: I beleeue hee haue them all at hiz fingers endz.'

[24] *Compota Thesauriorum*, vol. 4, p. 96.

[25] Thomas Warton, *The History of English Poetry from the Close of the Eleventh to the Commencement of the Eighteenth Century*, 3 vols (London, 1774–81).

[26] Warton, *History of English Poetry*, vol. 1, p. 89.

Et cantabat Joculator quidam nomine Herebertus canticum Colbrondi, necnon Gestum Emme regine a judicio ignis liberate, in aula prioris.[27]

(And in the hall of the Prior, a certain minstrel by the name of Herbert sang the song of Colbrond and also the *geste* of Queen Emma, who was freed by the judgment of flame.)

Warton points out that 'these were local stories'. We know the story of Colbrond as a lengthy episode in *Guy of Warwick* in which Guy fights the Danish giant Colbrond just outside Winchester,[28] and Queen Emma 'was a patroness of this church, in which she underwent the tryal of walking blindfold over nine red hot ploughshares.'[29] In this case, both the *canticum* and the *geste* appear to be sung, but there is no evidence of a musical instrument involved in the performance.

Warton's final fourteenth-century record does link a sung story with instrumental accompaniment. He quotes a passage describing the anniversary of Bishop Alwyne, in the year 1374 at the convent of St Swithin:

Et durante pietancia in aula conventus, sex ministralli, cum quatuor citharisatoribus, faciebant ministralcias suas. Et post cenam, in magna camera arcuata dom. Prioris, cantabant idem gestum, in qua camera suspendebatur, ut moris est, magnum dorsale Prioris, habens picturas trium regum Colein. Veniebant autem dicti jocularatores a castello domini regis, et ex familia episcopi …[30]

(And during the meal in the convent hall, six minstrels with four harpers were making their minstrelsy. And after dinner, in the large arched chamber of the Lord Prior, in which room was hung, as is customary, the great tapestry of the prior, containing pictures of the three kings of Cologne, they sang that same *geste*. Indeed, the said minstrels came from the castle of the Lord King, and from the household of the bishop …)

It is unclear what 'idem gestum' might be. Warton suggests 'some poetical legend of the prelate, to whose memory this yearly festival was instituted, and who was a Saxon bishop of Winchester about the year 1040.'[31] Andrew Taylor infers it might be a dramatic rendition of the story of Queen Emma sung by Herbert thirty-six years earlier.[32] But a more direct conclusion might be a performance of *The Three Kings of Cologne*, the story portrayed on the tapestry.[33] How better could minstrels from the king and the bishop honour the community linked with Bishop Alwyne

---

[27] Warton, *History of English Poetry*, vol. 1, p. 89; my translation.

[28] *Guy of Warwick* (stanzaic), lines 2791–3273.

[29] Warton, *History of English Poetry*, vol. 1, p. 89.

[30] Warton, *History of English Poetry*, vol. 2, p. 174; my translation.

[31] Warton, *History of English Poetry*, vol. 2, p. 175.

[32] Taylor, 'Fragmentation, Corruption, and Minstrel Narration', p. 50.

[33] Warton, *History of English Poetry*, vol. 2, p. 174, notes '[a]mong the Harleian manuscripts, there is an ancient song on the three kings of Cologne, in which the whole story of that favorite romance is resolved into alchemy.'

than by bringing to life one of St Swithin's most treasured possessions? The involvement of six minstrels and four harpers (or even six minstrels of whom four are harpers) makes a dramatic rendition of the tale seem highly likely.

A less detailed record of a 1432 performance at the Priory of Bicester in Oxfordshire suggests a similar situation:

> *Dat.* sex Ministrallis de Bokyngham cantantibus in refectorio *Martyrium septem dormientium* in Festo epiphanie, iv s.[34]

> (Paid to six minstrels from Buckingham for singing *The Martyrdom of the Seven Sleepers* on the Feast of Epiphany, four shillings.)

The story tells of seven people sealed into a cave at Ephesus by Emperor Decius, and after 372 years they are found alive and sleeping.[35] The thought of a dramatic performance of this tale is daunting. In a story involving so much sleeping, there would surely be more singing than acting; and, while the title emphasizes the importance of the number, it would be impossible for six performers to represent seven sleepers. What did the six performers do? It seems likely that some played instruments, but that information is not included in the record. Where did the entertainment fall on the drama/narrative spectrum?

These are, as far as I know, all the explicit records of musical narrative performance in late medieval Britain. Only two specifically link musical instruments with narrative, in one case two fiddles and in the other four harps. Neither record of instrumentally accompanied narrative performance involves fewer than two performers. Furthermore, all of the records come from just two sources.

But when we look at the phrasing of these references, it is easy to see how similar they are to countless others. How different, fundamentally, are 'tua fithelaris that sang Graysteil' from 'ana man and ane woman that sang'? The record keeper, who may not have been present at the performance, might easily have selected details he could observe to characterize each entry: the genders of one pair of performers, the instruments another pair happened to be carrying when they collected payment. Idiosyncratically, having witnessed a striking performance, a clerk might note a tale that is a personal favourite like *Gray Steel*. Similarly, how different are the six minstrels and four harpers of the 1374 St Swithin performance from the '12 ministrallis in festo Sci Cuthb.' noted in the Durham Priory records for 1375–6?[36] Given so many performers, a clerk might simplify the notation, merely counting the number of people receiving payment. Given twelve minstrels, some combination of singing and instrumental music is likely. When the historical documents rest silent regarding the nature of minstrel entertainment, why would we exclude the possibility of sung narrative with instrumental accompaniment when there is so little evidence that any other type of performance is more likely?

---

[34] Warton, *History of English Poetry*, vol. 2, p. 175; my translation.

[35] Warton, *History of English Poetry*, vol. 2, p. 175, observes, 'In the Cotton library, there is a Norman poem in Saxon characters on this subject; which was probably translated afterwards into English rhyme.' He notes a Greek source for the story.

[36] Chambers, *Mediaeval Stage*, p. 243.

Most scholars agree that performance of narrative would have been carried out normally by an individual minstrel or a pair of minstrels.[37] Terms like *gestour*, *rimour*, *mentour*, *disour*, *bourdour*, *tregatour*, and *joculator* are probably associated with narrative performance. Although historical records do not provide many instances of these terms,[38] several occurrences appear to link storytelling with instrumental music. In the description of the 1374 St Swithin feast, *joculatores* is used explicitly to describe both the *ministralles* and the *citharisatores*. In the mid-twelfth century, a performer named Warin is termed both *vielator* and *joculator*,[39] suggesting that he may have played the fiddle and performed narrative, though we cannot know if he did both at once. Similarly, 'Ricard le Rimour', one of the prince's five 'boy minstrels' at the 1306 Pentecost Feast, was sent away for several months to learn to play the crowd,[40] a bowed stringed instrument.[41] Other evidence indicates that Ricard also sang,[42] so we have here a possible convergence of singing, instrumental music, and storytelling. Ricard le Rimour seems to disappear from the records after 1306, but Richard was a common name; the 1306 payroll lists twelve minstrels with some form of that name.[43] One of these, Richard Rounlo, was the King's fiddle player, whom evidence shows to be a man of some standing and wealth. Constance Bullock-Davies infers that 'he seems to have fallen on evil times or found himself in reduced circumstances' by 1316, pointing to a gift of forty shillings 'To Ricard, the vielle-player ... as an aid in support of his wife and children.'[44] But the evidence could equally well support an identification of this Ricard as the former boy minstrel, who would now be a man around twenty-two, likely to have a new wife and children needing a start in life, and what would be more natural than to move from one bowed instrument, the crowd, to another, the fiddle? 'Ricard le Rimer', instead of disappearing or ceasing to 'rhyme', may simply have been redesignated by his instrument. Along similar lines, other rhyming minstrels may be indistinguishable in the records because they lacked a name conveniently alliterating with 'Rimer'. Finally, a reference in the Household Accounts of the Courtenays, Earls of Devon, lists a payment given 'au Tregatour & au harper', which suggests teamwork between a storyteller and an instrumentalist, a type of partnership hinted at, as we have seen, in such records as the payments to

---

[37] See, for example, Chesnut, 'Minstrel Reciters', pp. 53–8; and Taylor, 'Fragmentation, Corruption, and Minstrel Narration', pp. 48–54.

[38] For example, Rastall, 'Minstrels of the English Royal Household', in his inventory of minstrels attached to the royal household, documents only Robert Fool, *bourdour*; John Alisaundre, *rymour*; William Percival, *gestour*; and Alexander Mason, *geyster*.

[39] Southworth, *English Medieval Minstrel*, p. 45.

[40] Bullock-Davies, *Menestrellorum Multitudo*, pp. 148–50.

[41] Mary Remnant, *English Bowed Instruments from Anglo-Saxon to Tudor Times* (Oxford: Clarendon Press, 1986), p. 42–4.

[42] Bullock-Davies, *Menestrellorum Multitudo*, p. 149.

[43] Bullock-Davies, *Menestrellorum Multitudo*, pp. 1–6. I am assuming that 'Mons. Ricard le Vilour' and 'Mons. Ricard Le Vilour Rounlo' (who helped distribute payment) are the same person as 'Richard Rounlo', and I am counting 'Ricard de Haleford' only once.

[44] Bullock-Davies, *Menestrellorum Multitudo*, p. 158.

a lute player who accompanied his wife's singing, and to a 'jestour' who may have joined a lute player in presenting *Gray Steel*.

But the most common narrative performances are probably hidden in countless payments to individual minstrels.[45] These payments are most commonly noted in one of two ways: either employing a generic terms for an entertainer (minstrel, *histrio*, *mimus*, etc.), or designating a musical instrument (fiddler, luter, harper, etc.). In addition, association with a patron is frequently noted ('domini Regis', 'Comitis Lancastrie', 'domini ducis de Eboraco', etc.), and sometimes a name is given ('Ralph Hubard', 'Matheo', 'Ricardo de Quitacre', etc.). When a name alone is provided, we may not know if the remuneration covers service as a minstrel; and sometimes terms for instrumentalists are simply family names. Occasionally we have a bit more information, as in the 1495 payment of two shillings '[t]o a woman that singeth with a fiddle',[46] but these are rare. The verbs describing performance, when they appear, are often ambiguous, as the payment 'Cuidam ministrallo ludenti coram domino Priori in camera sua' (to a certain minstrel playing before the Lord Prior in his chamber).[47] Here one minstrel engages a small audience, but was this minstrel playing as an actor or playing an instrument or both? 'Making minstrelsy', a term frequently used to describe performance, covers a wide variety of entertainment, as evidenced by a payment to John de Coton for 'making his minstrelsy with snakes ("cum serpentibus")'.[48] Even if categories of performance were more clearly distinct, it would be cumbersome for any clerk to specify the simultaneous convergence of narrative, singing, and instrumental playing. There are intriguing hints, but the records cannot take us much further.

Romance References to Minstrel Performance

Most recent discussion of minstrel activity has drawn productively on contemporary romances to provide complementary evidence. Like the historical records, however, the romance texts can be misleading. In the past, extrapolating from a few passages created distortions, and much of the controversy surrounding the romances originated in unwarranted confidence in the romance narrators' claims to orality. Critics in various disciplines have called for balanced analysis of broad-based pools of information.[49]

[45] Rastall, 'Some English Consort-Groupings', p. 200, notes a 'high incidence of payments for solo minstrelsy;' and Andrew Taylor, 'Songs of Praise and Blame and the Repertoire of the *Gestour*', in *The Entertainer in Medieval and Traditional Culture: A Symposium*, ed. Flemming Andersen, Thomas Pettitt, and Reinhold Schröder (Odense: Odense University Press, 1997), pp. 47–72, at p. 51, comments: 'Moral and historical writings provide a wealth of references to *gestours* and *disours* well into the fifteenth century, while pay records are filled with references to harpers and fiddlers or crowders, all of whom were probably singers or reciters as well as just instrumentalists.'

[46] Quoted in Greene, *Early English Carols*, p. cxxxvi.

[47] From the Bursars' Rolls of Durham Priory under 1375–6, Chambers, *Mediaeval Stage*, p. 243.

[48] Bullock-Davies, *Menestrellorum Multitudo*, pp. 66–7.

[49] J. Michele Edwards, 'Women in Music to ca. 1450', in *Women and Music: A History*, ed. Karin Pendle (Bloomington: Indiana University Press, 1991), pp. 8–28, at p. 8, observes: 'No single type

Responding to the need for a more comprehensive information base, I have collected minstrel references in the Middle English verse romances. Instead of examining passages where the romances pretend to be performed by minstrels, I have gathered passages *about* minstrel performance. While there is some overlap, the distinction is an important one. Although the texts we possess are not medieval performances, they may accurately describe such performances. That is to say, in creating or maintaining an illusory performance shell for a romance, a writer is likely to draw on details of performance familiar in that culture. In a culture so filled with records of payment to many kinds of minstrels on many occasions, minstrel performance is not a nostalgic anachronism. Furthermore, there is enough evidence that related forms of some romances were performed by minstrels that we might reasonably expect to find useful information in the written artefacts.[50]

I have catalogued explicit references to minstrels and music performance in eighty-three Middle English verse romances. (See Appendix A.) Since the purpose of the collection is to find patterns that may illuminate narrative performance, some categories of music performance have been eliminated, most significantly musical signals associated with hunting or battle or the commencement of a course at a feast. There is a large number of these references to hunting horns, trumpets, pipes, shawms, and tabors, and it would be intriguing to look at these in the light of Helen Jeffries' discussion of the role of trumpeters,[51] but for now I simply note that musical signals on loud instruments are a substantive element in the romances, and they often intersect with the references included here; although not the subject of this study, they are a persistent presence.

In this catalogue I have not distinguished among the romances on the basis of provenance, relative chronology, or relationship among manuscripts; and I have not attempted to characterize the manuscript evidence, though I do consider minstrel references from all manuscript versions of each romance. This study focuses on elucidating the performed relatives of the romances, performances that could have been far distant in time and place from the extant manuscripts, involving relationships we might never anticipate, so the details of manuscript production are in some respects peripheral. Acknowledging that differentiation among this material may enhance its value in future studies, I will here treat the assembly of minstrel references from romances as a uniform body of information.

of resource provides comprehensive information … We can, however, bring together an array of resources: iconographic and literary references, wills and financial accounts, guild records and religious documents, didactic treatises and chronicles by travelers, tax records and song texts, and music treatises and manuscripts. Since there are problems in understanding and interpreting each type of resource, they can best be used to clarify each other.'

[50] For example, McGillivray, *Memorization*, points to evidence of memorial transmission in the variants of certain romances; and the '[m]oral and historical writings' that 'provide a wealth of reference to *gestours* and *disours* well into the fifteenth century' (Taylor, 'Songs of Praise and Blame', p. 51) frequently include lists of *gestour* topics that survive in written romances (Liu, 'Middle English Romance as Prototype Genre', pp. 348–9, quotes two of these). Several such lists can also be found among the minstrel references listed in Appendix A.

[51] Jeffries, 'Job Descriptions, Nepotism, and Part-Time Work'.

Sixty-one of the eighty-three romances contain qualifying minstrel references. Sixteen of these texts (around a fourth) contain at least one reference to rewards for minstrels.[52] Sometimes the language describes unspecified gifts or 'fee', but in many cases the nature of the gifts is indicated. In sixteen of the twenty-five instances, the payment includes clothing ('robes of pall' is a typical formula); in six cases minstrels receive horses; gold shows up in eight cases, silver in four, jewels in four, and rings in one. In the three cases where specific amounts of money are mentioned, the payments are large round numbers (£500 in one case, and £100 in two). At first these rewards seem unrealistic when we compare them with typical historical payments of nine shillings (in the Accounts of the Lord High Treasurer of Scotland), or two pence (in a Maxtoke Priory payment to a blind performer),[53] or maybe as much as twenty shillings (in a payment to Merlin the fiddle player).[54] But when we look at payments to large numbers of minstrels at feasts, a context more analogous to the romance feast contexts, we find a gift of £100 to the 426 minstrels who performed at the wedding of Princess Margaret in 1290,[55] and 200 marks paid to minstrels at the 1306 Pentecost Feast celebrating the knighting of the future Edward II.[56] While less than the £500 mentioned in *Ipomadon B*, these historical records approximate the £100 and a steed the eponymous hero of *Sir Degrevant* wins in a tournament and then gives to minstrels, or the gifts worth £100 given to minstrels at the wedding in *Sir Eglamour of Artois*.

Rewards of clothing to minstrels are similarly validated in historical documents. 'Sixteen tunics, with as many hoods' were purchased for minstrels in connection with a 1345 feast,[57] and scanning Constance Bullock-Davies' *Register of Royal and Baronial Domestic Minstrels, 1272–1327*, we find numerous payments for minstrels' clothing. Often the records are scant, as '20s. for his summer outfit',[58] but sometimes they are quite detailed:

> 27s. 6d. prest, to Adam, the King's Harper, being the price of 3½ ells of bluet cloth, 3½ ells of striped, and one lamb's fur; given to him by Ralph de Stokes, Clerk of the Great Wardrobe.[59]

While most of the payments in the register document either cash or clothing, some suggest a practice of bestowing other items of value. A fiddle player received a silver gilt cup worked with enamel valued at forty shillings, and the

---

[52] Instances where the reward is a queen (Ysonde or Heurodis) or where the recipient is a protagonist in disguise are excluded because they complicate the minstrel reward motif with other factors.

[53] Chambers, *Mediaeval Stage*, p. 245.

[54] Bullock-Davies, *Register*, p. 115.

[55] Bullock-Davies, *Menestrellorum Multitudo*, p. 12.

[56] Bullock-Davies, *Menestrellorum Multitudo*, p. 7.

[57] Clair Olson, 'The Minstrels at the Court of Edward III', *PMLA* 56.3 (1941): 601–12, at p. 605.

[58] Bullock-Davies, *Register*, p. 28.

[59] Bullock-Davies, *Register*, p. 30.

famous minstrel Adam was rewarded with a gold clasp worth sixty shillings.[60] Two harpers received a horse to carry their baggage.[61] Sometimes property was involved: the trumpeter John le Scot received eight acres of land, John le Leutour was given ten pounds toward building a house in London, and William de Morley was given a house.[62] In fact, 'Robes riche, gold and fe'[63] are not as far from reality as they might seem at first.

Still, romance rewards to minstrels generally exaggerate real life, and this may reflect a performance convention. A noble hero lavishly rewarding minstrels may stimulate a patron to emulate him. But generous payment to minstrels may serve a more fundamental purpose directed toward the entire audience, not just those responsible for determining the reward. High payment to minstrels in a story reinforces the value of minstrel entertainment, and audiences generally appreciate a performance more when they perceive the entertainers are highly paid.[64]

But, whether an artefact of a written or a performance tradition, the prominence of payment to minstrels in romances correlates with the historical records. In both bodies of material, payment to minstrels is something to be documented. As in the historical pay records, most of the romance rewards designate minstrels in general as the recipients (in sixteen cases), but some additionally specify instruments or storytelling or singing (in nine cases).[65] In both the romances and the historical documents, this is the way to record performance: minstrels were rewarded.

A preponderance of the romance references note the presence of minstrels at feasts (sixty instances), and almost half of these feasts celebrate weddings (twenty-four). Historically, feasts in general, and weddings in particular, were a focus of minstrel activity, so much so that in 1290 three minstrels were paid twenty shillings each for staying with the king instead of going to the Earl Marshal's wedding feast,[66] and such records are not uncommon. Laurence Wright has suggested a linking of minstrelsy with honour and joy in the twelfth century,[67] and continuation of this perspective would explain the large numbers of entertainers at important feasts. Wright surmises, 'the most important reason for employing minstrels was not because they entertained or performed useful secondary roles, but because they symbolized joy which in turn symbolized honour.'[68] The more

---

[60] Bullock-Davies, *Register*, pp. 213 and 177.

[61] Bullock-Davies, *Register*, p. 11.

[62] Bullock-Davies, *Register*, pp. 65, 95, and 19.

[63] *Guy of Warwick* (stanzaic), line 209.

[64] The actual amount is irrelevant. A school that struggles to pull together $50 is likely to appreciate a performance as much as feasters at a banquet paying $200, but performances done gratis are sometimes taken for granted.

[65] It is not surprising that the romances, unbound by place or time, do not specify the affiliation of the minstrels.

[66] Bullock-Davies, *Register*, p. 75.

[67] 'Laurence Wright, The Role of the Musicians at Court in Twelfth-Century Britain', *Art and Patronage in the English Romanesque* 8 (1986): 97–106.

[68] Wright, 'Role of Musicians', p. 100.

minstrels, the greater the joy their music symbolized and the more important the occasion they honoured with that music.

This valuation is expressed in the romances, where absence of minstrelsy indicates something seriously wrong. Before a dangerous mission, Emere feasts without minstrelsy;[69] all minstrelsy and feasting should cease if Gawain were to die;[70] no minstrelsy will induce Amis's lady to rejoice, because she has lost her husband;[71] King Richard's troops, sailing toward Jaffa, fear all is lost because they hear no minstrelsy;[72] the King of Hungary knows his daughter is grieving because she no longer plays the harp and sings;[73] and as Melusine departs, she bids farewell to the sound of instruments.[74] In three romances, minstrelsy is contrasted with battle; and four characters' isolation or grief is cast in high relief by the music they hear. The word *mirth* is used, sometimes indistinguishably, to mean making merry, making music, or making love. This inextricable linking of minstrels with celebration makes their presence inevitable in processions and welcoming parties (twenty-one references). Five instances portray minstrels travelling with noblemen. They are also ubiquitous before, during, and after battle. Most of the battle references are not included in the catalogue because they describe signals, mostly involving trumpet, shawm, pipe, and/or tabor. Ten references associated with battle, however, suggest the possibility of other types of minstrelsy.

These contexts for entertainment corroborate what we know of historical minstrels. In 1474 Prince Edward was greeted with music that apparently included harp, lute, dulcimer, pipes, organ, and children singing.[75] A minstrel was paid for entertaining the Lady Alianora while she was travelling between Ospringe and Canterbury in 1332/3,[76] and the harper Nicholas le Blond travelled with Edward I from London to Caerlaverock in 1300.[77] Edward I's minstrels received increased wages when they accompanied the king to war.[78] Not all of these battle minstrels played loud instruments: Edward III paid his fiddler and citoler wartime wages, suggesting that they, like his trumpeters, pipers, and taborers, had some role in the battle camp.[79]

In fact, minstrels performed in quite diverse situations. *The Hermit and the Outlaw* offers a realistic minstrel perspective:

---

[69] *Le Bone Florence of Rome*, lines 1009–12.

[70] *Lancelot of the Laik*, lines 2761–2.

[71] *Reinbrun*, stanza 70.

[72] *Richard Coer de Lyon*, lines 6745–53 and 6771–82.

[73] *The Squyr of Lowe Degre*, lines 715–16.

[74] *The Romauns of Partenay*, line 3856.

[75] John Stevens, *Music and Poetry in the Early Tudor Court* (Cambridge: Cambridge University Press, 1961), pp. 237–8.

[76] Bullock-Davies, *Register*, p. 121.

[77] Bullock-Davies, *Menestrellorum Multitudo*, p. 20.

[78] Bullock-Davies, *Menestrellorum Multitudo*, p. 20.

[79] Olson, 'Minstrels at the Court of Edward III', p. 610.

> A man that wylle synge or carpe,
> Be hyt wyth geterne or wyth harpe,
> Be hyt never so schrylle,
> Yyf a nothyr be ludder than he,
> Lytel lykyng ys in his ghe
> But men be faste and stylle.[80]

(When someone wants to sing or talk, whether with a gittern or a harp, even if the sound is quite shrill, if another is louder than he, he will express little pleasure unless people are quiet and still.)

While it can happen that a competitor will overwhelm a minstrel's performance by sheer volume, the minstrel prefers his audience to listen attentively in silence, and apparently holds a reasonable expectation that this will occur. While a large feast may not have accommodated a sustained narrative, both the romances and the written records describe a number of venues that would have afforded leisure for storytelling to interested listeners. In two cases in the romances, the action of the story interrupts a king when he is listening to a minstrel apparently outside of a feast context,[81] and minstrelsy occurs in 'chaumbre' or 'parlere' as well as 'halle' in the romances and the payment records. The minstrels paid to attend patrons on long trips, too, would have found ample opportunity to tell a story to an attentive audience.

To the extent we can test the romance references against historical documents, they present a realistic range of possibilities for minstrel performance. But the romances have been somewhat discredited for glamorizing the figure of the minstrel. Andrew Taylor observes:

> The image of the medieval minstrel that we have inherited is … composed from a host of stories in which minstrels played prominent or glamorous roles: King Alfred assuming the guise of a 'scop' to spy on the Norsemen, Taillefer riding to his death, Blondel scouring Europe to find Richard the Lion-heart, or even Rutebeuf's hand-to-mouth existence as celebrated in his autobiographical poems.[82]

Yet not one of these figures appears in a Middle English romance.

The case of Blondel is particularly instructive in illustrating a difference between francophone and anglophone treatments of minstrels. His story survives in a mid-thirteenth-century French account by the 'Minstrel of Reims'.[83] When King Richard is imprisoned in Austria, the legend tells, no one knows what has become of him. Now it happens that the king has raised a minstrel named Blondel

---

[80] Transcribed from BL Add. MS 37492, fol. 76v; my translation. While not strictly a romance, *The Hermit and the Outlaw* exhibits a number of romance features.

[81] *Horn Child*, lines 157–9, and *Sir Cleges*, line 481ff.

[82] Taylor, 'Fragmentation, Corruption, and Minstrel Narration', p. 38.

[83] Natalis de Wailly, ed., *Récits d'un ménestrel de Reims au treizième siècle* (Paris: Librairie Renouard, 1876), pp. 41–5.

from childhood, and this man travels to foreign lands to find the king. Hearing of a mysterious prisoner held by the Duke of Austria, Blondel offers his services at the castle. His experience is described in some detail: we hear a conversation with the widow where he lodges before going to the castle, we see him returning there to pick up 'sa viele et ses estrumenz' (his fiddle and his instruments), and we are told how much he pleases the duke and his household. Then at Easter, King Richard, imprisoned in a tower, sees Blondel in a garden below and reveals himself to his minstrel by singing a song which they had composed together and which no one else knows ('une chançon qu'il avoient faite entr'eus deus, at que nus ne savoit que il dui'). Blondel's response is to go to his room, kneel down and pick up his fiddle, and play a tune so compellingly that the duke seeks him out. While this fiddle playing does not immediately assist Richard, it emphasizes in vivid detail the intimate and potent link between Richard and Blondel. Later Blondel returns to England and informs the barons of his discovery of the king, and they set about rescuing King Richard.

The story of Richard's captivity is also told in the Middle English *Richard Coer de Lyon* (lines 652–94), and again an English minstrel takes an active role in the events, but this minstrel is no Blondel. Disguised as pilgrims, King Richard and two companions pause in their travels in 'Alemayne'. At a tavern, they are cooking a goose and drinking when an English minstrel comes in and asks if they want 'ony mynstralsy'. Richard, a rather irascible figure in this romance, asks him to leave, to which the minstrel responds:

> Ye are men unkynde,
> And yiff I may, ye schall forthynk.
> Ye gaff me neyther mete ne drynk!
> Ffor gentyl men scholde bede
> To mynstrall that abouten yede
> Off here mete, wyn, and ale:
> Ffor los ryses off mynstrale.
>
> (lines 670–6)

(You are unkind men, and if I can [bring it about], you will regret that you gave me neither meat nor drink! For noble men should give some of their meat, wine and ale to minstrels that travel about, for praise rises from minstrels.)

The minstrel thereupon goes to the King of Almayne, who is Richard's bitter enemy, and informs him of the identity of the three 'pilgrims'. The three are seized and cast in prison and remain there for some time. Evidently this experience teaches Richard to respect minstrels as guardians of 'los' (praise); at a feast honouring King Philip, Richard rewards heralds and minstrels so that they will 'bere his los', and as a result, 'thorwgh her cry his renoun ros' (lines 3773–81).

At first it might appear that a pejorative Middle English representation of minstrels has replaced the glamorized French portrayal, but there is only one other scoundrel among minstrels in Middle English romances, the Irish minstrel in *Sir Tristrem* who tricks King Mark into giving him Ysonde. While the minstrel in *Richard Coer de Lyon* seems vindictive, he may be set against the minstrel on the wall in *Sir Degrevant* who does not reveal when Degrevant sneaks into the earl's castle because 'Mynstrals are ay curtayse / Als thay ere kende to be' (Minstrels are always curteous, as they are known to be, Lincoln MS, lines 1587–8). Normally the Middle English romances are neutral about the morality of minstrels.

The association of minstrels with 'los', however, does occur in other romances. Minstrels carry information. When a minstrel visits their court, Baldwin's lady 'had myrth of his mouthe, / To here his tithand'.[84] A number of prologues link minstrels with the renown of romance heroes, who 'worship han goote in boure and halle',[85] and whose 'dedis ben in remembraunce';[86] because by hearing minstrels tell *gestes*, an uneducated person 'may lere / thynge that fryste he ne knewe'.[87] This informational function of minstrelsy is limned large in *Sir Cleges*. In MS Ashmole 61, when the impoverished Sir Cleges comes to present his miraculous cherries, the king is sitting in his chamber listening to a harper tell a tale. The king asks the harper, because he has travelled so far, if he can identify the visitor, and the harper immediately replies that this man was once the king's knight Cleges:

> The Kyng was sett in hys parlere,
> Myrth and revell forto here;
> Syre Cleges theder wente.
> An harper had a geyst i-seyd,
> That made the Kyng full wele a-payd,
> As to hys entente.
> Than seyd the Kyng to this herpere:
> 'Mykyll thou may ofte tyme here,
> Fore thou hast ferre wente.
> Tell me trew, if thou can:
> Knowyst thou thys pore man,
> That this dey me presente?'
> He seyd: 'My lege, with-outen les,
> Som-tyme men callyd hym Cleges;
> He was a knyght of youre.
> I may thinke, when that he was
> Full of fortone and of grace,
> A man of hye stature.'
>
> (MS Ashmole 61, lines 481–98)

(The king was seated in his chamber in order to hear mirth and revelry; Sir Cleges went thither. A harper had told a *geste* that pleased the king in being

---

[84] *The Avowynge of King Arthur*, lines 747–8.

[85] *Generides* (couplet version), line 18. A few lines later, 'Thei gate worship and grete los', line 22.

[86] *The Laud Troy-Book*, line 25.

[87] *Partonope of Blois*, lines 23–4.

what he had desired. Then the king said to this harper, 'You must often hear a great deal because you have travelled far. Tell me truly, if you can: do you know this poor man who has brought me a gift today?' [The harper] said, 'My liege, without lying, people used to call him Cleges; he was a knight of yours. I remember when he was replete with fortune and grace, a man of high stature.)

In the other manuscript of the romance, Advocates MS 19.1.11, the harper is actually singing a *geste* about Sir Cleges when that knight arrives. In this version, the king also asks for information on the grounds that the harper has travelled extensively, but this time he asks the whereabouts of Sir Cleges, the subject of the *geste*, or anything the harper might know about him. The harper, who apparently does not recognize Cleges, states only that he was once the king's knight, adding that 'we mynstrellys' miss him since he left the country:

> The kynge was sett in hys parlor
> Wyth myrth, solas and onor;
> Sir Cleges thedyr went.
> An harpor sange a gest be mowth
> Of a knyght ther be sowth,
> Hym-selffe, werament.
> Than seyd the kynge to the harpor:
> 'Werc ys knyght Cleges, tell me herr;
> For thu hast wyde i-went.
> Tell me trewth, yf thou can:
> Knowyste thou of that man?'
> The harpor seyd: 'Yee, iwysse!
> Sum tyme for soth I hym knewe;
> He was a knyght of youres full trewe
> And comly of gesture.
> We mynstrellys mysse hym sekyrly,
> Seth he went out of cunntre;
> He was fayr of stature.'
>   (Advocates MS 19.1.11, lines 481–98)

(The king was seated in his chamber with mirth, pleasure, and honour; Sir Cleges went thither. A harper was singing a *geste* about a knight who was actually there, himself, in fact. Then the king said to the harper, 'Where is this knight Cleges, tell me here, for you have travelled widely. Tell me the truth, if you can: do you know of that man?' The harper said, 'Yes, certainly! I used to know him, in fact. He was a very true knight of yours, and gracious in behaviour. We minstrels miss him sorely, since he went out of the country. He was of fair stature.)

Here we see a *geste* about a contemporary figure told by a harper (who may or may not play the harp as he narrates). Earlier in the tale, we have seen the hero of the *geste* lavishly rewarding minstrels, and now here we see one of those minstrels, who naturally misses the lucrative Christmas feasts, spreading the hero's fame.

Andrew Taylor provides strong evidence that carrying the praise or blame of contemporaries was an important function of minstrels.[88] He points to a number of extant song texts that might have served that function and documents several historical corroborations. He notes that in the fourteenth century, minstrels sometimes accompanied criminals to the stocks;[89] in *Chevalere Assigne*, the queen is taken to be burned to the accompaniment of music (lines 225–6).

In proclaiming the deeds of contemporaries, minstrels seem to have overlapped with heralds. Taylor notes that '[b]oth were expected to know blazons, to attend battles and tournaments, to keep track of which knights performed well, and to spread word of what they saw',[90] and Richard Rastall points out that often a *rex ministrallorum* was also a *rex haraldorum*.[91] Even as professions became more specialized in the fourteenth century, 'the duties of herald and minstrel must often have merged.'[92] We find evidence of shared responsibility for carrying news in the romances. Richard, after all, gives treasure to 'herawdes' as well as 'to dysours, to tabourrers, and to trumpours' to 'bere his los'. We see this combination in action in *Libeaus Desconus* when heralds and minstrels provide a play-by-play account of the fight between Libeaus and Geffron:

> Tabowres and trompours,
> Heroudes and dissoures,
> Her strokys con discrye.
> > (Lambeth Palace MS, lines 954–6)

(Taborers and trumpeters, heralds and storytellers, proclaimed their strokes.)

If this accurately describes a practice that may have taken place, would the 'heroudes and dissoures' have alternated with the 'tabowres and trompours'? The possibilities are complicated by the variant in BN MS XIII.B.29 and MS Ashmole 61, where the ones who 'discrye' the blows are:

> Mynstrals and trompours,
> Harpours and gestours,

---

[88] Taylor, 'Songs of Praise and Blame'. This practice was also common in France, as is evident from the 1395 ordinance forbidding 'à tous dicteurs, faiseurs de ditz et de chançons, et à tous autres Ménestriers de bouche et recordeurs de ditz' (all storytellers and makers of stories and songs, and all other minstrels of the mouth and performers of stories) from 'facent, dyent, ne chantent' (making, speaking, or singing) any 'ditz, rymes ne chançons' (stories, rhymes, or songs) that mention either the pope or the king in an unfavorable light (quoted in Wright, *Music at the Court of Burgundy*, p. 27).

[89] Taylor, 'Songs of Praise and Blame', p. 67.

[90] Taylor, 'Songs of Praise and Blame', p. 53.

[91] Rastall, 'Minstrel Court', p. 100.

[92] Taylor, 'Songs of Praise and Blame', p. 55. Similarly, McGee, *Ceremonial Musicians*, pp. 72–3, observes that in late medieval Florence, 'there was always a close link between the herald and the singing minstrel inasmuch as the praises usually took the form of sung poetry.'

The presence of harpers is puzzling, and it echoes questions raised by other historical and literary representations of coexisting loud and soft instruments at feasts. Would the harpers have played for small subgroups of the total audience at a formalized combat? Would they, on this occasion, have used their voices only and left their harps at home? Or would they have played their instruments loudly, as evidence indicates they could have done?[93] How would a combination of instrumentalists and speakers/singers formulate a story that is occurring simultaneously?

Storytelling is present in many romances, but it is not developed as fully as in the Continental romances. Thirty-three references in twenty-three romances include explicit mention of storytelling or storytellers. About half of these romances are in some form of tail-rhyme, and the other half are in couplets; only one alliterative romance includes a reference to narrative performance. While a number of factors might account for this distribution, it may be that alliterative verse was less strongly associated with minstrels and possibly less commonly performed by them. Terms used for storytellers (ignoring variant spellings) are: *minstrel*, *bourdour*, *glewman*, *gestour*, *disour*, *jogolour*, and *harpour*. Some of the passages listing terms for a variety of entertainers may distinguish between the storytellers and other minstrels: 'theo mynstral syngith theo jogolour carpith', 'disours and minstrels to singe and carpe', and 'minstrels of mouthe and mani dysour'.[94] In these cases it is difficult to tell if the terms *disour* and *jogolour* are being used exclusively or synonymously with *minstrel*. There are other instances in which *minstrels* clearly serve a narrative function: the storytelling harper in *Sir Cleges* describes himself as a minstrel; the narrator of *Emare* asserts that minstrels should begin their stories speaking of Jesus and then continues 'As I here synge in songe'; and in *Sir Degrevant*, it is minstrels who 'hafe haldyn up his name'.[95] Two of the romance narrators assert that they are telling the tale 'as y have herd menstrelles syng yn sawe' or 'as gestours tellys at bord'.[96] As in the broader European entertainment tradition, terms for performers elude definition, and words for singing and speaking intermingle and alternate freely.

The terms for the tales themselves, however, exhibit some consistency. In eight of the eleven instances where *romaunce* is used in a performance context, the term is explicitly linked with reading, and in the remaining three cases the mode of

[93] Judy Kadar, 'Some Practical Hints for Playing Fourteenth and Fifteenth Century Music', in *Historische Harfen: Beiträge zur Theorie und Praxis historischer Harfen* (Dornach: Eigenverlag der Musik-Akademie der Stadt Basel, 1991), pp. 120–32, at pp. 129–30, quotes the mid-fifteenth-century theorist Paulus Paulirinus, who describes a triangular harp plucked with the fingernails: 'It projects sound to a great distance, indeed farther than any other instrument aside from the trumpet, organ and portative. It may be combined with any musical instrument by plucking it louder or softer.' She also describes a way of producing such a sound: 'Using the fingernail (cut short) to pluck the string *près de la table* produces a metallic, clear sound and can be played much louder than any other means I have found. This sound can be even louder than playing with bray pins.'

[94] *The Lyfe of Alisaunder*, line 4715; *Sir Firumbras* (Fillingham), line 417; and *Guy of Warwick*, line 197.

[95] *Sir Cleges*, Advocates MS, line 496; *Emare*, lines 13–24; and *Sir Degrevant*, line 90.

[96] *Emare*, line 319; and *Libeaus Desconus*, MS Ashmole 61, fol. 57r.

presentation is not specified. All eleven instances of the term *geste*, on the other hand, refer to a story that is heard, told, or sung, as are the two references to a *tale* and ten of the eleven references to a *lay*. In *Havelok*, romance reading and the singing of *gestes* are set side by side as celebratory activities:

> Romanz-reding on the bok.
> Ther mouthe men here the gestes singe,
>
> (lines 28–9)

In *The Laud Troy-Book*, stories about heroes are made into *romaunces* and also turned into *gestes* by *gestours* at meals and great feasts. After a list of heroes we know from extant romances, the narrator observes:

> In romaunces that of hem ben made
> That gestoures often dos of hem gestes
> At mangeres and at grete festes.
>
> (lines 22–4)

Even more explicit, *Richard Coer de Lyon* contrasts romances in French that can be read with 'jestes' in English that can be heard (lines 5–28). What emerges is a consistent pattern of parallel treatment of the same body of narrative material. *Romaunces* are read, and *gestes* are heard, and both narrate the same stories. In this light, it is not surprising to find that in Beauvais in 1377 the two items one might confiscate from minstrels would be 'leur livre ou leur vièle' (their book or their fiddle),[97] the physical items needed for two different modes of story performance.

The two approaches to narration are further complicated when we look more closely at who performs in the romances. While the entertainment norm is clearly some form of minstrel performance, especially at feasts, both music and story performance are sometimes carried out by the nobility, not always in disguise as minstrels. By implication, the relationship between minstrel and patron may not be easily contained within a performer/audience model. We may learn more about the interface between minstrels and their patrons by looking carefully at the romances.

Some intriguing patterns emerge when we look at the nineteen romances in which characters in the tales are performers. Eight romances state that a noble character is a skilled musician, but we never see that person perform. Five of these characters are women: Florence plays the harp and the psaltery; Felice is 'lerned … in music'; Persevis plays the harp, sings, and dances; the daughter of Argus plays the harp, the fiddle, and the psaltery, and is capable of 'romance reding'; and Ysonde, already able 'romaunce to rede aright', is taught by Tristrem some options for performing lays ('what alle playes were / in lay') and to play and sing.[98] Four of the performers who remain silent in the story are men: Harlond likes 'to harp wele' and apparently is the one who teaches Horn 'of al gle … insight' and to

---

[97] Bernhard, 'Recherches sur l'histoire de la corporation des ménétriers', pp. 399.

[98] *Le Bone Florence of Rome*, lines 61–3; *Guy of Warwick* (couplet), Caius MS 107, line 91; *Partonope of Blois*, lines 7617–18; *Reinbrun*, stanza 12; *Sir Tristrem*, lines 1257–65, 1283–5, and 1608.

play the harp and read romance correctly; we do not see Horn perform in *Horn Child*; in *King Horn*, Athelbrus is apparently a musician, since the king asks him to teach Horn to play the harp and sing; and Degrevant, sings and plays the citole (or lute), the psaltery, the rote, the gittern, and the harp.[99] In these instances, skill in storytelling is sometimes linked with instrumental prowess, and both appear to be accomplishments typical of a male or female member of the nobility.

Among the noble characters in the romances, three men and six women are seen performing in the course of the tale. Each of the three men, Horn (in *King Horn*), Orfeo, and Tristrem, performs while disguised as a minstrel in order to win back the lady he loves. Horn and Orfeo both play the harp, and Tristrem plays the rote.[100] Among the six women, only the Armenian princess Josian earns her living disguised as a minstrel, and she does so only in the Auchinleck MS.[101] The other five ladies all perform in their own person in a non-professional capacity: the Carle's daughter plays the harp and sings romances in the hall for their visitor Gawain; La Dame Amour detains Libeaus with minstrelsy; in a bedchamber, a lady plays the harp for Degare, causing him to fall asleep; in a bedchamber, Loose-pine plays the psaltery while two maidens sing for Eger and then for Grime; and in her chamber, Myldor harps and sings for Degrevant.[102] All five of these ladies, except possibly La Dame Amour, are at some point sexually linked with a man who hears her performance, and three of the performances take place in a bedchamber. In the romances, performing music is symbolically associated with love for both men and women of the nobility.

It is difficult to tell to what extent courtiers actually learned performance skills. John Stevens points out that 'private music of its very nature scarcely gets even the barest mention in the records.'[103] He notes that King Henry V and Queen Katherine played the harp and that the henchmen of Edward IV were required to learn 'to harping, to pype, sing, daunce'.[104] In a 1474 set of regulations, the 'sonnes of nobles, lords and gentlemen' who were being brought up together with Prince Edward were to be 'taught in grammar, musicke, and other cunning',[105] and in the early sixteenth century, the two sons of James IV of Scotland received training in instrumental and vocal music.[106] Musical education was not restricted

---

[99] *Horn Child*, lines 43 and 286–8; *King Horn*, Laud Misc. MS, lines 247–50 and 255–6; *Sir Degrevant*, Lincoln MS, lines 33–40; Cambridge MS, lines 35–9.

[100] *King Horn*, Laud Misc. MS 108, lines 1579–98; *Sir Orfeo*, Auchinleck MS, lines 419–52; *Sir Tristrem*, lines 1809–1925. Both Orfeo and Tristrem are shown playing the harp at other points in the story.

[101] *Bevis of Hamptoun*, Auchinleck MS, lines 3905–18.

[102] *The Awntyrs off Arthure at the Terne Wathelyne*, MS Douce 324, lines 343–4; *Syre Gawene and the Carle of Carelyle*, lines 427–38; *Libeaus Desconus*, MS Ashmole 61, fol. 52v; *Sir Degare*, lines 835–45 and 858–60; *Eger and Grime*, Percy Folio, lines 263–72 and 851–62; *Sir Degrevant*, Lincoln MS, lines 1432–40.

[103] Stevens, *Music and Poetry*, p. 275.

[104] Stevens, *Music and Poetry*, pp. 277–8 and 273.

[105] Stevens, *Music and Poetry*, p. 273.

[106] Helena M. Shire, 'Music for "Goddis Glore and the Kingis"', in *Stewart Style, 1513–1542: Essays on the Court of James V*, ed. Janet Hadley Williams, pp. 118–41 (East Linton: Tuckwell Press, 1996),

to the upper ranks of the nobility. In thirteenth-century Italy, Brunetto Latini noted the presence of courtiers who expected money and clothing in return for entertainment,[107] and in twelfth-century England the knight Luc de la Barre appears to have provided regular amusement, though this apparently took the form of derisive songs.[108] Although not many records survive, middle-class involvement in music is verified by the wool merchant George Cely's payments to Thomas Rede for instruction in playing the harp and the lute in Calais in 1473–5.[109] More might be discovered by extrapolation from literary and historical sources about the degree to which the nobility were normally trained in music. In the meantime, the romances have proven trustworthy in other respects, and they may reflect a historical reality here.

When heroes or heroines perform in the romances, their music is symbolically linked to love. Yet within that symbolic function, we have a few hints of performance perspectives. When Myldor entertains Degrevant during supper (lines 1432–40), she sometimes harps and sometimes eats, showing authorial awareness that she could not do both at once and that a harp-playing lady would need to eat. *Sir Orfeo* is particularly sensitive to performance realities.[110] In the Auchinleck MS, Orfeo keeps his harp in a hollow tree and only takes it out in fair weather; a harp would be ruined in the rain. Similarly, a performer's voice echoes strongly in Orfeo's dialogue with the porter and his whimsical assurance to the King of Faerie that minstrels have to perform wherever they can, even where they are not welcome (Auchinleck MS, lines 379–84 and 419–34). But some of the vivid descriptions of performance we find in Anglo-Norman romances are not present in their Middle English counterparts. For example, the lengthy technical description of Horn's harp playing and singing in the *Roman de Horn*[111] is absent from either English version of the story, where three lines in *King Horn* state simply that he sits down, clenches his harp, and makes a *lai* (Laud Misc. MS 108, lines 1595–7).[112]

Professional minstrels appear in equally sketchy terms. Aside from the many minstrels who set the scene at a feast or other occasion, or who are characterized generically as performing romances, only six characters might be described as professional minstrels, and only two of these are seen unambiguously performing in the course of the story: the harper in *Sir Cleges* performs a story, and the Irish

---

pp. 126–7.

[107] McGee, *Ceremonial Musicians*, p. 73.

[108] Taylor, 'Songs of Praise and Blame', pp. 65 and 68.

[109] Alison Hanham, 'The Musical Studies of a Fifteenth-Century Wool Merchant', *The Review of English Studies*, New Series 8 (1957): 270–4.

[110] Perhaps coincidentally, of the romances I have memorized, I found *Sir Orfeo* the easiest to commit to memory and in some ways the most performable.

[111] Mildred Pope, ed., *The Romance of Horn by Thomas*, 2 vols, ANTS IX–X, XII–XIII (Oxford: Basil Blackwell, 1955–1964), lines 2830–45.

[112] It would be useful to compare a catalog of minstrel references in the Anglo-Norman romances with the Middle English references; the implications might elucidate some of the melding and disjunction between performance traditions in medieval England.

harper in *Sir Tristrem* performs 'a miri lay'.[113] The minstrel in *Richard Coer de Lyon* does not perform, though he would if Richard allowed it. We do not hear the minstrel on the wall play music in *Sir Degrevant*, and it is difficult to say definitely that when the minstrel in *The Avowynge of King Arthur* presents his tidings, the 'myrth of his mouthe' constitutes performance. The dwarf Theodolyne who accompanies the messenger damsel in *Libeaus Desconus* is described as a famous minstrel noted for playing many instruments and telling stories for ladies, but at no point does Theodolyne present a formal performance.

As Theodolyne travels with Ellen and Libeaus, however, there are possible hints of performance:

> They ryden forth all yn saght
> And tolde how knyghtes faght
> For ladyes bryght and schene.
> (MS Cotton Caligula A.ii, lines 1030–2)

(They rode forth peacefully and told how knights fought for bright and lovely ladies.)

This passage describes stories like the romances being told as travel entertainment within a small group, and there is no indication that Theodolyne is the sole storyteller. A little later, Ellen and Theodolyne tell what Libeaus has accomplished (the content of the romance to this point) to Lambard:

> Sche and the dwerk y-mene
> Tolde seven dedes kene
> That he dede dydyr-ward,
> And how that Syr Lybeauus
> Faught wyth fele schrewys
> And for no deth ne spared.
> (MS Cotton Caligula A.ii, lines 1663–71)

(She and the dwarf together told seven valiant deeds that he had done on the way there, and how Sir Libeaus had fought with many scoundrels and not held back for any threat of death.)

Why does it take two people to tell the story? Given the 'romance reading' skill of noblewomen illustrated above, could this passage reflect the kind of paired minstrelsy we have seen in the minstrel records? Similar terminology is used to describe the 'gle and game' at supper, this time between Lambard and Libeaus. The possibility of collaboration is suggested in five of the fourteen words:

> Lambard and Lybeauus yn fere
> Of aventurus that ther wer
> Talkede bothe yn same.
> (MS. Cotton Caligula A.ii, lines 1677–80)

---

[113] *Sir Cleges*, line 484; and *Sir Tristrem*, line 1832.

(Lambard and Libeaus talked companionably, both together, about adventures that had befallen.)

Since we have found the romances reliable in descriptions of performance to the extent we can verify them, we may also take this as a valid representation of a kind of informal story performance, possibly one that would require considerable training. We have seen evidence that minstrel performance of romance topics paralleled the reading aloud of romances. Here we see an embodiment of *geste* performance. Might it not be possible that some members of the nobility were trained in improvised story performance? This would fit well with the evidence we have seen that minstrels performed stories from the present as well as those from the past. In the romances there are many instances of storytelling as entertainment among the nobility; these passages do not appear in the catalogue of minstrel references because they are not clearly instances of performance, but it is worth considering that another mode of storytelling might become visible if we re-examine the records with different expectations.

The figure of the minstrel in Middle English romances is neither glorified nor very much developed: neither the affiliation of minstrels nor colourful terms such as *rex ministrallorum* occur in the romances. The minstrel references in the romances, like the manuscript evidence, do not reveal the hand that wields the harp or bow, but rather the hand of a writer who participates in a culture filled with minstrelsy: 'harping and piping', 'romanze reding', and 'gestes singe'.[114] Minstrelsy is firmly bound up with the romances, but the bond may be more fluid than we imagine.

Even today, entertainment is perhaps more diverse than is commonly imagined. It is not as difficult as it might be imagined to make up a sung story improvisationally and collaboratively, taking turns developing the plot, taking on different roles, and sometimes singing extended duos. It is challenging and stimulating, but easier and more intuitive with practice, and it provides excellent entertainment for travel or tedious tasks. It is intimate and private and would not be performed for a non-participant.

But what if this practice were a skill actively developed? It is easy to imagine Ellen, Theodolyne, and Libeaus entertaining themselves with stories on their forest roads, and not necessarily in the anecdotal style of our narrative communications over pizza and beer. In a world without electronic devices, where entertainment was ubiquitous at feasts, in bedrooms and sitting rooms, on trips, and even at war, a wide range of storytelling options must have been available and cultivated, 'in gestes song, or else in prose tolde wyth tonge'.[115] Where historical records naturally show no interest in informal storytelling, the romances touch on a wide range of performance situations and performers.

The performance world in the historical documents and the romances hints at an interface between public and private performance, between contemporary

---

[114] *Havelok*, lines 2325, 2327–8. Six references set reading and performing romances side by side as equivalent.

[115] *Partonope of Blois*, line 27.

praise and tales of past heroes. Verse is sometimes involved, and so are instruments, and the general approach to narrative must have been flexible enough to allow a minstrel to shift easily from fragmented opportunities at a feast, to lengthy entertainment for a king during his bloodletting,[116] to a long (and probably not memorized) story for a lengthy journey, to (possibly) collaboration with a patron or other minstrels, to upholding the 'los' of a patron.

When a king sat listening to a harper or to two fiddlers, what would he have heard and seen? The historical practice of narrative performance in Britain is elusive. While terms such as *disour* or *gestour* probably designate storytellers in both the historical records and the romances, more generic terms such as *minstrel* or *histrio* are in some cases used interchangeably, and performers described as instrumentalists, *harpour* or *fitheler*, are sometimes ascribed narrative functions. Payment records do not clarify the situation: they rarely describe performance content and do not appear to differentiate between narrative and drama. What evidence we have suggests that narrative performances were most commonly undertaken by one or two performers, often instrumentalists, but this can only be inferred. The romances, however, can take us a little further. With certain exceptions such as *Sir Orfeo*, the romances present a clerical perspective on minstrel performance, an audience perspective that lacks detail. But to the extent we can test them, the romance references to minstrels describe current practice. These passages validate a contemporary narrative function of minstrels, and they reiterate an assumed model of written and oral forms of romance, sometimes listing topics that survive as written romances. Although they are not themselves performances and rarely performance scripts, the romances give evidence of parallel minstrel performance. It is reasonable, then, to look to the romances as our best clue to the verbal component of minstrel narration, and that allows us to explore musical possibilities for romance performance. The most puzzling question is how a metred voice may have melded with instruments in narrative production, and it is through examining the musical instruments themselves that we may find some answers.

---

[116] E.g. Bullock-Davies, *Register*, p. 114.

3
Musical Instruments and Narrative

TAKEN as a whole, the Middle English verse romances associate themselves with instrumental music at a fundamental level, and information about instruments can extend our understanding of romance by delineating how music could have interacted with a text. The Middle English romances confirm traditional associations of plucked and bowed stringed instruments with narrative performance, suggesting strongest support for the harp and the fiddle, and to a lesser degree the lute. Remarkably detailed information on the medieval fiddle survives, and from a careful consideration of fiddle construction and tuning, we may derive principles of narrative accompaniment that can reasonably extend to other instruments, taking into account differences in sound production.

The fiddle is well adapted to playing the extant narrative melodies, which are generally syllabic and repetitive. Though most commonly confined to a narrow range, these melodies sometimes exhibit interval leaps, which are easily accommodated by the tuning structure of the fiddle; and sometimes shift to a different tonal centre, which can again be addressed by a documented adjustment in tuning. More important, fiddle tuning provides an answer to how medieval aesthetics of variation would have been applied to fiddle accompaniment of narrative by prescribing a structure of pitches that automatically creates a continually shifting framework of ancillary sound when a melody is played. Furthermore, the instrument offers numerous options for simple variation, either melodic or non-melodic, which can be carried out without distracting a performer's attention from the text. Fiddle accompaniment thus adds complexity to a text by interacting with it in fluid permutations of sonic background, never so abrupt as to distract, with transitions not necessarily coinciding with metrical structures. These principles can readily be applied to the harp and the lute, though with some modification based on differences among these instruments.

The fiddle, the harp, and the lute share certain features that further characterize performance practice. One significant commonality is a method of sound production that creates inherent patterns of strong and weak sounds, rhythms which must have interacted in some way with the strong and weak patterns of narrative verse.

To arrive at these understandings, however, it is necessary to consider the romances in a broader context. Unlike their francophone counterparts, the Middle English romances are not very specific about minstrel performance. Like the historical records, they rarely note the content of a performance. When the romances do mention narrative performance, though they often mention the presence of musical instruments, they do not specify how the instruments may have been involved. Yet it is possible to arrive at that involvement from other directions: by looking at consistent patterns in European narrative performance and by applying what we know of the instruments involved.

In fact, European tradition is generally corroborated in the Middle English romance, with the notable exception of a stronger emphasis on the harp in England. In the light of the general continuity of English culture with Continental culture discussed in Chapter 1, it is reasonable to draw on evidence from the Continent to extend our understanding of English practices except where we have reason to suspect differentiation.

Instruments Associated with Narrative

Medieval instruments were classified according to their sonority, whether they were *haut* or *bas*, that is loud or soft.[1] The eighty-three Middle English romances confirm this division, although the terms themselves ('hye and bas') are used on only one occasion.[2] In the fifteen passages that list four or more instruments, only two passages and a variant of another mingle *haut* and *bas* instruments.[3] All the rest list the loud instruments first and then the soft, or they include only loud or only soft.[4]

But how do storytellers relate to these categories? Speaking or singing minstrels are not in every case linked with soft instruments. In their *los*-spreading function, *disours* are twice linked with taborers, trumpeters, and heralds;[5] and in another case, taborers, trumpeters, and *jangelours* make so much noise that people wouldn't have been able to hear thunder.[6] A range in narrative volume is suggested in *The Lyfe of Alisaunder*, where at one feast, storytelling occurs in the noisy context of the pipe and tabor:[7]

---

[1] Edmund Bowles has demonstrated this division for the Continent, 'Haut and Bas: The Groupings of Musical Instruments in the Middle Ages' (1954), in *Instruments and their Music in the Middle Ages*, ed. Timothy J. McGee (Farnham: Ashgate, 2009), pp. 3–28; and Richard Rastall has suggested that it holds true in England at least from the late thirteenth century, 'Some English Consort-Groupings', p. 182.

[2] *The Romauns of Partenay*, line 945.

[3] The three exceptions remind us that the categories may not be as immiscible as we imagine. Loud and soft instruments were present together at major banquets, processions, and other occasions. We know very little of how instruments were combined in late medieval England (Rastall, 'Some English Consort-Groupings') or what minstrels may have attempted for familial or geographical reasons. Remnant, *English Bowed Instruments*, p. 153 and plate 91, notes a mid-fourteenth-century manuscript depiction of a fiddle and shawm playing together during combat; and, p. 71, she points to a record of payment to a fiddler, two trumpeters, and a nakerer, observing 'there is much pictorial evidence for the fiddle playing in small groups with the trumpet ..., so this quartet may actually have taken place.'

[4] Frequently variant instruments are listed in different manuscripts, but (with the one exception mentioned), the variants preserve *haut* and *bas* distinctions.

[5] *Libeaus Desconus*, Lambeth Palace Library MS 306, lines 954–5; and *Richard Coer de Lyon*, lines 3776–7.

[6] *The Lyfe of Alisaunder*, Lincoln's Inn MS 150, lines 3403–5.

[7] James Blades and Jeremy Montagu, *Early Percussion Instruments from the Middle Ages to the Baroque*, Early Music Series 2 (London: Oxford University Press, 1976), p. 7, include an image from

> Noyse is gret with tabour and pype,
> Damoysels playen with peren ripe.
> Ribaudes festeth also with tripe;
> The gestour wil oft his mouthe wype.
> (MS Laud Misc 622, lines 1573–6)

(The noise of pipe and tabor is loud. Damsels play with ripe pears; good-for-nothings feast on tripe; the storyteller often wipes his mouth.)

But in describing another feast, the same romance associates storytelling with the harp:

> Mery it is in halle to here the harpe;
> The mynstrales synge, the jogelours carpe.
> (MS Laud Misc 622, lines 4714–5)

(In the hall it is merry to hear the harp; the minstrels sing, and the jongleurs tell stories.)

In a society without amplification, a loud voice would be a valuable commodity. At a large feast or a tournament, or in a procession or battle camp, short bursts of loud information would be most appropriate for communicating events either past or present. For sustained narration in a chamber or for a smaller audience, the minstrel would probably switch to a quieter voice.

The association of storytellers with tabors is intriguing, because tabors, too, because of their versatility, resist classification as *haut* or *bas*.[8] Six romances refer to tabors in the same context as storytelling, and one of these hints at the possibility of storytellers accompanying themselves on the tabor:

> There mouthe men here the gestes singe,
> The gleumen on the tabour dinge.
> (*Havelok*, lines 1329–30)

(There people could hear the *gestes* sung, the gleemen beating on the tabor.)

There is some historical confirmation of this combination, a payment to two taborers 'and ane spelare with thaim'.[9] Although the medieval tabor varied in size and shape, iconographic evidence suggests this double-headed drum was invariably fitted with a snare and that it was played with one stick.[10] The one stick suggests simple rhythms, and the snare would cause a sharper rattle than the dull thud that results without it, enhancing verbal rhythmic structures.

---

a mid-sixteenth-century psalter portraying a pipe and tabor playing together with both loud and soft instruments: a trumpet, a harp, and a dulcimer.

[8] Rastall, 'Some English Consort-Groupings', p. 182.

[9] Thomas *et al.*, ed., *Compota Thesauriorum*, vol. 1, p. 326.

[10] James Blades, *Percussion Instruments and their History* (New York: Frederick A. Praeger, 1970), pp. 205–9; and Blades and Montagu, *Early Percussion Instruments*, pp. 4–7.

Noisy narrative appears to occupy a distinct niche. Certainly *bas* instruments would be favoured to accompany any involved narrative, where the verbal content would be of primary importance, yet not all 'soft' instruments took on this role. For example, although some wind instruments are classified as *bas*, there is no suggestion in the Middle English romances that they ever accompany narrative, and this accords with a very long European tradition in which soft winds were associated with other repertory. The Middle English romances emphatically point to the use of chordophones, stringed instruments, to accompany narrative, thus falling in with tradition dating back to ancient times that associates bowed and plucked instruments with the accompaniment of poetry.

In the romances, some passages suggests the possibility of the lute, but the harp and the fiddle are most consistently associated with narrative performance. This pattern matches English and Continental records that document practices of narrative accompaniment. These three instruments serve well to illustrate three different classes of stringed instruments: the lute is plucked or strummed with a plectrum;[11] the harp is plucked with the fingers, with the hands positioned on each side of the instrument; and the fiddle is bowed.[12] By examining common characteristics of these instruments and differences among them, we can derive some principles of accompaniment. But first we will look at the evidence for associating each instrument with narrative performance.

The Lute

The lute is a definite possibility for accompaniment of narrative in late medieval England. Two related instruments, the citole and the gittern, are less likely, though possible. The citole is mentioned eleven times in the romances, and the dwarf Theodolyne in *Libeaus Desconus,* who is a 'mery man of mouthe' (line 141), is accomplished on the citole (among other instruments) in one manuscript. Sir Degrevant is also skilled on the citole in one manuscript, on the lute in the other manuscript, and on the gittern in both.[13] An early-fourteenth-century English citole survives,[14] and one musician at the 1306 Pentecost feast was designated a

---

[11] Vladimir Ivanoff, 'An Invitation to the Fifteenth-Century Plectrum Lute: The Pesaro Manuscript', in *Performance on Lute, Guitar, and Vihuela: Historical Practice and Modern Interpretation,* ed. Victor Anand Coelho (Cambridge: Cambridge University Press, 1997), pp. 1–15, at p. 9, states, 'Numerous iconographical documents show that until at least around 1450, the lute was invariably plucked with a plectrum made from a bird's feather. Paintings and drawings show that lutenists generally held the plectrum between the index and middle fingers and plucked the strings with a shaking movement of the forearm and wrist.'

[12] For a complete survey of instruments used in late medieval England, see Mary Remnant, 'Musical Instruments in Early English Drama', in *Material Culture and Medieval Drama,* ed. Clifford Davidson (Kalamazoo, MI: Medieval Institute, 1999), pp. 141–94.

[13] Lincoln MS, lines 35–6, and Cambridge MS, lines 36 and 38.

[14] Matthew Spring, *The Lute in Britain: A History of the Instrument and its Music,* Oxford Early Music Series (Oxford: Oxford University Press, 2001), p. 5.

citoler,[15] but the citole was not commonly used after around 1350.[16] The gittern, mentioned five times in the romances, was 'usually associated with taverns and unruly behaviour',[17] and it may have been used to accompany the vulgar stories so repudiated in many sources, though the romances do not hint at this. Judging from the number of appearances in English carvings and paintings, the gittern was more popular in the fourteenth century, and the lute in the fifteenth century.[18]

The lute appears six times in the Middle English romances, in each case in just one manuscript, but there is historical support for linking the lute with narrative performance. Victor Coelho discusses a late-sixteenth-century Italian lute book containing 'songs without even a text, in which only an intabulated lute formula, or chordal scheme, is provided as an accompaniment to which any poem in *terza* or *ottava rime* (*stanze*) might be sung.'[19] As Douglas Alton Smith observes, this manuscript 'constitutes one of the best sources for learning how to re-create the old tradition of singing narrative or poetry to formulaic melodies and quasi-improvised lute accompaniment'.[20] At least in Italy, there is reasonable cause for linking the lute with narrative, and there is evidence of a tradition of singing improvised or memorized text with instrumental accompaniment.

The first record of the lute in Britain is a payment in the royal accounts to 'Jehan le leüteur' in 1276 or 1277.[21] From this point, a steady presence of one or two lute players is documented at court most of the time through 1500, when the lute began to gain ascendancy.[22] On Easter in 1496, the Royal Treasurer of Scotland noted payments to 'Jacob, lutar', and 'Lundoris the lutare'.[23] Earlier that month, a lute player was paid together with 'David Hay', who, since no instrument is listed, could be a singer or *gestour*. Teamwork between a lutenist and a storyteller is more emphatically implied in the 1508 payment to 'Gray Steill, lutare' and 'ane jestour',[24] and the pairing of a lutenist with another performer is documented outside the royal courts in the Durham payment 'In uno viro ludenti in uno loyt et uxori ejus cantanti' (to a man playing a lute and his wife singing).[25]

[15] Bullock-Davies, *Menestrellorum Multitudo*, p. 6.

[16] Spring, *Lute in Britain*, p. 5.

[17] Spring, *Lute in Britain*, p. 14.

[18] Spring, *Lute in Britain*, pp. 19–23.

[19] Victor Coelho, 'Raffaello Cavalcanti's Lute Book (1590) and the Ideal of Singing and Playing', in *Le Concert des voix et des instruments à la Renaissance*, ed. Jean-Michel Vaccaro (Paris: Centre National de la Recherche Scientifique, 1995), pp. 423–42, at p. 424.

[20] Douglas Alton Smith, *A History of the Lute from Antiquity to the Renaissance* (Fort Worth, TX: The Lute Society of America, 2002), p. 138.

[21] Smith, *History of the Lute*, p. 31.

[22] Smith, *History of the Lute*, pp. 30–1; and Rastall, 'Minstrels of the English Royal Households'.

[23] Thomas *et al.*, ed., *Compota Thesauriorum*, vol. 1, p. 326.

[24] Thomas *et al.*, ed., *Compota Thesauriorum*, vol. 4, p. 96.

[25] Chambers, *Mediaeval Stage*, vol. 2, p. 242.

The Harp

The harp, however, far outweighs the lute as a preference for romance accompaniment. More favoured in Britain than on the Continent, the late medieval harp may even have developed in England.[26] An initial glance at the minstrel references in romances would seem to suggest that the harp is the only option for narrative accompaniment. The harp is mentioned in forty-eight passages in the eighty-three Middle English verse romances, compared with eighteen references to the fiddle, sixteen to the psaltery, eleven to the citole, six to the lute, five to the rote, five to the gittern, four to the crowd, two to the rebec, and one to the dulcimer. The harp, too, is most explicitly associated with narrative.

When we examine the passages where the harp is linked with narrative, however, the image blurs. The Carle's daughter in *Syre Gawene and the Carle of Carelyle* does play the harp and sing romances, but the text presents these activities as a sequence:

> First sche harpyd, and sethe songe
> Of love and of Artorrus armus amonge.
>
> (lines 436–7)

(First she harped, and then she sang about love and about Arthur's chivalry.)

Similarly, although we see a harper singing a story to the king in *Sir Cleges*, at no point in either manuscript does the text state that he is playing a harp while he tells the story (lines 481–95). While one feast description in *The Lyfe of Alexander* may associate storytelling with the harp, three other storyteller references in that romance include no mention of an instrument,[27] and a fourth occurs in a context with tabors and trumpeters.

There are, however, three instances of a harper harping a lay, which may be a narrative song, as discussed in Chapter 1.[28] In *King Horn*, when Horn sits down on a bench and grasps his harp, he 'makede Reymyld a lay' (made a lay for Reymyld, Laud Misc. MS 108, lines 1591–2). In an analogous passages, the Irish Harper in *Sir Tristrem* harps 'a miri lay' (line 1832). In *The Lyfe of Alisaunder,* when Alexander enters the defeated Thebes and begins killing its inhabitants, a harper comes before him and makes a lay asking for mercy. This lay is quoted, possibly in abbreviated form, listing illustrious men and gods associated with Thebes (Lincoln's Inn MS 150, lines 2824–36). These lays may well refer to narrative performance, yet the romances do not claim for themselves instrumentally accompanied performance.

---

[26] Roslyn Rensch Erbes, 'The Development of the Medieval Harp: A Re-Examination of the Evidence of the Utrecht Psalter and its Progeny', *Gesta* 11.2 (1972): 27–36, at p. 33, states: 'Whether or not the English were responsible for this evolution in regard to an actual musical instrument must remain a subject for conjecture. The evidence of the art monuments suggests only that it is artists of an English manuscript who, in the process of copying a Carolingian manuscript, represent logical steps in the refashioning of the harp frame from an Eastern angle-type one to a typically medieval one. Some three or four hundred years later the latter design was still considered musically valid.'

[27] In a variant of one passage, a pipe and tabor are present (MS Laud Misc. 622, line 1573).

[28] I am using the spelling 'lay' to distinguish the Middle English use of the term from the French *lai*.

In no case does a romance narrator claim to accompany the story with the harp or any other instrument.[29]

The most memorable association of the harp with romance occurs in the prologues to *Lai le Freine* and *Sir Orfeo*. So similar are the two passages that editor A. J. Bliss has used the Auchinleck Manuscript prologue to *Lai le Freine* to substitute for the missing opening of *Sir Orfeo* in that manuscript. All three versions of the passage describe Breton lays as something we read in books. While *Lai le Freine* suggests that the 'layes ben in harping', both manuscripts of *Sir Orfeo* mention 'layes that ben of harpyng' or 'made of herpyngys', and, in fact, *Sir Orfeo* is a story *about* harping. *Lai le Freine* and one manuscript of *Sir Orfeo* say a little more about how the harp was involved in creation of lays. *Lai le Freine* links lay production with kings:

> In Breteyne bi hold time
> This layes were wrought, so seith this rime.
> When kinges might our yhere
> of ani mervailes that ther were,
> thai token an harp in gle and game,
> and maked a lay and gaf it name.
>
> (lines 13–18)

(These lays were created in Brittany long ago, as this rhyme says. When kings were able anywhere to hear about any marvels that befell, they took a harp playfully and made a lay and gave it a name.)

MS Harley 3810/1 attributes lay creation simply to the 'brytons', and is more explicit about initial textual involvement:

> In Brytayn this layes arne y-wrytt,
> Furst y-founde and forthe y-gete,
> Of aventures that fallen by dayes,
> Wherof Brytouns made her layes.
> When they myght owher heryn
> Of aventures that ther weryn,
> They toke her harpys wyth game,
> Maden layes and yaf it name.
>
> (lines 13–20)

(These lays were written down in Brittany, where they were first found and produced. They concern adventures that happened from day to day, about which the people of Brittany made their lays. Whenever they were able anywhere to hear about adventures that befell, they took their harps playfully, and made lays and gave them names.)

---

[29] There is one possible exception. Although editor L. F. Casson transcribes *Sir Degrevant* line 9 from CUL MS Ff.i.6 as 'And Y schall karppe off a knyght', the line could equally reasonably be transcribed, 'And Y schall harppe of a knyght'.

Sometime in the past, these lays were created with the harp and written down in books, and it is in books that we find them. Both the Auchinleck MS and MS Ashmole 61 conclude the story of *Sir Orfeo* with a further reference to the initial composition of the lay and what has survived into the present:

> Harpours in Bretaine after than
> Herd hou this mervaile bigan,
> And made her-of a lay of gode likeing,
> And nempned it after the king.
> That lay 'Orfeo' is y-hote:
> Gode is the lay, swete is the note.
> (Auchinleck MS, lines 597–602)

(Harpers in Brittany after that heard how this marvel began, and they made a delightful lay about it and named it after the king. That lay is called 'Orfeo'. The lay is good; the melody is sweet.)

In the past, harpers created the story, but what survives is the lay and its melody.

All versions of both romances agree in placing harper creation of lays in the past, but two versions of *Sir Orfeo* imply that the melody has survived in addition to the text we read in books. This reference to a melody, a 'note', has been discounted as a relic of a lost and distant oral tradition,[30] but the romances have been reliable on a number of other points, and *Sir Orfeo* is particularly sensitive to performance realities. The passages are very specific about which processes occur in the past and which in the present, and evidence of historical records is compatible with the notion of a sung memorized version of the story performed by contemporary minstrels, though those minstrels are not necessarily harpers; the harpers were in ancient Brittany.

The romance distinction between mythical past performance and current practice becomes clearer when we compare the passages describing Breton harpers in *Sir Orfeo* and *Lai le Freine* with the beginning of *The Laud Troy-Book*:

> Many speken of men that romaunces rede.
> That were sumtyme doughti in dede,
> The while that god hem lyff lente,
> That now ben dede and hennes wente:
> 15   Off Bevis, Gy, and of Gauwayn,
> Off kyng Richard, and of Owayn,
> Off Tristram, and of Percyvale,
> Off Rouland Ris, and Aglavale,
> Off Archeroun, and of Octovian,
> 20   Off Charles, and of Cassibaldan,
> Off Havelok, Horne, and of Wade; –
> In romaunces that of hem ben made

---

[30] See, for example, Roy Michael Liuzza, 'Sir Orfeo: Sources, Traditions, and the Poetics of Performance', *Journal of Medieval and Renaissance Studies* 21 (1991): 169–84, at p. 284.

> That gestoures often dos of hem gestes
> At mangeres and at grete festes.
> 25 Here dedis ben in remembraunce
> In many fair romaunce;
> But of the worthiest wyght in wede
> That evere by-strod any stede,
> Spekes no man, ne in romaunce redes
> Off his batayle ne of his dedis.
>
> (lines 11–30)

(Many people who read romances speak about men, now dead and gone away, who were once doughty in their deeds while God gave them life: about Bevis, Guy and Gawain, about King Richard, and about Owain, about Tristram, and about Percival, about Roland Ris and Aglovale, about Archeroun, and about Octavian, of Charlemagne, and of Cassibaldan, of Havelok, Horn, and of Wade. [These men appear] in romances that have been made about them, [romances] that *gestours* often turn into *gestes* for meals and great feasts. Their deeds are remembered in many fair romances, but of the worthiest creature in armour that ever bestrode any steed, no one either tells or reads in romance about his fighting nor his deeds.)

Many of the stories listed in this passage are included among the extant Middle English verse romances, and here they are described as being either read or else told by 'gestoures' at feasts. The balance between the two alternative modes of reception is maintained throughout and described as contemporary practice, and in this passage, story performance is not linked with any particular instrument. It is only in two Middle English romances that harpers are linked with Breton lay creation, and this process explicitly occurs in the distant past. In the Middle English romances there is no claim that the written romances were made by contemporary minstrels, and no unambiguous description of harp accompaniment of a contemporary romance.

One of the reasons for the prominence of harp references in the romances is the high incidence of noble characters who play the harp.[31] Three stories, *Sir Orfeo*, *King Horn*, and *Sir Tristrem* centre on harp playing heroes, and a number of ladies play the harp. These references account for twenty-two (just under half) of the harp references, but, as noted before, harp playing is here associated with love, not storytelling. While storytelling may well form part of the performance, narrative is not specified in any of these cases.

Thus, although the harp is clearly the instrument most associated with contemporary narrative performance in the romances, the association is not as overwhelming and exclusive as it might initially appear. Historical records do not clarify as much as we might expect because the terminology is frequently

---

[31] In fact, with the exception of the hunting horn, noble characters play only *bas* instruments, and women only stringed instruments.

ambiguous. Although Warton, in those few key passages that suggest harp accompaniment of narrative, confidently translates the Latin *cithara* as 'harp', we can only be certain that the term refers to a stringed instrument.[32] The extent of the potential for confusion is revealed in a comparison of fifteenth-century word lists in England:

> 'fidis' denotes a harp string in the *Catholicon* and a fiddler in *Nominale* A, while 'fidicen' is a harper in the former manuscript and a fiddler in the *Promptorium*. The word 'viella', which is normally taken to mean a fiddle ..., appears also in the *Promptorium* as a lute.[33]

Finally, although *cithara* consistently refers to a harp in these word lists, some of the twenty-four Elders of the Apocalypse, who in the Vulgate Bible play *citharae*, are shown in a twelfth-century painting at Hardham in Sussex playing rebecs and fiddles. Although no bows are shown, 'in England the plucking of such instruments seems to have been very rare indeed'.[34]

Despite the ambiguity, however, both the romances and contemporary historical documents indicate that the harp was more prominent in England than in mainland Europe in the Middle Ages, and it is likely minstrels would have used it for narrative performance. It is difficult to assess textual or iconographic harp evidence, though, because of the powerful symbolic associations of the harp. In art, the harp is strongly associated with David, particularly in his role as a *figura* of Christ.[35] This association is evident in the Towneley play of the Prophets, where King David, using language very similar to the medieval romance prologues, announces in tail-rhyme verse that he will sing a 'fytt'. (See Introduction.) A few lines later he states that he is making mirth 'with my harp and fyngers ten' (line 110). He is apparently narrating a fitt while playing a harp, but does this statement imply that contemporary harpers used all of their fingers to pluck the strings? Scholars theorize that medieval harpers used only the thumb, the index finger, and possibly the middle finger of each hand.[36] There are other cases where symbolism clearly overrides contemporary physical reality. Martin van Schaik has demonstrated that 'the tuning of the harp by David, symbolizes the imposition of order on the macrocosmos', and that in medieval illustration 'reality is almost

---

[32] Roslyn Rensch, *The Harp: Its History, Technique and Repertoire* (New York: Praeger Publishers, 1969), p. 70, reminds us, 'Regarding the term *cithara*, it must be emphasized that the Latin *citharisare*, like the German *harfen* and the Anglo-Saxon *hearpan* (of *Beowulf*), simply meant to play a stringed instrument. In literary sources the musical instrument intended by the term *cithara* or *cythara* varied, apparently according to both locale and era.'

[33] Remnant, *English Bowed Instruments*, p. 13.

[34] Remnant, *English Bowed Instruments*, p. 5.

[35] Martin van Schaik, *The Harp in the Middle Ages: The Symbolism of a Musical Instrument* (Amsterdam: Rodopi Editions, 1992), p. 58.

[36] See, for example, Susan Reit de Salas, 'Thumb-Under Technique on Gothic Harps', in *Historische Harfen: Beiträge zur Theorie und Praxis historischer Harfen*, ed. Heidrun Rosenzweig (Dornach: Eigenverlag der Musik-Akademie der Stadt Basel, 1991), pp. 120–32, at p. 117.

always subordinate to symbolism: the tuning pegs are not represented at the side but on the top of the neck'.[37]

Detailed discussion of the symbolism of the harp is not necessary here, but it is important to note the strong religious affiliation of many of the romances, particularly evident in the prologues and epilogues. Harp symbolism is even explicit, though in somewhat different terms, in *Roland and Vernagu*, where the harp is compared to the Trinity:

> As the harp has thre thinges,
> Wode and soun and strenges,
> And mirthe is ther tille,
> So is god persones thre,
> And holeliche on in unite,

> (lines 707–11)

(The harp has three features, wood and sound and strings, and mirth is therein; in the same way, God is three persons and wholly one in unity.)

It is easy enough to see Tristrem, Orfeo, and (to a degree) Horn as allegorical figures, but it is harder to see all the harp- and psaltery-playing ladies in the same terms; while the association of the harp with love may have religious resonance, the symbolic potential should not efface the possibility that noblemen and ladies actually played these instruments. Although a glance through the records indicates that women were not included among the minstrels who received regular wages at court,[38] women minstrels were sometimes hired on an occasional basis,[39] and in 1531 Henry VIII paid 7s. 6d. to a 'blynde woman being a harper'.[40] Richard Rastall has observed that the households of the queen and queen mother did not include a harper until the fifteenth century. He infers 'the psaltery seems to have been considered the most suitable plucked instrument for a lady's entertainment',[41] but if ladies commonly played the harp themselves, they would have been less likely to employ harpers. Since most of our documentation of music performance takes the form of payment records, musicianship among the nobility would go undocumented because no payment occurred. Howard Mayer Brown observes that in fourteenth-century Florence Francesco da Barberino regarded the harp as appropriate for young ladies:

> Young girls, he writes, ought to be taught to play appropriate musical instruments, and especially those that are not exclusively associated with

---

[37] Van Schaik, *Harp in the Middle Ages*, p. 58.

[38] Rastall, 'Minstrels of the English Royal Households'.

[39] The acrobat Matilda Makejoy, for example, was hired three times to perform at court, Bullock-Davies, *Menestrellorum Multitudo*, pp. 3 and 138.

[40] Southworth, *English Medieval Minstrel*, p. 168.

[41] Rastall, 'Some English Consort-Groupings', p. 184.

professional minstrels, the *giullari*. He singles out as especially suitable the psaltery (*mezzo cannone*), the fiddle (*viuola*) and the harp.[42]

The English romances frequently link skill on the harp with skill in romance reading. One male figure[43] and two female figures are assigned these attributes, and the Carle's daughter explicitly plays the harp and sings romances. Four other ladies are noted for harping and singing.

Certainly the harp is the front contender for accompaniment of the Middle English romance, but we have little access to what that harp accompaniment might have been like. Literary descriptions can shed some light on the instrument and playing technique. The eleventh-century *Ruodlieb*, for example, provides considerable detail:

> Pulsans mox laeua *digitis geminis*, modo dextra
> Tangendo chordas dulces reddit nimis odas,
> Multum distincte faciens uariamina quaeque,
>
> (lines 38–40)[44]

(Plucking now with two fingers of the left, now with the right, by intoning chords, he renders very sweet songs, producing many variations with great clarity.)

Nonetheless, we lack key information about the harp: physical evidence is sketchy,[45] and iconography is vexed with symbolic complexity. Even the string composition is open to debate.[46] We are left with evidence that does not clarify how the harp might have been used. We know that in Britain the harp varied dramatically in size and number of strings,[47] and that the harp was tuned diatonically with seven

---

[42] Howard Mayer Brown, 'The Trecento Fiddle and its Bridges' (1989), in *Instruments and their Music in the Middle Ages*, ed. Timothy J. McGee (Farnham: Ashgate, 2009), pp. 293–313, at p. 39.

[43] In *Horn Child* we are assured, 'Harpe and romaunce he radde aright' (line 286), while in *King Horn*, in the parallel context describing Horn's education, the king asks Athelbrus to 'Tech him of harpe and song' (Laud Misc. MS 108 line 156).

[44] Edwin H. Zeydel, ed. and trans., *Ruodlieb: The Earliest Courtly Novel (after 1050)*, University of North Carolina Studies in the Germanic Languages and Literatures 23 (Chapel Hill: University of North Carolina Press, 1959).

[45] Van Schaik, *Harp in the Middle Ages*, p. 11, points out that 'due to the fact that there are virtually no extant harps dating from medieval times, every statement about the actual characteristics of the instrument is, in fact, hypothetical.' Three harps do survive from the fifteenth century, all three wire-strung harps 'typical of the Irish harp evident in the works of art and noted in literature from about the twelfth century'; Roslyn Rensch, *Harps and Harpists* (Bloomington: Indiana University Press, 1989), p. 114.

[46] For example, Christopher Macklin, 'Approaches to the Use of Iconography in Historical Reconstruction, and the Curious Case of Renaissance Welsh Harp Technique', *Early Music* 35.2 (2007): 213–23, at p. 216, suggests: 'we may provisionally conclude that many of the compositions of the Welsh bards would have been heard on a Gothic bray harp having from 11 to 25 strings with a straight frontpillar and strings made of black horsehair, though instruments using gut strings were also apparently in frequent use.'

[47] Roslyn Rensch, *The Harp*, describes a wide variety of harps represented in English paintings and carvings of the late Middle Ages.

notes per octave.[48] The harp is thus too versatile to reveal much about accompaniment. So much medieval music can be played on a diatonically tuned harp (even some sharps and flats are possible),[49] that we cannot eliminate very many possibilities. More specific information is available about the fiddle, where the tuning and structure of the instrument introduce constraints that limit the options for how the instrument could have been used. These constraints may fill in gaps in our understanding of how the harp may have been used in narrative accompaniment.

The Fiddle

The fiddle had a strong presence at court in the late Middle Ages in Britain, and its prominence has been somewhat obscured by the manner in which instruments have been categorized and discussed. For example, in a chart of instrumentalists on the payroll of the 1306 Pentecost feast, Constance Bullock-Davies counts twenty-six harpers and thirteen fiddlers.[50] This two to one proportion, however, is the result of grouping *harpours* with *citharistes* (who may play harp, but may also play other stringed instruments such as the psaltery), but separating *vilours* or *vidulatores* from the other bowed stringed instruments, the *crouderes/crouthers* and the *gigours*.

As we have seen, there is considerable evidence of fiddle accompaniment of narrative in mainland Europe. In Italy the fiddle was used in the *cantare all-improvviso* tradition,[51] and in *c.* 1487 Tinctoris observed that in most parts of the world ('in plerisque partibus orbis') the 'viola cum arculo' (fiddle) is used 'ad historiarum recitationem' (for the recitation of stories).[52] The association is particularly pronounced in France. Christopher Page observes, 'The evidence is overwhelming that the preferred instruments for accompanying the voice in twelfth- and thirteenth-century France and Occitania were bowed instruments';[53] he provides numerous literary passages specifically illustrating fiddle accompaniment of the

---

[48] Kadar, 'Some Practical Hints', pp. 122–3. The expense records of the fifteenth-century English wool merchant George Cely, however, suggest alternative tuning structures. Cely notes payment in 1474 to Thomas Rede 'ffor to teke me to sett my harppe an nothyr way and ffor to teche me all my davnsys that same way' (for teaching me how to tune my harp another way and for teaching me how to play all my dances in that way [within that tuning structure]), Alison Hanham, 'The Musical Studies of a Fifteenth-Century Wool Merchant', *The Review of English Studies*, New Series 8 (1957): 270–4, p. 271.

[49] Kadar, 'Some Practical Hints', demonstrates a number of techniques for playing inflected modes on the gothic harp.

[50] Bullock-Davies, *Menestrellorum Multitudo*, p. 10.

[51] McGee, *Ceremonial Musicians*, 80–1. Regarding Minuccio's performance in the *Decameron*, for example, McGee demonstrates, 'There is little doubt that the instrument referred to as the *vivuola* is the five-string fiddle, and that the poetry is performed in the *cantare all-improvviso* tradition', p. 81.

[52] Anthony Baines, 'Fifteenth-Century Instruments in Tinctoris's *De Inventione et Usu Musicae*', *The Galpin Society Journal* 3 (1950): 19–26, at p. 24.

[53] Page, *Voices and Instruments*, p. 163.

chanson de geste, concluding, 'Je n'ai trouvé aucun témoignage de l'utilisation d'autre instruments' (I have found no testimony of the use of other instruments).[54] A 1377 ordinance from Beauvais confers on Jean de Puys the right to assign minstrels to perform *chansons de gestes* on appointed holidays, and the right to charge each minstrel in Beauvais a one-time fee of twelve pence; if they refuse to pay, he can take either their book or their fiddle, if they have one.[55] This peripheral reference to a minstrel's typical possessions confirms, not only that these minstrels who performed *gestes* relied on written books, but also that they typically possessed fiddles, and this association is confirmed in the tales themselves, tales which suggest a continuity between *chanson de geste* and *roman*. In a twelfth-century *chanson de geste*, jongleurs sing a *geste* on the fiddle ('Chil jougleour en cantent en vïele'); a minstrel in the *Roman de Silence* 'viiele un lai berton'; and the fiddlers in the *Roman de Flamenca* fiddle *lais* we know in narrative form.[56] Several romance protagonists sing while playing the fiddle: Josiane 'a chanter, / Notes et lais bien a vïeler'; Beton 'canta et vihola'; and Gerart 'chanter et vïeler ensemble' in a description of instrumentally accompanied narrative so unambiguous that we are given a *laisse* of the *chanson de geste* he performs.[57] Since there was considerable cultural interchange between England and France, and since many of the Middle English romances are translations of francophone originals, it seems reasonable that the instruments used to accompany narrative on the Continent, both the harp and the fiddle, and possibly the associated melodies, would have been adapted to the Middle English versions.

In England, the fiddle is extensively documented in solo performance, the situation where need would be most likely to impel self-accompaniment. Richard Rastall observes that 'there are more account-book payments to fiddlers than to any other type of minstrel', concluding that 'among the itinerant minstrelsy fiddlers were apparently most common'.[58] The historical evidence previously

---

[54] Christopher Page, 'Le Troisième Accord pour vièle de Jérôme de Moravie: Jongleurs et "anciens Pères de France" in *Jérôme de Moravie: un théoricien de la musique dans le milieu intellectuel parisien du XIIIe siècle*, ed. Michel Huglo and Marcel Peres, pp. 83–96 (Paris Editions Créaphis, 1992), p. 91.

[55] Bernhard, 'Recherches sur l'histoire de la corporation des ménétriers', pp. 398–9: Item ledit Jehan à cause dudit fief a de chescun jongleur venant et estant à Beauvèz, une foiz douze deniers de ceulx qui chantent en place, et se ils sont refusant de payer, il puet prendre leur livre ou leur vièle se ils l'ont. ¶ Item ledit Jehan puet donner la place et faire chanter de gestes à Beauvès, au lieu accoustumé, qui que il lui plaît, le jour de Noel, le jour de Pasques, le jour de Penthecoustes et leurs féeries. ¶ (Item, the said Jean, because [he holds] the said fief, has from each jongleur coming and staying at Beauvais, a one time [fee of] twelve pence from those who sing in the square, and if they refuse to pay, he can take their book or their fiddle if they have one. ¶ Item, the said Jean can grant [the right to perform in] the square and can have *gestes* sung by whomever he pleases at Beauvais in the accustomed place the day of Christmas, the day of Easter, the day of Pentecost, and their feast days.)

[56] Wilhelm Cloetta, ed., *Les Deux Rédactions en vers du Moniage Guillaume: chansons de geste du XIIe siècle*, 2 vols (Paris: Firmin-Didot, 1906), vol. 1, line 2072; *Silence*, line 2761; *Flamenca*, lines 603–4.

[57] *Bueve de Hantone*, lines 12087–8; *Daurel et Beton*, line 1505; *Roman de la Violette*, lines 1399–1405.

[58] Rastall, 'Some English Consort-Groupings', p. 186.

discussed for self-accompanied solo performance often involves the fiddle: the case of Warin, termed both *vielator* and *joculator*; of 'Ricard le Rimour', who played the crowd and may also have played the fiddle; and of the woman 'that singeth with a fiddle'. Although not an instance of solo performance, the payment to the 'tua fithelaris that sang Graysteil' is the most explicit documentation of instrumental accompaniment of romance, and it makes it clear that this type of performance was not unknown.

The fiddle is mentioned in eighteen passages in the Middle English romances. Fourteen of these passages also include the harp, and in eleven passages the harp and the fiddle are grouped in one line. In their usual offhand manner, the romances may link the fiddle with narrative performance. When they are disguised as minstrels, Horn and his companions are described as 'harperes, / jogelours and fithelers' in *King Horn*; and at a wedding feast in *The King of Tars*, there is melody 'of harp and fithel and of [gest]'. In *Libeaus Desconus* the dwarf Theodolyne, who is a 'noble dysour', plays the fiddle along with various other instruments. In *Reinbrun* the daughter of Argus's skill in 'romance reading' is linked with her skill on musical instruments including the fiddle; and the Armenian princess Josian, who in Continental versions of the romance performs narrative with the fiddle, in the Auchinleck Manuscript version of *Bevis of Hampton* plays the fiddle.[59] The harp and the fiddle are closely linked with song in three passages, and with *gestes* in two.

Other literary references connect the fiddle with narrative performance, so much so that in the C-text of *Piers Plowman*, 'fithele' is used metaphorically as a verb describing narrative performance: 'And fithele the withoute flaterynge of god Friday the geste' (and fiddle you, without flattery, the *geste* of Good Friday, *Passus* VII, line 106). The context of this passage, a comparison of frivolous minstrelsy with spiritual instruction that ought to occupy its place, provides a vivid (if satirically slanted) description of narrative entertainment, concluding with minstrels leading those who listen to them to Lucifer's feast, and his fiddling of a different sort of lay:

> There flaterers and foles with here foule wordes
> Leden tho that lythed hem to Luciferes feste
> With *turpiloquio*, a lay of sorwe and Luciferes fythele,
> *(Passus* VII, lines 114–16)

(There flatterers and fools with their foul words lead those who listened to them to Lucifer's feast with *turpiloquio*, a lay of sorrow, and Lucifer's fiddle.)

Literary evidence can be supplemented in the case of the fiddle by at least one fourteenth-century visual image. Although iconography does not normally elucidate narrative performance, a cluster of figures in the Macclesfield Psalter (fol. 9r)

---

[59] It may be significant that among ladies, only non-Westerners play the fiddle in the Middle English romances, possibly suggesting that ladies in England would not have played the fiddle. Even if this were the case, however, many female minstrels or women from lower classes may have played the fiddle. It is possible that the fiddle-playing heroines came into the romances in association with the Muslim women performers who had been brought into European courts as slaves. (See Chapter 1.)

strongly suggests a minstrel fiddling a romance. In a horizontal strip of margin below the text of the first Psalm, a man with a long sword and a tiny red buckler fights a golden-winged griffin twice his size. Balancing the griffin compositionally, a minstrel nearby plays a fiddle, to all appearances narrating the story of this romance-like combat.[60]

The fiddle is a realistic option for instrumental accompaniment of narrative in late medieval England. The evidence of the instrument's use for solo narrative performance in mainland Europe, and the high incidence in Britain of payment to fiddlers for unspecified performance, render this instrument particularly appropriate as a test case for how a single performer might have used an instrument to enhance memorized performance of narrative. By looking in some detail at characteristics of the instrument and what these features imply about playing technique and sound production, we can more fully understand options for accompaniment that would have been available to minstrels. The fiddle has a number of advantages over the harp for this purpose: several medieval fiddles have survived, representations of the fiddle are not as enveloped in symbolism as the harp, and the tuning of the fiddle is relatively well documented. The limitations imposed by the structure and tuning of the fiddle narrow the range of how the instrument might have been used to accompany narrative, thus allowing us to identify approaches to playing that are facilitated by the instrument and those that are rendered awkward. From this evidence we will be able to draw some inferences about narrative accompaniment that may extend to other instruments.

What the Fiddle Reveals about Narrative Performance

In late medieval Europe the broad class of bowed chordophones was variously termed *viële, viella, fidel, fithele, fiedel, fidula, vidula,* or other related terms.[61] Considerable evidence about the fiddle has been assembled: Werner Bachmann's impressive organological study of the origins of bowing through the early fourteenth century, Mary Remnant's careful iconographic survey of bowed instruments in England through the sixteenth century, Christopher Page's meticulously documented editions of treatises on tuning, and many focused studies that illuminate the structure and use of the instrument. In this book, I follow Mary Remnant and most anglophone musicologists in using the term *fiddle* to describe a late medieval instrument characterized by 'a clear distinction between the body and the neck' and 'a flat or nearly flat back'.[62] This instrument was prevalent in

---

[60] A facsimile of the manuscript is available in Stella Panayotova, ed. *The Macclesfield Psalter* (New York: Thames & Hudson, 2008).

[61] Werner Bachmann, *The Origins of Bowing and the Development of Bowed Instrument up to the Thirteenth Century* (London: Oxford University Press, 1969), p. 138, notes that 'the word "fidula" occurs repeatedly in early medieval texts, but until the turn of the millennium does not refer to a bowed instrument.' He also points out some of the difficulty in distinguishing between plucking and bowing, pp. 146–8.

[62] Remnant, *English Bowed Instruments*, p. 61. Pierre Bec, *Vièles ou violes? Variations philologiques et musicales autour des instruments à archet du moyen âge* (Paris: Editions Klincksieck, 1992),

England from the late-twelfth through the mid-sixteenth centuries,[63] making it contemporary with the Middle English romances, and it is probably the instrument described by the term *fiddel* or *fithele* in the documents we have looked at to this point.

We know from iconographic sources that the medieval fiddle exhibited a wide range of features. In the thirteenth century in England, fiddles were typically oval, elliptical, or possessing incurved sides.[64] The elliptical body became most common from the fourteenth century on, with fewer oval fiddles and an increased number with incurved sides. From the fourteenth century some fiddles had separately carved backs. Strings, almost always made of sheep gut, were normally attached to a tailpiece[65] and a flat pegbox;[66] usually a fiddle had three to six strings, and strings were sometimes paired. In the thirteenth century, fiddles often had a lateral *bordunus*, a string positioned away from the fingerboard. This feature appears to have faded out by the end of the fourteenth century in England, though it continued in Italy through the end of the fifteenth century.[67] From around 1300, some fiddles are portrayed with frets. Evidence from the fifteenth century is less complete because 'English artists preferred to decorate their margins with artificial foliage, instead of the general assortment of musicians and other characters who filled them in the previous century.'[68] In England the fiddle was usually held 'at or near the shoulder'.[69] A curved wooden bow, strung with horsehair and probably rubbed with rosin,[70] was used to sound the strings; from the twelfth century on, the bow curvature became less pronounced, narrowing the distance between the stick and the hairs and thus giving the player more

p. 332, points to the ambiguity created by applying the same term 'medieval fiddle' to the primitive instrument made of one piece of wood used up to the thirteenth century as well as to the 'classic' late medieval instrument made of several pieces of wood with much more complex workmanship. The term 'vielle' is sometimes used in Modern English to describe the instrument, but this word derives from a French form, and it creates its own ambiguity since the word means 'hurdy gurdy' in Modern French. The term 'fiddle' creates the least disjunction with the Middle English texts, which so consistently use closely related forms of this word.

[63] Remnant, *English Bowed Instruments*, p. xxiii.

[64] Iconographic information about the medieval fiddle is drawn from Remnant, *English Bowed Instruments*, pp. 61–3.

[65] From the fourteenth century, strings sometimes alternatively connected directly to an end projection or separate pins or to frontal stringholders like those on lutes, Remnant, *English Bowed Instruments*, p. 63.

[66] Christopher Page, 'An Aspect of Medieval Fiddle Construction', *Early Music* 2 (1974): 166–7, points out that twelfth- and thirteenth-century fiddles 'did not require a nut to direct the strings onto the plane of the fingerboard', but that 'it is only necessary to drill the holes sufficiently far up the shaft of each peg for the strings to be raised clear.'

[67] Timothy McGee, 'The Medieval Fiddle: Tuning Technique and Repertory', in *Instruments, Ensembles, and Repertory, 1300–1600: Essays in Honor of Keith Polk*, ed. Timothy McGee and Stewart Carter (forthcoming).

[68] Remnant, *English Bowed Instruments*, p. 3.

[69] Remnant, *English Bowed Instruments*, p. 67.

[70] Bachmann, *Origins of Bowing*, p. 86.

control.[71] Bridges appear to be low and flat, though curved bridges do exist.[72] The characteristics of English fiddles probably apply in France as well, where less detailed information is available.[73]

None of the extant bowed chordophones is as large as many of the fiddles represented in iconography. The physical instruments do, however, confirm the wide variety implied in pictorial and sculptural representations,[74] and they supply vital information about construction materials[75] and techniques. A fourteenth-century instrument from Elblag, Poland, provides physical evidence of paired strings and suggests the possibility of stopping the strings away from the fingerboard.[76]

[71] The five fiddles portrayed in the Macclesfield Psalter (*c.* 1325–35), unknown until 2004, provide new details about how the hairs were in some cases attached to the bow. See Jeremy Montagu, 'Musical Instruments in the Macclesfield Psalter', *Early Music* 34.2 (2006): 189–204.

[72] Bridge shape has attracted considerable controversy. Brown, 'Trecento Fiddle', p. 303, noting that 'more than 300 of the 350 pictures I have collected so far do not depict the shape of the bridge clearly', describes three types of fiddle bridge, 'flat, arched, or attached to the stringholder'. Mary Remnant, *English Bowed Instruments*, pp. 24–5, observes that, because of the perspectives of pictorial representation, we cannot always identify the shape of a bridge. Within those limitations, though, she characterizes most English bridges from the twelfth through fifteenth century as 'quite flat, and quite low in comparison to that of the modern violin', though curved bridges do exist. E. Segerman and D. Abbott, 'Jerome of Moravia and Bridge Curvature in the Medieval Fiddle', *Fellowship of Makers and Restorers of Historical Instruments Quarterly* 6 (1977): 34–6, at p. 34, suggest that a bridge 'could have been curved only on the right (or treble) side where, presumably, the melody would be played'. Appendix B explains why bridge curvature may not have mattered as much as has been assumed.

[73] Mary Springfels, 'The Vielle after 1300', in *A Performer's Guide to Medieval Music*, ed. Ross W. Duffin (Bloomington: Indiana University Press, 2000), pp. 302–16, at p. 310. Bachmann, *Origins of Bowing*, pp. 63–4, in a discussion of regional differences, describes shared characteristics in England and France.

[74] Frederick Crane, *Extant Medieval Musical Instruments: A Provisional Catalogue by Types* (Iowa City: University of Iowa Press, 1972), p. 15, observes that the instruments he classifies as medieval fiddles 'have very little in common, except that they presumably were played with a bow, and that all of those for which I have any information have bodies made of a single piece of wood'.

[75] For example, Mary Remnant, *English Bowed Instruments*, p. 2, discusses an unusual instrument from mid-fifteenth-century Bologna. Although it has a curved back like a rebec and idiosyncratically incorporates a body in two sections, each with its own soundboard, this instrument provides specific information about construction. The back, sides, and pegbox of the instrument are carved from a single piece of maple, and the instrument has four strings. The hairs are attached to a short bow with a fixed nut at the lower end and a cap at the tip. She points out that this type of fiddle developed into the Renaissance *viola da braccio*. For a detailed discussion of this instrument, see Marco Tiella, 'The Violeta of S. Caterina de' Vigri', *The Galpin Society Journal* 28 (1975): 60–70.

[76] All the instruments surviving from the fourteenth century are from central Europe, where, according to Bachman, *Origins of Bowing*, p. 64, fiddles of the twelfth and thirteenth centuries had 'a broad, almost circular body and a curiously thick-set appearance'. Three of the four instruments excavated at Novgorod, dating from the mid-eleventh through the mid-fourteenth centuries, have pegholes for three strings, and their basic shape places them in the rebec family. The Elblag fiddle, however, though crudely carved, fits Remnant's description of a fiddle. Dorota Popławska and Tadeusz Czechak, 'The Tuning and Playing of a Medieval Gittern and Fiddle from Elblag, Poland', *The Consort* 58 (2002): 3–12, at p. 9, describe the instrument as having 'a flat, uneven bottom and a short neck culminating in a peg box'. Four pegs inserted into four holes in the pegbox imply four strings. Of greatest interest here is the existence of a carved nut with four indentations, indicating

From a later era, the two fiddles preserved in the 1545 shipwreck of the *Mary Rose* are British in provenance and bear some similarity to instruments portrayed in fifteenth-century art.[77]

Implications for the sound of the instrument are of vital importance in a discussion of narrative accompaniment. Mary Remnant points out that 'with their very varying shapes mediaeval fiddles must have produced very different sounds'.[78] Medieval descriptions of the sound of the fiddle are difficult to interpret. Contemporary writers often describe the effect of the instrument rather than its sound. Tinctoris, for instance, raves that the fiddle and the rebec promote piety and inflame the heart with contemplation of heavenly joys ('animus meus ad affectum pietatis assurgit: quaeque ad contemplationem gaudiorum supernorum: ardentissime cor meum inflammant').[79] The fiddle is often characterized as merry or joyous,[80] but it could also express grief and pain, and it could be used to put people to sleep.[81] The sound of the fiddle was thought to have magical powers, sometimes associated with healing, but in some cases dangerous.[82] The range in effect thus seems as varied as the instrument itself.

The European fiddle appears to have been less strident than eastern bowed chordophones. In the mid-fourteenth-century *El Libro de Buen Amor*, the 'rabé gritador' (harsh rebec, stanza 1229) is contrasted with the fiddle, which is sweet and clear:

> where the strings would have fallen. The distances between the strings are 11, 4, and 13 mm. The middle two strings are thus paired, and the spacing between this course and the outer strings is fairly wide and not uniform. Furthermore, the distance between the strings and the fingerboard suggest that the strings 'would have been stopped with the fingertips or the nails, without pressing the string down to the fingerboard', p. 10. While the provenance is somewhat removed from England and France, this instrument helps verify of the arrangement of strings in courses, and suggests the possibility of stopping strings away from the fingerboard. This practice is supported by Brown's observation, 'Trecento Fiddle', p. 301, that in fourteenth-century Italian art a few fiddles 'are clearly pictured without any fingerboard at all', a characteristic that could be explained by off-board stopping.

[77] Mary Anne Alburger, 'The 'Fydill in Fist': Bowed String Instruments from the *Mary Rose*', *The Galpin Society Journal* 53 (2000): 12–24, has described the fiddles in considerable detail. She suggests that Fiddle One, at least, is probably intended to be flat, pp. 14–15. No neck, pegbox or peg has been found, but 'both fiddles have features associated with tailpiece attachment', p. 18. Markings on the soundboard of Fiddle One 'may indicate where the feet of a bridge or combined bridge and stringholder may have rested', p. 19.

[78] Remnant, *English Bowed Instruments*, p. 69.

[79] Baines, 'Fifteenth-Century Instruments in Tinctoris's *De Inventione*', p. 25.

[80] As in a description of musical instruments by Galfridus de Vim Salor in his *Medulla Grammatica Coloribus Rhetoricis* of *c.* 1200: 'Cymbala praeclara, concors symphonia dulcis, fistulae, somnifera cythara, vitulaeque jocosae' (the illustrious chime bells, the sweet concord of the hurdy-gurdy and of the flute, the sleep-inducing *cythara*, and the merry fiddle), quoted in Bachmann, *Origins of Bowing*, p. 134.

[81] Bachman, *Origins of Bowing*, pp. 134–5.

[82] Bachman, *Origins of Bowing*, pp. 134–5. In 1347, for example, the 'vileresse' Jehanne de Crotot was accused of having ensorcelled a cleric, Rokseth, 'femmes musiciennes', p. 474.

La viyuela de arco faz' dulces devailadas,
adormiendo a vezes, muy alto a las vegadas,
bozes dulces, sabrosas, claras et bien puntadas;
a las gentes alegra, todas las tiene pagadas.[83]

(The fiddle plays sweet dance rhythms, sometimes soporific, sometimes loud, with sweet, solid, clear, well-played sounds that delight and please everyone.)

In fact, the adjective most commonly employed to describe the fiddle, some form of the word *sweet*, is also the term generally used to describe any music (and also to characterize most romance heroes and heroines). In the *Nibelungenlied*, for example, Volker makes sweet music on his fiddle ('videlte süeze dœne', stanza 1705);[84] and Gerart in the *Roman de la Violette* produces a 'douch son' (line 1405). But what might *sweet* mean in a world that favours bray pins, snares, and shawms? In this world, the brass jingles on a tambourine also make a 'dulce sonete' (sweet sound),[85] so assuredly the notion of *sweet* would not have suggested the smooth and even tones of the modern violin or viola. Medieval writers describe birdsong as sweet, and most birdsong has a raucous quality that would not be out of place on a children's play field.

More specific evidence about tone quality is rare, but there are some hints. The Middle English prose *Life of St Brandan* compares the fluttering sound of a bird's wings to the merry sound of the fiddle: 'and he with flykerynge of his wynges made a full mery noyse lyke a fydle'.[86] This comparison implies some form of rapid fluctuation in the tone of the instrument, a whirring or buzzing sound or possibly rapid bow changes.

As far as they go, medieval descriptions of the fiddle confirm Mary Remnant's expectation of considerable diversity in sound, and modern reproductions of fiddles corroborate this. One instrument can produce a harsh bark, a breathy sigh, an exotic surge, a textured singing voice, or a brutal scrape.

Certain physical commonalities, however, do govern the instrument in any embodiment using any playing technique. Of primary importance is the back and forth nature of the fiddle's sound production. Every bow stroke is achieved either with movement of the arm downward and outward, away from the instrument (downbow), or upward and inward, toward the instrument (upbow). Because the downward stroke is assisted by gravity, it tends to be stronger. This binary characteristic of the instrument is of vital importance in relation to narrative since it juxtaposes an inherent pattern of strong and weak sounds on the rhythms of the text.

Furthermore, bow changes on any permutation of this instrument cannot go

---

[83] References to this text are from Juan Ruiz, *Libro de Buen Amor*, ed. Raymond S. Willis (Princeton, NJ: Princeton University Press, 1972); my translation.

[84] Helmut de Boor, ed., *Das Nibelungenlied* (Wiesbaden: F. A. Brockhaus, 1979).

[85] Juan Ruiz, *Libro de Buen Amor*, stanza 1232.

[86] Thomas Wright, ed., *St Brandan: A Medieval Legend of the Sea* (London: T. Richards, 1844), p. 40.

unnoticed, as they can on a modern violin. Every time the bow changes direction, there is a moment of sonic instability combined with a scratchiness that can be emphasized and accented for effect or minimized. The result is a built-in rhythmic structure that must in some way accord with the rhythm of the narrative. These rhythmic characteristics pose special challenges for English verse, as we will see in the following chapter.

Bowing is an inviolable identifying feature of the fiddle, an unvarying characteristic. But ironically, another vital commonality of medieval fiddles is revealed in the startling range in instrument shape, bow construction and string arrangement. This variety in instrument construction furnishes strong evidence of a highly robust approach to the instrument. We see a way of thinking about the fiddle that can accommodate a wide range of equipment: instruments of diverse shape, size and manner of construction; strings of varying gauge and number, sometimes paired and sometimes single, sometimes including an off-board string and sometimes not; bridges of varying curvature; fingerboards present or absent; frets present or absent; bows of varying length, curvature, and method of attaching hairs. The contemporary treatises on tuning the instrument provide a structure that explains and unifies what at first appears to be an impossibly diverse situation. Because tuning structures are complex and technical, only some of the more significant aspects will be summarized here. For a fuller discussion of medieval fiddle tunings and implications for narrative performance, see Appendix B.

The most detailed discussion of tuning is provided by Jerome of Moravia, who wrote his *Tractatus de Musica* in Paris toward the end of the thirteenth century. Jerome describes the fiddle as having five strings, and he proposes three different ways of tuning the instrument. None of the tunings invites unadorned melodic playing; when only one string at a time is sounded, the arrangement of pitches creates awkward gaps in melodies or abrupt skips across strings. All the systems of tuning facilitate playing clusters of strings, normally two or three strings in the low, middle, or high range, though in some cases individual strings can be isolated or all five sounded together. Although bridge curvature has sometimes been cited as a crucial feature in fiddle construction, in practice it has little impact on playing within Jerome's tunings. Various options become possible or disappear according to the structure of the instrument and bow, but the overall approach remains consistent.

There is a robust quality to Jerome's approach to the instrument that survives considerable variation in string gauge, length, and arrangement; bow type; instrument shape; and style of construction. This is essential. Given the irrefutable variation in the instrument, any historical approach to the fiddle must be resilient enough to accommodate a wide range of embodiments. Jerome even specifies two different approaches to construction: the first tuning is designed for an instrument with one string positioned away from the fingerboard, and Jerome specifies that the player does not apply fingers to this string; the second tuning requires a fiddle with all five strings positioned over the fingerboard, and Jerome specifies how to finger each string; the third tuning does not specify the positioning of strings. Jerome's tunings thus assume and accommodate variety in instruments, and a wide range of fiddles can be played with the fairly uniform approach facilitated by these tunings.

Jerome's approach to the fiddle does not allow production of every pitch, but rather it creates a flexible and strategic structure of drones (unvarying pitches), and multiple pitches sometimes doubled at the octave, sometimes doubled in unison, sometimes following the melody (when the fingers stop two strings at once). The term *drone* has pejorative connotations, but medieval fiddle drones create a fluid substrate for melody and story. Rather than producing an unvarying root in a hacksaw-like approach to accompaniment, the drones provide a spectrum of shades which combine with the melody in multifarious patterns. The simple melodies of medieval narrative, far from tedious, abound in myriad combinations with word sounds and interactive pitches.

The most important key to narrative accompaniment supplied by Jerome is the principle of small-scale variation. While considerable complexity is possible, it is always accomplished within simple patterns. The patterns, furthermore, shift continually. No approach lasts very long, and changes in sound do not necessarily align with melodic phrasing. As a melody moves from one string to another, the surrounding drones shift as well, and this does not always occur at cadences. Furthermore, parallel fifths or fourths or octaves can be maintained only while the melody inhabits one string.

Within this overarching principle of kaleidoscope transformation, Jerome's three tunings appear to meet different needs.[87] The first tuning is well suited to a less skilled instrumentalist; it can produce a simplified form of a melody, or a rhythmic drone while the player or another musician sings a melody, and the instrument offers multiple easy ways of varying simple accompaniment. The second tuning is adapted for a more accomplished player; though it offers fewer automatic variation features, it covers a broader range, accommodates more developed melodic playing, and invites advanced techniques such as parallel intervals or polyphonic lines. The third tuning, the most problematic, appears to facilitate shifts from one tonal centre to another, thus making it possible to play some of the extant narrative melodies (such as *Aucassin et Nicolete*) that cannot otherwise be accomplished on the fiddle.

As we saw in Chapter 1, variation was a fundamental principle of both text and music composition in the Middle Ages, and we find in the construction and tuning of the fiddle how this principle would have been applied instrumentally. Jerome's tunings offer an energizing elasticity to the fiddle, and sometimes subtle effects are possible and natural without requiring much thought.

Once we are aware of the characteristics of fiddle technique, it becomes possible to recognize references in the Middle English romances that may describe such technique. Engagement with this tradition of fiddle playing becomes evident in the passage from *Bevis of Hampton* in which Princess Josian plays the fiddle. This is the most developed description of performance on the fiddle in the romances. When her companion, Saber, falls sick in Greece, Josian, already in disguise, buys

---

[87] See McGee, 'Medieval Fiddle'.

a fiddle and earns their sustenance by playing the instrument every day in the city. She continues to earn money as a minstrel for six months until Saber recovers:

> 3905 While Josian was in Ermonie,
> She hadde lerned of minstralcie,
> Upon a fithele for to play
> Staumpes, notes, garibles gay;
> Tho she kouthe no beter red,
> 3910 Boute in to the bourgh anon she yed
> And boughte a fithele, so saith the tale,
> For fourti panes of one menestrale;
> And alle the while that Saber lay,
> Josian everiche a day
> 3915 Yede aboute the cite with inne,
> Here sostenaunse for to winne.
> Thus Josian was in swiche destresse,
> While Saber lai in is siknesse.
>
> (Auchinleck MS, lines 3905–18)

(While Josian was in Armenia, she had studied music, and she had learned to play estampies, melodies, and cheerful 'garibles' on a fiddle. When she could think of no better solution, she went at once into the city and, as the story tells, she bought a fiddle for forty pence from a minstrel.)

As we have seen, Josian's musicianship is a firm part of the *Bevis* tradition in mainland Europe. (See Chapter 1.) In Continental versions of the story, we see her fiddling and singing while her companion plays the harp (with the two instruments paired as they frequently are in the Middle English romances). Even more significantly, in one late-thirteenth-century version she sings a *chanson de geste* about herself; thus a character in the story sings the story she inhabits. Guiraut del Luc's invocation of 'el son Beves d'Antona' as a melody commonly known provides solid historical evidence that some form of the *Bevis* story was sung.

The Middle English version does not specify that Josian sings, though we have seen that historical descriptions of performance rarely include all features. The text specifies that she plays 'staumpes' (the dance form *estampie*, a form which normally included a text), 'notes' (melodies, a term sometimes applied to narrative melodies, as in *Sir Orfeo*, line 602), and 'garibles gay'. The term *garibles* is obscure. The Oxford English Dictionary, citing this passages as the only instance, indicates that the word is 'related to the OF verb *guerbloier, guebloier*, to play or sing in some special fashion, probably the same word as *werbler*, to quaver with the voice … ?A flourish in music.' Henry Holland Carter speculates on these grounds that the term may refer to an 'arbitrary change in a piece of music, a variation, ornament, or flourish'.[88] Alan Hindley *et al.* translate *guerbloiier* as 'warble,

---

[88] Henry Holland Carter, *A Dictionary of Middle English Musical Terms* (Bloomington: Indiana University Press, 1968).

twitter; trill'.[89] The word suggests an instrumental form of the ornamentation Timothy McGee documents in *The Sound of Medieval Song*.

A passage from Gautier de Coinci may shed further light on the term 'garible'. Among the ways one can honour God with song are:

> En l'orguener, ou werbloier,
> ou deschanter, ou quintoier[90]

(To sing organum or to *werbloier* or to sing discant or to *quintoier*)

Since *garible* is probably related to *werbloier*, here employed in the same context as organum, discant, and 'fifthing', it seems possible that Josian's 'garibles' may have involved playing parallel intervals on her fiddle.[91] However we interpret the term, it shows continuity with a tradition of fiddle ornamentation, a tradition that is strongly linked with narrative accompaniment.

What we know about the medieval fiddle confirms what extant narrative fragments of notated music suggest: that narrative melodies were generally syllabic and repetitive. Although the melodies we know are often confined to a narrow ambitus, they sometimes incorporate interval leaps, and these leaps often conform to the tuning structure of the fiddle. These melodies have horrified modern readers, who speculate that medieval audiences must have had a higher tolerance for repetition than we. When such a melody is tied to a narrative text, however, the repetition furnishes a scintillating background, shaping itself around elements in the story without distracting. Each leaf of an aspen tree is round with a serrated edge and a slight point at the end, with veins branching from a central rib, the same pattern for every leaf. Yet some leaves twist quickly in a breeze and some more slowly; sunlight shines through some and reflects off others; some glow against pale bark and others float in blue sky; some cluster together and others tremble alone. The myriad embodiments of a pattern give a unified structure and harmony to the tree. The same is true of a story sung to a simple melody; the music creates an intricate shape for the tale, an organic structure modelled of clustering, shifting, blending, twisting, screeching, sighing, iterations of one melody.

The fiddle carries in its structure the genetic information for how such a narrative melody might have grown, how the fiddle might have enhanced the storyteller's living mosaic of shifting tesserae. Any melody sounded on the instrument carries with it a shifting spectrum of drones. Different features become available depending on the instrument and the ambitus of the melody. Some melodies on some fiddles can be played in different octaves, and passages can be played in parallel octaves or fifths or doubled in unison by stopping two strings at once. An off-board string, bowed or plucked or possibly stopped with the left thumb for microtone ornamentation, can extend the palette of textures. Many of the

---

[89] Alan Hindley, Frederick W. Langley, and Brian J. Levy, *Old French–English Dictionary* (Cambridge: Cambridge University Press, 2000).

[90] Quoted in Sarah Fuller, 'Discant and the Theory of Fifthing', *Acta Musicologica* 50 (1978): 241–75, at p. 243.

[91] See Appendix B for a fuller discussion of 'fifthing'.

embellishments described in medieval descriptions of singing can be applied on the fiddle. In this manner, the principle of variation is built into the instrument, and the fiddle and the voice provide two different agents of variation; in symbiotic combination, they provide an endless range of expressive possibility. The simple melody frees rather than limiting, and the fiddle adds its protean voice to the telling of a tale.

Implications for Instrumental Accompaniment of Narrative

The principles of accompaniment derived from fiddle construction and tuning can reasonably be applied to other instruments associated with narrative accompaniment, illuminating the long tradition of how narrative poetry was to be presented and accompanied, regardless of which instrument did the accompanying. Fiddle construction and tuning point to a shifting fabric of ancillary sound, drones and concordant pitches in simple patterns of variation somewhat independent of melodic phrasing. This principle and specific applications revealed by the fiddle tunings can readily be applied to harp or lute accompaniment of narrative. The parameters of each instrument, however, render certain approaches to accompaniment more idiomatic.

The lute is percussive, generating a sharp attack followed by a rapid decay, much more rapid on gut strings than on modern composite strings, but the instrument can create the illusion of sustain by rapid reiteration of pitches. The plectrum invites binary patterns: any note or chord must be generated by either a downstroke or an upstroke, and thus it is convenient to establish rhythmic structures. The medieval lute is capable of strumming chordal patterns or articulating a melody, or combining the two.[92] It should be noted, however, that what we term 'chords' is probably more akin to drones in medieval thought, and thus the instrument shares certain capacities with the fiddle.[93]

Although we associate the sound of the harp with the clear, bell-like tone of the modern instrument, Ron Cook provides strong evidence that bray pins, crooked pegs which create a buzz when a string is plucked, were common as early as the thirteenth century and were the norm for British harps in the fifteenth century.[94] He suggests that for softer playing, a lighter touch may have been employed 'so as

---

[92] Ivanoff, 'An Invitation to the Fifteenth-Century Plectrum Lute', p. 10, notes 'ample evidence of a performance technique on the plectrum lute that combines single-line and chordal playing', and he indicates, 'Pieces employing the originally plectrum-based technique of strumming full chords and connecting them with single-line passages echoed well into the sixteenth century', p. 15.

[93] On the lute it is most convenient either to pluck one string or course at a time or to strum all the strings, rather than playing groups of strings as on the fiddle. The lute is tuned differently from the fiddle, and the frets make it convenient to finger multiple strings simultaneously to achieve concordances that must be supplied by open strings on the fiddle.

[94] Ron Cook, 'The Presence and Use of Brays on the Gut-Strung Harp through the 17th Century: A Survey and Consideration of the Evidence', *Historical Harp Society Bulletin* (1998): 2–39. In 1474 George Cely notes payment to his music teacher Thomas Rede for stringing and 'bray pynnyng' a harp: Hanham, 'Musical Studies', p. 272.

to minimize the effect of the brays',[95] but a buzzy tone would still be characteristic of the instrument. The harp can produce an isolated melody more easily than the lute or the fiddle, but while chordal playing is possible, on the diatonically tuned harp it requires individual selection of each pitch, whereas the lute and fiddle tunings are structured to facilitate multiple concordant pitches.[96] Harp playing is not limited by the binary upstroke or downstroke of a single tool. By utilizing multiple plucking tools (the fingers), the harpist can develop complex interactive rhythmic patterns in counterpoint with the rhythms of the text, selecting strong or weak fingers to build in musical nuances and phrasing,[97] and adding fifths or octaves or drones for structure.[98]

The medieval fiddle shares with the lute the binary limitation of the upward or downward movement of a single sounding tool, in this case the bow, and thus can easily create rhythmic patterns, but unlike the other two instruments, the fiddle is a sustaining instrument. The sound continues and can be inflected and modified after the initial attack; the duration of the attack and of the sustain can be adjusted, as can the pitch. The fiddle can embellish words and phrases with sustained swells and tonal shifts, or accent textual patterns with percussive rhythms.

While medieval narrators may have sung or chanted, or employed a quicker or slower delivery, or utilized more or fewer dramatic inflections, certain realities pervade any approach. In narrative performance, far more than any other musical performance, the primacy of the text is vital; the purpose is to communicate a story. Any model of medieval instrumental accompaniment must allow the instrument to enhance the text rather than compete with it or obscure it. Three instrumental features potentially interfere with narrative clarity: volume, timbre, and positioning of attacks. The volume can be adjusted by the player on all three instruments, though it should be noted that bray pins on the harp increase the volume. The timbre, or tone quality, is a more complex feature. The plucked gut strings of the harp and the lute enhance the higher overtones of the sonic range,

---

[95] Cook, 'Presence and Use of Brays', p. 15.

[96] Spring, *Lute in Britain*, p. 26, observes, 'No specific directions on how to tune the lute survive from England before the late fifteenth century', but he speculates, based on sources from outside England, 'that in the fourteenth century the lute, like the gittern, was tuned in rising fourths, which indeed is the normal tuning of the Arabic 'ūd both today and in medieval times'. He adds, 'We know that by the end of the fifteenth century the tuning by fourths had given way to a tuning of fourths around a major third.'

[97] Salas, 'Thumb-Under Technique', p. 117, suggests that three fingers were used, of which the thumb is strong, the index finger weak, and the middle finger strong, but not as strong as the thumb, p. 117. The passage from *Ruodlieb* quoted above may alternatively imply use of only the thumb and the index finger. Either way, the principle would remain the same, though the rhythmic options would differ.

[98] Howard Mayer Brown, 'The Trecento Harp', in *Studies in the Performance of Late Mediaeval Music*, ed. Stanley Boorman (Cambridge: Cambridge University Press, 1983), pp. 35–73, at p. 50, provides evidence that, at least in fourteenth-century Italy, harps were probably tuned diatonically, and he concludes that 'all of them could play at least some single lines from the written repertoire, and that most were capable of playing two or more melodic lines simultaneously, and even of playing chords or drones' (p. 55).

and these higher frequencies tend to have a rapid decay, allowing the relatively sustained sound of the voice to maintain prominence. At the same time, they rely on relatively frequent attacks to maintain a presence. The fiddle with its capacity for sustain can present a less complex texture, but its tone quality is similar enough to the voice that it can be difficult to distinguish instrument from voice.

The positioning of attacks in relation to the text also significantly affects the clarity of the text. When the attack of a note coincides with a key syllable, the meaning can be obscured, especially when multiple notes are sounded simultaneously. Each instrument suggests a characteristic approach to solving this problem. In simplified terms, the lute creates a musical grid to contain the words, and the harp weaves wreathes of notes around the words, while the fiddle surges and recedes beneath the words.[99]

But neither syllables nor notes are uniform. One vital aspect of all three instruments associated with narrative accompaniment is a technique of sound production that results in alternation of strong and weak sounds. The medieval plectrum was rough on one side and smooth on the other, rendering a strong–weak pattern when a line is played with alternating strokes. Harp fingering moves between the strong thumb and the weaker fingers. The strong downbow stroke on the fiddle alternates with the weaker upbow stroke. All three instruments create inherent patterns of strong and weak sounds, not the smooth, flowing, even sounds associated with modern performance technique. Some form of strong–weak contrast is thus built into each accompanying instrument, and the resulting rhythms must in some way have interacted with the inherent rhythms of narrative verse. To understand how this may have worked in England, we must turn to rhythmic structures of the Middle English romance.

---

[99] To hear Joseph Baldassarre's accompaniment of *The Tournament of Tottenham* on a replica of a fifteenth-century lute, see The Quill Consort, *Three Medieval Romances* (Boise, ID: Silver Quill Recordings, 1992). To hear Laura Zaerr's accompaniment of the same romance on the gothic harp, see *Sentimental and Humorous Romances* (Provo, UT: The Chaucer Studio, 2007). For a contrast between Laura Zaerr's harp accompaniment, and Shira Kammen's accompaniment on a medieval fiddle, see the TEAMS video recording of excerpts of *Sir Gawain and the Green Knight* (Provo, UT: The Chaucer Studio, 2002). For my self-accompaniment of *The Tournament of Tottenham* on the fiddle, see *Music and Medieval Narrative* (Provo, UT: The Chaucer Studio, 2011).

4

Metre, Accent, and Rhythm

COMPLICATED patterns dance through Middle English verse, rhythms so flexible they appear 'deregulated'.[1] The following discussion draws on music theory to explicate both characteristics of this rhythmic complexity and principles that govern it. By distinguishing categories of accent and articulating how different types of accent establish simultaneous rhythms in the text itself, we may come to appreciate and understand choices that might otherwise be dismissed as 'scribal corruption'.

This approach, grounded in music theory, is more clearly justified when we consider the intimate connection between verse and music in the development of rhythm in medieval Europe and the integral involvement of music in the poetry that influenced Middle English verse. In this context, the thirteenth-century English song 'Edi beo thu' models how lines with varying number of syllables can be set to a melody in triple metre, and how initial and final unstressed syllables group with preceding or subsequent stressed syllables, establishing line structures that do not consistently align with metrical structures.

Linguistics as well as music can provide a means of recognizing and understanding the simultaneous rhythmic patterns that structure Middle English verse. Variation in one rhythmic structure provides energy without a loss of continuity when other rhythmic structures are maintained; recurrence of a disrupted pattern brings greater satisfaction than continuous reiteration of the pattern. Furthermore, we find evidence that where metre is strong, as in the tail-rhyme romances, we should expect discontinuities in the prosody.

Finally, this chapter will conclude with instances of rhythmic variation in the manuscripts of the Middle English romances. These passages exhibit rhythmic flexibility suggestive of an improvisatory approach to transmission grounded in a performance tradition, where ephemeral links and transitory patterns, similar to those facilitated by fiddle tunings, create a rhythmic polyphony that accords with the aesthetic we find in music of that era. By approaching the rhythmic patterns intrinsic to Middle English verse in musical terms, we gain insight into how the rhythms of an accompanying musical instrument might enhance those patterns.

Middle English Verse

The Middle English verse romances may be grouped roughly according to their metrical structure. About a third are in couplets composed of four-stress lines,

---

[1] Referring to the late-thirteenth-century *Floris and Blauncheflur*, M. L. Gasparov, *A History of European Versification*, trans. G. S. Smith and Marina Tarlinskaja (Oxford: Clarendon Press, 1996), p. 183, observes, 'Deregulated verse of this kind held the field in English poetry for a century and a half.'

a structure adapted from the Old French and Insular French (Anglo-Norman) octosyllabic couplets. Another third are in some form of tail-rhyme stanza, typically constructed of *aab* units[2] in which a couplet of four-stress lines is followed by a three-stress line, which provides the rhyme that ties together the stanza. A twelve-line stanza rhyming *aabccbddbeeb* is the most common English tail-rhyme form. The last group, alliterative verse, is rooted in Germanic accentual verse. It is composed of four-stress lines, frequently incorporating more unstressed syllables than the other verse forms. The first three stressed syllables of each line normally alliterate, and each line is divided into two half-lines or hemistiches, each carrying two stressed syllables. Sometimes alliterative verse is structured into elaborate stanzas of varying line length, in many cases incorporating rhyme. All three categories show considerable variation, and sometimes the metrical structure changes within a romance.

Middle English verse[3] might best be characterized as *ictic*, that is, the metrical designs are based around the *ictus*, the beat or prominent syllable.[4] A line operates within a pattern of beats rather than a specified number of syllables or feet, though some romances are more syllabically structured than others. The Middle English language is phonologically suited to ictic verse. Martin Duffell observes:

> [I]ctic verse is indifferent to the loss of word-final schwa and of weak syllables in syncope; it allows either accentuation of French loan words; it allows any monosyllable to represent a beat, making versifying easier in an increasingly monosyllabic language.[5]

The alliterative long line is particularly variable within a four-stress verse design, offering such patterns as this:

> Sum covettis and has comforth to carpe and to lestyn
> Of curtaissy, of knyghthode, of craftis of armys,
> Of kyngis at has conquirid and ovircomyn landis;

---

[2] In discussions of verse, lower-case letters in italics are used to indicate rhyme structure. Each letter identifies a line by is ending sound; when a letter is repeated, the corresponding lines rhyme.

[3] Jeremy Smith, "'The Metre Which Does Not Measure': The Function of Alliteration in Middle English Alliterative Poetry', in *Approaches to the Metres of Alliterative Verse*, ed. Judith Jefferson and Ad Putter, Leeds Texts and Monographs, New Series 17 (Leeds: University of Leeds School of English, 2009), pp. 11–23, at pp. 22–3, reminds us that 'Middle English varieties developed over four centuries in different directions at different speeds. … "Middle English" is thus a portmanteau-term, encapsulating a period of processual change.' He points out that the verse we encounter reflects 'the kind of experimentation we must expect during a period when the linguistic basis of verse was changing'.

[4] A number of models have been developed to describe rhythmic features of verse, making it possible to enhance simple characterization of syllables as 'stressed' or 'unstressed' with more subtle analysis of the acoustic correlates of stress: pitch, volume, and duration. These features, however, frequently describe performance instances rather than the inherent rhythmic properties of a text, properties present in any performance but reflected or held in tension in a range of ways.

[5] Martin Duffell, *A New History of English Metre* (London: Modern Humanities Research Association and Maney Publishing, 2008), p. 81.

> Sum of <u>wir</u>schip, <u>iwis</u>, <u>slike</u> as tham <u>wyse</u> lattis,
> And sum of <u>wanton</u> <u>wer</u>kis, <u>tha</u> that ere <u>wild</u>-hedid;[6]

(Some crave and have comfort when they tell or listen to stories of chivalry, about knighthood, about skill in arms, about kings who have conquered and overcome lands; some, indeed, [like to hear] about honour, such people as they consider wise; and some [prefer to hear] about self-indulgent deeds, those that are wild-headed.)

The second line maintains a triple rhythm of a stressed syllable followed by two weaker syllables, a pattern established in the second half of the first line; the third line stretches to a galloping quadruple arrangement of hoof beats; no matter how you scan them, the last two lines are a mixed bag, each concluding with three syllables tumbling from stronger to weaker, whimsically jumbling honour with wantonness.

Romances in couplets and tail-rhyme also incorporate varying numbers of unstressed syllables, though generally within a narrower amplitude. A typical pattern is:

> <u>Tho</u> she <u>kou</u>the no <u>be</u>ter <u>red</u>,
> Boute <u>in</u> to the <u>bourgh</u> <u>anon</u> she <u>yed</u>
> And <u>boughte</u> a <u>fi</u>thele, so <u>saith</u> the <u>tale</u>,
> For <u>four</u>ti <u>panes</u> of <u>one</u> men<u>es</u>trale;
> And <u>alle</u> the <u>while</u> that <u>Saber</u> lay,
> <u>Josian</u> <u>everiche</u> a <u>day</u>
> <u>Yede</u> a<u>boute</u> the <u>cite</u> with <u>inne</u>,
> Here <u>sostenaunse</u> <u>for</u> to <u>winne</u>.
> (Auchinleck MS, lines 3909 16)

(When she could think of no better solution, she went at once into the city and, as the story tells, she bought a fiddle for forty pence from a minstrel. And all the while that Saber lay [sick], Josian went around the city every day to win their sustenance.)

Only the last line could be described as regular iambic tetrameter, with a weak–strong arrangement of syllables. While generally one or two weaker syllables intervene between accented syllables, the end of the fourth line, 'For fourti panes of one menestrale', creates ambiguity about whether to assign the third stress to 'o-' or 'me-'. If 'o-' is stressed (as indicated above), it is followed by three weaker syllables; if 'me-' is stressed (as is normal for the word 'menestrale'), it is preceded by four weaker syllables. Both contenders can be accented, introducing five stresses into the line, 'For <u>four</u>ti <u>panes</u> of <u>one</u> <u>menestrale</u>', and this raises some questions about correspondence rules for verse that will be addressed later.

Rhythmic complexity is even more evident when we compare versions of a

---

[6] *The Alliterative Alexander Fragment C* or *Wars of Alexander*, lines 8–12. Stressed syllables are underlined. Other interpretations of inherent stress are possible in some places, and that ambiguity is typical of Middle English verse.

single romance. Variants among manuscripts exhibit remarkable freedom, especially at the level of the weaker syllables. A couplet from *Floris and Blauncheflur* illustrates a typical pattern:

> The <u>kin</u>ges <u>hert</u> was <u>al</u> in <u>ca</u>re,
> That <u>sawe</u> his <u>so</u>ne for <u>love</u> so <u>fa</u>re.
> (Trentham MS, lines 253–4)

> And the <u>kin</u>ges <u>herte</u> is <u>ful</u> of <u>ca</u>re
> That he <u>sikth</u> is <u>so</u>ne vor <u>love</u> so <u>fa</u>re.
> (CUL MS Gg.4.27.2, lines 55–6)

(The king's heart was full of concern to see his son so affected by love.)

While the final -e's (in 'sawe' and 'herte') could be handled differently to foster rhythmic consistency, the rhythms still contrast. The two lines in the Trentham Manuscript begin with one weak syllable ('The' and 'That'), and in the Cambridge MS with two ('And the' and 'That he'). Although a minor difference, it transforms perception of the rhythm of the couplet, and it illustrates a pervasive characteristic among the manuscripts.

Sometimes rhythmic variation appears to be mingled with scribal corruption, as in this couplet from *Sir Orfeo*:

> <u>Sum</u> ben of <u>wele</u> and <u>sum</u> of <u>wo</u>,
> And <u>sum</u> of <u>joy</u> and <u>merthe</u> al<u>so</u>;
> (Harley MS 3810, lines 5–6)

> <u>Som</u> of <u>werre</u> and <u>som</u> off <u>wo</u>,
> <u>Som</u> of <u>myr</u>thys and <u>joy</u> al<u>so</u>;
> (MS Ashmole 61 lines 11–12)

(Some [Breton lays] are about well being [Ashmole: war] and some about sorrow, and some about joy and also mirth.)

In the Harley manuscript, 'wele' (well being) and 'wo' (sorrow) contrast effectively in meaning; but in the Ashmole manuscript, the bitterness of both 'werre' (war) and 'wo' is nicely balanced by the more cheerful 'myrthys' and 'joy'. However we interpret the relationship of the manuscripts, one of them exhibits a substantive change in one word that could be viewed as a corruption. At the same time, simple rhythmic variation at the level of weak syllables is indicated in the Harley manuscript by 'ben' in the first line and 'and' in the second, and in the Ashmole manuscript by the final syllable of 'myrthys'.

The tail-rhyme romances are notoriously variable. A somewhat restrained instance is the following description of feast entertainment from the Northern Version of *Octavian*:

> With <u>gud</u> <u>myr</u>this <u>tham</u> <u>e</u>mange,
> <u>Har</u>pes, <u>fe</u>thils and <u>full</u> faire <u>son</u>ge,
> <u>Cy</u>toles and <u>saw</u>tr<u>ye</u>,

<u>Till</u> the <u>seven</u>y<u>ghte</u> was <u>gone</u>
With <u>alkyn</u> <u>wel</u>this <u>in</u> that <u>wone</u>,
Of <u>myr</u>this and <u>mynstralsye</u>.
(Thornton MS, lines 199–204)

(… with good mirth among them until the week was over: harps, fiddles, and very lovely song, citoles and psalteries, with abundance of all kinds of mirth and minstrelsy in that dwelling.)

Wyth <u>gode</u> <u>metys</u> <u>them</u> <u>amonge</u>,
<u>Harpe</u>, <u>pype</u> and <u>mery</u> <u>songe</u>,
Bothe <u>lewte</u> and <u>sawtre</u>.
<u>When</u> the <u>sevyn</u> <u>nyght</u> was all <u>goon</u>
Wyth <u>allkyn</u> <u>welthe</u> <u>in</u> that <u>won</u>,
And <u>mery</u> <u>mynstralsy</u>,
(CUL MS Ff.2.38, lines 196–201)

(… with good food among them – harp, pipe, and merry song, both lute and psaltery. When the week had passed with all kinds of abundance in that dwelling, and merry minstrelsy, …)

In both versions, there is a tension between the normal stress on the first syllable of 'sawtre' and the emphasis on the second syllable implied by the rhyme scheme. Although the list of instruments varies, the rhyming words at line endings remain constant. One of the intriguing features of both versions is the ambiguity about which syllables are intrinsically stressed. An argument could be made that '<u>full</u> <u>faire</u> <u>songe</u>' presents a sequence of three stressed syllables. Similarly, it would be reasonable to scan 'Wyth <u>allkyn</u> <u>welthe</u> in that <u>won</u>' so that it has only three stressed syllables. Even though Middle English poetry may be characterized as 'ictic', there is demonstrable evidence of variation in the number of beats per line. Among couplets with four stresses, a line might carry only three,[7] or both lines might carry three;[8] or, among tail-lines with three stresses, a tail-line might carry only two.[9] Additional stresses are common in alliterative poetry,[10] or, alternatively, four stresses can stretch across as many as sixteen syllables.[11]

In addition to many deviations from the number of stresses established within a text, the tail-rhyme romances also contain numerous perturbation of the stanza design. Sometimes three lines are missing from a stanza;[12] sometimes three lines are added;[13] sometimes, as in the case of *The Weddynge of Sir Gawen and*

---

[7] E.g.: <u>Orfeo</u> <u>mest</u> of <u>ani</u> <u>thing</u> / <u>Loved</u> the <u>gle</u> of <u>harping</u>; (*Sir Orfeo*, Auchinleck MS, lines 25–6).

[8] E.g.: <u>Sholde</u>, at <u>her</u> bygynnyng,/ <u>Speke</u> of that <u>ryghtwes</u> <u>kyng</u> (*Emare*, lines 16–17).

[9] E.g. 'Be <u>north</u> and be <u>southe</u>' (*Libeaus Desconus*, Cotton Caligula MS A.II, line 135).

[10] E.g. 'The <u>king</u> <u>castes</u> up his <u>sheld</u> and <u>covers</u> him <u>fair</u>' (*Alliterative Morte Arthure*, line 1110).

[11] E.g. 'Ther was <u>clynkyng</u> of <u>cart</u>-sadellys and <u>clattiryng</u> of <u>connes</u>' (*The Tournament of Tottenham*, line 163).

[12] E.g. the Lambeth Palace MS of *Libeaus Desconus*, between lines 2123 and 2124.

[13] E.g. in the last stanza of *Emaré*, lines 1033–5.

Dame Ragnell, we can recognize a tail-rhyme construction, but lines leap to seven stresses or shrink to two, and stanzas bloat with extra lines or expurgate all tail-lines, while orphan lines or couplets are stranded in bewildering intersections of scrambled rhyme.

In the context of these examples, Greek terminology describing regular patterns of stressed and unstressed syllables flounders; iambic and trochaic feet, mired in explanations and exceptions, stagger to a halt. The flexibility of the Middle English language invites rhythmic ambiguity; and an unprecedented profusion of hetero-rhythmic bouquets blossom where more sober syllables had marched.

Ad Putter argues for editions that 'recover what the original author wrote', expressing concern that the 'tail-rhyme romances are getting left behind, and will seem, as other forms of verse are being tidied up, even more of a prosodic mess.'[14] Yet, while some scribal variation is clearly the result of carelessness, the pervasiveness of rhythmic transformation carries the scent of performance, even when transmission is purely textual. The prevailing aesthetic fosters improvisation over rigid adherence to a source. So while it may be the goal of an editor to recover the original version, this study listens for echoes of uttered romance, and in the romances, scribal variation tells an articulate tale of rhythmic improvisation.

The continuity of the Middle English romances with contemporary performance traditions becomes evident when we consider how concepts of rhythm developed in medieval Europe. Verse and music are consistently discussed together, and to consider verse alone creates distortions. Both music theory and linguistics offer ways of thinking about accent that can elucidate transformations in Middle English verse, especially within an awareness of the cultural influences operating in medieval England.

Rhythm in Verse and Music

Martin Duffell distinguishes verse from other utterances as being 'numerically regulated', involving 'some form of counting'.[15] He states, 'Rhythm is produced when a series of events occurs at what is perceived by the human ear as regular intervals.' He further classifies rhythm as either primary (consisting of undifferentiated iterations, as the ticking of the clock) or secondary, which is 'the language of patterning metres', in which lines 'contain two different types of event in a regular sequence'.[16] A contrast between more and less prominent events can be created through contrasts in pitch, volume, duration, or a combination of these. Lerdahl and Jackendoff present the idea in terms of music: 'Fundamental to the idea of meter is the notion of periodic alternation of strong and weak beats.'[17] In both

---

[14] Ad Putter, 'Metre and the Editing of Middle English Verse: Prospects for Tail-Rhyme Romance, Alliterative Poetry, and Chaucer', *Poetica* 71 (2009): 29–47, at pp. 29 and 43.

[15] Duffell, *New History of English Metre*, p. 7.

[16] Duffell, *New History of English Metre*, p. 18.

[17] Fred Lerdahl and Ray Jackendoff, *A Generative Theory of Tonal Music* (Cambridge, MA: MIT Press, 1983), p. 19.

music and verse, rhythm is created by regularly occurring patterns of strong and weak sound events.

In the sixth century Cassiodorus linked speech with the pulse of the human body through musical rhythm: 'loquimur vel intrinsecus venarum pulsibus commovemur, per musicos rithmos armoniae virtutibus probatur esse sociatum' (Our speech and the pulse of our veins are proved to be related through musical rhythms to the virtues of harmony).[18] About a century later, in his highly influential *Etymologiae*, Isidore divided music into three aspects, two of which concern the arrangement of sound in words:

> Musicae partes sunt tres, id est harmonica, rythmica, metrica. Harmonica est quae decernit in sonis acutum et gravem. Rythmica est quae requirit incursionem verborum, utrum bene sonus an male cohaereat. Metrica est, quae mensuram diversorum metrorum probabili ratione cognoscit, ut verbi gratia, heroicon, iambicon, elegiacon, et cetera.[19]

> (The parts of music are three: harmonics, rhythmics and metrics. Harmonics discerns the high and the low in sounds. Rhythmics is that which inquires after the joining of words, whether the sound hangs together well or ill. Metrics is that which knows the measure of the different metres by proven theory; as, for example, of the heroic, the iambic, the elegiac, etc.)

Margot Fassler has demonstrated that, in the late twelfth and early thirteenth centuries, the development of modal rhythms in music (patterns of long and short note values) was linked with the development of sung Latin poetry.[20] It becomes clear that the history of verse structure alone does not provide adequate background for understanding Middle English verse. The rhythmic structure of music must be considered as well.

Theorists such as David Abercrombie use the note values of standard musical notation to represent the rhythms of English verse, suggesting that stresses function in the same way as musical beats. Following this general approach, we might express the rhythmic structure of the beginning of *The Weddynge of Sir Gawen and Dame Ragnell* as shown in example 4.1. Notated in this way, the rhythmic pattern resembles some of the contemporary music, vacillating between duple and triple rhythms. While the romances operate in a very different tradition, we should not forget that they might be influenced by a similar aesthetic. The creators, transmitters, and audience of the romances were not hermetically separated from the creators, transmitters, and audience of the rhythmically sophisticated music of the fourteenth and fifteenth centuries.

But why should the passage be conceived in triple time? Within the same structure of stressed syllables, an equally plausible rendition might be that shown in

---

[18] Quotation and translation from Arthur Glowka, 'The Function of Meter According to Ancient and Medieval Theory', *Allegorica* 7 (1982): 100–9, at p. 105.

[19] Quotation and translation from Margot E. Fassler, 'Accent, Meter, and Rhythm in Medieval Treatises "De rithmis"', *The Journal of Musicology* 5.2 (1987): 164–90, at pp. 167–8.

[20] Fassler, 'Accent, Meter, and Rhythm', p. 173.

Example 4.1 A possible rhythmic structure for *The Weddynge of Sir Gawen and Dame Ragnell*, lines 1–3, in triple meter

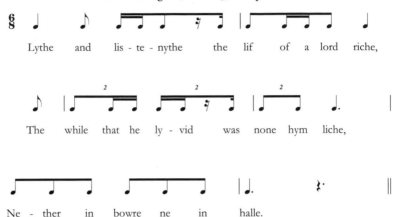

(Listen, and hear about the life of a noble lord. While he lived there was no one like him either in chamber or in hall.)

example 4.2. These two alternatives suggest a serious concern with this temporal approach. Must the unstressed syllables always coincide with time-lengths subdivided in simple ratios? Verse rhythm may not fall into exact duple or triple patterns. It becomes evident, too, that examples 4.1 and 4.2 attempt to describe particular performance instances rather than intrinsic characteristics of the language. Derek Attridge argues that a metrical system 'should operate neither on the minutiae of phonetic detail (which are a property of individual performances) nor on purely abstract categories, but on the perceptual realities of linguistic rhythm.'[21] He advocates simply classifying syllables as either stressed or unstressed, especially since this 'probably corresponds to an actual process of simplification which occurs in the perception of regular rhythm'.[22]

Recognizing a distinction between rhythms intrinsic to a text and rhythms introduced in performance, however, does not remove a fundamental challenge in our understanding of Middle English verse: How was metre realized? We might expect to derive insight from music notated for verse, either Middle English song or the Continental traditions so influential in England, but equal controversy reigns here too. There is no clear agreement about how to perform monophonic secular songs: some argue for an implied pattern of long and short notes (applying the rhythmic modes), some favour a more declamatory approach (following the inherent rhythms of the text), and some urge an isosyllabic approach which allots

---

[21] Derek Attridge, *The Rhythms of English Poetry* (London: Longman, 1982), p. 151.

[22] Attridge, *Rhythms of English Poetry*, p. 156. Attridge's system accommodates considerable complexity in addressing the positioning of syllables.

Example 4.2 An alternative rhythmic structure for *The Weddynge of Sir Gawen and Dame Ragnell*, lines 1–3, in duple meter

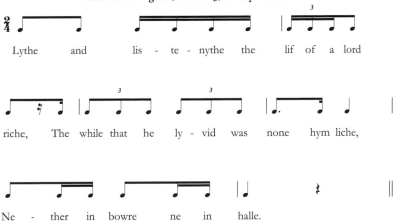

roughly equal time value to each syllable.[23] Though generally favouring an isosyllabic approach, John Stevens sensibly observes that 'the various genres require various rhythmical interpretations', an awareness rendered more complex by the 'intermingling of monophonic and polyphonic repertoires'.[24]

The characteristics of the French language exacerbate the ambiguity. Roger Pensom summarizes the received view:

> Verse-accent in Modern French ... accords no prosodic status to the word ... The fact that it is impossible, according to this view, to pin the ictus on to any prosodic element within the 'curseme' ... helps to explain the complete lack of consensus about what French metre, if it exists, really is.[25]

Old French verse is normally described in terms of a set number syllables of undifferentiated weight, but the last counted syllable of each line or hemistich (half-line) must be accented, and this accented syllable may be followed by an unaccented syllable, creating variation in the actual number of syllables in each line. There are, in fact, several ways in which the number of syllables can vary, and this has profound implications for musical setting: when the number of syllables varies, the text setting for a melody can never be the same from line to line or

---

[23] For a summary of this discussion, see Elizabeth Aubrey, 'Non-Liturgical Monophony: Introduction', in *A Performer's Guide to Medieval Music*, ed. Ross W. Duffin (Bloomington: Indiana University Press, 2000), pp. 105–14, at pp. 106–10.

[24] Stevens, *Words and Music*, p. 416.

[25] Roger Pensom, *Accent and Metre in French: A Theory of the Relation between Linguistic Accent and Metrical Practice in French, 1100–1900* (Bern: Peter Lang, 1998), p. 11.

stanza to stanza. This variability is further complicated by word accent, which was more prominent in Old French than Modern French; it is clear that it operates in some Old French verse in the construction of a periodically repeating pattern of stressed and unstressed syllables.[26] The elasticity we find in Old French verse may be even more characteristic of Anglo-Norman poetry, which sometimes requires 'fierce editing' to turn it into octosyllabics.[27] M. Dominica Legge observed regarding *Gui de Warewic*, 'The state of the versification in the extant manuscripts reduced Professor Ewert to despair.'[28]

In Latin, too, we find patterns that defy our expectations of regularity. The musical rhythmic modes articulated in the mid-thirteenth century are based on patterns of long and short duration, and they are described in terms of quantitative Latin poetry in metres structured around contrasts in syllable length: first mode, trochaic (long–short); second mode, iambic (short–long); third mode, dactylic (long–short–short); fourth mode, anapaestic (short–short–long); fifth mode, spondaic (long–long); and sixth mode, tribrachic (short–short–short). Yet, ironically, in the twelfth and early thirteenth centuries, during the time the rhythmic modes were being developed, rhythmic Latin poetry based on word accent rather than duration was gaining prominence. Margot Fassler argues compellingly that the rhythmic modes developed from patterns of consonance and dissonance in polyphony, thus from a feature of music rather than poetry, and these patterns were only later applied to monophonic music. Because polyphonic music is built around relationships between simultaneously occurring melodic lines, the intervals between concurrent pitches can be sequenced into patterns of strong (consonant) and weak (dissonant) sound events. Monophonic music, involving only one melodic line, would not have this capacity. Fassler concludes:

> In the monophonic genres, rhythmic patterns were created primarily by stress accent; in the polyphonic genres of the early Ars antiqua, rhythmic patterns were created by alternating consonant and dissonant intervals and by making the consonant intervals long and the dissonant intervals short.[29]

She demonstrates that John of Garland 'tried to make the beat or ictus the governing force of individual lines of rhythmic poetry', but that he encountered difficulty with poetry of a 'quasi-iambic cast':

> In classical iambic meter, the ictus falls on the second half of the foot, or on the long. When this meter gets transformed into rhythmic poetry where longs and shorts no longer matter, the beat or ictus still falls on the strong or second half of the foot. Thus iambic lines are 'up-beat' lines. But the natural

[26] See David Maw, 'Accent and Metre in Later Old French Verse: The Case of the Polyphonic *Rondel*', *Medium Aevum* 75.1 (2006): 46–83, at p. 50.

[27] R. C. Johnston, 'On Scanning Anglo-Norman Verse', *Anglo-Norman Studies* 5 (1983): 153–64, at p. 155.

[28] M. Dominica Legge, *Anglo-Norman Literature and its Background* (Oxford: Clarendon Press, 1963), p. 170.

[29] Fassler, 'Accent, Meter, and Rhythm', pp. 189–90.

force of the Latin language usually puts the accent on the first syllable of two-syllable words.[30]

As a result we find irregularities in Latin rhythmic verse. Thus Latin poetry and music together offer the developing Middle English romance genre both a tolerance of rhythmic variation and two different ways to create patterns of emphasis: duration and stress.

Since Old French, Anglo-Norman, and Latin are profound forces in the development of Middle English verse, it is significant to find among these influences stress-based verse, variation in number of syllables, and two techniques for establishing metre. On the principle that 'good metre looks for a match with the natural spoken rhythms of the language', Roger Pensom makes a strong argument that in some cases in the late medieval French lyric, 'the rhythmic structure of the melody changes from stanza to stanza in parallel with the metre of the verse.'[31] In a detailed analysis of the late-thirteenth-century *rondel*, David Maw suggests either 'the rhythmic form of a melody may undergo significant change against a constant metre in different performances' or, following Roger Pensom, the melody may exhibit 'a variable modal rhythm which responds to the changing pattern of di- and trisyllabic feet in the verse'.[32] In either case, the musical setting of a verse text must be transformed in some way from stanza to stanza or line to line. The melody must accommodate a varying arrangement of syllables.

'Edi beo thu': Rhythmic Implications of an English Melody

We might then reasonably look for an English melody that can make such accommodations, since this might reveal something of the way verse and music interact rhythmically. Karl Reichl recognizes the historical validity of applying a contrafactum, a melody from another source, to a Middle English romance text, but he concludes that no appropriate melody survives. His discussion, however, is limited by two stipulations, that 'it is essential that there is a text with music whose metrical structure is identical to that for which a music is sought', and that the music should not have 'wide ambitus, interval leaps, [or a] poly-motif melody'.[33]

But, though not English, the music for *Aucassin et Nicolete* (example 4.3) serves as evidence that neither limitation need apply to sung narrative.[34] The *A* and *B* melodic phrases applied to the heptasyllabic lines of *Aucassin et Nicolete*

---

[30] Fassler, 'Accent, Meter, and Rhythm', p. 183.

[31] Roger Pensom, 'Performing the Medieval Lyric: A Metrical-Accentual Approach', *Performance Practice Review* 10.2 (1997): 212–23, at pp. 215 and 219.

[32] Maw, 'Accent and Metre', p. 74.

[33] Reichl, 'Comparative Notes', pp. 66–7.

[34] Non-mensural notation is used in the manuscript, though a rhythmic mode may have been applied. Stevens, *Words and Music*, p. 227, summarizes a complex range of options: 'Either the rhythm is neutral, and subservient to verbal accent, or it is metrical, with regular groups of twos or of threes.' This transcription adheres to the manuscript's non-mensural notation (BN, MS français 2168).

Example 4.3 *Aucassin et Nicolete*

suggest a pairing of lines,[35] but the assonating verse structure is not organized in couplets, and in a number of cases an odd number of seven-syllable lines renders pairing impossible. The metrical structure of the *laisse* is thus not identical with the melodic structure, though the manuscript provides irrefutable evidence this melody was applied to this text. Furthermore, the ambitus of the *A* and *B* phrases spans a seventh, which extends to an octave and a third when we include the *C* phrase of the final shorter line; a leap of a fifth is required to move from the *B* phrase to the *C* phrase; and even if we consider the *A* and *B* phrases as one melodic motif, the *C* phrase with its different tonal centre introduces a second and very different motif in the melody. All of the features rejected by Reichl are present in this narrative melody, which is here applied to a text akin to many of the romances in both form and subject matter.[36]

The same is also true of many of the melodies Ewald Jammers includes in his collection of 'Epische Formeln und Strophen'. The *Jungeres Hildebrandslied* (in a verse form similar to the *Nibelungenlied*) is particularly compelling with its ambitus of an octave and a step, its leap of a sixth, and its shifting melodic structure reminiscent of the *lai*.[37]

In the light of these narrative melodies, the late-thirteenth-century English lyric 'Edi beo thu' (example 4.4) is a reasonable contrafactum for a Middle English romance, despite Reichl's rejection of it for its range of a seventh, frequent interval leaps of a fifth, and three different melodic motifs.[38]

---

[35] In this discussion, capital letters in italics are used to designate melodic form. Each letter identifies a melodic phrase; reoccurrence of a phrase is indicated when the corresponding letter is repeated.

[36] For further discussion of *Aucassin et Nicolete* and narrative melody, see Chapter 1 and Appendix B.

[37] Jammers, *Ausgewählte Melodien*, p. 76. Eberhard Kummer has recorded all of *Das Nibelungenlied* (Provo, UT: The Chaucer Studio, 2006) to this melody.

[38] The text is transcribed from a facsimile of Oxford, Corpus Christi College, MS 59, fol. 113v; the musical transcription, transposed to accommodate fiddle tuning, follows the rhythmic interpretation in Dobson and Harrison, *Medieval English Songs*, p. 258.

Metre, Accent, and Rhythm

Example 4.4 'Edi beo thu'

A
1. E - di be - o thu, he - ve - ne que - ne,

B
2. fol - kes fro - vre and en - gles blis,

A
3. mo - der un - wem - med and mai - den cle - ne,

B
4. swich in world non o - ther nis.

C
5. On the hit is wel eth sene

C
6. of al - le wim - men thu ha - vest thet pris.

A
7. Mi swe - te le - ve - di, her mi bene

B
8. and reu of me yif thi wille is.

(May you be blessed, Queen of Heaven, consolation of people and angels' bliss, mother unblemished, pure maiden; there is no other such in the world. In you it is easily seen that of all women you have that praise. My sweet lady, hear my plea, and have pity on me if that is your will.)

Example 4.5 Varying number of syllables set to the same melodic phrase:
'Edi beo thu', lines 4 and 20

4.		swich	in	world	non	o -	ther	nis.
20.	and	he - o - re	sou-le	to a - le - sen	for	on.		

Syllabic flexibility in the text setting is already demonstrable in the original Middle English song text, so much so that editors Dobson and Harrison, justifying their emendation to restore metrical regularity, describe the text in terms of scribal corruption, terms similar to those applied to many of the romances:

> Words are given in forms not intended by the poet, or in the wrong order; little words that do not much affect the sense are omitted or added; in several places the syntactical construction is altered. These are common signs of memorial transmission, but in the circumstances the variations from metrical regularity are probably due to conscious revision (for the worse) by the versifier(s) of Llanthony. That the irregular metre is the fault of those who transmitted or copied the text, and not of the original author, is shown by the ease with which the metrical scheme can be deduced from the extant words and from the music, and in most places by the obviousness of the emendations which restore regularity.[39]

Whoever wrote this unique manuscript clearly does not place 'metrical regularity' as a priority. On the contrary, the versifier has gone to some effort to introduce rhythmic complexity. Within the first stanza, we see melodic phrases transformed to accommodate varying arrangements of syllables. For example, 'Edi beo thu, hevene queene' (line 1) occupies the same melody as 'moder unwemmed and maiden clene' (line 3). This comparison demonstrates how a melody in a triple metre can conform to Middle English verse. In each group of three beats in the music, a stressed syllable occupies the first one or two beats, depending on the number of unstressed syllables that follow, each of which is granted one beat. It doesn't matter whether those three beats incorporate one, two, or three notes. Thus in line 1, the first syllable of 'Edi' occupies two beats, but the first syllable of 'hevene' lasts only one beat. If a stressed syllable were followed immediately by another stressed syllable, it would occupy three beats, however the beats were distributed among pitches.

If it were argued that each melodic phrase in the stanza is distinct, then still each new stanza must fit this same melody; line 20 in stanza 3 must be set to the same melody as line 4 in stanza 1 (example 4.5). In the sequence of three unstressed syllables in the middle of line 20, the '-o' and 'a-' could either be treated as one syllable or the beat could be divided into two quick notes. An additional note can easily be added at the beginning or end of a line to accommodate an unstressed syllable.

---

[39] Dobson and Harrison, *Medieval English Songs*, p. 167.

Example 4.6 An alternative rhythmic interpretation of 'Edi beo thu', lines 7 and 8

There is, however, another possibility for construing metre. The editors observe that the musical notation for this song is 'not entirely non-mensural, but neither did the scribe make consistent use of mensural note-forms'.[40] They opt for a mensural transcription and emend both the text and the music to accommodate it. They observe, however, that in order to infer metrical regularity, 'a number of longs (seven in the upper voice, six in the lower, four of which coincide) must be transcribed as if they were breves, and one breve in the lower voice must be transcribed as though it were a long.'[41] If, however, the note durations are interpreted as written, especially where the two lines agree, they enhance the meaning of the text. In line 1 'hevene' is emphasized, as is 'levedi' in line 7. More profoundly, the last measure of line 7 and line 8 is given greater clarity by employment of a hemiola. In the process, the plea for Mary to listen ('her mi bene') stands out, and her 'wille' in the last line is rescued from the insignificant position accorded it in the regularized rendition.[42] The extra-metrical notes introduced by this rearrangement can be shortened to accommodate the variation. The last two lines of the song might thus be rendered as in example 4.6. Modern standard notation is limited to precise subdivisions of duration, but what is suggested in the manuscript seems less rigidly defined, entirely improvisational and motivated by the text, and the varying rhythms and arrangement of meaning in subsequent stanzas would suggest alternative rhythmic interpretation of the pitches.[43] We have then

---

[40] Dobson and Harrison, *Medieval English Songs*, p. 302.

[41] Dobson and Harrison, *Medieval English Songs*, p. 302.

[42] The fifteenth-century theorist Giorgio Anselmi advocates introducing delays into a melody as a kind of rhetorical gesture: 'Quemadmodum enim defatigatum auditorem sepius ioco quodam lenit orator et gratum reddit, sic auditorem cantus doctus cantor moras quasdam cantabilibus intermiscens vocibus avidum magis et intentum ad reliquas cantilene partes iniciendas facit. Moras has sive quietes a cantu pausas nominant.' (For just as the orator often soothes the weary listener with some joke and makes him well disposed, so the trained singer mixes some delays (*moras*) with the melody and makes the listener more eager and attentive to the rest of the phrases of the song. These morulas, or rests, are called pauses in a song.) (Quotation and translation from McGee, *Sound of Medieval Song*, pp. 78 and 168.)

[43] If the rhythm notated for stanza 1 were applied to stanza 4, for example, inappropriate emphasis would be placed on the unstressed syllables of 'heovene' and 'ilke' in the last two lines: Thu schalt us into heovene lede;/ welle swete is the ilke dew. (lines 31–2).

an English example of a song melody that evidently accommodated just the rhythmic variation we find in the Middle English romances.

Reichl points out that the metrical structure of 'Edi beo thu' is identical to the so-called Stanzaic *Morte Arthur*, which has a stanza consisting of four-stress lines rhymed *abababab*.[44] It is very easy to sing *Le Morte Arthur* to the melody of 'Edi beo thu'. But as soon as this is attempted, a significant difference in the stanza structure becomes evident. The melodic setting is *ABABCCAB*, with a slight variation incorporated into the *A* phrase when it recurs after *C*. The rhyme structure thus matches the melodic structure except during the *C* phrases. The *C* melody brings its two lines of text to prominence partly by its relative infrequency and partly by its insistence on the fourth and its doubled repetition of the cadence of the *B* melody. In 'Edi beo thu', the lines sung to the *C* melody most often contrast in some way with the rest of the stanza, presenting a comparison (stanzas 1 and 2) or initiating a direct appeal (stanzas 3, 4, and 5) or intensifying a comparison or appeal (stanzas 6, 7, and 8). No such distinction is evident in the stanzas of *Le Morte Arthur*. In some cases the fifth and sixth lines do fortuitously stand out, but on the whole the melodic emphasis of those lines would be inappropriate.

Another approach to the melodic structure is possible, however, and supported by prior evidence: the *C* melody can be employed selectively to enhance textual emphasis. Ernoul le Vielle's late-thirteenth-century *Lai de Notre Dame*, like *Aucassin et Nicolete*, uses three short melodic phrases, but in this case, the melody is notated for all twenty-six lines of the *lai*. John Stevens observes that 'phrase *A* is always followed by phrase *B*; phrase *B* can, however, stand on its own (e.g. lines 9–13); phrase *C* rounds off a section.'[45] In the *Lai de Notre Dame*, then, we have clear evidence of an asymmetrical pair of melodic phrases, one phrase occurring less frequently than the other and requiring that the other immediately follow, and this provides a historical precedent for arranging melodic lines in varying configurations to accommodate a lengthy text.

Because the melodic phrases in 'Edi beo thu' are always paired (*AB* or *CC*), the melody can be applied to verse in rhymed couplets. When this is done, the *CC* melodic pattern can provide asymmetrically spaced variation in a sequence of *AB* patterns, and a performer can use the highlighting *C* melody to underscore important ideas.

'Edi beo thu' has a further advantage for our understanding of the rhythms of Middle English poetry; the song is polyphonic, with a second melodic line notated just below the first. This second line suggests a possible approach to instrumental self-accompaniment by specifying both pitches and durations designed to enhance the primary melody.

A performer can easily sing *Bevis of Hampton* to the first melody while playing the second melody on a fiddle tuned to Jerome of Moravia's second tuning system.[46] In example 4.7 (lines 3905–12), Josian's companion has fallen

---

[44] In this discussion lower case letters indicate poetic form, and capital letters melodic form.

[45] Stevens, *Words and Music*, p. 227.

[46] The result is only slightly different using Jerome of Moravia's first tuning. The first tuning has a

Example 4.7 *Bevis of Hampton*, lines 3905–12, set to the melody of 'Edi beo thu'

continued overleaf

Example 4.7 *continued*

(While Josian was in Armenia, she had studied music, and she had learned to play estampies, melodies, and cheerful 'garibles' on a fiddle. When she could think of no better solution, she went at once into the city and, as the story tells, she bought a fiddle for forty pence from a minstrel.)

sick in Greece, and they have run out money. Having learned to play the fiddle in Armenia, the disguised Princess Josian ventures into the city and buys a fiddle from a minstrel for forty pence. For six months she goes through the city earning their sustenance as a minstrel. Although the notation is complicated by the drones, the instrumental melody spans only a third and is played with just two fingers.

Variation is built into the 'Edi beo thu' music with its relatively less frequent *CC* phrase, whether it is applied arbitrarily to every fourth couplet or whether it is applied selectively. If the passage in example 4.7 were continued, the *B* melody might recur after two rather than three iterations of the *AB* melody to link Josian's journeys out into the city.[47] The texture of drones provides additional variety; although the fiddle melody is played entirely on one string, the player can modify the number and intensity of drones. In example 4.7, drones at a higher pitch bring out a convergence of the romance performance with Josian's fiddle playing. In these lines as well, the polyphonic association of 'garibles' is hinted at by a touch of 'fifthing'. (See Chapter 3 and Appendix B.) Further variation can be introduced, as discussed in Appendix B, by either the voice or the instrument or a combination of the two.[48]

Perhaps most important, this polyphonic setting reveals a way to enhance textual clarity. By changing the bow direction on the offbeats, as indicated by the slur marks in example 4.7, the performer displaces the fiddle articulation from the semantically more important stressed syllables. This non-synchronous approach to instrumental accompaniment has important implications for metre because the changes in bow direction, by their very nature, provide an accent, an event of relative high prominence in the sound patterns of the fiddle. If this accent occurs in conjunction with the stressed syllables in a text, it hampers comprehension but reinforces semantic emphasis; but if the bow change accent occurs between textual accents, does it set up a competing rhythm? To address this dilemma, we will need to consider the nature and function of accents.

A Wave–Particle Model of Middle English Verse

Lerdahl and Jackendoff describe three types of accent in music. A *phenomenal accent* is:

> any event in the musical surface that gives emphasis or stress to a moment in the musical flow. Included in this category are attack points of pitch-events,

further advantage in that a less experienced fiddle player could ignore the melody and play drones following the bowing pattern in example 4.7, using the approaches to variation described in Appendix B. In Jerome's third tuning, the instrumental line must be played an octave lower, and the drones do not shift.

[47] For the text of the passage, see Appendix A under *Bevis of Hampton*. Lines 3909–10 and 3915–6 would be set to the *CC* melody.

[48] A minstrel would be likely to emphasize the fiddle playing in this passage with one or more instrumental insertions.

local stresses such as sforzandi, sudden changes in dynamics or timbre, long notes, leaps to relatively high or low notes, harmonic changes, and so forth.[49]

In terms of a narrative text, *phenomenal accent* might describe similar patterns in the vocal inflection of a text, both those required by the text and those introduced in a performance instance. Except for harmonic changes, all the musical events mentioned above could easily describe the techniques applied in spoken delivery to structure information and to signal relative prominence of semantic content, but also to realize the emphasis inherent in the language itself (stressed and unstressed syllables). Phenomenal accents, then, are in some cases motivated by the information contained in a text, varying from one performance instance to another; but in other cases built into the language itself and thus a part of any performance instance. A *structural accent*, in contrast, is 'an accent caused by the melodic/harmonic points of gravity in a phrase or section – especially by the cadence, the goal of tonal motion'.[50] Rhyme and assonance serve an analogous function in verse, aurally marking ends of lines (cadences) and creating structural links among lines. Finally, a *metrical accent* is 'any beat that is relatively strong in its metrical context'. Lerdahl and Jackendoff clarify the relationship between metrical accent and phenomenal accent:

> Phenomenal accent functions as a perceptual input to metrical accent – that is, the moments of musical stress in the raw signal serve as 'cues' from which the listener attempts to extrapolate a regular pattern of metrical accents. If there is little regularity to these cues, or if they conflict, the sense of metrical accent becomes attenuated or ambiguous. If on the other hand the cues are regular and mutually supporting, the sense of metrical accent becomes definite and multileveled.[51]

The beats that make up a metrical pattern, they explain, are inferred from phenomenal accents. Beats have no duration and must be equally spaced, and a metrical structure must be built on 'periodic alternation of strong and weak beats'.[52] In medieval poetry, alliteration, unlike rhyme and assonance,[53] is linked with metre, underscoring the stressed syllables that establish a four-beat line structure.

As this analysis shows, not all points of prominence are tied to metre. In verse, the metrical structure does not account for all accents, only for a pattern of relative strong and weak beats. Other rhythmic structures may operate simultaneously, and other accents may occur as long as they do not consistently violate the metrical beat structure.[54] Short-term divergence between phenomenal accentuation and

---

[49] Lerdahl and Jackendoff, *Generative Theory*, p. 17.

[50] Lerdahl and Jackendoff, *Generative Theory*, p. 17.

[51] Lerdahl and Jackendoff, *Generative Theory*, p. 17.

[52] Lerdahl and Jackendoff, *Generative Theory*, p. 19.

[53] Duffell, *New History of English Metre*, pp. 12–13, provides a clear paradigm describing all categories of phoneme repetition.

[54] Ronald Waldron, 'Measured Discourse: The Fourteenth-Century Alliterative Long Line as a Two-Tier System', in *Approaches to the Metres of Alliterative Verse*, ed. Judith Jefferson and Ad

metrical accentuation results in 'syncopation, ambiguity, or some other kind of rhythmic complexity'.[55]

Furthermore, the structural groupings aurally marked by rhyme in Middle English verse are often offset from the metrical structure. Verse lines frequently begin before the beat or end after the beat, yet the integrity of their offset rhythm does not conflict with the regular beat of the verse design. In example 4.7 above, then, the fiddle reinforces the structural framework of the lines, a majority of which begin on an offbeat with an unstressed syllable. Lerdahl and Jackendoff suggest:

> A metrical pattern can begin anywhere and end anywhere, like wallpaper. But once metrical structure interacts with grouping structure, beats do group one way or the other. If a weak beat groups with the following stronger beat it is an *upbeat*; if a weak beat groups with the previous stronger beat it is an *afterbeat*.[56]

In example 4.7 a metrical structure is established by phenomenal accents in the text, but the line structure (here reinforced by the fiddle) is frequently offset, the accent created by the beginning of a line coinciding with an upbeat, and the ending coinciding with an afterbeat. It is at the level of the unstressed syllables that variety is created within the unvarying framework of the metre. Understood in this light, the rhythmic transformations of the Middle English romance scribes energize a text, not merely providing variety, but introducing complex overlays of rhythmic structure.

Phrases thus become significant rhythmic components. Jan Ziolkowski makes a strong case that the early medieval musical neumes in manuscripts of Latin hexameter epics were tied to phrasing. The musical neumes break off, he observes, at 'major transitions in sense':

> This prevalence lends support to the idea that at least when employed for the hexameter passages, the song or chant was syllabic and that the stresses, pitches, or lengths of the syllables were not the major determinants in the nature of the melodies; the crucial factors were the expressive values of the words and the middles and ends of the lines, which often coincided with the sense units into which those words fitted.[57]

Ziolkowski suggests that one of the purposes of music notation may have been to provide information about phrasing. In Gregorian chant 'textual and musical

Putter, Leeds Texts and Monographs, New Series 17 (Leeds: University of Leeds School of English, 2009), pp. 235–54, at p. 252, argues that: 'poetry in the fourteenth-century alliterative long line, like later verse forms in English, requires of the reader the ability to 'hear' (mentally) two prosodies simultaneously: that of the meaningful discourse linguistically realized in the poetry and the underlying rhythm of four chief stresses signaled by alliteration, and to respond to a continuous complex interaction between those two prosodies.'

[55] Lerdahl and Jackendoff, *Generative Theory*, p. 18.

[56] Lerdahl and Jackendoff, *Generative Theory*, p. 28.

[57] Jan Ziolkowski, *Nota Bene: Reading Classics and Writing Melodies in the Early Middle Ages*, Publications of the Journal of Medieval Latin 7 (Turnhout: Brepols, 2007), p. 116.

cadence correlate closely, so that musical duration coincides with what would be commas, colons, and full stops in punctuation.'[58] The expressive context for music in narrative is verified by the passages chosen for musical setting, typically passages containing direct address. 'Speeches that give utterance to the passions of women in matters of love are singled out for close attention',[59] and this emphasis coincides with a focus of romance writing. In this precedent, the rhythms of speech are intensified by music.

But this introduces a complication in our understanding of Middle English verse. How do metrical accents (tied to syllable stress) relate to structural accents (tied to phrasing) when both must be realized as phenomenal accents? Are the metrical beats truly isochronous, that is, do that occur at evenly spaced intervals? If so, what are the implications for phrasing? A number of theorists insist that for music to be metred, the beats must be equally spaced,[60] but others present a broader notion. Duffell suggests, 'Rhythm is produced when a series of events occurs at what is perceived by the human ear as regular intervals.'[61] What we perceive may be very different from measurable reality.

Computer analysis leads us to crave consistency. Our model for verse and music is an inflexible grid of events occurring regularly across a continuum of time; when music is notated, we expect to see the beginning and ending of every pitch. But in practice, a variety of rhythmic factors apparently perturb isochronous progression of metrical accents without interfering with our perception of a regular beat. Fred Cummins, for example, shows 'nontrivial and systematic deviations from isochrony' in sequences of words with a strong-weak rhythm.[62] Reuven Tsur more emphatically demonstrates that equal timing is refuted by 'an ever-growing amount of measurements'.[63] In our music training, we carefully combat such irregularities; the old mechanical metronomes and tuning forks are too imprecise, and we govern our music with electronic timekeepers and tuners. But in the medieval world, removed from the incorruptible rhythms of traffic signals and the unvarying tones of toothbrushes, the creators of verse and music were habituated to the more flexible pulse of chant.

Ziolkowsky's work provides a musical precedent for the medieval romances, a historical record of music tied to the expressive aspects of narrative, operating within a metrical framework, but apparently interacting with text in a similar way to Gregorian chant. And Ziolkowski further points out a 'misimpression that Gregorian chant and related forms lack, and have always lacked, expressive value'.[64]

---

[58] Ziolkowski, *Nota Bene*, p. 85.

[59] Ziolkowski, *Nota Bene*, p. 161.

[60] See Lerdahl and Jackendoff, *Generative Theory*, p. 19.

[61] Duffell, *New History of English Metre*, p. 18.

[62] Fred Cummins, 'Interval Timing in Spoken Lists of Words', *Music Perception: An Interdisciplinary Journal* 22.3 (2005): 497–508, at p. 507.

[63] Reuven Tsur, *Poetic Rhythm: Structure and Performance* (Berne: Peter Lang, 1998), p. 296.

[64] Ziolkowski, *Nota Bene*, p. 165.

The notion of a flexible pulse, responsive to phrasing, may be helpful with the alliterative long line divided into two hemistiches. By this I do not mean that a chant-like melody would have been applied to the alliterative verse. In fact, for this discussion of rhythm it is not necessary to distinguish between sung and spoken delivery. Rather the ebb and flow of energy in the alliterative long line is congruent with what we know of the antiphonal settings of the Psalms. Unfortunately, we have little evidence for how late medieval singers understood the rhythms of chant,[65] but however it is understood, a musical pattern is applied to passages of highly variable length. In the psalm-tones two cadences occur in each 'line'; the mediant cadence ends at a higher pitch, and the termination ends at the final, the stable foundation of the mode. This pattern matches a way we might read an alliterative long line, with a higher pitch just before the caesura, and a lower at the end of the line. While it is possible to fit the unstressed syllables of alliterative verse into a grid of regularly spaced stressed syllables, the melodic structure of Gregorian chant suggests a possible rhythmic structure based on phrasing contours, with variable duration from line to line.

A notated musical example cannot demonstrate a realization of this approach effectively. As Leonard Meyer points out, 'a score which contained *all* of the information communicated by a particular performance – every nuance of duration, pitch, dynamics, timbre, etc. – would not only be unreadable, but would take years to write down and months to decipher',[66] but it is just such nuances that would give shape to this rhythmic approach to the alternating hemistiches. It may be helpful to imagine stringing wild rose hips and madrone berries[67] into a chain. The rose hips, fragrant and tangy, are longer and smoother, a deeper shade of red. The madrone berries, almost perfectly round, are rougher in texture and a brighter red. Each bead has its own integral structure, varying in size and shape and texture and colour, but on the string the wild rose hips alternate with madrone berries, and we recognize the distinction even when an individual rose hip is smaller than a madrone berry or a berry is a deeper red than a rose hip. Because half-line berries and rose hips vary so markedly, the metrical beats they contain are constrained in their relative position. They cannot maintain even spacing with respect to each other within such diverse structures.

But berries are solid forms, static and immutable. A better analogy might be a 'wave–particle duality'. A Middle English verse design propagates a wave function of verse lines, and this function predicts where a metrical beat particle is likely to be found, two metrical particles suspended in each hemistich wave. But the concept from quantum mechanics is too rigid, the probabilities too inviolable. In Middle English alliterative verse, the waves are fluid, like ocean waves, formed in varying size, shape and velocity, shifting in our perception even as they move

---

[65] For a summary of the dilemma, see Richard H. Hoppin, *Medieval Music* (New York: Norton, 1978), pp. 88–90.

[66] Leonard B. Meyer, *Explaining Music: Essays and Explorations* (Berkeley: University of California Press, 1973), p. 13.

[67] The madrone is a North American tree of the Arbutus genus, related to the European strawberry tree, and bears similar fruit.

past us. These shifting shapes each contain two (or in some cases three) beats, and these vary significantly in their placement within the half-line waves. Simultaneously the metrical beats give an illusion of regularity to the waves they inhabit, and the structurally recognizable waves provide a cue for inferring regularity. The beats, despite their measurably diverse spacing, are perceived as even.

This interpretation is supported by the experiments of Darwin and Donovan, who demonstrate that listeners hear alliterating stressed syllables as occurring at equal time intervals even when they are objectively unequal, as in a sentence like 'He turned up by ten talking of terrorism', where the /t/ sound does not occur at regular intervals.[68] This evidence is crucial in our understanding of alliterative verse. In our rhythmic models, we do not have to cram varying syllables into equal units of time; the alliteration will ensure that time units are perceived as equal. In fact, even when we believe that we are spacing stressed syllables evenly, a simple experiment with a metronome exposes the illusion.

The verse and music that strongly shaped Middle English alliterative verse, the manuscript variants, and modern theory all point strongly to a high degree of rhythmic complexity in the romances, the phenomenal accents of which form a flexible framework of structural and metrical accents. With alliterative poetry then, a fiddle could reinforce the wave pattern of contrasting half lines with its binary up and down bowing pattern, the first hemistich marked by a downbow and the second by an upbow. This structural rhythm does not always coincide with the metrical rhythm, which is established internally between the articulation points of the wave sequence of differentiated hemistiches.

Rhythmic Structures in the Tail-Rhyme Stanza

Once we understand how stress functions in alliterative verse, it is easy to see how the principle extends to other forms of Middle English verse, where the varying unstressed syllables also render isochronous delivery improbable. But here we are forced to recognize that the regular progression of metrical beats can be systematically disrupted. This occurs in the tail-rhyme stanza with its characteristic 'unrealized' beat, the void stress position following each three-stress line. Intriguingly, it is here that we have the best evidence for musical performance of Middle English romance. Rhiannon Purdie, in her recent study of tail-rhyme romances, discusses 'an unusual, inconvenient and instantly recognisable manuscript layout used by some English scribes to display Anglo-Norman and, later on, Middle English tail-rhyme poems'.[69] She terms this layout 'graphic tail-rhyme',

---

[68] Cited in Tsur, *Poetic Rhythm*, p. 300. C. I. Darwin and A. Donovan, 'Perceptual Studies of Speech: Isochrony and Intonation', paper presented at the Conference on Language Generation and Understanding, Bonas, 1979; and A. Donovan and C. I. Darwin, 'The Perceived Rhythm of Speech', paper presented at the ninth International Congress of Phonetic Sciences, Copenhagen, 1979. It is, of course, possible to space the /t/ sounds equally in the example given, but this was not the realized delivery in the test case.

[69] Purdie, *Anglicising Romance*, p. 7.

an arrangement which places tail-lines to the side and links rhymes by means of bracketing lines. She suggests that this visual organization 'may well be influenced by the expected mode of performance', and 'the use of graphic tail-rhyme may have been encouraged by an ill-recorded and intermittent tradition of setting the texts that employed it to music.'[70] In support, she observes:

> Where graphic tail-rhyme has the advantage over regular columns of verse is in indicating at a glance the precise metrical shape of the stanza, not only the stanza divisions but which lines are long and which are short. While a reader (whether performing or solitary) has no particular need to be reminded that, for example, the next section will contain two eight-syllable lines followed by a four-syllable one, a musician or singer needs this infor-mation in order to match the words to appropriate musical phrases, whether they are working with a known melody or something more improvised. It is noticeable that, in the manuscripts of later Middle English literature, graphic tail-rhyme is most often encountered in copies of lyrics: this would seem to support the notion that graphic tail-rhyme was at least sometimes employed with the expectation of musical performance.[71]

A musical performance is supported by the apparent origin of the tail-rhyme stanza form in the sung Latin Victorine sequence, associated with the twelfth-century Adam de Saint-Victor.[72] Here a stanza pattern rhyming *aabccb* is constructed of units of two rhyming lines of eight syllables followed by a seven-syllable line containing three stressed syllables. A related form, also occurring in Middle English romance, is a stanza constructed of triplets followed by tail-lines. Numerous Middle English translations of Latin Victorine hymns attest to the influence of this form, and these translations are sometimes transcribed in graphic tail-rhyme.

The melodies of the Victorine sequences, however, do not provide useful contrafacta for Middle English tail-rhyme romances. The rhythmic interpreta-tion of the melodies is vexed with controversy. While the Latin tail-line appears to carry three stresses, ending in a dactyl, the melody suggests four stresses, assigning emphasis to the final syllable. The Middle English translations substantiate this. While the translations in many cases preserve the exact number of syllables of the Latin originals, the Middle English seven-syllable tail-lines carry four stresses.[73] The unrealized fourth beat of the typical Middle English tail-line can thus not be considered a characteristic of the Victorine stanza.

The general concept of a *cauda* (literally 'tail') in a different metre, however, is evident in a number of musical contexts. The Latin sung clausulae are described by Margot Fassler as:

---

[70] Purdie, *Anglicising Romance*, p. 78.

[71] Purdie, *Anglicising Romance*, p. 79. A reciter not engaged in a musical performance would not need so marked a signal.

[72] Purdie, *Anglicising Romance*, p. 26.

[73] Purdie, *Anglicising Romance*, p. 27.

categorized by how many different rhymes they have. A monotongus rhythmic clausula has one rhyme or tone ..., a diptongus has two rhymes, and a triptongus has three. Both the latter types can have caudae at the end, lines that are different from the others in the clausula, in syllable count, in accent pattern, and in rhyme (or in a combination of these). Thus the caudae serve to punctuate individual clausulae, but also to relate them.[74]

Clearly this concept of a contrasting line serving to punctuate verse units and link them into a stanza was vital in the development of the tail-rhyme stanza, and this concept comes from a sung tradition. Furthermore, thirteenth-century music theorist John of Garland 'includes caudae in his discussion of the differentiae, interpreting them under the aegis of variation',[75] and variation, as I have suggested, is a governing principle in narrative performance. The concept of the *cauda* is thus linked with embellishment.[76]

As suggestive as the connections are, however, Latin song does not illuminate the rhythms of the English tail-rhyme stanza, again because there is so little consensus about the rhythmic construction of medieval monophony. We can, however, find some answers in modern studies of verse. Richard Cureton confirms that we can simultaneously perceive phrasal rhythms and metrical rhythms and that they do not always coincide. In fact, the most strongly metrical poetry often exhibits the most flexible phrasing:

> If meter were a normative prosody, one would expect that the strongest meters would occur in response to the most continuous and rigidly repetitive phrasings, but just the opposite is the case. In forms such as rap, where meter is very strong, the linguistic prosody is often wildly discontinuous, flexible, and non-repetitive, running in high syncopation to the meter. It is also just the metrically strong tetrameter meters ... that can have prosodically 'unrealized' beats.[77]

In the tail-rhyme stanza, like rap, the metre is strong, and, as the manuscript evidence shows, the prosody is 'often wildly discontinuous, flexible, and non-repetitive'. Here, too, metrical prominence regularly coincides with a void. The implications are profound in revealing the function of rhythm in the stanza.

In their discussion of English folk verse, Hayes and MacEachern discuss three-stress lines occurring after one or more four-stress lines, demonstrating that 'in return for the aid their cadentiality provides in articulating quatrain structure, the shorter line types impose a sacrifice in the clarity with which the beat structure

---

[74] Fassler, 'Accent, Meter, and Rhythm', p. 176.

[75] Fassler, 'Accent, Meter, and Rhythm', p. 186.

[76] This association may be substantiated and extended by the use of the term *cauda* also to refer to 'extended passage(s) of textless melisma' in the polyphonic conductus (Stevens, *Words and Music*, p. 57).

[77] Richard D. Cureton, 'A Disciplinary Map for Verse Study', *Versification* 1 (1997), <http://www.arsversificandi.net/backissues/vol1/essays/cureton.html> (8 January 2011).

of the line is realized.'[78] Perception of a regular beat is vital to the operation of metre, yet in fact, not just the stanza structure, but the metre itself is more fully realized through this disruption. Reuven Tsur observes, 'It will be found that the suspension of the regular beat (by deviation from metric pattern) is frequently handled by temporarily shifting the focus of attention to another "architectonic level", where regularity is patent, while "metrical set" becomes, temporarily, an "off-sequence" process.'[79]

This shift in attention is described by Jonathan Kramer in terms of two modes of duration perception: the *still-spectator* mode is a nonlinear memory process that includes 'the cumulative perceiving, encoding, storage, and retrieval of … information', while the *active-listening* mode is a linear 'participation in continually changing materials and relationships' that includes 'ongoing timing of metric data'. Both modes 'feed back into present perceptions', a present that is 'the meeting ground of memory and anticipation, both of which color perception'.[80] The interplay between these two modes enriches the experience of listening to verse; in tail-rhyme verse we are reminded of the larger experience of the stanza structure (accessed through memory) when the tail-line jolts us out of the regular progression of metrical beats.

In the tail-rhyme stanza, suspension of metre is built into the verse design, but disruption can enhance metre in a performance instance as well. Reuven Tsur suggests, 'If the higher unit (the line) is strongly established in perception, it tolerates a great number of deviations at the lower levels.'[81] He discusses this in terms of the concept of *recurrence* developed by Leonard Meyer to describe patterns in music:

> Recurrence is repetition which takes place after there has been a departure from whatever has been established as given in the particular piece. There can be a return to a pattern only after there has been something different which was understood as a departure from the pattern. Because there is departure and return, recurrence always involves a delay of expectation and a subsequent fulfilment.[82]

Tsur's evidence suggests that regularly realized metrical rhythm produces saturation in the listener, while disruption in metre gives rise to 'strong cravings for fulfilment.' When the metre is reaffirmed, 'the resulting satisfaction is stronger than the undisturbed reiteration of regular metre.'[83] Recurrence, not reiteration, makes the realization of metre most exquisite. Tsur applies this as follows:

---

[78] Bruce P. Hayes and Margaret MacEachern, 'Quatrain Form in English Folk Verse', *Language* 74.3 (1998): 473–507, at p. 505.

[79] Tsur, *Poetic Rhythm*, p. 299.

[80] Jonathan D. Kramer, *The Time of Music* (New York: Schirmer, 1988), pp. 365–7.

[81] Tsur, *Poetic Rhythm*, p. 298.

[82] Leonard B. Meyer, *Emotion and Meaning in Music* (Chicago: University of Chicago Press, 1956), p. 151.

[83] Tsur, *Poetic Rhythm*, p. 298.

Poetic rhythm is determined by an internal standard, an abstract pattern which can successively be confirmed, disconfirmed and reasserted by language. In this process, duration can be utilized as an acoustic cue for, e.g., perceived prominence or discontinuity. Fairly long pauses do not necessarily destroy the rhythm of a verse instance, but have a 'double-edged' effect. If the verse line is well-established as a coherent perceptual whole, it tends to reassert itself in perception against the interruption; if not, it tends to fall into pieces.[84]

Pauses, however, are infinitely variable, and it becomes evident that analysis of how the stressed and unstressed syllables of a passage realize verse design cannot tell us much about the rhythms of specific performance instances of that passage. Yet extant texts can reveal some inherent rhythmic patterns, and they may go far in substantiating an aesthetic of rhythmic variation. Whether or not manuscript versions reflect specific performances, they provide clear evidence of insistence on an aural aesthetic of variation that could not be produced by simply reading aloud.

Rhythmic Variation in Middle English Romance Manuscripts

Attridge and others emphasize the distinction between rhythmic variation created in performance and rhythmic variation inherent the language of a text, but this presupposes a stable text. What if the performance transforms the text itself? When this occurs, the distinction between a verse instance and a performance instance becomes blurred. Taken as a whole, the manuscripts of the Middle English romances show evidence of rhythmic variation that transforms both metre and stanza structure in accordance with the principles discussed above.

Returning to the wave–particle duality model of verse rhythm, the structural waves and the metrical particles of the stanza are continually perturbed by the phenomenal accents of rocks and coral, wind, moon, and the wakes of boats and whales. These phenomenal accents both shape the waves and particles into a verse design that we infer, and perturb that verse design. Calm, regular waves and the regular drift of particles become tedious, but interruption of those patterns followed by a return to structure gives satisfaction.

It may be helpful to look at the rhythmic evidence in some of the tail-rhyme romances, since the tail-rhyme design incorporates both metre and a stanza structured in terms of rhyme.[85] *Sir Cleges* was probably composed in the late fourteenth or early fifteenth century, but the two manuscript instances come from the late fifteenth century, around the time when the two fiddlers were paid to sing *Gray Steel*. While the text of the Advocates manuscript is problematic, some of the very

---

[84] Tsur, *Poetic Rhythm*, p. 330.

[85] While the same features of rhythmic variation occur among the romances in couplets, the results are not as extreme because of the simpler design. The same is true of the unrhymed alliterative long lines, where patterns of alliteration, line length, and phrasing alternate in salience.

features that have been seen as corrupt can alternatively be seen as appropriate improvisations involving suspension and recurrence of rhythmic features.

Neither manuscript indicates stanza divisions, but Ashmole 61 uses graphic notation to link three-line tail-rhyme units. In this case, graphic notation is used, not to indicate rhyme structure, but rather to mark out the fundamental three-line units consisting of a couplet followed by a tail-line. The stanza design is typical of Middle English tail-rhyme, $aa_4b_3cc_4b_3dd_4b_3ee_4b_3$, where the subscript numbers indicate the number of stresses in the preceding lines.

The Kyng was sett in hys parlere,	The kynge was sett in hys parlor
Myrth and revell forto here;	Wyth myrth, solas and onor;
Syre Cleges theder wente.	Sir Cleges thedyr went.
An harper had a geyst i-seyd,	An harpor sange a gest be mowth
485 That made the Kyng full wele a-payd,	Of a knyght ther be sowth,
As to hys entente.	Hym-selffe, werament.
Than seyd the Kyng to this herpere:	Than seyd the kynge to the harpor:
'Mykyll thou may ofte tyme here,	'Were ys knyght Cleges, tell me herr;
Fore thou hast ferre wente.	For thu hast wyde i-went.
490 Tell me trew, if thou can:	Tell me trewth, yf thou can:
Knowyst thou thys pore man,	Knowyste thou of that man?'
That this dey me presente?'	The harpor seyd: 'Yee, iwysse!
He seyd: 'My lege, with-outen les,	Sum tyme for soth I hym knewe
Som-tyme men callyd hym Cleges;	He was a knyght of youris full trewe
495 He was a knyght of youre.	And comly of gesture.
I may thinke, when that he was	We mynstrellys mysse hym sekyrly,
Full of fortone and of grace,	Seth he went out of cunntre;
A man of hye stature.'	He was fayr of stature.'
(Ashmole)[86]	(Advocates)

The rhythmic variation is evident; comparing the two passages line by line, only eight of the eighteen lines can reasonably be scanned with an identical pattern of stressed and unstressed syllables.

However, the most intriguing structural and metrical perturbation emerges when we compare Ashmole, lines 493–5, with Advocates, lines 492–4. The two passages contain analogous content, the harper's reply when the king asks for information about Cleges, but the lines occupy very different positions in the stanza structure. In the Ashmole manuscript, the minstrel answers the king's question with a complete tail-line unit beginning a new stanza, establishing the linking rhyme with its final word 'youre'. In the Advocates manuscript, however, the minstrel clambers into the previous stanza, interrupting the king with his exuberant praise of Cleges. In the process, he populates the final three-stress tail-line position in the stanza with a four-stress line which does not rhyme with anything: 'The harpor seyd: "Yee, iwysse!"' While an editor might simplify the harper's words to 'Ywis', producing a three-beat line, that is not what this scribe

---

[86] For translations of these passages, see Chapter 2.

has done. We have seen that the tail-rhyme form builds metrical suspension into its verse design, disrupting the regular progression of metrical beats with a three-stress line followed by an 'unrealized' beat to establish a strong sense of cadence, reinforcing the structure. In this stanza, however, the four-beat metrical structure is maintained while the stanza structure, normally marked by both rhyme and an unrealized beat, is here suspended. We have seen ample evidence of metrical recurrence, where a pattern of beats emerges, then disappears within a higher structural fabric, creating tension followed by satisfaction when the metre is reaffirmed. Here we have recurrence at the higher level of stanza structure: the tail-rhyme stanza structure, having been established, is suspended while the metrical beat is anomalously maintained; then in the following stanza structural regularity is restored. As the structure we respond to in our still-spectator mode is suspended, we shift to our active-listening mode.

A slightly different application of the principle of maintaining one rhythm while disrupting another may be seen in the transition from tail-rhyme stanzas to couplets in the early versions of *Bevis of Hampton*, particularly in the late four-teenth-century British Library Egerton MS 2862.

> With her ship there gon they lond;
> Thre marchauntes gan then found
> To that citee.
> With hem they toke childe Bevoun,
> For to selle him in the toun
> For gold plente.
>
> With selver cheynes they him gyrte.
> To lede him they were aferde,
> Eche held on him honde.
> For him to have grete bygete,
> They lad him throughout every strete,
> On his hed a roos garlonde.
>
> And they ne myght no man fynde
> To bye the child of cristen kynde,
> So dere they gan him hold,
> Tyl ther com a kinges stewarde
> That was hende and no negarde,
> An tyl him they him sold.
>
> The steward went to the kyng
> And presented him wyth the childe so yyng.
> The king ther of was glad and blyth
> And thankyd him ther of mony syth.[87]

(They landed their ship; three merchants then set out for that city. They took

---

[87] My transcription. This manuscript is followed closely by Biblioteca Nazionale MS XIII.B.29. The passage corresponds roughly to Auchinleck MS line 515ff.

with them the child Bevis, planning to sell him in town for a large quantity of gold. They bound him with silver chains. Because they were afraid to lead him behind them, each held him by a hand. Expecting to get a large sum of money for him, they led him through all the streets with a garland of roses on his head. But they could find no one to buy this child of Christian people because they regarded him as too precious, until a king's steward came who was courteous and no niggard, and they sold Bevis to him. The steward went to the king and presented him with the young child. The king was glad and blithe, and thanked the steward many times.)

Here the transition from tail-rhyme stanzas to couplets is gradual. The first stanza in the passage follows the tail-rhyme form most characteristic of *Bevis*, with two-stress tail-lines. The second stanza maintains the rhyme structure while extending the tail-lines from two stressed syllables to three and then four, rendering the end of that stanza metrically equivalent to couplets, though the rhyme scheme still follows the tail-rhyme pattern of *aabccb*. The third stanza draws back to three stresses in each tail-line. After this, the text switches to couplets, but the first line carries only three syllables. The scribe, operating in terms of a performance tradition, prepares a listening audience for the metrical shift by training them to accept a range of metrical possibilities, shifting either the number of stresses or the rhyme structure while maintaining the other. At no point do all the rhythmic patterns shift at once. Because multiple rhythms operate simultaneously, a shift can occur in one rhythm while the salient rhythm of the moment stays steady.

The unique manuscript of *The Weddynge of Sir Gawen and Dame Ragnell* is one of the most metrically egregious romance texts. As Ad Putter avers, this poem is 'patently corrupt' and far removed from 'the poet's original',[88] yet there is a felicity in many of the metrical irregularities that indicates purpose. Rather than classifying every anomaly in the poem as a result of carelessness, we can find motivation in the evidence of overlapping rhythmic patterns of varying salience. The rhythmic irregularities indicate an improvisatory performance approach to text.

One of the most editor-harrying passages occurs as King Arthur describes his encounter with Sir Gromer in Ingleswood Forest and his promise to return in one year with an answer to the question, 'What do women love best?':

> And also I shold com in none oder araye,
> Butt evyn as I was the same daye.
> And yf I faylyd of myne answere,
> I wott I shal be slayn ryghte there.
> 180 Blame me nott thoughe I be a wofulle man;
> Alle thys is my drede and fere.'
> 'Ye, Sir, make good chere.
> Lett make your hors redy
> To ryde into straunge contrey;

---

[88] Putter, 'Metre and the Editing of Middle English Verse', p. 33.

185   And evere wheras ye mete owther man or woman, in faye,
       Ask of theym whate thay therto saye,
       And I shalle also ryde anoder waye
       And enquere of every man and woman and gett whatt I may
       Of every man and womans answere;
190   And in a boke I shalle theym wryte.'
       'I graunt', sayd the Kyng as tyte;
       'Ytt is welle advysed, Gawen the good,
       Evyn by the Holy Rood.'
       Sone were they bothe redy,
195   Gawen and the Kyng, wytterly.
       The Kyng rode on way and Gawen anoder
       And evere enquyred of man, woman, and other,
       Whate wemen desyred moste dere.
       Somme sayd they lovyd to be welle arayd,
200   Somme sayd they lovyd to be fayre prayed,
       Somme sayd they lovyd a lusty man
       That in theyr armys can clypp them and kysse them than.
       Somme sayd one, somme sayd other;
       And so had Gawen getyn many an answere.
205   By that Gawen had geten whate he maye
       And come agayn by a certeyn daye.

                         (lines 176–206)

(And also I should come dressed in no other way, but exactly as I was that same day, and if I am wrong in my answer, I know I will be slain right there. Do not blame me if I am a woeful man! All this is what I dread and fear.' 'Yes, sir, cheer up. Have your horse prepared to ride into foreign countries, and everywhere you meet either men or women, in faith, ask them what they say about it. And I shall also ride in another direction and inquire of every man and woman and get what I can of every man and woman's answer, and I shall write [the answers] in a book.' 'I agree', said the king at once. 'It is well advised, Gawain the Good, by the Holy Rood.' Soon they were both ready, Gawain and the king truly. The king rode one way and Gawain another, and each enquired of men, women, and others, what women desired most dearly. Some said they loved to be well dressed; some said they loved to be beseeched respectfully; some said they loved an energetic man that could embrace them in their arms and kiss them. Some said one thing; some said another; and so Gawain acquired many answers. When Gawain had gotten what he could, he returned by a set day.)

The sudden omission of tail-lines after several regular tail-rhyme stanzas creates the impression that Arthur is interrupting himself, stumbling in his narrative of the frightening encounter with its alarming implications for the future. This impression fades as we adjust to the new pattern, but that pattern does not remain consistent.

The entire passage can be described as a series of couplets with three evenly spaced orphan lines (lines 180, 189, and 198). These lines call attention to themselves by their violation of the rhyme pattern. In line 180, 'Blame me nott thoughe I be a wofulle man', Arthur's anxiety shatters the sequence of information with his emotional realization of his situation. The non-rhyming word, 'man', also emphasizes Arthur's gender; he is a man trying to answer a question about women, and the contrast between 'man' and 'woman' is reiterated four times in the passage (lines 185, 188, 189, and 197). In the next orphan line, 'Of every man and womans answere' (line 189), the high-stakes goal of finding an answer jars against the enveloping couplets. It also establishes a resonance with line 180 by repetition of the word 'man'. Finally, the last orphan lines in the passage, 'Whate wemen desyred moste dere' (line 198), restates the question itself. Key ideas are thus emphasized by departure from rhyme scheme, but those deviations are themselves structured into a rhythm, with eight lines in couplets intervening between each orphan line.

This is not, however, the only organizing principle in the passage. Improvised stanza forms materialize and fade, and loose alliances govern desultory rhythms. When the lines are arranged into stanzas, and when two long lines are divided, the structuring patterns are easier to see. These structures are not regular enough to appease an editor, but in an oral context they create a satisfying web of resonating features.

> And also I shold com in none oder araye,
> Butt evyn as I was the same daye.
> And yf I faylyd of myne answere,
> I wott I shal be slayn ryghte there.
> 180   Blame me nott thoughe I be a wofulle man;
> Alle thys is my drede and fere.'
>
> 'Ye, Sir, make good chere.
>
> Lett make your hors redy
> To ryde into straunge contrey;
> And evere wheras ye mete owther man
> 185   or woman, in faye,
> Ask of theym whate thay therto saye,
> And I shalle also ryde anoder waye
> And enquere of every man and woman
> and gett whatt I may
>
> Of every man and womans answere;
>
> 190   And in a boke I shalle theym wryte.'
> 'I graunt', sayd the Kyng as tyte;
> 'Ytt is welle advysed, Gawen the good,
> Evyn by the Holy Rood.'
> Sone were they bothe redy,
> 195   Gawen and the Kyng, wytterly.

> The Kyng rode on way and Gawen anoder
> And evere enquyred of man, woman, and other,
> Whate wemen desyred moste dere.
>
> Somme sayd they lovyd to be welle arayd,
> 200   Somme sayd they lovyd to be fayre prayed,
> Somme sayd they lovyd a lusty man
> That in theyr armys can clypp them and kysse them than.
> Somme sayd one, somme sayd other;
> And so had Gawen getyn many an answere.
>
> 205   By that Gawen had geten whate he maye
> And come agayn by a certeyn daye.

The passage initiates its break from tail-rhyme form with line 178, which carries four stresses instead of the three we expect in a tail-line, and the line then cements its transitional status when it becomes the first line of a couplet. At the same time, however, lines 176–81 continue to function as a tail-rhyme stanza; line 178 is still perceived as a tail-line, rhyming with 181. In the stanza form, as in the couplet sequence, line 180 violates the rhyme scheme, though it is structurally linked with the previous line by its position in an otherwise relatively regular tail-rhyme stanza. Although the rogue line asserts its independence of two alternative rhyme designs, it is still contained within a stanza design. When one rhythm is interrupted, another is maintained.

The couplet design and the stanza design do not align; as the stanza pattern is dropped with line 182, the couplet pattern recurs after the divergence in line 180. Again, one set of expectations is realized while another set is denied. Line 182 may also establish a loose structuring principle for the entire passage based on rhyme. As discussed above, line 178, calling attention to the word 'answere', is followed by a quick succession of three rhyming lines, broken only by the renegade line 180. Line 182, 'Ye, Sir, make good chere', the last of these '-ere' lines, stands apart from the previous stanza structure, and it may form a rhyme link with line 189, 'Of every man and womans answere', bracketing the intervening stanza. This link may extend to the final line of each of the following sections, 'What wemen desyred moste dere' (line 198) and 'And so had Gawen getyn many an answere' (line 204), using rhyme both to structure groups of lines and to reinforce key ideas.

If the long lines 185 and 188 are divided, lines 183–8 fall into a rough tail-rhyme pattern rhyming *aabcccbc*. The two-stress lines create an impression of tail-rhyme construction, though the design differs from the poem's typical stanza form in the addition of the *b* lines and two stresses rather than three in the tail-lines. In these lines there is considerable variation in number of stressed syllables per line, but where the metrical patterns flounder and are temporarily off-line, a rhyme structure holds the passage together.

Lines 190–8 can be construed as a sequence of couplets concluding in a triplet. There is a natural break after 193, the conclusion of the conversation between Arthur and Gawain. Their preparation for their journey is accomplished in two abrupt lines of three stresses each. While the rhyme scheme stays constant, the metre shifts to three stresses. Line 196 appears to return to four stresses, but the following line, linked by rhyme, moves to five stresses, introducing a troubling violation of expectation with its addition of 'other' to our expected gender categories. Then line 198, with its three stresses, is perceived as a return to tail-rhyme structure, though the rhyme, on 'dere', links it with both the preceding couplet, and the thematic 'answere', rhyme that frames sections in this passage.

The irregular passage concludes with eight lines in couplets, lines 199–206. In this section we see again the establishment of a pattern, deviation from that pattern and satisfying recurrence. Lines 199–201 establish a regular rhythmic pattern beginning 'Somme sayd they lovyd ...' Line 202 breaks not only the word repetition, but also the metrical regularity of the lines, filling up the line with unstressed syllables. The following lines moves the opposite direction, incorporating only three unstressed syllables among its four stresses, while its partner, line 204, moves to five stressed syllables, as above using the extra stress to emphasize the thematic word 'answere'. Throughout, the couplet structure established in the preceding lines is maintained by means of rhyme. Then, as Gawain returns to Carlisle, with its predictable patterns, we have a satisfying return to metrical regularity in the couplet 205–6, and the passage is followed by recurrence of the tail-rhyme stanza back at Carlisle.

In *The Weddynge of Sir Gawen and Dame Ragnell*, marked irregularities in verse form tend to coincide with times of emotional anxiety. As lines break free of the highly flexible tail-rhyme stanza structure, they continue to establish and vary rhythmic structures, engaging both metre and rhyme in establishing overlapping continuities and disjunctions. Understandably, these variations are horrifying in a written context; couplets and tail-rhyme stanzas are mutually exclusive when they are realized with any consistency. The presence of such fragmentary rhythmic structures in the manuscript indicates exactly the kind of willingness to embrace improvisation, the lack of concern with permanent repercussions, that we would expect in a performance context. These rhythms are as ephemeral as the drones on a fiddle. They might seem illusory except that there are too many patterns, too consistently overlapping. The most likely explanation is a fundamental bent toward improvisation somewhere in the background of this version.

Flexible Realization of a Metrical Verse Design

The available evidence indicates a highly flexible rhythm in all three general categories of Middle English romance: couplets, alliterative verse (unrhymed, rhymed, and stanzaic), and especially tail-rhyme stanzas. While stressed syllables can be forced to align with equally spaced beats, the rhythms in the manuscripts and perception-oriented theory of verse indicate a more organic structure. Beats flow with the rhythms they inhabit, rhythms that transform even the language that carries them. These rhythms create patterns dancing among each other, patterns that satisfy most fully when they break and then reform.

It is easy to see why this possibility has not been pursued: it is very difficult to notate such rhythms. Audio recordings, rather than any modern notation system, best document these rhythmic structures. Further, there are no absolutes, no single correct way of scanning, and it is not enough to scan, not even enough to mark relative prominence of syllables. There are governing limitations and preferences, but so many variables and so many possibilities that notation is useful to a very limited extent, and it is no longer surprising to find no notated music for a Middle English romance. In fact, graphic tail-rhyme layout may well be the most useful approach: within that framework, rhythms can be improvised.[89]

This has profound implications for how a minstrel might have incorporated an instrument. Perhaps the wave–particle theory can apply to music as well. If the verse is fluid, the fiddle cannot linger in a rigid frame of evenly spaced bow changes. In fact, such an approach quickly reveals the impracticality of equal-timing in verse delivery. Rather than sawing out even bow strokes, a fiddle could enhance the rhythmic structures of a performance instance, sometimes sweeping along structural units (lines or hemistiches), sometimes tracing phrasing, sometimes marking each syllable with a light touch or brushing stressed syllables for emphasis, and sometimes reinforcing duple or triple patterns or sudden divergence from an established pattern and then its re-emergence. The same principles can be readily adapted to other instruments as well. One of the most intriguing results of this exploration is an awareness of how rhythmic variation in the text provides potential for flexibility and rhythmic sophistication in performance.

But how that might be accomplished requires a different approach. The next chapter suggests how we might reasonably extrapolate from all of the evidence presented to this point. We know with some certainty that in late medieval England romances were sometimes performed from memory accompanied by a musical instrument. Documentation of fiddle construction and tuning indicates some parameters for that instrumental accompaniment. Notated narrative melodies from mainland Europe provide the notion of a simple melody, in some cases constructed of two or more contrasting phrases, which could be varied in a number of ways. Finally, the extant manuscripts of Middle English romance persistently incorporate rhythmic variation that reflects a performance aesthetic. In fact, the rhythms of the romances strongly suggest an elastic embodiment of a metrical verse design. Historical performance, incorporating all of this evidence, can extend our understanding of the organic rhythms of Middle English verse.

---

[89] When I went back and looked at my performance text for *The Weddynge of Sir Gawen and Dame Ragnell*, I found that I had not written out the melody I was singing, but I had drawn lines to mark the rhyme structure, falling naturally into the graphic tail-rhyme convention.

5

Music and the Middle English Romance

The Contribution of Historical Performance to the Study of Narrative

Where a scholar asks, 'Were the Middle English romances performed by minstrels?' a performer asks, 'How could they have been performed?' The questions are different, but both scholar and performer work toward answers by drawing on available documents from the past. Both try to put aside modern perspectives as they construct understanding from evidence that is incomplete, complex, and ambiguous. Historical performance cannot uncover information that is not available in the documents scrutinized by scholars; it can, however, point out connections a scholar might miss. A performer is forced to summon together wide ranging information about instruments, vocal delivery, texts, melodies, and rhythms. In the process, bits and pieces of information that have been overlooked emerge, and contexts that have been ignored are re-established.

The normal processes of scholarship *could* demonstrate that the ornamentation in the melody for the German narrative *Titurel* falls on unstressed syllables; *could* recognize that *Titurel*, like many of the Middle English romances, represents a translation of a French romance into a stress-based language; *could* determine that the first line of the melody fits the English alliterative long line, a poetic tradition with Germanic roots; and *could* infer the possibility of melodic ornamentation of unstressed syllables in Middle English alliterative romances. The processes of scholarship could accomplish this, but are not likely to do so. A scholar interested in Middle English alliterative verse would not turn to a melody for a German poem, and a musicologist would find nothing attractive in Middle English alliterative poetry. A performer, on the other hand, trying to understand how alliterative poetry could be performed, is very likely to work through that sequence of links. Once a connection between the *Titurel* melody and alliterative poetry is suggested, it can have significant implications beyond performance: an ornamentation pattern applied to unstressed syllables might well illuminate the recent evidence of rhythmic constraints in alliterative poetry,[1] constraints which are intimately bound up with the functioning of unstressed syllables.

Along similar lines, a performer experimenting with Middle English tail-rhyme stanzas, recognizing that French songs are sometimes influenced by word stress, is likely to discover that the thirteenth-century French *trouvère* song 'Volez

---

[1] See Hoyt N. Duggan, 'The Shape of the B-Verse in Middle English Alliterative Poetry', *Speculum* 61.3 (1986): 564–92; Hoyt N. Duggan, 'Extended A-Verses in Middle English Alliterative Poetry', *Parergon* 18.1 (2000): 53–76; Ad Putter, Judith Jefferson, and Myra Stokes, *Studies in the Metre of Alliterative Verse*, Medium Aevum Monographs New Series 25 (Oxford: Society for the Study of Medieval Languages and Literature, 2007); and Judith Jefferson and Ad Putter, ed., *Approaches to the Metres of Alliterative Verse*, Leeds Texts and Monographs New Series 17 (Leeds: University of Leeds School of English, 2009).

vous que je vous chant' matches the tail-rhyme stanza structure. Having made that initial connection based on form, a performer is uniquely situated to notice that 'Volez vous' shares a detailed literary trope with a passage in the tail-rhyme romance *Sir Launfal*. This link opens the potential for exploring other thematic ties between songs and the romances and exposes the danger of distinguishing too sharply between literature and music. Chaucer's work has been considered in this way,[2] but the approach has not yet extended to the romances.

Some evidence concerning the performance of the Middle English romance would be nearly impossible to discover without attempting actual performance using historically informed instruments and approaches. Only by playing a medieval fiddle is anyone likely to realize a connection between the two fiddlers who played *Gray Steel* and the extant melody: the *Gray Steel* melody fits the fiddle tunings so precisely that varied accompaniment can be produced with little effort, even by an inexperienced musician. This pragmatic evidence both lends more credence to the possibility that the melody is a relic of a medieval version, and provides a means of exploring how cadences can be emphasized by displacing the accent in a sequence of pitches. Again, further consideration of these possibilities could affect editorial practices, and it could help explain what advantage medieval minstrels might have perceived in instrumental accompaniment of a romance.

A fiddle is an encumbrance. Holding a fiddle severely limits gesturing, and its sound competes with the voice. Yet in late medieval England the references to 'harping' or 'fiddling' a story are realistic and pervasive, and the available historical documents support a practice of instrumentally accompanied narrative. There must have been powerful motivation, then, to use a fiddle to tell a story. The foregoing chapters and Appendix B indicate how an instrument can enhance the riotous rhythms that somersault merrily through the Middle English romances. It remains now to be seen how the voice participates. This chapter addresses what we can determine about vocal delivery of minstrel *gestes*, what the voice might do that could that could either stand alone or engage with instrumental accompaniment.

The following discussion is based on research motivated by performance experiments. The findings are all possibilities, not unassailable certainties. Combined, however, the results compellingly narrow the options for how *gestes* could have been performed by minstrels. If we accept that the romances participate in a performance tradition, it is incumbent on us to understand that tradition as specifically as we can. It is not enough to imagine a text in performance without clarifying the characteristics of performance; even in our minds, words are utterly transformed in an operatic delivery, an ecclesiastical chant, a country western drawl, or a romantic flowing melody with plinking accompaniment. By failing to scrutinize what we mean by performance, we allow distorting assumption we are not even aware of to impose constraints on our imagined performance.

---

[2] See, for example, Steven Guthrie, 'Meter and Performance in Machaut and Chaucer', in *The Union of Words and Music in Medieval Poetry*, ed. Rebecca A. Baltzer, Thomas Cable, and James I. Wimsatt (Austin: University of Texas Press, 1991), pp. 72–100.

The possibilities presented here move toward a more accurate representation of minstrel performance of the Middle English romance by piecing together the evidence we have.

Combining Voice and Fiddle

When a song is composed, thirteenth-century theorist Johannes de Grocheio explains, the text is the raw material, and an appropriate melody is applied later to give it shape:

> Modus autem componendi haec generaliter est unus, quemadmodum in natura, primo enim dictamina loco materiae praeparantur, postea vero cantus unicuique dictamini proportionalis loco formae introducitur. Dico autem *unicuique proportionalis* quia alium cantum habet cantus gestualis et coronatus et versiculatus ut eorum descriptiones aliae sunt.[3]

> (There is generally one way of composing these things, as in nature, for in the first place the poems are prepared beforehand, serving as the raw material, and then a correctly designed melody is introduced into each poem, serving as the form. I say 'correctly designed into each [poem]', because the *cantus gestualis*, *coronatus*, and *versiculatus* all have their own kinds of melody just as their descriptions are different.)

De Grocheio clarifies this composition process for us when he uses the same terminology to describe playing the fiddle. The composer and the fiddler each *introducit formam* (introduces form). The composer introduces a melody to give shape to a text; similarly, a good fiddle player introduces every musical shape.[4] Both composing and playing involve the creation of musical form out of the raw material of a text or pre-existing song. Playing the fiddle well and applying music to narrative verse both mean continually introducing musical shape, an ongoing process of creation.

We have seen how the principle might have applied to fiddle accompaniment: playing the fiddle is a process of continual variation. The fiddle, with its evanescent drones, can romp along with metrical stresses; or roll out wavering sheets of varying intensity and timbre; or twirl with the phrasing, out of sync with the beat; or skid across every syllable; or stabilize a melody. Because the application of melody to text is described in the same terms as fiddle accompaniment, the approach to narrative delivery may be similar. De Grocheio states that the *chanson de geste* (*cantus gestualis*) repeats one melody for each line of a *laisse*.[5] The number

---

[3] Page, 'Johannes de Grocheio', p. 29.

[4] Page, 'Johannes de Grocheio', pp. 31–2, my translation: 'Bonus autem artifex in viella omnem cantum et cantilenam et omnem formam musicalem generaliter introducit' (A good fiddle player generally produces every *cantus* and *cantilena* [the two broad categories of song] and introduces every musical shape).

[5] Page, 'Johannes de Grocheio', pp, 27–8: 'Idem etiam cantus debet in omnibus versiculus reiterari.' (The same melody must be repeated in every versicle).

of lines is determined by the length of the text itself (the raw material) and by the wishes of the person creating the song.[6] De Grocheio distinguishes here between the text and the 'compositor', implying that the creator of the song may transform the text itself. The process of composition appears to be, not a written endeavour, but an ongoing creation in performance. This interpretation explains the absence of extant *chanson de geste* melodies; the composition process is in the subtle embellishments and responses to patterns in the text. Like fiddle playing, singing can give shape to the raw material of the text, accepting reiteration of a melody not in slavish literal terms, but as a means of applying strategic transformations in an ongoing engagement with improvisatory variation.

De Grocheio's distinction between the textual *materia* and the *cantus*[7] shaped from it seems very much like the distinction we found in the Middle English romances between the romances in books and the *gestes* created from them by minstrels. De Grocheio may supply a means of understanding the process English minstrels employed when they turned romances in books into performed *gestes*. This possibility, however, requires that we know something about the vocal delivery of narrative in medieval Europe.

Paul Zumthor, like many others, has noted the ambiguity of terms that describe singing and speaking: '[W]here is the frontier between song and non-song? It is a fluctuating border, whose precise location is of little importance.'[8] But although the location of the boundary may not be important, the location of a performance mode on that continuum is significant if we are to understand how music may have interacted with text and how a text may reflect that interaction.

Medieval English terms used to describe minstrel performance are notoriously inconclusive; words for singing and for speaking are often used interchangeably. Timothy McGee, writing about singer-reciters in late medieval Italy, identifies a source of confusion that may apply to English terminology as well:

> The confusion as to how they presented their material originates with modern scholars who equate *recitare* with the modern English 'recite', coupled with the assumption that the common practice of later centuries – of presenting poetry in a spoken format – was also the custom of the late Middle Ages.[9]

The position of narrative performance on the continuum of speaking and singing may further clarify the indeterminate use of language in medieval documents. McGee explains:

---

[6] Page, 'Johannes de Grocheio', pp. 27–8: 'Numerus autem versuum in cantu gestuali non est determinatus sed secundum copiam materiae et voluntatem compositoris ampliatur' (The number of verses in a *chanson de geste* is not fixed and may be extended according to the abundance of the raw material and the wish of the one who makes the song).

[7] De Grocheio uses the term *cantus* to refer both to a melody and to the song resulting from the application of that melody to text.

[8] Zumthor, 'Vocalization of the Text', p. 275.

[9] McGee, *Ceremonial Musicians*, p. 79.

... it would seem that then, as now, writers have difficulty finding terms that distinguish between full-blown melody and the more modest melodic form such as that employed in a simple psalm-tone setting. It is this latter style that is the probable basic mode of performance for the herald, in which the melodic content is more or less subservient to that of the text.[10]

A very basic melodic structure subservient to a text is consistent with the paucity of notated narrative melodies, and it explains the blurring of terms to describe narrative performance. This explanation, too, is consistent with de Grocheio's model for narrative performance.

In the English tradition, alternative modes of performance appear to have been available. 'Romanz-reding on the bok' (reading romances out of a book) is set side by side with entertainment at feasts, where 'mouthe men here the gestes singe' (people can hear the tales sung).[11] *Romaunces* and *gestes* present the same stories, but *romaunces* are read and *gestes* are sung.[12] While there are many ways to tell a story, minstrels are likely to sing verse renditions of a story: people learn from an old tale 'whanne hyt ys in gestes songe, / or els in prose tolde wyth tonge' (when it is sung in *gestes* or else told with the tongue in ordinary language).[13] At the same time, references to 'romanz-reding' are often presented in the context of musical accomplishments, and a simple sung rendition read from a book seems possible, and it is consistent with graphic tail-rhyme notation indicating stanza grouping. Today it is possible to go through life spending very little time singing, but singing was much more a part of everyday life in the Middle Ages, and it would have been easier then for amateur performers to move from speaking to singing.

Whatever the other performance options, it is evident that, at least on some occasions, English minstrels sang tales derived from romances. The fragments of narrative melodies from France, Germany, and England characterize what that singing would have been like and explain the ambiguity of the verbs used to describe that mode of vocal delivery. The fragments also indicate that specific pitches were involved.

The involvement of specific pitches in vocal production has direct impact on instrumental accompaniment. When the narrative is shaped by a melody, an instrument can engage with that narrative by means of concordant or discordant pitches in addition to the rhythmic interactions discussed in the previous chapter. Either singer or instrument may at times veer toward 'non-song', but the two voices relate to one another in terms of both pitch and rhythm.[14]

The sound of narrative is vital to our understanding of a performance context

---

[10] McGee, *Ceremonial Musicians*, p. 79.

[11] *Havelok*, lines 28–9. Appendix A includes a number of other illustrations of the contrast.

[12] See Chapter 2 for further discussion of this distinction and of the range of story performance options implied in historical documents and internal references in the Middle English romances.

[13] *Partonope of Blois*, lines 26–7.

[14] Experimentation confirms that self-accompaniment is more feasible with sung vocal delivery than with spoken delivery. However it is played, a fiddle produces specific pitches; but the pitches of normal speech inflections are irretrievably unrelated to any pitches the fiddle emits. I found I could

for the Middle English romances. Timothy McGee has provided copious documentation demonstrating that ornamentation was a requisite and assumed element of singing. He concludes:

> In order to imagine the sound of the medieval voice one must realize that the rapid articulation, pulsating notes, sliding pitches, and non-diatonic tones were a part of the basic technique, and not just unusual and colourful sounds that were introduced into a vocal style that was otherwise similar to the modern practice.[15]

The concept of a minstrel repeating a melody unswervingly is not at all in keeping with medieval aesthetics. Similarly, post-romantic models of flowing, even melodies do not match the evidence. Middle English verse is strongly defined in terms of accented and unaccented syllables. Furthermore, all of the instruments linked with narrative accompaniment are structured to produce strong/weak patterns.

Our model for minstrel performance of the Middle English romance can thus be defined in reasonably specific terms. We should envision a simple melody, embellished improvisationally, that can accommodate the rhythms created by the stressed and unstressed syllables in Middle English verse. This narration is optionally accompanied by an instrument, also characterized by improvised variation, interacting with the narration both at the level of rhythm (metrical articulation and broader structural patterns) and at the level of pitch relations, moving between consonance and dissonance.

We can say more about the melodies based on the characteristics of Middle English verse. Typically, these poems insist on rhythms that do not recline comfortably in pre-established and inflexible melodies. The melodies must float free of a metrical grid work. They may provide a structure of accents that generally aligns with the romance texts, but they cannot insist upon isochronous recurrence of those accents. The romance text will thus create natural variation in a simple melody. The rhythm is dictated by the text, and it sometimes has a duple feel and sometimes a triple feel, and sometimes something more complex.

This remains an abstract possibility, however, unless such melodies can be found. If music exists that conforms to the uniform characteristics of narrative song in Europe, that matches what we know of narrative performance in England, that can stand alone or interact with an instrument, that can adapt to Middle English verse, then we have a chance of discovering how music may have interacted with the romance texts, how assumptions about performance may have shaped the transformation introduced into the extant versions of the romances.

Such melodies do exist, and the justifications for applying them vary considerably. Here are some possibilities for how the Middle English romances may have been sung. The melodies are monophonic, requiring no co-ordination with other simultaneous melodies, and their non-mensural notation, free of isochronous

---

not simultaneously produce both speech and a fiddle melody; the combination of disparate sound events bewildered me. It is very easy, on the other hand, to play the fiddle while singing.

[15] McGee, *Sound of Medieval Song*, p. 118.

sequences of beats, can adapt to the varying rhythmic demands of the texts. Where it is relevant, potential for fiddle accompaniment is considered. The fiddle serves well as a representative instrument; principles drawn from fiddle accompaniment could be adapted and applied to other instruments.[16] Although ornamentation is an essential component of medieval vocal performance, embellishment is notated here only where it is supported by specific evidence. Together, these illustrations approach the question of minstrel performance from many angles, presenting a composite vision of what minstrel performance may have been like in late medieval England.

Unrhymed Alliterative Long Lines

Among the Middle English romance verse forms, unrhymed alliterative long lines are to a performer a tangle of blackberry brambles with plump fruit far within: the syllable count varies wildly, the alliteration is unpredictable, and the lines are not structurally related by rhyme. Insistent on its identification with Germanic tradition, alliterative verse yet draws on topics and techniques from French romance. Several contrafacta, melodies from other contexts, can be applied to alliterative verse, but it is difficult to determine which are most historically reasonable. In the Middle Ages the relation between words and music was largely a matter of convention,[17] and we have no idea which conventions might have operated for alliterative verse. There are too many cultural convergences, and is tempting to flinch away from the challenge. But, as with any thorny bramble, abrupt movement yields only scratches, while a calm hand may emerge unscathed bearing fruit.

We have extensive manuscript evidence for an improvisational approach to these romances. Ruth Kennedy notes, for example, that 'in the two "best" manuscripts of *The Awntyrs of Arthure* (Douce and Thornton) the two scribes can only agree on the same rhythm in any line of the poem 45% of the time.' She observes:

> We are used to this sort of corruption in the manuscripts of octosyllabic romances, but perhaps there we have come to accept a high degree of oral variation. But here we are dealing with 15th-century copies of quite late texts of a high degree of literary self-consciousness.[18]

The evidence indicates that 'oral variation' does in fact operate in this literary context. In conjunction with the documentation of a narrative performance tradition extending into the sixteenth century in England, the rhythms of these romances sketch an aural landscape of medieval English narrative.

The irregular syllable structure of the verse renders very few approaches

---

[16] All of the musical examples in this chapter have been transposed to fit the framework of the fiddle.

[17] See Hughes, *Style and Symbol*, p. 279ff.

[18] Ruth Kennedy, 'New Theories of Constraint in the Metricality of the Strong-Stress Long Line as Applied to the Rhymed Corpus of Late Middle English Alliterative Verse', in *Métriques du moyen age et de la renaissance: actes du colloque international du Centre d'Études Métriques*, ed. Dominique Billy (Paris: L'Harmattan, 1999), pp. 131–44, at pp. 137–8.

actually feasible. Although Anglo-Saxon poetry resonates strongly in its Middle English counterpart, an approach such as Thomas Cable's musical setting of *Beowulf* cannot be applied because it relies on a limited number of rhythmic patterns,[19] and the Middle English alliterative romances that survive are far more rhythmically complex and generally contain more syllables.[20] Benjamin Bagby's freer declamatory approach to *Beowulf* is more practical and would be effective with modern audiences.[21] His performance reminds us of the indistinct boundary between music and non-music, though it does not match the characteristics indicated for late medieval narrative.

It is possible to set alliterative lines to psalm-tones, and it is not unheard of to apply sacred music in secular contexts.[22] A few lines suffice to give the general idea (example 5.1).[23] This type of melody drawn from the church liturgy bears some similarity to our best example of a *chanson de geste* melody, from *Robin et Marion*, which fits alliterative long lines very comfortably (example 5.2).[24] The drawback to both these melodies is the sharp division between hemistiches, or half-lines. While Middle English alliterative poetry is generally constructed in half-lines, the full line often functions as a syntactic unit.[25] A sharp and persistent melodic divide feels like a violation of the integrity of the line, especially after repetition for a dozen lines or so.

Some of the extant German *Töne* offer melodic settings of four-stress narrative structured in half-lines, and these may suggest some viable solutions. The most promising melodies are set in stanza structures, and none can be applied without considerable modification. Still, substantial evidence points to the adaptability of melodies to diverse metrical structures.[26] Wolfram von Eschenbach's unfinished early-thirteenth-century German romance *Titurel* is based on Chrétien de Troyes'

---

[19] Thomas Cable, *The Meter and Melody of Beowulf* (Urbana: University of Illinois Press, 1974). The musical approach Cable describes is 'noncommittal', specifying contours rather than melodies, p. 104.

[20] For a concise summary of characteristics of Middle English alliterative metre, see Malcolm Andrew and Ronald Waldron, eds., *The Poems of the Pearl Manuscript: Pearl, Cleanness, Patience, Sir Gawain and the Green Knight*, 2nd edn (Exeter: University of Exeter Press, 1987), pp. 46–9.

[21] *Beowulf: The Epic in Performance* (Helsingborg, 2006). A clip from Benjamin Bagby's performance of *Beowulf* may be viewed at <http://www.bagbybeowulf.com/video/index.html> (1 May 2012).

[22] Hughes, *Style and Symbol*, p. 481, observes, 'By the application of new words and rhythms, some medieval plainsongs were transformed, complete, into secular songs.

[23] The music for example 5.1, tone 8, is drawn from the *Liber Usualis* (Tournai and New York: Desclée, 1961), p. 117, and Hoppin, *Medieval Music*, p. 82. On the fiddle, this example works with Jerome's first or second tuning structure. The low G functions as a mandatory drone between the open *d* final and the open *g* reciting tone.

[24] See Chapter 1 for a discussion of extant narrative melodies. The music for example 5.2 is derived from Stevens, *Words and Music*, p. 224. He observes that the manuscript notation is non-mensural, and that different notes are tailed in different manuscripts. A number of rhythmic transcriptions have been proposed.

[25] See Andrew and Waldron, *Pearl Manuscript*, p. 46.

[26] In a more heavily documented arena, motets transform melodic material almost out of recognition. See, for example, Hughes, *Style and Symbol*, pp. 343–5.

Example 5.1 *The Alliterative Alexander Fragment C or Wars of Alexander,*
lines 1–3, set to psalm-tone 8

Example 5.2 *The Alliterative Alexander Fragment C or Wars of Alexander,* lines 1–3,
set to the *chanson de geste* melody from *Robin et Marion*

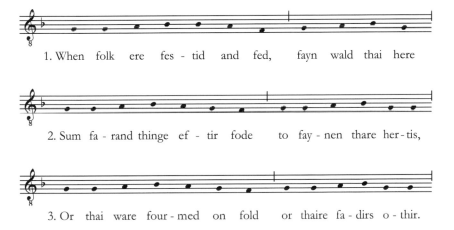

late-twelfth-century French *Conte du Graal.* A late-thirteenth-century continuation called *Der jüngere Titurel* (*The Newer Titurel*) contains a carefully notated
melody in Vienna Nationalbibliothek MS 2675.[27] The author, tentatively identified
as Albrecht von Scharfenberg, hopes 'daz iz ir aller herzen tugnde bringe, diez
lesen oder hoeren, der iz sage oder in dem done singe' (that it [the story] may
bring excellence to the hearts of those who read or hear this, to those who recite it

---

[27] The music appears at the beginning of the manuscript (fol. 1v), and the stanza chosen is Sigune's
love lament, an intriguing choice in light of the tendency toward neumation of women's love
laments in early medieval manuscripts of Latin narrative. See Ziolkowski, *Nota Bene*, p. 161ff.

or sing it to the melody).[28] Like many of the English romances, *Titurel* is intended to be read or heard, spoken or sung; and, also like many English romances, this narrative reflects a French tradition transformed in a stress-based Germanic language. The parallel offers an approach to treating English narrative. The original melody appears in example 5.3.[29]

I do not suggest that this stanza melody would have been used for alliterative English verse; lines 2 and 4 are too long, and line 3 is not structured in half-lines. Nonetheless, setting alliterative English long lines to this melody can be instructive in indicating patterns that may have applied to English verse. Not least, this melody solves the problem of the half-lines, allowing connection, but accommodating separation. Furthermore, Wolfram's original *Titurel* is so metrically irregular that it is difficult to describe a characteristic stanza form,[30] and a compelling argument can be made that Wolfram's *Titurel* may have been sung to this melody.[31] The many contemporary variations indicate that the melody was highly adaptable, a characteristic required by the Middle English romances.

Lines 1, 2, and 4 have essentially identical melodies in the initial half-lines, each ending with an ornament moving down a third.[32] The pattern that emerges is a syllabic setting of the first half-line with minor ornamentation to signal the break in the middle of the line, and we are given two different examples of ornaments. The second half-line offers a greater challenge. Line 1 provides an excellent model for an open line ending, calling for a second line to provide a closed cadence. This answering melody can be adapted to the English alliterative line by leaving off the original cadence that appears in lines 2 and 4.[33] Lines 1 and 3 provide further information about handling line endings; in both, an unstressed syllable preceding the final word is given a characteristic shape, moving above and then below the

---

[28] Quotation from Stevens, *Words and Music*, p. 216; translation by Maria Dobozy, personal communication, 5 August 2011.

[29] Example 5.3 is based on Stevens, *Words and Music*, p. 216, and the facsimile in Wolfram von Eschenbach, *Titurel*, ed. Helmut Brackert and Stephan Fuchs-Jolie (Berlin: Walter de Gruyter, 2002), p. 513. Translation by Maria Dobozy, personal communication, 5 August 2011; in line 2, either caesura placement is possible. She observes, 'The scene here is a pieta with Sigune sitting in the linden tree with the dead Schiontulander across her lap as described in Wolfram's *Parzival* (249, 11).'

[30] See Alexander Sager, *Minne von Mæren: On Wolfram's 'Titurel'*, Transatlantic Studies on Medieval and Early Modern Literature and Culture 2 (Göttingen: Vandenhoek and Ruprecht Unipress, 2006), p. 23.

[31] See Stevens, *Words and Music*, p. 216; and Karl H. Bertau and Rudolf Stephan, 'Zum sanglichen Vortrag mittelhochdeutscher strophischer Epen', *Zeitschrift für deutsches Altertum und deutsche Literatur* 87 (1957): 253–70. Maria Dobozy, personal communication, 5 August 2011, notes, 'It has been shown that the melody is written into the manuscript about 100 years later than the *Jüngere Titurel* manuscript itself [dated around 1300], but the melody in variations is found in so many other contexts that it is easy and safe to assume it was popular and therefore rather older than the *Jüngere Titurel* manuscript, so that it may actually have been composed by Wolfram himself.'

[32] Line 4 demonstrates how fewer syllables can be accommodated by truncating the melody. In this case, the first note is omitted.

[33] Comparison of lines 2 and 4 also demonstrates how variation in number of syllables can be accommodated within a repeated pitch.

Example 5.3 *Der jüngere Titurel* melody

1. Ia-mer ist mir ent-sprun - en___ ach mein lait ist___ves - te

2. O-we clag hat be-twun-gen mein sen-des hercz ouf dir-re lin-den

3. Ho-her mut trost vreu - de___ mus sich___dec - ken

4. Suf-czen trau-ren wai-nen wil ich han um di-sen wer-den

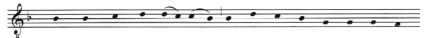

es - te___

rec-ken___

(Sorrow has welled up inside of me oh my sorrow is unmoving. / Alas, lamentation has overpowered my grieving heart out on the branch of this linden tree. / High spirits, solace and joy must disband. / Sighing, mourning, wailing are all I can now do for this worthy warrior.)

structural pitch. In fact, throughout the *Titurel* melody, we see ornamentation is normally applied to unstressed syllables, particularly near line or half-line endings. Semantically important syllables are left uncluttered and therefore clearer, and the ornaments can be executed quickly so they do not interfere with the phrasing. There is evidence of similar ornamentation of unstressed syllables near cadences in England in the manuscript of the narrative 'Als I lay on Yoolis Night'.[34] The *Titurel* melody has a further advantage in allowing a performer to pause at

[34] Dobson and Harrison, *Medieval English Songs*, p. 275.

the caesura (the break in the middle of the line) or to move through without hesitation.

Thus, *Titurel* offers a considerable accumulation of solid information, though it requires some adaptation to apply it to a passage of alliterative long lines.[35] Example 5.4 shows one possible rendition of the beginning of *The Alliterative Alexander Fragment C* or *Wars of Alexander*. This setting readily invites fiddle drones, melodic playing, parallel fourths, fifths and octaves, and a kaleidoscope of variations. The voice, too, is free to ornament following the general pattern suggested by the original *Titurel* melody.[36]

Example 5.4 suggests a way of treating alliterative long lines, a pattern of open and closed melodies, not necessarily in strict alternation, with the caesuras marked by one pattern of ornamentation and the line endings by another. This approach addresses the challenges of this metre: the undifferentiated lines, the variable number of syllables (and even stresses) in each line, and the requirement that some lines move through the caesura without a pause. If this possibility is incorporated into discussions of the prosody of the alliterative long line, it may help illuminate the characteristic rhythmic patterns that have been observed.

Tail-Rhyme and Other Stanza Forms

Tail-rhyme stanzas offer a different set of challenges. As in alliterative verse, the number of syllables fluctuates, but here the lines are linked into stanzas by rhyme, and the stanzas are heterometric, varying in the number of stressed syllables, or beats, per line.[37] Any melody, then, must be able to reflect this complex structure. As we have seen, the Latin Victorine sequences, apparently an important source for the English tail-rhyme stanza, do not provide useful contrafacta because the melodies imply four stresses in every line, and thus they do not accommodate the three-stress tail-lines. There is, however, a melody that applies aptly to the tail-rhyme stanza and can be adapted to the most convoluted metrical and rhythmic anomalies. The thirteenth-century French reverdie 'Volez vous que je vous chant' is constructed in lines of seven syllables, with six syllables normally for lines 3 and 6, and the music for the third and sixth lines implies three stresses rather than four.[38] Example 5.5 shows the second stanza of 'Volez vous'.

The text of the *trouvère* song describes a lady clothed in spring flowers and leaves, riding a mule. When courtiers ask about her background, she announces

---

[35] For instance, in example 5.4, lines 3 and 10 are a variation constructed from *Titurel*, lines 2–3.

[36] In example 5.4, I have intentionally preserved some features modern performers and audiences might find uncomfortable, such as the elaboration of the final unstressed syllable in lines 3 ('othir') and 12 ('hedid').

[37] Some tail-rhyme stanzas contain four stresses in each line, but this is the exception.

[38] This is based on the understanding discussed in Chapter 4 that word stress often influences French monophonic song. Hans Tischler, who transcribes the music metrically, maintains consistent four-beat lines by stretching out the last word of lines 3 and 6, Samuel N. Rosenberg and Hans Tischler, ed., *Chanter m'estuet: Songs of the Trouvères* (London: Faber Music, 1981), p. 30. Example 5.5 is derived from this edition, but with the metrical structure removed.

Example 5.4 *Der jüngere Titurel* melody adapted to *The Alliterative
Alexander Fragment C* or *Wars of Alexander*, lines 1–12

1. When folk ere fes - tid and fed, ___ fayne wald thai here

2. Sum fa - rand thinge ef - tir fode ___ to fay - nen thare her - tis,

3. Or thai ware four - med on fold or thaire fa - dirs o - thir. ___

4. Sum is leve to lythe ___ the le - sing of ___ sayn - tis

5. That lete thaire li - fis be lorne for oure lord sake,

6. And sum has lang - inge of lufe lays to ___ her - ken,

7. How le - dis for thaire lem - mans has lang - or en - du - red.

8. Sum co - vet - tis and has com - forth to carpe and to ___ les - tyn

continued overleaf

Example 5.4 *continued*

9. Of cur - tais - sy, of knyght - hode,   of craf - tis   of   ar - mys.

10. Of kyng - is   at has con - qui - rid   and o - vir - co - myn — lan - dis;

11. Sum of wir - schip,   i - wis, —   slike as tham wyse lat - tis,

12. And sum of wan - ton wer - kis,   tha that ere wild - he - did; —

(When people have feasted and are fed, they are eager to hear some pleasant thing after their meal to delight their hearts, [something from] before either they or their fathers were shaped on earth. Some like to hear about the redemption of saints that let their lives be lost for our Lord's sake; and some long to hear love stories, how people endured distress for their lovers; some crave and have comfort when they tell or listen to stories of chivalry, about knighthood, about skill in arms, about kings who have conquered and overcome lands; some, indeed, [like to hear] about honour, such people as they consider wise; and some [prefer to hear] about self-indulgent deeds, those that are wild-headed.)

Example 5.5 'Volez vous que je vous chant', stanza 2

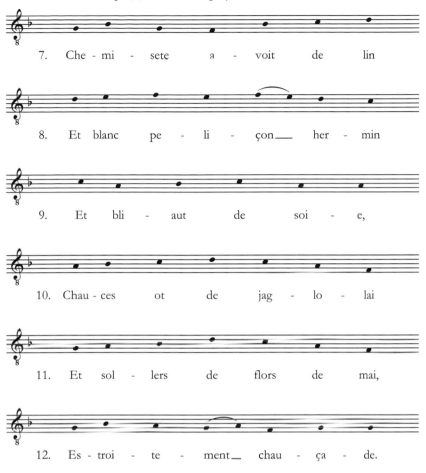

7. Che - mi - sete   a - voit   de   lin

8. Et   blanc   pe - li - çon___   her - min

9. Et   bli - aut   de   soi - e,

10. Chau - ces   ot   de   jag - lo - lai

11. Et   sol - lers   de   flors   de   mai,

12. Es - troi - te - ment___   chau - ça - de.

(She was wearing a linen undertunic, a white ermine mantle and a silk tunic. She was shod in close-fitting reed stockings and shoes of May flowers.)

that her father is a nightingale and her mother a siren, and she is greeted by a man who wants to marry her. A strikingly similar scene occurs in *Sir Launfal*, when the magnificently dressed fairy Triamour arrives on horseback and is united with Launfal. Both texts focus on an other-world lady involved in a love relationship with a man. In both, the lady rides to her beloved in a public setting, and her clothing and then her mount are described in detail. The verse form is also similar; *Sir Launfal* is composed in tail-rhyme stanzas.

The ultimate source of the English romance, Marie de France's *Lanval*, also shares this literary trope, but the Middle English text is somewhat removed from Marie's text. This leaves open the possibility of other francophone influences, such as a musical tradition associated with 'Volez vous', a sources which matches more closely in poetic form. The distance between Marie's octosyllabic couplets and the English tail-rhyme romance may be seen by comparison of a few couplets from Marie's version with the roughly analogous passage from *Sir Launfal*. Marie writes:

> Ele iert vestue en itel guise
> De chainse blanc e de chemise
> …
> Le cors ot gent, basse la hanche,
> Le col plus blanc que neif sur branche;
> …
> Sis manteus fu de purpre bis;
> Les pans en ot entur li mis.
>
> (lines 559–60, 563–4, and 571–2)

(She was dressed in this fashion: in a white linen shift … Her body was elegant, her hips slim, her neck whiter than snow on a branch, … Her cloak, which she had wrapped around her, was dark purple.)

The English *Sir Launfal* provides this version:

> The lady was clad yn purpere palle,
> Wyth gentyll body and myddyll small,
> That semely was of syght;
> Her matyll was furryd with whyt ermyn,
> Yreversyd jolyf and fyn –
> No rychere be ne myght.
>
> (lines 943–8)

(The lady was clad in purple cloth, with a slender body and a small waist that was lovely to see. Her mantle was trimmed with white ermine, splendidly and precisely lined; none could be richer.)

The mantle 'furryd with whyt ermyn' in the passage from *Sir Launfal* resonates with the 'blanc peliçon hermin' in 'Volez vous' more than with Marie's mantle of 'purpre bis'. Introduction of 'Volez vous' into the mesh of related traditions exposes the flimsiness of our modern division between music and literature. A text other

Example 5.6 *Sir Launfal*, lines 943–8, set to the melody of 'Volez vous que je vous chant'

than Marie's, one we would not normally associate with the romance tradition, here shares with an English romance both a literary trope and a verse form.

Tail-rhyme stanzas can readily be set to the melody of 'Volez vous'. More sylla- bles are involved in the English verse form, but the original song points the way to handling additional syllables; the positioning of the stressed syllables remains constant in the melody. Example 5.6 shows a passage from *Sir Launfal* set to the melody of 'Volez vous'. The melody is remarkably plastic, shaping itself comfort- ably to the natural rhythms of English tail-rhyme verse. While this song does not fit the fiddle framework of drones as conveniently as the others discussed in this chapter, the dissonance created in the middle of the melody can be ener- gizing. It is not clear how much dissonance would have been tolerated or even sought out in late medieval England, but even if the song were inappropriate for the fiddle, that would not disqualify it as a valid contrafactum for tail-rhyme romances.[39] The song can be adapted to the twelve-line stanza structure of *Sir Launfal* by the simple expedient of repeating the melody, and anomalies in stanza form and metre can be adjusted along the way without difficulty.[40]

Some stanza forms, however, cannot be accommodated by a contrafactum. *The Tournament of Tottenham* provides an instructive test case, since the stanza design is so complex. Editor Erik Kooper describes the structure as follows:

> It has a rhyming quatrain and a triplet (called the wheel), each followed by a single line, rhyming with each other, giving the rhyme scheme: aaaab–cccb. The meter of the quatrain is four-beat, i.e., it has four stressed syllables. That of the other lines is more difficult to establish. Normally speaking the triplet consists of three-beat lines, while the b-lines are even shorter with two or one beat only.[41]

An excellent case can be made for performance of this romance, a humorous tale in which rough peasants carry out a mock tournament. Not only are both fifteenth-century manuscripts written using graphic indication of stanza structure,[42] but there is a 1432–3 record of payment 'lusoribus ludentibus in Castro de la Tornment de Totyngham' (to performers for performing the *Tournament of Tottenham* in [Rougement] Castle).[43] Furthermore, psycholinguistic evidence indicates that memorial transmission effectively accounts for the types of textual transposition and incorporation exhibited in one of the manuscripts.[44]

While I am aware of no convenient contrafactum, it is possible to construct a melodic framework by drawing on typical patterns of medieval monophonic song. Fabrication of a melody within the parameters established for narrative accompaniment, while it cannot reconstruct a medieval performance version, can allow us to explore how music can interact with a complex stanza structure. The experiment reveals how a melody highlights aspects of the text, but also how the text transforms the melody. Example 5.7 shows a chameleon melody that readily takes on the character of the most wildly striped or dappled or jagged stanza a minstrel might present.[45] The melody accommodates a variety of phrasing constructions.

---

[39] The dissonance can be reduced, and even eliminating by placing fingers simultaneously on the third and second strings to create parallel fifths. See the discussion of 'fifthing' in Appendix B. The same technique can be applied to the top two strings when the melody shifts to the second string to produce parallel fourths.

[40] In performance these variations do not feel like anomalies.

[41] Erik Kooper, ed. *Sentimental and Humorous Romances* (Kalamazoo, MI: Medieval Institute Publications, 2006), p. 217.

[42] This is based on direct consultation of BL MS Harley 5396 and CUL MS Ff.5.48.

[43] Cooke, '*Tournament of Tottenham*', p. 2. While this performance may not have drawn on the same text as the extant romance, it is likely to have presented some form of the story.

[44] See Linda Marie Zaerr and Mary Ellen Ryder, 'Psycholinguistic Theory and Modern Performance: Memory as a Key to Variants in Medieval Texts', *Mosaic* 26.3 (1993): 21–35. The errors I made in the early stages of memorizing the romance correspond strikingly with the textual variants in the Cambridge manuscript.

[45] The beginning of this melody is loosely based on Cantiga 189, Higinio Anglés, ed., *La Música de las Cantigas de Santa María des Rey Alfonso el Sabio: Facsímil, Transcripción y Estudio Crítico*, 2 vols

Example 5.7 *The Tournament of Tottenham*, stanza 1

1. Of all thes kene con - que - rours to carpe it were kynde,

2. Of fele fegh - tyng folk fer - ly we fynde,

3. The tur - na - ment of To - ten - ham have we in mynde.

4. It were harme sych har - dy - nes were hol - den by - hynde,

5. In sto - ry as we rede,

6. Of Haw - kyn, of Her - ry,

7. Of Tom - kyn, of Ter - ry,

8. Of them that were dugh - ty

9. And stal - worth in dede.

(It is natural to talk about all these fierce conquerors. We find marvels about many fighting folk. We have in mind *The Tournament of Tottenham*. It would be a pity to denigrate such hardiness as we read in this story, about Hawkyn, about Harry, about Tomkyn, about Terry, about those who were doughty and stalwart in their deeds.)

Example 5.8 *The Tournament of Tottenham*, stanza 2

10. It be-fel in To-ten-ham on a dere day

11. Ther was mad a schar-tyng be tho hy-way.

12. The-der com al the men of tho con-tray,

13. Of Hys-syl-ton, of Hy-gatte, and of Ha-ke-nay,

14. And all the swete swyn-kers.

15. Ther hop-ped Haw-kyn,

16. Ther daun-sed Daw-kyn,

17. Ther trum-ped Tom-kyn

18. And all were trewe dryn-kers.

(It happened in Tottenham on a splendid day that there was a festival on the high road. All the men of that region came there, from Islington, from Highgate, and from Hackney, and all the sweaty workers. There Hawkyn hopped; there Dawkyn danced; there Tomkyn trumpeted; and they were all true drinkers.)

For example, the fifth line can be tied either to the first four lines or the following four, or, as in this case, it can adhere equally to both halves. The music assists memory of the text, and it facilitates slipping from one stanza to another to cover memory gaps. A fiddle can offer a natural break between stanzas by repeating or elaborating motifs from the melody, enhancing the rhythmic patterns inherent in the text.

The melody invites variation. A change to the melody in the second line transforms the entire stanza (example 5.8).[46] Comparison of examples 5.7 and 5.8 illustrates how the text itself also transforms the melody. In example 5.7, the lines beginning with the unstressed 'Off' (6–8) produce a very different rhythm from the analogous lines in example 5.8 beginning with the stressed 'Ther' (15–17). In addition to starting on an upbeat, the 'Off' lines bear two stressed syllables each, while the 'Ther' lines each bear three. The potential for transformation is further increased when we remember that any given performance can emphasize or de-emphasize metrical stresses.

Special features in the text can be highlighted by alternate related melodies. The mock epic character of this poem craves a grandiose melody (example 5.9).[47]

In a performance by a number of players, a lengthy, text-free battle could be instrumentally accompanied; and in any performance, voice and fiddle together could tug one way and another with the combatants, illuminate dissipated husbands with disapproval, limp to a wedding, and conclude in grand celebration. The irregular rhythms of the text are enhanced, rather than compromised, by the musical setting. The engagement of the text with music demonstrates a purpose that may have motivated the people who transcribed romances in late medieval England.[48]

Couplets and the Miscibility of Form: The Case of 'Gray Steel'

To this point, I have largely ignored the romances in couplets except to demonstrate that they can be sung to the melody for 'Edi beo thu'.[49] Many musical settings are practical and reasonable for couplets. It is only with couplets, though, that we have an extant melody, not a contrafactum, assigned to a specific romance text. Here we find clear indication of a music convention applied to a Middle English romance.

(Barcelona: Diputación Provincial de Barcelona, 1943), vol. 1, pp. 176–7, and vol. 2, pp. 209–10. The musical examples associated with *The Tournament of Tottenham* represent a specific performance recorded in *Music and Medieval Narrative* (Provo, UT: Chaucer Studio, 2011).

[46] After this passage, with its drunken dancing, a fiddler might play a brief staggering dance.

[47] In this example, a fiddle can elaborate the inflation of the event by playing parallel fourths above the melody.

[48] For a video of this hypothetical performance of *The Tournament of Tottenham*, see *Music and Medieval Narrative* (Provo, UT: The Chaucer Studio, 2011).

[49] See Chapter 4.

Example 5.9 *The Tournament of Tottenham*, lines 87–90

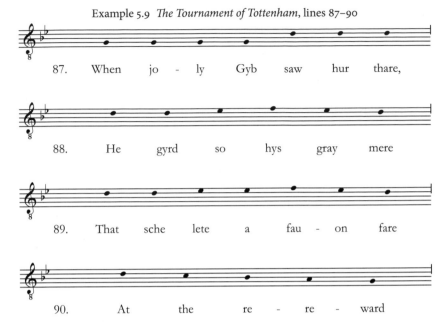

87. When jo - ly Gyb saw hur thare,

88. He gyrd so hys gray mere

89. That sche lete a fau - on fare

90. At the re - re - ward

(When jolly Gyb saw her there, he squeezed his gray mare so tightly that she let go a fart at her rear end.)

I was tempted to ignore *Gray Steel* because both the romance and the melody exist only in seventeenth-century forms,[50] but the convergence of evidence is compelling. *Gray Steel* (*Eger and Grime*) offers a melody for a romance known to exist in the fifteenth century, two versions of that romance, and a fifteenth-century reference to two fiddlers singing it. Application of the principles discussed in Appendix B reveals further justification for pursuing *Gray Steel*: the melody fits admirably into Jerome of Moravia's second fiddle tuning,[51] and the music can accommodate a range of verse forms. Example 5.10 shows the melody as preserved in George Farquhar Graham's nineteenth-century transcription of the Straloch Manuscript.[52]

[50] Purser, 'Greysteil', p. 144, argues that 'there is nothing in the Straloch 'Greysteil' that strikes this listener's ear as being incompatible with the late fifteenth century', and he makes a case that two performers could more conveniently present a long narrative. A recording of about nineteen minutes of the Huntington-Laing version sung by Andy Hunter with clarsach accompaniment by William Taylor is available on *Graysteil: Music from the Middle Ages and Renaissance in Scotland* (Dorian, 1997). This recording uses the lute harmonies from the Straloch manuscript, which Purser, p. 147, points out 'are not consistent with or even clearly suggestive of the harmonies that might have been provided by the fiddlers'. The recording does, however, effectively illustrate a number of the principles of variation discussed in Appendix B.

[51] This is not a characteristic of the collection as a whole; other pieces in the Straloch Manuscript do not conform to the medieval fiddle tuning as conveniently.

[52] National Library of Scotland MS Advocates 5.2.18.

Example 5.10 *Gray Steel*

The evidence of the preceding chapters justifies removing the mensural nota-tion (which may have been imposed at a later time), while preserving the pattern of stressed pitches (those that fall on the first and third beats of each measure), aligning these with stressed syllables. This frees the melody to shape itself to the rhythms in the text.[53] In the extant lute song, there are three melodic phrases, arranged (when we comply with the repeats) *ABABCBCB*. A fiddle player would not need to apply any fingers at all to accompany the recurrent *B* phrase, which functions as a comfortable rest pattern, rocking between the two top strings. Both the *A* and *C* phrases begin with the second finger applied to a *g* string, in one case the lower middle string, and in the other the higher top string.[54] All three melodic motifs fall easily under the fingers and can be executed without concentrated thought, and they can be simplified by a less experienced player.[55] Furthermore, the entire melody can be played an octave lower with exactly the same fingerings.[56]

Each melodic phrase accommodates one couplet of text. While it is possible to follow the extant lute melody literally, it is more likely a narrator would draw on phrases as a palette.[57] All three phrases end in the same stepwise-descending four notes. The *B* phrase, lingering within the four notes of the cadence, repeats the same motif twice, thus reiterating the cadence. The *A* phrase, in a lower range but with dramatic leaps of a sixth and a seventh, contrasts with the *C* phrase, in a higher range characterized by pitch repetition. The *B* melody serves as an effective transition between the lower *A* and the higher *C*, and its neutrality serves as a foil for the other two.

Example 5.11 is a reasonable application of the melody to lines 263–72 of the Percy folio version of *Gray Steel* (*Eger and Grime*).[58] The *A* melody contains two dramatic leaps upward, the higher note falling on an unstressed syllable. This pitch accent reinforces phrasing units that generally begin with unstressed syllables: 'of hew and hyde', 'by the bedside', 'upon her knee', and 'full love somelye'. The consistency of the melody in reflecting the phrasing of *Eger and Grime* provides further validation for using it with the romance.

A performer is free to express the phrasing invited by the text. The stressed syllables are marked to make it easier to see how the metrical structure interacts

[53] A residue of such a version may be preserved in the manuscript. In measure 7, a quarter note replaces the two eighth notes that occur in the three other instances of this pattern (measures 5, 13, and 15), providing exactly the sort of variation that would accommodate a varying number of unstressed syllables.

[54] The vocal range of this melody is high because the tonal centre is *d'* rather than the more common *g*. I have a fairly low vocal range, so I tuned my instrument down a major third from my usual setting. It is possible that when the minstrels in *Silence* change their instruments to 'une altre atempreüre' (another tuning, line 2763), they are simply tuning to a different pitch level. A retuning would be worth the effort for a lengthy narrative.

[55] Both the *A* and *C* phrases can be played with second finger on *b* for the first two measures and then first finger on *a* for the second two. The melody is particularly convenient in that the second and third fingers are placed close together on every string.

[56] In the lower octave, the low re-entrant *G* string is a mandatory drone in the *B* phrase.

[57] For a justification of this approach, see the discussion of 'Edi beo thu' in Chapter 4.

[58] Letters notated above the lines correspond to melodic phrases from example 5.10.

Example 5.11 *Eger and Grime*, Percy Folio lines 263–72, set to the *Gray Steel* melody

A

263. The la - dye **fayre** of **hew** and **hyde,**

264. Shee **sate downe** by the **bed - side;**

A

265. Shee **laid** a **sou** - ter u - **pon** her **knee,**

266. Ther - **on** shee **plaid** full **love** som - **lye,**

B

267. And **yett** for **all** her **sweet__** **play** - inge,

268. Of - **times** shee **had** full **still__** **mour** - ninge;

C

269. And her **2** **may** - dens **sweet** - lye **sange,**

270. And **oft** the **wee** - ped, and their **hands wrange;**

continued overleaf

Example 5.11 *continued*

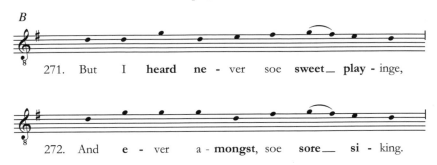

B

271. But I **heard** **ne** - ver soe **sweet**__ **play** - inge,

272. And **e** - ver a - **mongst**, soe **sore**__ **si** - king.

(The lovely lady sat down by the bedside. She laid a psaltery on her knees, and on it she played beautifully. Yet, for all her sweet playing, she often mourned silently; and her two maidens sang sweetly, and often they wept and wrung their hands. I never heard such sweet playing, but always throughout such grievous sighing.)

with the phrasing structure both in the text and in the melody. If a fiddle follows phrasing structures, it competes less with the semantically important stressed syllables, which are frequently internal. If the performer focuses on the text and the phrasing in that text, and uses the instrument to reinforce phrasing, the metre will take care of itself, realized in a variety of ways. If, however, the fiddler jabs at every beat, the instrument can become an obstruction, either drawing attention to the uneven spacing of the stressed syllables or forcing them into a rigid pattern where they do not fit.

The melody can easily be used to enhance parallels in the text. In example 5.11, the same melody is used for both the couplets that contrast lovely playing with bitter mourning (lines 267–8 and 271–2). Within each couplet, 'sweet play-inge' is echoed by 'still mourninge' or 'sore siking'. The ease with which the melody highlights textual features again provides support for its application, and in this case it is not a contrafactum, but a melody actually linked to this story.

The melody is highly flexible. It can be adapted to the parallel passage from the Huntington–Laing version of the story (example 5.12).[59]

The *Gray Steel* melody may also provide a clue to the tail-rhyme stanza. There is some evidence that an earlier version of the poem was set in tail-rhyme stanzas.[60] When we apply the melody to the beginning of the Auchinleck version of *Bevis of Hampton*, it is natural to echo the ending of each couplet (identical for any of the three melodic phrases) by attaching the ending of the *B* phrase to the two-stress tail-lines, but it is here that the pattern of accents plays a crucial role. If the last

[59] In example 5.12, to maintain a parallel with example 5.11, the C melody directly follows A without the more usual intervention of the B melody. This is a situation that might naturally have occurred in the course of improvisation, especially where a couplet may have been dropped.

[60] Caldwell, ed., *Eger and Grime*, pp. 42–3.

Example 5.12 *Eger and Grime*, Huntington-Laing lines 345–50, set to the *Gray Steel* melody

(She laid a breast-plate on her knee, and on it she played accurately about love. Her maidens sang sweetly to this instrument, but the lady sighed often throughout. Her every expression showed she had something heavy in her heart.)

four notes of the *B* phrase are applied to the two-stress tail-line, the stresses tend to fall on the same pitches as in the cadences of the *A* and *C* phrases, yielding the result shown in example 5.13.

By simply echoing the cadence of the couplet, the tail-line loses its identity, its culminating character. Furthermore, the only way to distinguish the cadence of the first half of the *A* phrase from the identical second half is this repetition of the ending. But if the metrical accent pattern of the *Gray Steel B* phrase is followed, rather than simply the sequence of four notes, the tail-line takes on a unique and

Example 5.13 The *Gray Steel* melody adapted to *Bevis of Hampton*, lines 1–6, without shift in metrical accent pattern

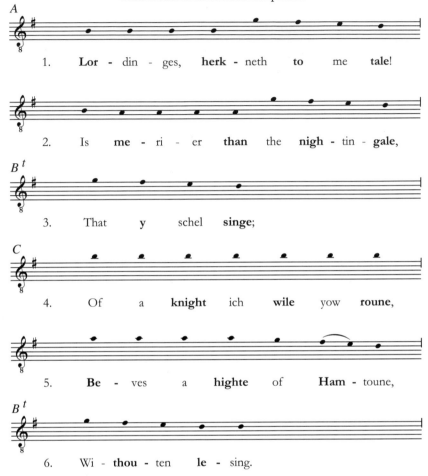

A

1. **Lor** - din - ges, **herk** - neth **to** me **tale!**

2. Is **me** - ri - er **than** the **nigh** - tin - **gale,**

B *t*

3. That **y** schel **singe;**

C

4. Of a **knight** ich **wile** yow **roune,**

5. **Be** - ves a **highte** of **Ham** - toune,

B *t*

6. Wi - **thou** - ten **le** - sing.

(Ladies and Gentlemen, listen to my tale! I shall sing a song merrier than a nightingale. In fact, I want to tell of a knight called Bevis of Hampton.)

recognizable character.[61] All that is required is setting the two stressed syllables of the tail-line to the *g'* and *e'* rather than the *f'* and *d'* (example 5.14). The only difference is the offsetting of the stressed syllables in the tail-lines, but this detail transforms the tail-line into a recognizable structural feature with a character different from its couplet companions. The *B* melodic phrase would not be used for couplets (except, perhaps for effect) because doing so would spoil the identity

---

[61] In notation of examples, I largely ignore word-final schwas at the ends of lines. These can be easily added as additional notes. It is worth observing, however, that it is possible to sing a final -e so that it is present as a syllable, but so understated as hardly to deserve its own notated pitch. It should not be assigned a separate pitch at the end of a tail-line.

Example 5.14 The *Gray Steel* melody adapted to *Bevis of Hampton*, lines 1–6, with shift in metrical accent pattern

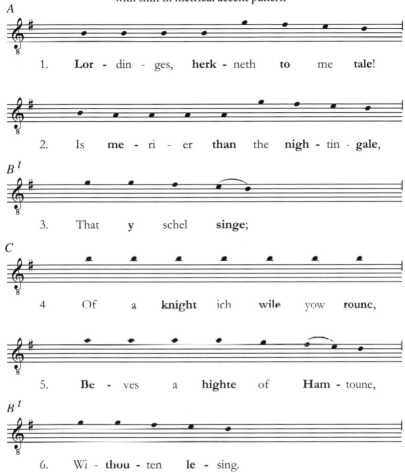

of the tail-lines. While the tail-line in example 5.13 lures a performer to plunge ahead breathlessly to the next line, example 5.14, ending on an afterbeat, almost demands a pause before the next line, a pause that is vital when so many lines begin on an upbeat, an unstressed syllable.

Here, too, 'irregularities' create no difficulty. In example 5.14, lines 4 and 5 scan most comfortably with only three stresses, and the melody conforms. This flexibility makes sense of the switch to couplets later in the manuscript.[62] Just as the text moves comfortably from tail-rhyme to couplets, so does the melody.

The rhythmic modification of the descending cadence provides a key to other

[62] For a discussion of the metre change, see Linda Marie Zaerr, 'Meter Change as a Relic of Performance in the Middle English Romance *Sir Beves*', *Quidditas* 21 (2000): 105–26.

tail-rhyme stanza designs. In the *Gray Steel* melody, every half phrase except the first half of *C* ends with a descending scale from *g* to *d*. As I have shown, the accented pitches in the *B* phrase are offset from the *A* and *C* phrases. Since the *B* phrase consists of a two-measure repeated pattern, by working with one pattern and truncating the beginning, we can adapt the *B* melody to fit a three-stress tail-line. The *Gray Steel* melody, then, adheres very comfortably to the most common tail-rhyme stanza, yielding a melodic form *ABtABtCBtCBt* or *ABtCBtABtCBt*, where *Bt* refers to the modified cadential motif drawn from the *B* phrase. Musical phrases may be applied differently to enhance the text following the principles discussed above.[63] In this arrangement of the *Gray Steel* melody, the *B* phrase is reduced to a kind of cadential extension of the *A* or *C* melody. The second stanza of *Emare* might thus be sung as shown in example 5.15.

On a fiddle it is easy to maintain this pattern since every couplet begins with the second finger applied to a *g* string, and either melodic phrase can be played on any of the three *g* strings on the instrument. The tail-line may be simplified to a rocking between *d* and *g* in either available octave. While it is impossible to determine the extent to which the melody that survives preserves original features, features such as the relationship of the melody to the fiddle tuning structure and the offset accent in the *B* melody suggest specific ways a melody could have interacted with a romance text in late medieval England.

Recognizing Traces of Performance

The laborious notation of musical settings above makes it evident why medieval scribes would not have written down such melodies. The differences from one example to another can seem trivial and obvious, and considerable repetition is necessary to point out differences. Why would anyone take the trouble to write down something a minstrel could do so easily without notation? If a pre-existing melody doesn't come to mind, it takes so little effort to make one up. It is small wonder that no Middle English romance text includes notated music.[64]

This is not to say that all trace of musical performance has disappeared, as I hope the discussion above indicates. There are bits of information that can take us closer to understanding musical settings of the Middle English romances. A thorough collection and analysis of medieval narrative melodies would provide

---

[63] For instance, in example 5.15, lines 16, 17, and 22 each contain three stressed syllables, a pattern most comfortably accommodated by the *C* melody.

[64] The experience of performance confirms the predictability of the absence of notated music. It is very difficult to think as a scholar in the midst of performance. Moving away from notated music and text to an integrally woven memorized performance, which must be worked out aurally, makes it increasingly challenging to think of how one might notate the rhythm or even the pitches. In performance mode, it becomes difficult even to distinguish between stressed and unstressed syllables.

Example 5.15 The *Gray Steel* melody adapted to *Emare*, lines 13–24

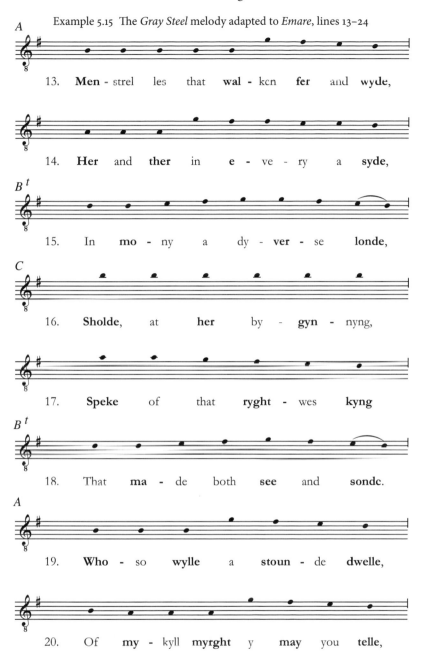

A

13. **Men** - strel les that **wal** - ken **fer** and **wyde,**

14. **Her** and **ther** in e - ve - ry a **syde,**

B^t

15. In **mo** - ny a dy - **ver** - se **londe,**

C

16. **Sholde,** at **her** by - **gyn** - nyng,

17. **Speke** of that **ryght** - wes **kyng**

B^t

18. That **ma** - de both **see** and **sonde.**

A

19. **Who** - so **wylle** a **stoun** - de **dwelle,**

20. Of **my** - kyll **myrght** y **may** you **telle,**

continued overleaf

Example 5.15 *continued*

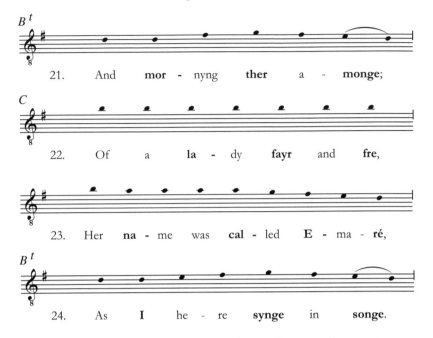

21. And **mor** - nyng **ther** a - **monge;**

22. Of a **la** - dy **fayr** and **fre,**

23. Her **na** - me was **cal** - led **E** - ma - **ré,**

24. As **I** he - re **synge** in **songe.**

(Minstrels, who walk far and wide, here and there and in every direction, in many different lands; these minstrels should, when they begin, speak of that righteous king who made both sea and sand. Whoever will linger a while, I may tell you of great mirth mingled with mourning, of a fair and gracious lady who was called Emaré, as I here sing in song [or 'as I hear sung in song'].)

an invaluable tool for further study.[65] In co-ordination, a survey of tropes shared between romances and extant songs would enhance awareness of overlap and shared traditions.

In the meantime it is enough to acknowledge a body of evidence that may not look like what we are used to. Studying the crystalline structure of a rock, we may not notice the lichen growing on its surface. Counting the petals of a flower (five or four or three), we may not see the moss that fosters its growth. Looking for deer trails, we may miss the glistening track of a slug. That melodies behave as they do and interact with romance texts as they do provides grounded information; it remains for us to learn to integrate this information into our understanding of the Middle English romance.

---

[65] It would be interesting, for example, to look again at some of the ballad melodies, since some ballads clearly come from a tradition shared with Middle English romances. See Fowler, *Literary History of the Popular Ballad*.

6

Conclusions

The Minstrel's Craft and the Immediacy of Audience

Mylsone the harper, trying to ignore the smell of roasting meat at an Easter feast, squeezes between two trumpeters, shoving the fiddler Adam Boyd in front of him. Mylsone jokes with the feasters about their rich basins and platters and goblets, and then he and Adam sing how Floripas flung feasting vessels made of gold and silver over the wall to distract attackers. A very young lady throws her goblet across the table, giggling with a friend as it clatters on the floor.[1]

A 'brokin bakkit' (broken backed) fiddler in the Church of St Andrew plays a brief melody for seven young soldiers hurrying past, but they ignore her.[2]

On the long road to Bury St Edmunds, in the mid-May drizzle (too wet for a harp), Nicholas le Blund rides beside the king, stretching out the story of Sir Bevis. He adds a fight with a griffin, and allows Ascopard to roar for a long time about the strange land of giants because the king is laughing so hard. He carefully leaves out that awkward episode about the fictional king's corrupt son, but he keeps in the horse race. When he mentions Arundel, he describes the horse the king is riding, and he lets Arundel be the horse who carries Bevis away from Damascus and swims in the sea. When John Forster rides closer, the minstrel elaborates the story of the fisher and the forester who raise the infant twins. Then, as the king hunches into his wet cloak and an inn appears ahead, Nicholas rushes through the tournament to a quick and happy conclusion and the whimsical burial of lord, lady, and horse. A few months later, the king jokes about Arundel as he grants Nicholas a hundred and eight shillings six pence for a horse.[3]

In our culture, it is easy to forget what 'audience' would have meant to a minstrel, never the same from one performance to another, or from one minstrel to another. We are used to crafting books for an audience of scholars or an audience of students or a general audience. It is this recent understanding of audience that has led us to accept recordings as accurate documents of performance. A video of *The Weddynge of Sir Gawen and Dame Ragnell* may have an audience of students today, but what is their relationship with the performer? A young woman with wet hair in a towel calls to a roommate and eats Hawaiian pizza while watching a down-loaded file on a laptop with tinny sound. Thirty-seven sophomores slump before a massive projection screen in a large room with minute desks. Nothing they do

---

[1] Dickson *et al.*, eds, *Compota Thesauriorum*, vol. 1, p. 326, records twenty-eight shillings paid 'to Adam Boyd, fithelar, and Mylsone the harpare' among a series of payments 'to thir menstralis, giffin for thair Pasche reward'.

[2] Although Dickson *et al.*, eds, *Compota Thesauriorum*, vol. 1, p. 333, notes nine shillings paid 'to the brokin bakkit fithelar in Sanctandrois', that fiddler may not always have been so fortunate.

[3] Bullock-Davies, *Register*, p. 12, documents a series of payments and money for a horsse to harper Nicholas le Blund in 1299 as he travelled with the King to the siege of Caerlaverock.

and nothing in their world transforms the performance; the performer does not interact with them directly. In this respect the video is much like the romance manuscripts in creating an illusion of performance. This is not to discount the value of recordings; they can accurately preserve physical and aural dimensions of performance. What they do not preserve is the one element the romances insist is most essential: the identifying feature of minstrelsy is the bond between minstrel and audience.

The 'I' and the 'you' are so emphatically chiselled across the written romances that it is easy to miss the obvious, that what distinguishes a minstrel's craft is living relationship among particular human beings. So fundamental is this relationship to the romances themselves that we see it replicated in the written forms, woven into the fabric of the genre.

Historical Performance Revisited

Whether or not the romances were ever presented by minstrels, live performance today serves as a reminder of the relational framework embedded in the texts and the transformative impact of a performance community on textual material. But the power of performance can be misdirected or misinterpreted, which helps explain why it has been viewed with such suspicion in the Middle Ages and today. In a sense, it is cheating to bring alive a medieval tale in the golden light of a carpeted lounge. Performance is compelling, but it cannot substitute for logical thought, and performing *The Tournament of Tottenham* from memory while playing the fiddle does not constitute evidence that the romance was performed in late medieval England. Historical performance can, however, work together with logical construction of evidence, substantiating, refining, and extending what scholarship discovers.

It is important, however, to distinguish between historical performance, grounded in what we know of medieval practice, and other performance approaches to the medieval romance. A group of graduate students redesigned part of *Floris and Blauncheflur*, performing it as an episode from *The Bachelor*, a 'reality' television show in which, like the Emir, a rich man uses a flower to select a wife from among a group of eligible young women living in community with him. The juxtaposition demonstrated cogently that such gender relations exist in our culture; yet it said nothing of how the romance might have been performed in its medieval context. This mode of performance shares with a number of theoretical approaches to literature the potential to create a fresh perspective, to reinterpret elements present in a text. Performance as a heuristic device is a powerful tool, but it has little to do with the medieval world of minstrel entertainment.

Similarly, performance does not have to be tied to medieval content to provide relevant perspectives on the 'mirth of minstrelsy'. If we accept that narratives were sometimes sung by minstrels with instrumental accompaniment, then the experience of singing any narrative while playing an instrument for a live audience may indicate certain universal realities of performance. Such experience can make sense of some of the medieval evidence by demonstrating the ephemeral nature of performance, the ways two performers can interact, and the elements that override textual considerations. Any performer is in a position to understand the power of the audience in shaping performance, the malleability of material, and the enforced and intuitive flexibility of the performer. These realities can explain the vagueness of the records, some characteristic ways orality and textuality interact, the fluidity of story movement between poetry and ordinary language, and the crystallized remnants of improvisation. At the same time, there are distinct limits to the information offered by this approach; it is not possible to arrive at a specific model of English minstrel narrative through a generic performance perspective.

Historical performance, in contrast, attempts to understand the entertainment of the past by replicating what we know of it. One of the challenges we face in this endeavour is the global character of performance. That is to say, any performance is complete; it cannot omit features that are historically uncertain. All approaches to the past are fraught with uncertainty, with chinks and large gaps in our understanding. Scholarship clearly and meticulously specifies where we are certain, the basis of that certainty, and where the evidence is unclear. When we speculate, we articulate the pieces of solid information that have led to that speculation. Performance, in contrast, presents every feature as unequivocal. Any text must be articulated in one way only, and the instrument at any given moment can produce only one pattern of sound. There is no means of specifying the basis of performance choices: which features are grounded in historical evidence, which features are reasonably extrapolated from a variety of evidence, and which features are simply made up because they have to be one way or another. In performance, the missing pieces must be filled in, and it is not possible to tag features with relative degrees of certainty. We may not know how minstrels used facial expressions, but a performer's face must carry some expression, even if that expression is blank. A singer cannot offer a rhythmic interpretation without pitch inflection, cannot sing just the two lines for which a melody is clearly indicated in the manuscript.

Yet a performer's global assembly of information about the Middle English romances and about performance in late medieval England provides valuable evidence which can be communicated outside the performance context. In preliminary notes and in discussion after the fact, performers can explicate their work, discussing which features are historically informed and the extent to which they are justified, clarifying how the entertainment they produce functions as a replica of medieval entertainment.

Bruce Haynes points out that a replica of a musical instrument 'is not necessarily a clone of an original. It is one on which the maker does not make intentional changes; there are no deliberate differences and no compromises to modern taste.'[4] This principle applies to historical performance of romance. The goal is to construct a performance which accords with everything we know of historical, literary, linguistic, and musicological evidence, without flinching away from sensibilities different from our own. Performance cannot recreate the past any more

---

[4] Haynes, *End of Early Music*, p. 161.

than scholarship can. This does not mean that all it can offer is entertainment after a conference banquet, the pleasure of text brought to life.

Daniel Leech-Wilkinson, supports the value of performance in the field of musicology, observing that 'other fields within medieval music studies work very largely with speculations, making claims for historical accuracy that cannot possibly be proved though are not necessarily wrong.' The value of performance, he goes on to say, is 'to break down the walls built unnecessarily around historical musicology to protect it from doubt, letting people inside emerge to find a far wider range of approaches and uses for musicology'.[5] The same might be said of romance performance, which can impel scholars to reconsider assumptions, to acknowledge areas of doubt, to scrutinize alternatives, and to attempt new approaches within a broader landscape of information and connections. These functions can be more clearly defined and discussed than the vague and unspecified inspiration sometimes attributed to historical performance. As the previous chapters have indicated, romance performance does not have to be a tree-shaped room freshener dangling in the window; it can offer precise and focused results.

The evidence of feasibility is no trivial contribution to scholarship. When historical performance demonstrates that the Middle English romances can be sung and self-accompanied on a fiddle – without compromising what we know of the historical context, the romances themselves, and contemporary music – this surely moves toward an answer to one of the questions posed by scholarship. Could the romances have been sung and instrumentally accompanied? Performance provides a certainty: the Middle English romances could have been sung by minstrels with instrumental accompaniment.

Performance can also serve to corroborate hypotheses produced by scholarship. When Rhiannon Purdie suggests that 'the possibility of musical performance may have encouraged some scribes to set out their texts in graphic tail-rhyme',[6] experimentation can produce a mode of performance that renders notated pitches superfluous, but relies on continual awareness of the rhyme structure that delineates stanzas. That is to say, a performer can exhibit a form of music that accords with the hypothesis.

Similarly, an extensive body of evidence demonstrates that variation was fundamental in the production of both music and narrative. Singing *The Tournament of Tottenham* can illuminate this evidence by demonstrating how a text can transform a melody. In sung performance, the poem offers a variety of phrasing groupings and shifting rhythmic patterns within the complex stanza design.

Historical performance can serve a more specific purpose in extending and elaborating observations produced by scholarship. When Karl Reichl points out that the thirteenth-century English song 'Edi beo thu' shares a metrical structure with the *Le Morte Arthur*,[7] performance can corroborate that the romance can be sung to this melody, but it can go further in providing evidence that the melody

---

[5] Leech-Wilkinson, *Modern Invention of Medieval Music*, p. 261.

[6] Purdie, *Anglicising Romance*, p. 80.

[7] Reichl, 'Comparative Notes', p. 67.

distorts the text at times by uniformly emphasizing the fifth and sixth lines of each stanza. Examining the manuscript from a performance perspective, we can see that the anomalous rhythmic structures in both text and music serve to enhance the meaning of the text and provide melodic variation based on textual considerations. Experimentation can go on to demonstrate how aptly the melody applies to romances in couplets and why it is easy for a singer to play the second melodic line on the fiddle. When Reichl argues that the melody for 'Edi beo thu' should not be applied to narrative poetry because of its 'wide ambitus, interval leaps, [and] polymotif melody', a performer would be aware of a range of narrative melodies that possess these characteristics, and could thus argue for a broader range of historical possibilities.

Drawing in this way on a wide range of material without making sharp generic distinctions, a performer is positioned to find connections that might be overlooked by scholars. The thirteenth-century French trouvère song 'Volez vous' may seem far removed from the Middle English romance tradition, but it shares both a literary trope and a metrical structure with *Sir Launfal*. The shared features provide support for applying the melody to English tail-rhyme romances. While the connection does not offer certainty, it does offer evidence of a specific nature.

In more general terms, performance can at times address questions raised by scholarship. The work of Hoyt Duggan, Ruth Kennedy and others points to scribal corruption of alliterative poetry at the metrical level. Reconsidering the metre of Middle English romances in performance terms, drawing on scholarship from both music and linguistics, can help explain why 'each copyist sabotaged the metre in his own characteristic way'.[8] Performance informed by principles drawn from medieval treatises and theoretical understanding of rhythm can reveal non-synchronous rhythmic patterns interacting in dynamic tension. Recitation of the texts, particularly in combination with instrumental accompaniment, can show why scribes, governed by an aesthetic of rhythmic variation and steeped in a world rich in rhythmically complex performance, would have naturally varied the rhythmic patterns of the poetry they interacted with.

Musical instruments themselves can expose other poetic features. Employing historical instruments together with verse can illuminate the types of musical interactions these instruments invite and show how instrumentalists may have applied aesthetic principles in combining text and music. The tuning structure of the medieval fiddle significantly limits how the instrument can be played, and once those limitations have been accepted, the remaining options offer clear evidence of how the instrument could have been used: melodic or rhythmic accompaniment moves in a dynamic milieu of shifting drones. An obscure word such as 'garible' applied to fiddle music in a Middle English romance, placed in the light of the French term *guerbloier*, together with a passage in which Gautier de Coinci sets the word parallel to organum, discant, and 'fifthing', can demonstrate continuity with European tradition and confirm the practice of improvisation using the parallel intervals implied by the tuning of the medieval fiddle. Occurring in

---

[8] Kennedy, 'New Theories of Constraint', p. 134.

a romance, in a description of a protagonist performing as a minstrel, the term may indicate a metaperformance element, possibly describing how a minstrel performing a *geste* might play the fiddle.

In some cases, significant evidence emerges only in performance with an instrument. The treasurer's accounts of James IV show that *Gray Steel* (*Eger and Grime*) was sung by two fiddlers at the Scottish court in 1497, and it points to two seventeenth-century versions of the romance, and a lute song titled *Gray Steel*. Either version of the romance can be sung to the extant melody, but this does not advance our understanding. Unexpectedly, performance reveals that the *Gray Steel* melody is ideally shaped to the tuning structure of the medieval fiddle, rocking from one open string to another and requiring only very simple and repetitive finger placement. Further, on the fiddle, the melody facilitates variation in octave without modification of fingering. Although we still cannot be certain what resemblance this melody bears to fifteenth-century versions, we have concrete evidence of features that support some resemblance, and these features further corroborate what we know of medieval aesthetics of variation. More fundamentally, the instrument itself provides clear evidence of how the fiddle would most likely have been used to accompany *Gray Steel*. The melody also offers information about how music may have fostered cadentiality in verse by displacement of accent.

If historical performance is taken seriously as an endeavour that can collaborate with scholarship, it may substantially enhance our understanding of the Middle English romance. Ample evidence indicates that during the thirteenth through fifteenth centuries minstrels performed *gestes* similar in form and content to the romances preserved in manuscripts. The form of the few specific historical records demonstrates why such references are so elusive: terminology is ambiguous, payments specify people rather than performance contexts, and cross referencing demonstrates how often key features (from our standpoint) are missing. While, as Andrew Taylor has demonstrated,[9] large-scale feasts were not a context where an elaborate tale could be developed, more routine meals with smaller audiences may have provided an appropriate venue for extended story performance. Professional entertainment on journeys and private performances for individuals or small groups are also well attested in both historical documents and romance references. Enough records survive to verify that stories were sometimes sung by minstrels and that they were sometimes accompanied by musical instruments.

This evidence provides strong motivation for understanding the performance tradition of late medieval England more fully and accurately, since that tradition is clearly intertwined with the textual artefacts that survive, the romances preserved in manuscripts. Performance can test the tensile strength of a text, stretch it and push it and twist it to see how it behaves. Melodies interact with texts in distinct ways; by exploring these interactions, we may learn more about the texts. The demands of performance enforce scrutiny of assumptions. When the rhythms of Middle English romances appear to hinder performance, a performer might look again at assumptions about rhythm. Sensitive to the flexibility of

---

[9] Taylor, 'Fragmentation, Corruption, and Minstrel Narration'.

performance, a performer may read the records of performance with an awareness of looser boundaries. The enforced interdisciplinarity of performance offers a valid approach to a culture that did not separate music and literature, or drama and narrative, or narrative and lyric. A performer is also continually forced into awareness of the verities of narrative performance: the plot is of prime importance, and musical elements must enhance and not detract from the audience's understanding of what happens in the story or the performer's ability to focus on that content.

Implications

The study of medieval romance is incomplete if we leave out awareness of possible musical performance, and this may have an impact on our editing practices. Scribes are sometimes careless and do corrupt texts. In many cases it is reasonable to seek to recover a poet's original. Even if we accept a uniform distinction between poet and scribe, though, there is no particular reason a poet would be more in tune with literary conventions or more sensitive to nuances in the language than a scribe would be. Both may be influenced by performance conventions, and both may apply transformations typical of performance with varying degrees of success.

In the face of almost systematic resistance of metrical regularity in many of the romance manuscripts, a policy of emending *metri causa* should be reconsidered carefully; it could easily result in oversimplification of a complex and sophisticated practice.[10] Any improvisation can be seen as a corruption, but we do not normally speak of jazz in terms of systematic corruption of original songs. By accepting some level of rhythmic ornamentation as a structuring value in the Middle English romances, we may come closer to accepting the context of the romances and appreciating and assessing where improvisatory embellishments are successful.

In fact, variation appears to be fundamental in medieval culture: in composition, transmission (whatever form that may have taken), and performance. Timothy McGee notes that 'to the medieval mind there was no real separation between the basic goals of the two activities – composition and performance – and that the instructions were often similar for both audiences because they were intended to produce similar results: embellishment of a basic framework.'[11] Elements in Middle English romances that seem simplistic or repetitive, may in fact be incomplete, missing an integral musical dimension. Metrical irregularities

---

[10] Jennifer Fellows, 'Editing Middle English Romances', in *Romance in Medieval England*, ed. Maldwyn Mills, Jennifer Fellows, and Carol Meale (Cambridge: D. S. Brewer, 1991), pp. 5–16, at p. 16, advocates 'not an excessively conservative scribolatry, but at least a movement *away from* traditional editorial assumptions as to the desirability of pursuing archetypes and *towards* a greater respect for scribal intentions and the individuality of variant texts. If we try to reduce every Middle English romance to a single "correct" version, we shall lose a great deal.'

[11] McGee, *Sound of Medieval Song*, p. 5.

may be the residue of sophisticated rhythmic variation that make sense only with music. While many romances may never have been performed by a minstrel, they still invite an imagined embodiment, but that embodiment must be informed.

If we acknowledge the possibility that musical performance may have had an impact on any of the romances, then it is not enough to conjure faint wraiths of minstrel performance, shaped by modern assumptions and varying from person to person. We have not been content to imagine a 'scribal context' for the romances in this way; we have not accepted a uniform and vaguely understood concept of scribal transmission. Instead, we have sought to understand the context of manuscript production, predilections of particular scribes, relationships between manuscripts, and doing so has enriched our understanding of the romances, delineating characteristics while acknowledging a complexity in the manuscript tradition. In the same way, it is irresponsible simply to imagine a 'performance context' for the romances. To acknowledge that minstrels performed *gestes* closely related to the extant romances, and yet to abandon the construction of that performance to unconstrained imagination would be to stifle a vital line of inquiry. It is incumbent on us to characterize minstrel performance of narrative as clearly as we can and then seek to determine where and how it may have shaped particular romances.

This study has drawn on evidence from historical documents and references to minstrels in the Middle English romances to demonstrate that minstrels performed narrative in late medieval England, setting that practice in the context of a broader European tradition. Amid a complex and interconnected performance tradition, English minstrels, most commonly solo or in pairs, performed *gestes* closely linked with written romances, sometimes playing musical instruments, in particular the harp or the fiddle. Characteristics of English narrative performance are documented in extant narrative melodies, theoretical discussions of rhythm and ornamentation, musical notation in manuscripts of Middle English songs, and detailed information about fiddle construction, tuning and playing technique. Although it is impossible to recover the performances themselves, enough evidence exists to allow us to construct a realistic model of minstrel performance of narrative. A simple melody, continually varied in both vocal and instrumental realizations, interacts with text within simultaneous and sometimes non-synchronous rhythmic structures, establishing patterns and then breaking them and returning to them. Both text and melody are malleable, responsive to the story itself. Together, these features demystify a vital dimension of the 'mirth of minstrelsy'.

Appendix A

Minstrel References in the Middle English Verse Romances

THIS appendix is intended to provide a comprehensive catalogue of explicit references to minstrels and music performance in Middle English verse romances. While numerous scholars have discussed minstrel references, they have frequently focused on phrases that imply oral presentation (such as 'Lythe and lystenyth' or 'I shall yow tell'). This collection does not include such references unless they are specific about minstrel performance. Since the purpose of the collection is to find patterns that may illuminate narrative performance, some categories of music performance have been eliminated. The catalogue does not include references to church bells ringing or liturgical singing, and it similarly excludes musical signals associated with hunting or battle or the commencement of a course at a feast. Bird song, angel song, siren song, and general references to joy and mirth and melody are not included, nor are general references to lamentation as song. References to courtiers dancing or revelling or entertaining each other are present only when they specifically refer to instrumental music. All other references to musical performance are included, as are all explicit references to 'minstrels' or 'minstrelsy' or music for processions, and references to musical instruments when they do not serve a signal function or are not simply being carried from one place to another. Explicit descriptions of narrative performance are included except when characters appear to be telling one another what has happened to them. When references elude these parameters, decisions about inclusion are based on overall consistency.

The romances are listed alphabetically, and each listing is followed by qualifying passages contained in that romance. A context and brief summary is provided for each reference, and difficult words or phrases are glossed. It should be noted, however, that in some cases the closest modern equivalent may distort a concept. For example, *bourdour* is most efficiently translated 'storyteller', but that translation excises the notion of singing as a mode of story delivery. Quotations are drawn from a standard edition of each romance except where an asterisk notes my transcription. When multiple manuscripts exist, only one instance of each passage is listed unless there is substantive variation, in which case each variant is represented. When a manuscript contains a reference not included in the edition, the passage is included with the manuscript citation; and when several manuscripts are transcribed in an edition, the manuscript quoted in each passage is specified. Romances that do not contain a qualifying reference are listed at the end of the catalogue.

With an aim of accessibility in mind, thorns and yoghs are given their modern equivalents, i/j and u/v are normalized, ampersands are expanded, and capitalization and punctuation have been made consistent. Because of the fragmentary nature of the references, stanza structure is not indicated.

The Alliterative Alexander Fragment C or *Wars of Alexander*

After a feast some people want to hear one kind of story and some another:

When folk ere festid and fed, fayn wald thai here		*gladly*
Sum farand thinge eftir fode to fayn[en] thare hertis,		*pleasant; delight*
Or thai ware fourmed on fold or thaire fadirs othir.		*before; earth*
Sum is leve to lythe the lesing of sayntis		*eager to listen to; redemption*
5 That lete thaire lifis be lorne for oure lord sake,		*lost*
And sum has langinge of lufe lay[e]s to herken,		*love stories*
How ledis for thaire lemmans has langor endured.		*anguish*
Sum covettis and has comforth to carpe and to lestyn		*tell*
Of curtaissy, of knyghthode, of craftis of armys,		
10 Of kyngis at has conquirid and ovircomyn landis;		*that have*
Sum of wirschip, iwis, slike as tham wyse lattis,		

such people as they consider wise

And sum of wanton werkis, tha that ere wild-hedid;

self-indulgent deeds; wild-headed

Bot if thai wold on many wyse, a wondire ware it els,

It would be a wonder if they did not desire many different styles [of story]

For as thaire wittis ere within, so thaire will folowis.

(lines 1–14)

Among other wonders, Alexander sees the muses:

The muses of musike and the merke how it was made first.

(line 2239)

Jupiter is a 'joglour':

And Jupiter that joglour sum jape bos have;

And it is necessary to have some foolish gift for Jupiter, that joker

(line 4655)

Amis and Amiloun

Minstrel entertainment at a fourteen-day feast:

Ther was mirthe and melodye	
And al maner of menstracie	*minstrelsy*
Her craftes for to kithe;	*display*

(lines 103–5)

Variant:

Her gestys for to kithe

(BL MS Harley 2386)*

Arthour and Merlin

Minstrelsy at a feast in Arthur's court:

Ther were trumpes and fithelers	*trumpeters and fiddlers*
And stivours and tabourers	*bagpipe players and taborers*
	(lines 6557–8)

The Avowynge of King Arthur

Arthur sends his minstrel as a spy to find out how Baldwin behaves as a dinner host:

705	Thenne the king cald his mynstrelle	
	And told him holly his wille –	
	Bede him layne atte hit were stille –	*asked him to dissemble to keep it secret*
	That he schuld furth fare	
	To Baudewins of Bretan.	
710	'I cummawunde the, or thou cum agayne,	*command; before*
	Faurty days, o payne,	*upon penalty*
	Loke that thou duelle thare;	
	And wete me prevely to say	*let me know secretly*
	If any mon go meteles away.	*without food*
715	For thi wareson for ay,	*You will receive a lasting reward,*
	Do thou me nevyr more.'	*even if you never do anything more for me.*
	Then the mynstrell weyndus on his way	
	Als fast as he may.	
	Be none of the thryd day	*noon*
720	He funde thaym atte the mete,	*at table*
	…	
	Thenne he wente to the dece	*dais*
	Before the pruddust in prece.	*the most noble in the assembly*
	That lady was curtase,	
	And bede him stille stonde.	
745	He sayd he was knoun and couthe,	*well known and renowned*
	And was comun fro bi southe,	*the south*
	And ho had myrth of his mouthe	*she*
	To here his tithand.	*news / stories*
	A sennyght duellut he thare.	*He stayed there for a week*
750	Ther was no spense for to spare.	*No expense was spared*
	Burdes thay were nevyr bare,	*boards (tables)*
	Butte evyr covurt clene.	*completely covered (with food)*
	Bothe knyghte and squiere,	
	Mynstrelle and messyngere,	

755 Pilgreme and palmere
  Was welcum, I wene.   *believe*

                                           (lines 705–20 and 741–56)

The Awntyrs off Arthure at the Terne Wathelyne

At Arthur's feast after the appearance of the ghost, a musician comes in with a lady leading a knight:

  There come in a soteler with a symballe,   *citole player with a cymbal*
                                              (MS Douce 324, line 343)

Variants:

  Righte yn so come syphoners and symbale   *musicians and cymbalists*
                                             (Lambeth Palace Library MS 491)

  two setolers   *citole players*
                                                  (Thornton MS)

Bevis of Hampton

Living as a fugitive as a shepherd in the fields, Bevis hears minstrelsy from his home:

  Trompes he herde and tabour   *trumpets; tabor*
  And meche blis.
                                            (Auchinleck MS, lines 383–84)

Princess Josian earns a living as a minstrel while Saber is sick:

3905 While Josian was in Ermonie,   *Armenia*
  She hadde lerned of minstralcie,
  Upon a fithele for to play   *to play the fiddle*
  Staumpes, notes, garibles gay;   *estampies, melodies,*
                                               cheerful parallel intervals

  Tho she kouthe no beter red,   *When she could think of no better solution,*
3910 Boute in to the bourgh anon she yed   *city; went*
  And boughte a fithele, so saith the tale,   *as the story tells*
  For fourti panes of one menestrale;   *for forty pence from a minstrel*
  And alle the while that Saber lay,   *lay (sick)*
  Josian everiche a day
3915 Yede aboute the cite with inne,   *went about within the city*
  Here sostenaunse for to winne.   *to earn their sustenance*

Thus Josian was in swiche destresse,   *such hardship*
While Saber lai in is siknesse.   *lay sick*

(Auchinleck MS, lines 3905–18)

Le Bone Florence of Rome

Florence's accomplishments include playing the harp and the psaltery:

Be that she was XV yere olde,   *fifteen*
Wel she cowde as men me tolde,   *she was able to play well*
Of harpe and sawtyre.   *on the harp and the psaltery*

(lines 61–3)

When the embassy from Garcy rides into Rome their bridles make minstrelsy:

Thorow the towne the knyghtys sange,
And evyr ther bryght brydyls range,   *bridles*
Makeyng swete mynstralcy;

(lines 166–8)

Before he sets out to capture Garcy, Emere feasts without minstrelsy:

Then they wysche and to mete be gone, *washed their hands; went to the meal*
'Of mynstralcy we kepe none,   *We will have no minstrelsy*
We have no space to sparc;   *leisure*
Nodur harpe, fedyll, nor geest',   *neither harp, fiddle, nor story*

(lines 1009–12)

Minstrelsy at the wedding feast with gifts to minstrels:

There was grete myrthe of mynstrals stevyn,   *music*
And nobull gyftys also gevyn,
Bothe golde and robys schene;   *beautiful*

(lines 2155–7)

Chevalere Assigne

Music when the queen is brought out to be burned:

And noyse was in the cyte · felly lowde,   *very loud*
With trumpes and tabers · whenne they here up token   *her*

(lines 225–6)

Duke Roland and Sir Otuel of Spain

Minstrels lived in that land, but they could not tell everything about the deeds of Charlemagne and his court; they were occupied with trivial entertainment:

25	Mynstrells in that lande gan duelle,	*lived*
	Bot alle the sothe thay couthe noghte tell	
	Of this noble chevalrye.	
	How that Cherlles with his swerde gan melle,	*Charlemagne; fight*
	Bot suche a Menske hym be-fell	*honour*
30	That come hym Sodeynly.	
	They tentede to thaire daunsynge	
	And also to thaire othir thynge,	
	To make gamen and glee.	
	Burdours in to the haulle thay brynge,	*storytellers*
35	That gayly with thaire gle gan synge,	*music*
		(lines 25–36)

Eger and Grime

The lady Loosepine entertains the wounded Sir Eger by playing the psaltery; two maidens sing; all three mourn:

	The Ladye fayre of hew and hyde,	*colour and complexion*
	Shee sate downe by the bedside;	
265	Shee laid a souter upon her knee,	*psaltery*
	Theron shee plaid full love somlye,	*beautifully*
	And yett for all her sweet playinge,	
	Oftimes shee had full still mourninge;	
	And her 2 maydens sweetlye sange,	
270	And oft the weeped, and their hands wrange;	*wrung*
	But I heard never soe sweet playinge,	
	And ever amongst, soe sore siking.	*sighing*
		(Percy Folio, lines 263–72)

Loosepine plays the psaltery for the newly arrived Grime after supper in a bedchamber; two maidens sing; all mourn:

	The Ladye lovesome of hew and hyde	*lovely*
	Sett her downe by his bed side,	
	Shee layd a sowter upon her knee,	*psaltery*
	And theron shee playd full love somlye,	
855	And her 2 mayds full sweetlye sang,	
	And ever they wept and range their hands.	*wrung*
	Then spake Gryme to that Ladye fayre:	

'Of one thing, Madam, I have great Marveile,
  For I heard never soe sweet playinge,
860 And ofentimes soe sore weepynge.'
  Shee commanded her sowter to be taken her froe,
  And sore she wrange her hands 2:

                                              (Percy Folio, lines 851–62)

Earl Gare and a hundred knights welcome Eger and Grime with minstrelsy before
Grime and Loosepine's wedding:

  With a 100 Knights in royall array
  Mett Egar and Grime in the way,
  With much myrth of Minstrelsye,
  And welcomed them into that countrye;

                                              (Percy Folio, lines 1401–3)

Emare

Minstrels should begin by singing of Jesus, as I have begun, and now I will sing of
Emaré:

  Menstrelles that walken fer and wyde,
  Her and ther in every a syde,
  In mony a dyverse londe,
  Sholde, at her bygynnyng,
  Speke of that ryghtwes kyng   *righteous*
  That made both see and sonde.   *sea; sand*
  Who-so wylle a stounde dwelle,   *linger a while*
  Of mykyll myrght y may you telle,   *great mirth*
  And mornyng ther a-monge;   *mourning*
  Of a lady fayr and fre,
  Her name was called Emare,
  As I here synge in songe.   *as I here sing in song / as I hear sung in song*
                                                         (lines 13–24)

Minstrels are portrayed on Emaré's cloak together with lovers Ydoyne and Amadas:

  And menstrellys wyth her glewe.   *music*
                                                          (line 132)

I have heard minstrels sing of Emaré's time at sea:

  As y have herd menstrelles syng yn sawe,   *story*
                                                          (line 319)

When Sir Kadore holds a feast for his king, there is minstrelsy:

> Ther was myche menstralse,
> Trommpus, tabours and sawtre,   *trumpets, tabors, and psaltery*
> Bothe harpe and fydylleyng.   *harp and fiddling*
>
>   (lines 388–90)

Minstrels are among the features of the wedding feast for the king of Galys and Emaré:

> And mony a ryche menstralle.
>
>   (line 468)

Generides (couplet version)

Anyone can combat idleness by singing, reading, or speaking romances:

> A man that hath litel to doone,
> Werk he may make him soone;
> Ne thar him nat be idel long   *He does not have to be idle for long*
> That any werk wil underfong, –   *if he wants to undertake any work*
> 5   Neither lewd man ne clerk, –   *uneducated person nor scholar*
> That he ne may find him werk,
> Forto sing, or forto rede,
> Or for to speke of sum old dede
> That here before hath be wroght,   *that was done before*
> 10 Which unto this day be on thoght,
> Of doughtie men that sum tyme were,
> How noble that thei hem bere, –
> Guy of Warwik, and Tristram also,
> Bevis of Hampton, and othir moo,
> 15 Percyvale, and curteys Gaweyn,
> And othir knightes as Sir Oweyn, –
> I ne may reken hem all
> That worship han goote in boure and hall,   *gotten; chamber*
> And, for here ladies sake, to and froo
> 20 Suffred grete sorow and woo;
> And at the last, to here purpos,
> Thei gate worship and grete los.   *praise*
>
>   (lines 1–22)

After battle Generides is greeted outside the town with celebration:

> Bi his armes thei him knew,
> For joye anoon the trompes thei blew;
> The Soudon, kinges, erles, and barouns,   *sultan*
> And the bisshops with processiouns,

Old and yong of the citie that might,
Went ayeinst him, as it was right,
With daunsing, singyng, and al solempnitie,
So was he broght in to the citie.

(lines 3133–40)

Generides (stanza version)

After battle Generides is greeted outside town with minstrelsy:

And all the citezens uppon the playn,
With mynstrellys of many a dyverse sownd,
Preletys, prestys, with riall precession,   *royal*
And childryn syngeng in the fressest wise,   *freshest manner*
With merthis moo thanne I canne now device.   *more*

(lines 3559–63)

Gest Historiale of the Destruction of Troy

The people of Troy welcome Helen with minstrelsy:

With synging, and solas, and sitals amonge;   *citoles*
With myrthes of mynstralsy, musike with all;
Daunsyng of damsele, dynnyng of trumpys,

(lines 3435–7)

Priam rules by reason, and he will hear solemn or happy songs:

Songis of solemnite and songes of myrthe
He wold herkon full hertely in his high wit.

(lines 3871–2)

Golagros and Gawane

At a feast before battle:

The meriest wa[r] menskit on mete at the maill,
     honoured at dinner during the meal
With menstralis myrthfully makand thame glee.

(lines 215–16)

Guy of Warwick (couplet)

Felice, the daughter of Rohaud, Earl of Warwick, is learned, and her learning includes music:

> Lerned she was in musyke;
>
> (Caius College MS 107, line 91)

Guy of Warwick (stanzaic)

Minstrels at the two-week wedding feast of Guy and Felice:

190 Ther was mirthe and melody	
And al maner menstracie	
As ye may fortheward here.	
Ther was trumpes and tabour,	
Fithel, croude, and harpour	*crowd (musical instrument)*
195 Her craftes for to kithe;	*display*
Organisters and gode stivours,	*organists; bagpipe players*
Minstrels of mouthe and mani dysour	*storyteller*
To glade tho bernes blithe.	*delight; happy men*
Ther nis no tong may telle in tale	
200 The joie that was at that bridale	*wedding*
With menske and mirthe to mithe,	*honour; be seen*
For ther was al maner of gle	*entertainment*
That hert might thinke other eyghe se	*eye*
As ye may list and lithe.	*listen and hear*
205 Herls, barouns, hende and fre	*earls*
That ther war gadred of mani cuntré	
That worthliche were in wede,	*clothing*
Thai goven glewemen for her gle	*gave gleemen*
Robes riche, gold and fe,	
210 Her giftes were nought gnede.	*stingy*
On the fiftenday ful yare	
Thai toke her leve for to fare	
And thonked hem her gode dede.	

(lines 190–213)

Guy of Warwick (fifteenth-century)

Minstrels at the wedding of Guy and Felice:

> There were mynstrels on all manere
>
> (line 7101)

Havelok

When Havelok becomes king, minstrelsy and romance reading and singing are among the celebratory activities:

Harping and piping ful god won,	*great abundance*
…	
Romanz-reding on the bok.	
Ther mouthe men here the gestes singe,	*might; stories sung*
The gleumen on the tabour dinge;	*beat*
…	
Ther was so mike yeft of clothes	*so great gift*
That, thou I swore you grete othes,	*even if*
I ne wore nouth ther-offe trod.	*I would not be believed*
	(lines 2326, 2328–30, and 2337–9)

Horn Child

Harlond (the children's teacher) likes hunting, and playing the harp and chess:

> To harpe wele and play at ches
>
> (line 43)

When Hatholf hears of the attack of kings from Ireland, he asks the harper to stop, since now another kind of playing is more appropriate:

He bad the harpour leven his lay:	
'For ous bihoveth another play,	
Buske armour and stede.'	*prepare*
	(lines 157–9)

Horn's education includes harp playing and romance reading:

Harpe and romaunce he radde aright:	*read correctly*
Of al gle he hadde insight,	*entertainment*
That in lond ware.	*was*
	(lines 286–8)

Ipomadon B or The Lyfe of Ipomydon

When the king knights his son, there is a tournament and a forty-day feast, and minstrels are rewarded:

> Mynstrellys had yiftes of golde,
>
> (line 548)

Minstrels at the wedding feast:

> Trumpes to mete gan blow tho,
> Claryons and other menstrellis mo;   *clarions*
> Tho they wasshe and yede to mete,   *went to the meal*
> And every lord toke his sete;
> Whan they were sette, all the route,   *company*
> Menstrellis blew than all aboute,
> Tille they were servyd with pryde
> Of the fryst cours that tyde;
>
>   (lines 2253–60)

Payment to wedding feast minstrels:

> Ipomydon gaff in that stound
> To mynstrellis V C. pound,   *five hundred*
>   (lines 2269–70)

King Horn

The king asks Athelbrus his steward to teach the child Horn to harp and sing (among other skills):

> Tech him of the harpe,
> Wit his nayles sharpe   *sharp fingernails*
> Biforn me for to harpen,
> And of the cuppe serven,
>
> …
> Horn child thou underfonge;   *undertake*
> Tech him of harpe and songe.
>   (MS Laud Misc. 108, lines 247–50 and 255–6)

Variant – description of harp playing:

> and toggen o the harpe   *pluck*
>   (MS Harley 2253, line 247)

To rescue Rymenhild from her wedding feast Horn and his companions gain entrance to the castle as minstrels. Horn plays a lay that causes Rymenhild to grieve:

>   To herpe he gan drawe,   *took up his harp*
> 1580 And wyght hys tweye felawe,   *with; two*
>   Knyghtes swythe felle,   *very worthy*
>   And schurde hem in pelle.   *dressed them in fur*
>   Wyt swerdes he hem gyrte
>   Anouen here schirte.   *over their shirts*

1585 He wenden on the grauel	*went; gravel (walkway)*
Toward the castel.	
He gonne murye synge,	*began to sing merrily*
And makede here glewinge.	*their music*
That Fykenyld myght yhere;	*hear*
1590 Hearkede wat hye were.	*inquired what they were*
Men seyde hyt harperes,	*said they were*
Jogelours and fitheleres.	*entertainers*
He dude hem in lete;	*had them let in*
At halle dore he sete.	
1595 Horn set on the benche;	
Hys harpe he gan clenche.	
He makede Reymyld a lay,	
And Reynyld makede weylawey.	*(a woeful song)*

(MS Laud Misc. 108, lines 1579–98)

Variant – identification of minstrels:

Hi sede hi weren harpurs,	
And sume were gigours.	*fiddlers*

(CUL MS Gg.4.27.2, lines 1591–2)

The King of Tars

Although the daughter of the King of Tars pretends to forsake Christianity, no minstrel could change her real faith:

Wher that sche was, bi northe or southe,	
No minstral with harp no crouthe	*crowd (musical instrument)*
No might chaunge hir thought.	

(lines 508–10)

Minstrelsy in the sultan's court to celebrate his wedding with the daughter of King of Tars:

For ther was melodi with the mest	
Of harp and fithel and of [gest]	*story*
To lordinges of renoun	
Ther was yeven to the menstrels	*given*
Robes riche and mani juweles	*jewels*
Of erl and of barouon.	

(lines 556–61)

Lai le Freine

When Breton kings heard a marvel, they took a harp and made a lai:

We redeth oft and findeth ywrite,		
and this clerkes wele it wite,		*these scholars know it well*
layes that ben in harping		*stories*
ben yfounde of ferli thing.		*strange*
5	Sum bethe of wer and sum of wo,	
	and sum of joie and mirthe also,	
	and sum of trecherie and of gile,	
	of old aventours that fel while;	
	and sum of bourdes and ribaudy,	*jokes; frivolity*
10	and mani ther beth of fairy.	
	Of al thinges that men seth,	*see*
	mest o love for sothe thai beth.	*are*
	In Breteyne bi hold time	*in old*
	This layes were wrought, so seith this rime.	*created; says*
15	When kinges might our yhere	*anywhere; hear*
	of ani mervailes that ther were,	
	thai token an harp in gle and game,	
	and maked a lay and gaf it name.	
	Now of this aventours that weren yfalle	
20	y can tel sum ac nought alle.	*I; but not*
		(lines 1–20)

Lancelot of the Laik

If Gawain were to die, all minstrelsy and feasting should cease:

… and gladschip aucht to ses,	*ought to cease*
Baith menstrasy and festing at the des;	*dais*
	(lines 2761–2)

The Laud Troy-Book

At feasts, *gestours* often tell *gestes* about the heroes people read of in romances:

Many speken of men that romaunces rede.	*Many who read romances speak of men*
That were sumtyme doughti in dede,	*once*
The while that god hem lyff lente,	*gave them life*
That now ben dede and hennes wente:	*gone hence*

15 Off Bevis, Gy, and of Gauwayn,	
Off Kyng Richard, and of Owayn,	
Off Tristram, and of Percyvale,	
Off Rouland Ris, and Aglavale,	
Off Archeroun, and of Octovian,	
20 Off Charles, and of Cassibaldan,	
Off Havelok, Horne, and of Wade; –	
In romaunces that of hem ben made	
That gestoures often dos of hem gestes	*make them into*
At mangeres and at grete festes.	*meals*
25 Here dedis ben in remembraunce	
In many fair romaunce;	
But of the worthiest wyght in wede	*creature in clothing*
That evere by-strod any stede,	
Spekes no man, ne in romaunce redes	
Off his batayle ne of his dedis.	

(lines 11–30)

The people of Troy greet Helen with a procession and minstrelsy:

Ther was gadered alle the toun	*gathered*
With mochel joye and processioun,	*great*
With alle musik and menstrasye	

(lines 2991–3)

When the siege has been set, there is music all night in the Greeks' camp:

The fires yeven a gret lyght,	*gave*
As of hit hadde ben day-lyght.	
Mynstralles her pipes hente	*took up*
And alle other of instrumente,	
Thei nakered, piped, and blew,	
Unto that the cokkes crew.	*cocks crowed*

(lines 4695–4700)

Music when the Trojans agree to a truce:

Then myght men here many glewes,	*hear many kinds of entertainment*
Pipe and Trompe, and many nakeres,	
Synfan, lute, and citoleres;	*symphonia (musical instrument)*
Ther was so many a daunce.	
Thei made tho gret purvyaunce	*provision*
Off corn and hay, of wyn and otes,	
And thei songen wel merie notes;	

(lines 8214–20)

The Greek leaders would rather discuss plans than hear harp music:

> And that thei myght to-gedur carpe; –   *talk*
> Hit were him levere then note of harpe.   *they preferred*
>
> (lines 8283–4)

The King of Troy sets an image of gold on an altar to the accompaniment of music:

> He sette hit there with mochel song,
> With ffythel, harpe, and mynstrasie,   *fiddle; minstrelsy*
> With mychel merthe and melodye.
>
> (lines 9558–60)

Celebration when Pirrus comes to the Greeks:

> Then myght men here a mechel dyn   *great din*
> Off trompes, pipes, and other glues   *entertainment*
> Among the Gregais and the Grues.
> Gret was the murthe and the melody
> That ther was of menstralcy;
>
> (lines 16594–8)

Libeaus Desconus

The dwarf Theodeleyn, companion to the messenger damsel Elene, is a renowned instrumentalist and storyteller:

> Teandelayn was hys name:
> Well swyde sprong hys name,   *widely known*
> Be north and be southe;
> Myche he couthe of game   *He was skilled at entertainment*
> Wyth sytole, sautrye yn same,   *citole; psaltery*
> Harpe, fydele and crouthe.   *crowd*
> He was a noble dysour   *storyteller*
> Wyth ladyes of valour:
> A mery man of mouthe.
>
> (MS Cotton Caligula A.II, lines 133–41)

Variant instruments:

> Fiddle, crowde, and sowtrye   *psaltery*
> (He was a merry man of mouth),
> Harpe, ribble, and sautrye.   *rebec; psaltery*
>
> (Percy Folio, p. 319)*

Minstrels proclaim the fight between Libeaus and Geffron:

> Her shaftis brosten asondre,   *burst*
> Her dyntis ferden as thonder   *sounded like*

That cometh oute of the skey;
Tabowres and trompours,   *taborers; trumpeters*
Heroudes and dissoures,   *heralds; storytellers*
Her strokys con discrye.   *proclaim*
    (Lambeth Palace Library MS 306, lines 951–6)

Variant performers:

Mynstrals and trompours,
Harpours and gestours,
    (BN MS XIII.B.29, p. 88)*

La Dame Amoure's sorcerous melody:

For the faire lady
Cowthe more of sorcerye   *was able to accomplish more sorcery*
Than other suche fyve;
She made hym suche melodye
Off all maner mynstralsye
That any man myght discryue.   *describe*
    (Lambeth Palace Library MS 306, lines 1485–90)

Variant – diverse melody:

Off many a diverse melody
    (MS Ashmole 61, fol. 52v)*

When Libeaus enters the two clerics' magical castle, he is greeted in the hall by loud instruments:

Trompes, schalmuses   *trumpets; shawms*
He seyth be-for the hyegh deys   *sees; high dais*
Stonde yn hys syghte.
    (MS Cotton Caligula A.II, lines 1762–4)

Variants:

Trumpys, hornys, sarvysse,   *shawm*
Right by-for that highe deys,
He herde and saughe with sight,   *saw*
    (Lambeth Palace Library MS 306, lines 1836–8)

Trumpetts, hornes, and shaumes ywis,
he found before the hye dese,
he heard and saw with sight.

    (Percy Folio, p. 342)*

> Trumpis, pipis, and schalmys
> He hurde bifore the highe deys
> And sawe ham with sight.
>
> (BN MS XIII.B.29, p. 108)*

In the hall of the magical castle, Libeaus sees minstrels with soft instruments, with a torch burning in front of each:

Of mayne mor ne lasse	*household staff*
1775 Ne sawe he body ne face	
But menstrales y-clodeth yn palle.	*clothed in fine cloth*
Wyth harpe, fydele and rote,	
Orgenes and mery note,	
Well mery they maden alle;	
1780 Wyth sytole and sawtrye,	
So moche melodye	
Was never wyth-inne walle.	
Be-fore ech menstrale stod	
A torche fayr and good,	
Brennynge fayre and bryght.	

(Cotton Caligula A.II, lines 1774–85)

Variant instruments:

With harpe, lute and roote	*rote*
And orgone noyse of note,	*sound of organ notes*
Grete gle they maden all;	*music*
With sotill and sawtery,	*citole; psaltery*
Suche maner mynstralsye	

(Lambeth Palace Library MS 306, lines 1851–5)

> With harp, fiddle, and note,
> And alsoo with organ note,
> Great mirth they made all;
> And alsoo fiddle and sautrye.
> Soo much of minstralsye
> Ne say he never in hall.
>
> (Percy Folio, p. 342)*

> With setoll and with sawtry,
> And every maner mynstralci,
> Grete gle they made alle.
> Harpe, pipe, and rote,
> Organs mery of note,
> Was wrete in that walle.
>
> (BN MS XIII.B.29, p. 108)*

Harpe, pype, and rote,
Orgoyne vois with note,
Gret gleo made thay alle;   *music*
with sytole and sawtry,
and such maner mynstralcy,
was never wyght in wold.   *creature*
                                        (Lincoln's Inn MS 150, fol. 11v)*

With fydell and with sautre,
And ilke maner of myntralse,
Grete gle made thei all.
Herpe, pype, and rote,
Orgeynus mery of note,
Was within the walle.
                                        (MS Ashmole 61, fol. 55v)*

When Libeaus sits on the dais in the magical castle, the torches are quenched and
the minstrels are gone:

He sette hym an that deys:
The menstrales wer in pes,   *quiet*
That were so good and trye;   *trusty*
The torches that brende bryght
Quenchede anon ryght: *extinguished*
The menstrales wer aweye.
                                        (Cotton Caligula A.II, lines 1801–6)

Libeaus fights with Mabon, as storytellers tell at meals:

He ranne to mabon ryght
Full fast gan thei fyght
As gestours tellys at bord   *storytellers; at meals*
                                        (MS Ashmole 61, fol. 57r)*

Minstrels receive gifts at the wedding of Libeaus and the Lady of Synadoun:

The menstrales yn bour and halle   *chamber and hall*
Hadde ryche yftes wyth-alle,
And they that weryn un-wrest.   *poor*
                                        (MS Cotton Caligula A.II, lines 2116–18)

The Lyfe of Alisaunder or *King Alisaunder* (couplets)

Olimpias wants to hold a rich feast, including 'jugoleris':

Of knyghtis and ladies honeste
Of burgeys and of jugoleris   *entertainers*

And of men of eche mesteris   *all crafts*

(Lincoln's Inn MS 150, lines 156–8)

Minstrelsy in the town in honour of Olimpias:

> Orgles tymbres al maner gleo   *?organ; timbrel*
> Was dryuen ayeyn that lady freo

(Lincoln's Inn MS 150, lines 189–90)

Music for the wedding of Philip and Cleopatra of Assyria:

> At theo feste was trumpyng
> Pipyng and eke taboryng
> Sytolyng and ek harpyng
> Knyf pleyng and ek syngyng
> Carolyng and turmentyng   *tourneying*

(Lincoln's Inn MS 150, lines 1035–39)

Variant instruments:

> At the fest was harpyng,
> And pipyng and tabournyng,
> And sitollyng and trumpyng,
> Knijf-pleyeyng and syngyng,

(Bodleian MS 1414, lines 1039–42)

Storytelling at a feast to celebrate Philip's reunion with his wife Olimpias:

> There was gynnyng aneowe feste
> And of gleomen mony ageste.   *a story*

(Lincoln's Inn MS 150, lines 1145–6)

Feasting to celebrate Alexander's assurance of his parentage:

> Now bygynnith geste hende
> Murthe is gret in halle
> Damoselis plaien with peoren alle   *all the damsels play with pears*
> Teller of jeste is ofte myslike   *tale; displeased*
> Ribaud festes al so with tripe   *the carouser also feasts on tripe*

(Lincoln's Inn MS 150, lines 1568–72)

Variant performers:

> Now agynneth gestes hende.
> Noyse is gret with tabour and pype,
> Damoysels playen with peren ripe.
> Ribaudes festeth also with tripe;
> The gestour wil oft his mouthe wype.

(MS Laud Misc. 622, lines 1572–6)

After a statement that Alexander provides for Darius's female relatives, a list of lovely images includes music:

> Mury is the styvour   *bagpipe player*
> Mury is the twynkelyng of the harpour
> (Lincoln's Inn MS 150, lines 2555–6)

When Alexander enters the defeated Thebes and begins killing the people, a harper comes before him and makes a lay asking for mercy (but to no effect: Alexander kills every man, woman and child):

> 2825 To fore the kyng com an harpour
>   And made a lay of gret favour   *a verse narrative*
>   In whiche he saide with mury cry
>   Kyng on ows have mercy   *us*
>   Here men was y bore Amphion
> 2830 Fadir of godis everychon
>   Aliber the god of wyne
>   And Hercules of kynne thyne
>   Here hadde the godes of nortour   *upbringing*
>   This toun thow schalt kyng honoure
> 2835 Ayeyns heom thy wraththe adant   *subdue*
>   Yef heom mercy and pes heom grant   *them*
>   (Lincoln's Inn MS 150, lines 2825–36)

Noise of music before battle would drown out thunder:

> No scholde mon have herd the thondur
> For the noise of the taboures
> And the trumpours and jangelours   *entertainers*
> (Lincoln's Inn MS 150, lines 3403–5)

It is enjoyable to hear minstrels in the hall, but Alexander enjoys hearing of unknown lands:

> Mury hit is in halle to here the harpe
> Theo mynstral syngith theo jogolour carpith   *entertainer tells tales*
> Yet thoughte mury kyng Alisaunder
> Of uncouth londis to here sclaunder   *to hear news of unknown lands*
> (Lincoln's Inn MS 150, lines 4714–17)

Feast entertainment:

> Murye they syngyn and daunces maken
> Dysours dalye reisons craken   *storytellers jest and crack jokes*
> (Lincoln's Inn MS 150, lines 5713–14)

Morte Arthure (alliterative)

King Arthur arranges for the Roman senator to be entertained by minstrels after feasting:

> With myrthe and with melodye of mynstralsy noble.
>
> (line 242)

The Roman camp is noisy with German dancers and pipes:

> For dauncesyng of Duchemen and dynnyng of pypez,   *Germans*
> All dynned fore dyn that in the dale hovede.
>
> (line 2030–1)

Octavian (Northern version)

Minstrelsy at a feast held by the Emperor of Rome:

> With gud myrthis tham emange,   *among*
> Harpes, fethils and full faire songe,
> Cytoles and sawtrye,
> Till the sevenyghte was gone
> With alkyn welthis in that wone,   *all manner of abundance; dwelling*
> Of myrthis and mynstralsye.
>
> (Thornton MS, lines 199–204)

Variant instruments:

> Harpe, pype and mery songe,
> Bothe lewte and sawtre.   *lute*
> (CUL MS Ff.2.38, lines 197–8)

When Florent is conducted to his knighting ceremony, his adoptive father Clement beats the minstrels:

> Byfore the emperoure the childe was broghte,
> A kyng one aythir syde.   *on each side*
> The kyng of Fraunce byfore hym yode   *went*
> With mynstralles full many and gode,
> And lede hym up with pryde.
> Clement to the mynstralles gan go
> And gafe some a stroke and some two:
> There durste noghte one habyde.   *abide*
> (Thornton MS, lines 1057–64)

The company of kings take their leave from feasting with music:

> With trowmpes and with lowde songe
> Ilke a man wente to his owun londe,
> With joye and mekill pryde.
>
> (Thornton MS, lines 1620–2)

Octavian (Southern version)

Minstrelsy at the Paris wedding of the Emperor and Florence:

> Ther myghth men here menstralcye,
> Trompys, taborus and cornettys crye, *cornets*
> Roowte, gyterne, lute and sawtrye, *rote*
> Fydelys and othyr mo;
> In Parys greet melodye
> They maden tho.
>
> (lines 67–72)

Minstrels win clothes at Florent's wedding:

> Ryche robes be four and fyyf, *five*
> Ther menstralles wonne; *earned*
>
> (lines 1269–70)

Tales from Rome and France at the wedding:

> Ther was many a ryche jeste *tale*
> Of Rome and Fraunce
>
> (lines 1275–6)

The mantles Clement has taken hostage for the wedding expenses are given to the minstrels:

> The knyghtys logh yn the halle, *laughed*
> The mantellys they yeve menstrales alle; *gave*
>
> (lines 1297–8)

Otuel a Knight

When Otuel is defeated and agrees to become a Christian, Charlemagne celebrates with minstrelsy:

> And makeden murthe and meloudie,
> Of alle maner of menestrausie,
>
> (lines 631–2)

Otuel and Roland

Minstrelsy at Charlemagne's feast in Paris:

> the kyng with hys knyghtys alle
> wenten to parys in-to hys halle
> with moche melodye:
> he held fest ryche and ryall,   *royal*
> for-sothe in the kyngys halle,
> with myrthe and mynstrelsye.
>
> (lines 626–31)

Charlemagne takes the defeated Garcy to Paris with trumpets and dancing:

> Charlys of hym tok goode hede,
> And to parys he dude hym lede,
> with trumpes and daunsyng.
>
> (lines 1677–79)

Partonope of Blois

The unlearned can benefit from old stories that teach us how to behave by hearing them either sung or told in ordinary language:

> To the lewed also, parde,   *uneducated*
> Is goode sum-tyme for to here.   *hear*
> For by herynge he may lere   *by hearing he may learn*
> Thynge that fryste he ne knewe;   *at first*
> And to soche folke olde thynge ys new,
> Whanne hyt ys in gestes songe,   *sung in stories*
> Or els in prose tolde wyth tonge.
>
> (lines 21–7)

Persevis, a damsel in the castle in Salence where Partonope is recovering, is skilled in music, but doesn't like love:

> She couthe wele harpe, singe, and daunce,
> But of love toke she noone hede.
>
> (lines 7617–18)

Final wedding music:

> Many trompe now dothe ther sowne,   *sound*
> Also taketh up many a claryoun.
> Pipes and makers so many assemble,   *?nakers*
> As though all the worlde shuld tremble.
>
> (lines 12164–7)

Reinbrun

The daughter of Argus king of Africa is skilled in minstrelsy:

> Meche she kouthe of menstralcie,
> Of harpe, of fithele, of sautri,
> Of romaunce reding.

(lines 142–4)

No minstrelsy will make Amis's lady rejoice because she has lost her lord:

> For hire lord that she hath lore: *lost*
> Joie ne worth hire never ther-fore   *befell her*
> For non menstralcie.

(lines 829–31)

Richard Coer de Lyon

Initial description of making romances and reading them:

5	It is ful good to here in jeste	
	Off his prowesse and hys conqueste.	
	Ffele romaunses men maken newe,	*Many*
	Off goode knyghtes, stronge and trewe;	
	Off here dedys men rede romaunce,	*their*
10	Bothe in Engeland and in Ffraunce:	
	Off Rowelond, and off Olyver,	
	And off every Doseper;	*paladin*
	Off Alisaundre, and Charlemayn;	
	Off kyng Arthour, and off Gawayn,	
15	How they were knyghtes goode and curteys;	
	Off Turpyn, and of Oger Daneys;	
	Off Troye men rede in ryme,	
	What werre ther was in olde tyme;	*war*
	Off Ector, and off Achylles,	
20	What folk they slowe in that pres.	*slew; battle*
	In Frenssche bookys this rym is wrought,	
	Lewede men ne know it nought –	*uneducated*
	Lewede men cune Ffrensch non,	*do not understand French*
	Among an hondryd unnethis on –;	*scarcely one among a hundred*
25	Nevertheles, with glad chere,	
	Ffele off hem that wolde here	
	Noble jestes, I undyrstonde,	*tales*
	Off doughty knyghtes off Yngelonde.	*England*

(lines 5–28)

Variant:

> Miri it is to heren his stori
> 5   And of him to han in memorie,
> That never no was couward.
> Bokes men maketh of Latyn,
> Clerkes witen what is ther in,   *know*
> Bothe Almaundes and Pikard;
> 10   Romaunce make folk of Fraunce
> Of knightes that were in destaunce,   *armed conflict*
> That dyed thurch dint of sward: *through; sword*
> Of Rouland, and of Oliver,
> And of the other dusse per,   *paladins*
> 15   Of Alisander, and Charlmeyn,
> And Ector, the gret werrer,   *warrior*
> And of Danys le fiz Oger,
> Of Arthour, and of Gaweyn.
> As this romaunce of Freyns wrought,   *created*
> 20   That mani lewed no knowe nought,
> In gest as so we seyn;   *tale*
> This lewed no can Freyns non,
> Among an hundred unnethe on;   *scarcely one*
> In lede is nought to leyn.   *In the land this is not to be hidden.* [*idiom*]
>   (Auchinleck MS, lines 4–24)

Minstrels are present when Princess Cassadorien and her father the King of Antioch disembark and are greeted by King Henry:

> And menstralles with mekyl pryde.

>   (line 148)

Disguised as pilgrims, King Richard and two companions stop in 'Alemayne'. They go to dinner at a tavern, and when they have drunk well, a minstrel comes in and asks if they want to have any minstrelsy. When Richard asks him to go away, the minstrel says they will regret not providing food and drink, since worthy men give minstrels food, wine, and ale; for praise arises from minstrels. The minstrel, who is English, has recognized the three travellers, and he informs the Emperor, who takes them captive:

> Whenne they hadde drunken wel, afyn,
> A mynstralle com ther in,
> 665   And saide: 'Goode men, wyttyrly,   *truly*
> Wole ye have ony mynstralsy?'
> Rychard bad that he scholde goo;
> That turnyd hym to mekyl woo.   *great*
> The mynstralle took in mynde,
> 670   And sayde: 'Ye are men unkynde,

And yiff I may, ye schall forthynk.   *regret*
Ye gaff me neyther mete ne drynk!
Ffor gentyl men scholde bede   *offer*
To mynstrall that abouten yede
675 Off here mete, wyn, and ale:
Ffor los ryses off mynstrale.'   *praise*
He was Ynglysch, and wel hem knew,   *English*
Be speche, and syghte, hyde and hewe.   *complexion and colour*
Forthe he wente in that tyde   *time*
680 To a castell there besyde,
And tolde the kynge all and some,
That thre men were to the cyte come;
...
To hym sayd the kynge: 'Iwys,
That thou haste tolde yf it sothe is,   *if what you have said is true*
Thou shalte have thy warysowne,   *reward*
And chose thyselfe a ryche towne.'
    (Gonville and Caius College Cambridge MS 175/96, lines 651–82 and 691–4;
                    switches to Wynkyn de Worde edition at line 679)

Variant:

Whenne the gos was rosted well,   *goose*
In ther cam a mynstrell,
And if hit hure wille were,   *their*
Of his myrthe for to hure.   *hear*
Ric. hym answerde and scyde: 'Nay,   *Richard*
We mote eten and go oure way!'   *must*
'Ye buthe uncurteys, so me thenke,   *are*
Ye ne biddeth this mynstrel no drynke!
Ye were well better by this day!'
Thus by himselfe he gan to say.   *to himself; said*
His way he taketh faire and wel,
Tille he com to the castell,
Ther the kyng of Almayne was;
And to the porter he made his pas,   *way*
And seyde: 'Wende in an hyying,   *Go quickly*
And sey thus to my lorde the kyng:
Ther buth icom upon his londe   *have come*
Thre palmers, ich understonde,
The strongest men in Cristiante,
And ic wol telle whiche they be.   *I*
...
The porter yede into the halle,
And tolde the lorde thes wordes all.
The kyng was glad of that tythyng,   *tiding*

He swor his othe by hevene kynge,
The mynstrell that hath do this dede,
Full well he shall have his mede.   *reward*

(College of Arms MS Arundel 58, fol. 252v)

After a feast, Richard rewards storytellers and other performers so they will carry his praise:

Afftyr mete, thoo they were glad,
Rychard gaff gyfftes, gret wones,   *plenty*
Gold, and sylvyr, and precyouse stones;
To herawdes, and to dysours,   *heralds; storytellers*
To tabourrers, and to trumpours
Hors and robes to bere his los;   *carry his praise*
Thorwgh here cry his renoun ros,   *their; rose*
Hou he was curteys and ffree.

(lines 3773–80)

As Richard and his ships approach Jaffa, they hear no sound of minstrelsy; they grieve until a wayte plays his 'flagel' (small flute or whistle-pipe):

6745 Kyng R. unto Jaffe was come,   *Richard*
With hys galeyes alle and some.
They lokyd towarde the castel,
They herde no pype ne flagel.   *prob. flageolet*
They drowgh hem nygh to the lande
6750 Yiff they myghte undyrstande;   *(To see) if*
And they ne cowde nought aspye,
Be no voys of menstralsye,   *sound*
That quyk man in the castel ware.   *living*
...
Thus waylys Kyng R. ay   *Richard; continually*
Tyl it were spryng al off the day: *beginning*
A wayte ther com in a kernel,   *crenel*
And pyped a moot in a flagel.   *little bit*
6775 He ne pypyd but on sythe,   *just one time*
He made many an herte blythe.   *glad*
He lokyd doun, and seygh the galeys,   *saw*
Kyng R. and his naveys.   *ships*
Schyppys and galeyes wel he knew;
6780 Thenne a meryere note he blew,
And pypyd: 'Seynyours! or suis! or sus!   *Lords! Wake up! Wake up!*
Kyng R. is icomen to us!'

(lines 6745–53 and 6771–82)

Roland and Vernagu

Roland compares the Trinity to a harp:

> As the harp has thre thinges,
> Wode and soun and strenges,   *wood and sound and strings*
> And mirthe is ther tille,
> So is god persones thre,
> And holeliche on in unite,   *wholly one*
>   (lines 707–11)

The Romauns of Partenay (Lusignan)

Minstrelsy for the wedding of Melusine and Raymond includes loud and soft instruments:

> In that place was had ful gret mynstracy;
> Both hye and bas instrumentes sondry;   *loud and soft*
>   (lines 944–5)

The nobles of Luxemburg greet Anthony and Raynold with instrumental sound:

> Of whome the instrumentes sounded at end,
>
> …
>
> To the sounde that thes instrumentes gan make;
> The nobles and gentiles comyng thaim agayne.
>   (lines 1817 and 1821–2)

When Melusine departs, she bids farewell to the sound of instruments:

> Adieu, the suete sound of ech instrument!   *sweet*
>   (line 3856)

The Seege of Troye

At Alisaunder's wedding with Elayne, the minstrelsy contrasts with Elayne's grief:

> Ther was joye and melodye
> Of alle skynnes menstracye,   *kinds of*
> Of trompe, tabour, harpe, and crouth,   *crowd*
> And mony mury dissour of mouth;   *storyteller*
> Ther weore yeve many yeftes, for theo nones, *given; gifts; on the occasion*
> Of gold, seolver, and preciouse stones.
> Theo murgere that ilke mon made   *the merrier; each*
> Theo more sorowe Dame Elayne hade.
>   (Lincoln's Inn MS, lines 803–10)

Variant performers:

> Trompes, nakers, and crowth,
> And mony a mery song with mouth;
>
> (Egerton MS, lines 805–6)

> Cruppe and tabur, harp and sautrie –   *?crowd*
>
> (Arundel MS, lines 805)

The Siege of Jerusalem

When Vespasian is cured of his wasps, the celebration includes 'piping':

> Than was pypyng and play,
>
> (line 257)

After battle against Jerusalem, although they are wounded, the Romans feast with music and dancing:

> Bot daunsyng and no deil with dynnyng of pipis
> And the nakerer noyse alle the nyght-tyme.
>
> (lines 855–6)

Sir Cleges

Minstrels at Sir Cleges's Christmas feasts are richly rewarded:

> Mynstrellus wold not be-hynd,
> Myrthys wer thei may fynd,   *where*
> That is most to ther pay.   *that pleases them most*
> Mynstrellus, when the fest was don,
> Schuld not with-outyn gyftes gon,
> That wer both rych and gode,
> Hors and robys and rych rynges,
> Gold and sylver and other thynges,
> To mend with ther mode.   *to improve their mood*
>
> (MS Ashmole 61, lines 46–54)

Sir Cleges hears minstrelsy as he mourns his lost wealth:

> And as he walkyd uppe and done
> Sore sygheng, he herd a sowne   *sighing; sound*
> Off dyverse mynstralsy,
> Off trumpers, pypers, and nakerners,
> Off herpers, notys and gytherners,
> Off sytall and of sautrey.

Many carrals and grete dansyng   *carols*
In every syde herd he syng,

(MS Ashmole 61, lines 97–104)

Variant instruments:

Of trompus, pypes and claraneres,   *clarions*
Of harpis, luttes and getarnys,
A sotile and sawtre

(MS Advocates 19.1.11)

A harper sings a geste to the king; when the king asks him to identify the poor visitor, the harper recognizes Cleges:

The Kyng was sett in hys parlere,   *chamber*
Myrth and revell forto here;
Syre Cleges theder wente.
An harper had a geyst i-seyd,   *tale; recounted*
485 That made the Kyng full wele a-payd,   *pleased*
As to hys entente.
Than seyd the Kyng to this herpere:
'Mykyll thou may ofte tyme here,   *You may often hear many things*
Fore thou hast ferre wente.   *because you have travelled far.*
490 Tell me trew, if thou can:
Knowyst thou thys pore man,
That this dey me presente?'
He seyd: 'My lege, with-outen les,   *liege; lies*
Som-tyme men callyd hym Cleges;   *Once*
495 He was a knyght of youre.   *yours*
I may thinke, when that he was
Full of fortone and of grace,
A man of hye stature.'

(MS Ashmole 61, lines 481–98)

Variant – The harper's geste is about Sir Cleges; the king asks for news of Cleges, and the harper says minstrels miss him since he went away:

An harpor sange a gest be mowth
Of a knyght ther be sowth,   *from the south*
Hym-selffe, werament.   *in truth*
Than seyd the kynge to the harpor:
'Were ys knyght Cleges, tell me herr;   *Where; here*
For thou hast wyde i-went.
Tell me trewth, yf thou can:
Knowyste thou of that man?'
The harpor seyd: 'Yee, iwysse!
Sum tyme for soth I hym knewe;
He was a knyght of youres full trewe

And comly of gesture.
We mynstrellys mysse hym sekyrly,   *assuredly*
Seth he went out of cunntre;   *since*
He was fayr of stature.'

(MS Advocates 19.1.11)

Sir Degare

The lady or her maiden plays the harp for Degare in a chamber while he drinks wine:

Into the chaumbre he com ful sone.   *soon*
The leuedi on here bedde set   *lady*
And a maide at here fet   *feet*
And harpede notes gode and fine;
Another broughte spices and wine.
Upon the [bed] he set adoun
To here of the harpe soun.   *sound*
For murthe of [the] notes so sschille   *clear or high-pitched*
He fel adoun on slepe stille:
So he slepte al that night.

(Auchinleck MS, lines 836–45)

Variant – The lady is the only performer:

The lady was both fayr and brygth.   *bright*
Sche set hur amyddys the bed ryght;
Sche harpyd the notys good and fyn.
A mayd fyllyd the pese wyth wyn,   *cup*
And Syr Degare set hym down
to here of the harpys sown.
Thorow the notys that sche harpyd schryll   *clear / high-pitched*
He fyl down and sclept hys fyll.   *slept*

(MS. Rawl. Poet 34, f. 15v)*

In response to the lady's teasing about falling asleep, Degare blames the harp:

For godes love foryif hit me!   *forgive*
Certes, the murie harpe hit made;   *Certainly; caused it*
Elles misdo nowt [I] ne hade.   *otherwise I would not have done wrong*

(Auchinleck MS, lines 858–60)

Variant – The harp or the wine caused him to sleep:

The notys of thy harp yt mad
Other ells the good wyn that y hadd.

(MS. Rawl. Poet 34, fol. 16r)*

Sir Degrevant

Sir Degrevant is a skilled musician:

> He was faire and free,
> And gretly gaf hym to glee:
> To cetoyle and to sawtree
> And gytternyng full gaye;
> Wele to playe on a rotte,   *rote*
> To syng many newe note,
> And of harpyng, wele I wote,
> He wane the pryse aye.
>
> > (Thornton MS, lines 33–40)

Variant instruments:

> To harp and to sautre
> And geterne full gay;
> Well to play on a rote,
> Off lewtyng, well y wote,   *luting*
> And syngyng many seyt not   *sweet note*
> > (CUL MS Ff.i.6)

Degrevant rewards minstrels, and they spread songs about him:

> Gestis redy for to calle
> To here mynstralls in haulle,
> He gafe tham robis of palle,
> Bothe golde and fee;
> In ylke lande whare he come,   *each*
> When he went oghte fra home,
> Thay hafe haldyn up his name
> With mekill melody;
>
> > (Thornton MS, lines 85–92)

Degrevant pays minstrels from his tournament winnings:

> A hundrethe pownde and a stede   *hundred pounds; horse*
> He sent mynstrals to mede;   *reward*
> Of gyftis was he [n]ever gnede   *stingy*
> In wele na in waa.   *woe*
> > (Thornton MS, lines 1173–6)

Degrevant gives battle spoils to minstrels:

> Sir Degrevaunt tuke the stede,
> Gaff hym mynstrals to mede,
>
> > (Thornton MS, lines 1345–6)

Myldor entertains Degrevant during supper:

> And ever Mildor sett
> And harped notys full suete,
> And otherwhile scho ete
> Als hir will ware.
> Scho sang songes a-bove,
> And other mirthis ynewe,   *enough*
> In the chambyrs of love
> Thus thay sla kare.   *slay care*
>
> (Thornton MS, lines 1432–40)

The minstrel (in contrast with the foresters) holds his peace about the lovers:

> The waytis blewe one the walle,
> The Erlis awen mynstralle
> Thow thay went to the haulle,
> And thare thay gun habyde.   *abide*
> The mynstralle helde his pesse,   *peace*
> To no man he it sayse
> (Mynstrals are ay curtayse
> Als thay ere kende to be).   *as they are believed to be*
>
> (Thornton MS, lines 1581–8)

Variant:

> So dud the weyt on the wall,   *watchman*
> The Eorlus owne mynstrall
> Sey tham wende to the hall,
> And wyst nevere what hyt mende.
> The pypere haldus hys pays,
> Tyl no man he hyt says
> (Mynstralus shuld be cortays
> And skyl that thei ben).   *it is reasonable*
>
> (CUL MS Ff.i.6)

A dance representing the paladins is performed at the wedding of Degrevant and Myldor; gifts are given to minstrels:

> Thare come in a daunce
> Alle the dugepers of France;
> Me thynk swylke a purveance   *such a provision*
> Was gay to be-halde.
> …
> Alle the mynstrals in the haulle
> He gaffe tham robis of palle,

And other gyftis with-alle –
Germentes alle halle.

(Thornton MS, lines 1869–72 and 1877–80)

Sir Eglamour of Artois

Minstrels are rewarded at the final double wedding:

> Mynstrelles co[m]e fro fere lond: *far*
> Thay hadde ryche gyftes, I unthurstond:
> In hert they were lyght.
>
> …
>
> Mynstralles that were ther in that stownd   *time*
> Ther gyftus were worth an hondred pownd,
> The boldere myght they spende.

(MS Cotton Caligula A.ii, lines 1363–5 and 1372–4)

Sir Firumbras (Fillingham)

As the French return home, the joy of hearing minstrelsy is compared with the joy of fighting Saracens:

> Ful mery it is to here the harpe,
> Dysours and mynstrels to synge and to carpe.   *storytellers*
> 'Ful mery it is', thought Roulond,
> 'To fyght a-yen the sarsins and to don hem schond.'   *destruction*

(lines 416–19)

Sir Gawain and the Green Knight

The Christmas feast is introduced with music:

> Then the first cors come with crakkyng of trumpes,   *blaring*
> Wyth mony baner ful bryght that therbi henged;
> Nwe nakryn noyse with the noble pipes,   *noise of nakers*
> Wylde werbles and wyght wakned lote,   *wavering pitches; lively;*
>   *awakened noise*
> That mony hert ful highe hef at her towches.   *lifted; phrases of music*

(lines 116–20)

The Christmas feast involves all kinds of food and minstrelsy:

> Wyth alle maner of mete and mynstralcie bothe,

(line 484)

At the Christmas feast in Bertilak's hall, there is music:

> Trumpez and nakerys,
> Much pypyng ther repayres;   *is present*
>
> (lines 1016–17)

Minstrelsy at the feast after the third hunt:

> With merthe and mynstralsye, wyth metez at hor wylle,
>
> (line 1952)

Sir Gowther

Music and dancing at the victory feast after the second battle contrasts with tired Gowther lying down:

> They pypud and trompud in tho hall,
> Knyghtus and ladys dancyd all
> Befor that mynstralsy.
> Syr Gwother in his chambur ley,   *lay*
> He lyst nowdur dance ne pley,   *desired neither to*
> For he was full wery,   *weary*
>
> (MS Advocates 19.3.1, lines 529–34)

Sir Isumbras

Isumbras rewards minstrels:

> Glewmen he luffede wele in haulle   *Entertainers; loved*
> And gafe tham riche robis of palle,   *fine fabric*
> Bothe golde and also fee.
>
> (lines 19–21)

Variants:

> Menstralles he lovyd wel in halle
>
> (Gonville and Caius College Cambridge MS 175)*

> Harpers loved hym in hall
> With other mynstrelles all,
> For he gave them golde and fee.
>
> (MS Douce 261)*

> He loved wyll gle men in hall
>
> (MS Advocates 19.3.1)*

> Sylver, golde, and fee.
>
> (MS Cotton Caligula A.II)*

And gyftys of glytering gold.

(MS Ashmole 61)*

Isumbras sees minstrels riding with knights:

As he went hym selvun a lone	*himself alone*
Of mynstrell he herd gud wone	*a great many*
On every syde	
Then he saw rydand in felde	
mony semely undur schelde	
That knythtis wer hym thoghth	*seemed to him to be knights*

(MS Advocates 19.3.1, fol. 52r [near Schleich line 432])*

Musicians rewarded at reunion feast:

Trompetys and pypys all
That wer that tyme in hall
hadun robys mony folde

(MS Advocates 19.3.1, fol. 55v [near Schleich line 10])*

Isumbras and his family are welcomed with music:

With gret honour thei dyd them welcom,	
With trumpys, pype, and with schalmewon,	*shawms*

(MS Ashmole 61, lines 805 6 [near Schleich line 787])*

Sir Landeval

Landeval clothes minstrels:

Landevale clothys the pore gestes,	*gestours*

(line 172)

Sir Launfal

Launfal clothes minstrels:

Fyfty clodede gestours	*clothed*

(line 430)

Minstrels play when Guinevere and her ladies come down to dance with the knights:

They hadde menstrales of moch honours,	
Fydelers, sytolyrs and trompours –	
And elles hyt were unryght;	*otherwise it would not be right*

(lines 667–9)

Sir Orfeo

In the spring, the Britons made diverse narrative lays set to harp music:

	The Brytans, as the boke seys,	
	Off diverse thingys thei made ther leys:	
	Som thei made of herpyngys,	*harping*
10	And som of other diverse thingys;	
	Som of werre and som off wo,	*war*
	Som of myrthys and joy also;	
	Som of trechery and som of gyle,	
	Som of happys that felle som-whyle,	*occurrences; befell*
15	And som be of rybawdry,	
	And many ther ben off fary;	*Faerie*
	Off all the venturys men here or se	
	Most off luffe, for-soth, thei be,	*love*
	That in the leys ben i-wrought,	
20	Fyrst fond and forth brought.	
	Off aventours that fell som-deys	
	The Bretonys ther-of made ther leys,	
	Off kyngys that be-fore us were;	
	When thei myght any wondres here	
25	They lete them wryte as it wer do,	
	And ther-among is Syr Orfewo	

(MS Ashmole 61, lines 7–26)

Variant:

	We redyn ofte and fynde y-w[ryte,]	
	As clerkes don us to wyte,	*give us to understand*
	The layes that ben of harpyng	
	Ben y-founde of frely thing:	*strange*
5	Sum ben of wele and sum of wo,	
	And sum of joy and merthe also;	
	Sum of bourdys, and sum of rybaudy,	*jokes* or *tricks*
	And sum ther ben of the feyré;	
	Sum of trechery, and sum of gyle,	
10	And sum of happes that fallen by whyle;	
	Of alle thing that men may se	
	Moost to lowe, forsothe, they be.	*love*
	In Brytayn this layes arne y-wrytt,	
	Furst y-founde and forthe y-gete,	
15	Of aventures that fallen by dayes,	
	Wherof Brytouns made her layes.	
	When they myght owher heryn	*anywhere*
	Of aventures that ther weryn,	

They toke her harpys wyth game,
20   Maden layes and yaf it name.
Of aventures that han be-falle
Y can sum telle, but nought all:
Herken, lordyngys that ben trewe,
And y wol you telle of Syr Orphewe.

(MS Harley 3810, lines 1–24)

Orfeo honours harpers and himself plays the harp:

He was, for-soth, a nobull kyng,	
That most luffyd gle and herpyng;	
Wele sekyr was every gode herper	*certain*
30 To have off mekyll honour.	
Hym-selve he lernyd forto herpe,	*harp*
And leyd ther-on hys wytte so scherpe;	*sharp*
He lernyd so wele, wyth-outen les,	*lying*
So gode herper never non was.	
35 In all thys werld was no man bore	*born*
That had Kyng Orfeo ben be-fore	
(And he myght hys herpe here)	
Bot he wold wene that it were	
A blyssed-full note of Paradys,	*blissful melody from*
40 Suche melody ther-in is.	

(MS Ashmole 61, lines 27–40)

In good weather Orfeo plays the harp during his ten-year exile; animals and birds are drawn to the sound of his music:

His harp, where-on was al his gle,	
He hidde in an holwe tre,	*hollow*
And when the weder was clere and bright	*weather*
270 He toke his harp to him wel right	
And harped at his owhen wille.	*own*
In-to alle the wode the soun gan schille,	*wood; sound; resound loudly*
That alle the wilde bestes that ther beth	
For joie abouten him thai teth,	*draw near*
275 And alle the foules that ther were	
Come and sete on ich a brere,	*briar*
To here his harping a fine	
– So miche melody was ther in;	
And when he his harping lete wold,	*stop*
280 No best bi him abide nold.	*beast*

(Auchinleck MS, lines 267–80)

Variant – includes tuning the harp before playing:

> And temperyd hys herpe wyth a mery sounne,   *tuned*
>
> (MS Ashmole 61, line 274)

Sometimes Orfeo sees groups of dancers and minstrels in the wilderness:

> Knightes and leuedis com daunceing   *ladies*
> In queynt atire, gisely,   *skilfully*
> Queynt pas and softly;   *elegant step*
> Tabours and trunpes yede hem bi,   *trumpets*
> And al maner menstraci.
>
> (Auchinleck MS, lines 298–302)

Variant instruments:

> Taberis and pypes yeden hem by,
>
> (Harley MS 3810)

Disguised as a minstrel, Orfeo gains entrance at the King of Faerie's castle:

> Orfeo knokketh atte gate;
> The porter was redi ther-ate,
> And asked what he wold have y-do.
> 'Parfay!' quath he, 'Icham a minstrel, lo!   *indeed; I am*
> To solas thi lord with mi gle,
> Yif his swete wille be.'
>
> (Auchinleck MS, lines 379–84)

Variant – Orfeo promises entertainment to the porter instead of the king:

> To solas the with my gle
> – The merier schalt thou be.
>
> (Harley MS 3810)

Orfeo, as a minstrel, comes before the King of Faerie. When challenged, he points out that minstrels cannot be particular about where they play. The king is so impressed by his harp playing, he asks Orfeo to name his reward:

> 'O lord', he seyd, 'yif it thi wille were,
> 420 Mi menstraci thou schust y-here.'   *should hear*
> The king answerd: 'What man artow   *are you*
> That art hider y-comen now?   *are come hither*
> Ich, no non that is with me,
> No sent never after the.
> 425 Seththen that ich here regni gan   *since; rule*
> Y no fond never so fole-hardi man
> That hider to ous durst wende,   *dared*
> Bot that ichim wald of-sende.'   *unless I sent for him*
> 'Lord', quath he, 'Trowe ful wel,   *believe*

430 Y nam bot a pouer menstrel;   *I am only*
   And, Sir, it is the maner of ous   *it is our custom*
   To seche mani a lordes hous:
   Thei we nought welcom no be,   *although we are not welcome*
   Yete we mot proferi forth our gle.'   *must offer*
435 Bifor the king he sat adoun
   And tok his harp so miri of soun,
   And tempreth his harp as he wele can,   *tunes*
   And blisseful notes he ther gan,   *began (to play)*
   That al that in the palays were
440 Com to him forto here,
   And liggeth adoun to his fete,   *lie*
   Hem thenketh his melody so swete.   *His melody seems so sweet to them.*
   The king herkneth and sitt ful stille;
   To here his gle he hath gode wille.
445 Gode bourde he hadde of his gle;   *delight*
   The riche quen al-so hadde he.   *queen; she*
   When he hadde stint his harping   *stopped*
   Than seyd to him the king:
   'Menstrel, me liketh wele thi gle.
450 Now aske of me what it be,
   Largelich ichil the pay: *I will pay you generously*
   Now speke and tow might asay.'   *you can test this*
                                    (Auchinleck MS, lines 419–52)

Orfeo maintains his minstrel disguise with his beggar landlord and his own wife:

   (To him and to his owhen wiif)   *own wife*
   As a minstrel of pouer liif,
                                    (Auchinleck MS, lines 485–6)

Variant:

   As an herpere off pore lyffe,
                                    (MS Ashmole 61, line 475)

Orfeo, disguised as a foreign harper, asks for help from his steward, who takes him home. Orfeo plays among the minstrels in his own hall, and his steward recognizes his harp. Orfeo makes up a story about finding the harp where a man had been killed by wild animals:

   And, as he yede in the strete,
510 With his steward he gan mete,
   And loude he sett on him a cric:
   'Sir steward!' he seyd, 'Merci!
   Icham an harpour of hethenisse: *foreign parts*
   Help me now in this destresse!'

515   The steward seyd: 'Com with me, come!
      Of that ichave thou schalt have some.   *I have*
      Everich gode harpour is welcom me to
      For mi lordes love, Sir Orfeo.'
      In the castel the steward sat atte mete,
520   And mani lording was bi him sete.
      Ther were trompours and tabourers,
      Harpours fele, and crouders: *crowders*
      Miche melody thai maked alle,
      And Orfeo sat stille in the halle
525   And herkneth; when thai ben al stille   *quiet*
      He toke his harp and tempred schille.   *tuned it accurately*
      The blissefulest notes he harped there
      That ever ani man y-herd with ere:
      Ich man liked wele his gle.
530   The steward biheld, and gan y-se,
      And knewe the harp als blive: *quickly*
      'Menstral!' he seyd, 'So mot thou thrive,
      Where hadestow this harp and hou?
      Y pray that thou me telle now.'
535   'Lord!' quath he, 'In uncouthe thede,   *unknown country*
      Thurch a wildernes as y yede,
      Ther y founde in a dale
      With lyouns a man to-torn smale,   *a man torn to small pieces by lions*
      And wolves him frete with teth so scharp;   *devoured*
540   Bi him y fond this ich harp,   *same*
      Wele ten yere it is y-go.'   *ago*

                    (Auchinleck MS, lines 509–41)

The Queen is brought into town in a procession with minstrelsy:

      And seththen, with gret processioun,   *afterward*
      Thai brought the quen in-to the toun,
      With al maner menstraci.
      Lord! Ther was grete melody!

                    (Auchinleck MS, lines 587–90)

Concludes with a statement that Breton harpers made this lay, a good story with a sweet melody:

      Harpours in Bretaine after than   *Brittany*
      Herd hou this mervaile bigan,
      And made her-of a lay of gode likeing,
      And nempned it after the king.   *named*
      That lay 'Orfeo' is y-hote: *called*
      Gode is the lay, swete is the note.   *melody*

                    (Auchinleck MS, lines 597–602)

Sir Torrent of Portyngale

Minstrelsy at a feast in the court of the King of Provyns:

Menstrelles was them a-monge,	
Trompettes, harpys, and myrre songe,	*merry*
Delycyous nottis on hyght.	*melodies*
	(lines 942–4)

Variant instruments:

With harpe, fedyll and songe,	
	(MS Douce, line 943)

Minstrelsy at a feast at the jousts at Jerusalem:

Tho they held a gestonye,	*celebration*
With all maner of mynstralsye,	
Tyll the Sevynth day.	
	(lines 2374–6)

Sir Tristrem

Music is prominent among the accomplishments Rohand teaches Tristrem:

He taught him ich a lede	*every song (lied)*
Of ich maner of glewe	*every style of music*
And everich playing thede,	*?every country's style of playing*
Old lawes and new.	*?both the old rules and the new*
	(lines 289–92)

After his first meal at King Mark's court, Tristrem surpasses a harper in performance:

An harpour made a lay	
That Tristrem aresound he.	*berated*
The harpour yede oway,	*gave way (to Tristrem)*
'Who better can, lat se.'	*let us see*
555 'Bot Y the mendi may,	*Unless I can surpass your performance*
Wrong than wite Y the.'	*I blame you wrongly*
The harpour gan to say,	
'The maistri give Y the	*I give you the victory*
Ful sket.'	*quickly*
560 Bifor the kinges kne	
Tristrem is cald to set.	
Blithe weren thai alle	
And merkes gun thai minne,	*distinguishing characteristics;*
	observe (in Tristrem)

Token leve in the halle
565 Who might the child winne.
Mark gan Tristrem calle,
Was comen of riche kinne;
He gaf him robe of palle   *cloak*
And pane of riche skinne
570 Ful sket.
His chaumber he lith inne   *goes into*
And harpeth notes swete.

(lines 551–72)

Wounded Tristrem plays music in the boat:

In his schip was that day
Al maner of gle
And al maner of lay
In lond that might be.

(lines 1189–92)

Tristrem's musical accomplishments and rich instruments astonish the Irish:

His gles weren so sellike   *marvellous*
That wonder thought hem thare.   *it seemed to them*
His harp, his croude was rike,   *precious*

(lines 1224–6)

Tristrem's skill as a musician makes him desired in private chambers, and he
teaches the king's daughter until no knight can equal her:

He made his play aloft;   *He began to play his music*
His gamnes he gan kithe.   *entertainment; demonstrate*
1250 Forthi was Tristrem oft
To boure cleped fele sithe   *called many times to a chamber*
To sete.
Ich man was lef to lithe,   *eager to listen*
His mirthes were so swete.
1255 The king had a douhter dere;
That maiden Ysonde hight   *was called*
That gle was lef to here   *was eager to hear music*
And romaunce to rede aright.   *and to read romances correctly*
Sir Tramtris hir gan lere   *teach*
1260 Tho with al his might   *then*
What alle pointes were,   *techniques*
To se the sothe in sight,
To say.
In Yrlond nas no knight   *Ireland; there was*
1265 With Ysonde durst play,   *dared to complete with Ysonde in playing*

(lines 1248–65)

Tristrem teaches Ysonde options for performing lays:

> Ysonde he dede understand
> What alle playes were
> In lay.

(lines 1283–85)

When Tristrem's identity is discovered, he asserts he taught Isonde to play and sing:

> Tho Y Tramtris hight,
> Y lerde [MS lerld] the play and song,   *taught*

(lines 1607–8)

An Irish Harper wins Ysonde with his harping; Tristrem wins her back with his rote playing:

Fram Irlond to the King	
1810 An harpour com bituen.	*arrived*
An harp he gan forth bring,	
Swiche no hadde thai never sen	
With sight.	
Himself, withouten wen,	*doubt*
1815 Bar it day and night.	
Ysonde he loved in are,	*honourably*
He that the harp brought.	
About his hals he it bare;	*neck*
Richelich it was wrought.	*richly*
1820 He hidde it evermare,	*always*
Out no com it nought.	
'Thine harp whi wiltow spare,	*Why won't you play your harp*
Yif thou therof can ought	*if; can perform anything*
Of gle?'	
1825 'Out no cometh it nought	
Withouten giftes fre.'	*generous*
Mark seyd, 'Lat me se	
Harpi hou thou can	*how you can play the harp*
And what thou askest me	
1830 Give Y schal the than.'	
'Blethely', seyd he;	*Gladly*
A miri lay he bigan.	
'Sir King, of giftes fre,	
Herwith Ysonde Y wan	
1835 Bidene.	*forthwith*
Y prove the for fals man	
Or Y schal have thi Quen.'	*unless*
…	

Tho was Tristrem in ten	*in distress*
1850 And chidde with the King:	*scolded*
'Gifstow glewemen thi Quen?	*Do you give your queen to entertainers?*
Hastow no nother thing?'	*Don't you have anything else (to give)?*
His rote, withouten wen,	*rote*
He raught bi the ring;	*seized*
1855 Tho folwed Tristrem the ken	*bold*
To schip ther thai hir bring	
So blithe.	
Tristrem bigan to sing,	
And Ysonde bigan to lithe.	*listen*
1860 Swiche song he gan sing	
That hir was swithe wo.	*very sorrowful*
Her com swiche lovelonging,	
Hir hert brast neighe ato.	*almost broke in two*
Th'erl to hir gan spring	
1865 With knightes mani mo	
And seyd, 'Mi swete thing,	
Whi farestow so,	
Y pray?'	
Ysonde to lond most go	
1870 Er sche went oway.	*before*
'Within a stounde of the day	*brief time*
Y schal ben hole and sounde.	
Ich here a menstrel; to say,	*hear*
Of Tristrem he hath a soun.'	
1875 Th'erl seyd, 'Dathet him ay	*damn him forever*
Of Tristrem yif this stounde.	
That minstrel for his lay	
Schal have an hundred pounde	
Of me	
1880 Yif he wil with ous founde,	*go with us*
Lef, for thou lovest his gle.'	
His gle al for to here	
The levedi was sett on land	
To play bi the rivere;	
1885 Th'erl ladde hir bi hand.	
Tristrem, trewe fere,	*companion*
Mirie notes he fand	*played*
Opon his rote of yvere	*ivory*
As thai were on the strand	*shore*
1890 That stounde.	*time*
Thurch that semly sand	*Through; lovely sound*
Ysonde was hole and sounde.	
Hole sche was and sounde	

Thurch vertu of his gle.
1895 Forthi th'erl that stounde,
Glad a man was he.
Of penis to hundred pounde   *two hundred pounds in coins (pence)*
He gaf Tristrem the fre.
To schip than gun thai founde;   *go*
1900 In Yrlond wald thai be
Ful fain,   *gladly*
Th'erl and knightes thre
With Ysonde and Bringwain.
Tristrem tok his stede
1905 And lepe theron to ride.
The Quen bad him her lede
To schip him biside.
Tristrem dede as hye bede;   *did as she asked*
In wode he gan hir hide.   *He hid her in the woods*
1910 To th'erl he seyd, 'In that nede
Thou hast ytent thi pride,   *lost*
Thou dote.   *fool*
With thine harp thou wonne hir that tide;
Thou tint hir with mi rote.'   *lost*
1915 Tristrem with Ysonde rade   *rode*
Into the wode oway.
A loghe thai founden made   *dwelling*
Was ful of gamen and play.
Her blis was ful brade,   *plentiful*
1920 And joieful was that may.   *woman*
Seven night thai thare abad   *remained*
And seththen to court com thai.   *afterward*
'Sir King',
Tristrem gan to say,
1925 'Gif minstrels other thing.'   *something else*
(lines 1809–37 and 1849–1925)

Minstrels at the wedding of Boniface and a lady from Lyon:

Ther was miche solas
Of alle maner soun
And gle
Of minestrals up and doun
Bifor the folk so fre.

(lines 2856–60)

Back in England Tristrem harps a song in praise of Ysonde:

> Tristrem made a song
> That song Ysonde the sleighe   *sang; wise*
> And harped ever among.   *continuously while she sang*
>   (lines 3026–8)

The Squyr of Lowe Degre

The King of Hungary notes, among symptoms of grief, that his daughter no longer harps and sings:

> Ye were wont to harpe and syng,   *accustomed to*
> And be the meriest in chambre comyng;
>
>   (lines 715–16)

To cheer up his daughter the King of Hungary promises her a hunting trip, and she will have minstrelsy when she rides out hunting:

> Ye shall have harpe, sautry, and songe,
> And other myrthes you amonge;
>
>   (lines 751–2)

The King of Hungary promises that after her hunting trip, his daughter will have entertainment, both secular and sacred:

> Whan you come home, your men amonge,
> Ye shall have revell, daunces, and songe,
> Lytle chyldren, great and smale,
> Shall syng as doth the nyghtyngale.
> Than shall ye go to your evensong,
> With tenours and trebles among;
> …
> Your quere nor organ songe shall wante   *choir; lack*
> With countre-note and dyscant, *polyphonic lines; descant*
> The other halfe on orgayns playeng,
> With yonge chyldren full fayre syngyng.
>   (lines 777–82 and 789–92)

The King of Hungary includes a musical barge trip in his plan to cheer up his daughter:

> A barge shall mete you full ryght
> With twenti-thre ores full bryght,   *oars*
> With trompettes and with claryowne,
> The fresshe water to rowe up and downe.
>
>   (lines 811–14)

In the King of Hungary's cheering-up plan, mariners sing on a larger ship on salt water:

> Your maryners shall synge arowe   *mariners; in a canon*
> 'Hey how and rumbylawe.'
>
>   (lines 823–4)

The King of Hungary's cheering-up plan concludes with minstrels staying up to play if his daughter cannot fall asleep:

> And yf ye no rest may take,
> All night minstrelles for you shall wake.
>
>   (lines 851–2)

There is mirth and melody of many instruments when the squire is united with the daughter of the King of Hungary:

> There was myrth and melody
> With harpe, getron, and sautry,   *gittern*
> With rote, ribible, and clokarde,   *rebec; chimes*
> With pypes, organs, and bumbarde,   *shawm*
> With other mynstrelles them amonge,
> With sytolphe and with sautry songe,   *citole*
> With fydle, recorde, and dowcemere,   *recorder; dulcimer*
> With trompette and with claryon clerc,
> With dulcet pipes of many cordes: *sweet; notes / concordant intervals*
> In chambre revelyng all the lordes,
> Unto morne that it was daye.
>
>   (lines 1069–79)

Syre Gawene and the Carle of Carelyle

The Carle's daughter plays the harp and sings stories in the hall at supper (before sleeping with Gawain):

> Then sayde the Carle to that bryght of ble,   *face*
> 'Wher ys thi harpe thou schuldist have broght wytt the?
> Why hast thou hit forgette?'
> Anon hit was fett into the hall,   *At once; fetched*
> And a feyr cher wyttall   *chair as well*
> Befor her fador was sett.   *She was seated before her father.*
> The harpe was of maser fyne;   *maple*
> The pynnys wer of golde, I wene;   *tuning pegs*
> Serten, wyttout lett   *delay*
> First sche harpyd, and sethe songe   *then sang*

Of love and of Artorrus armus amonge,
How they togeydor mett.

(lines 427–38)

When Arthur returns with Gawain to the Carle's castle, they are greeted with music:

Trompettis mette hem at the gate,
Clarions of silver redy therate,
Serteyne wythoutyn lette –
Harpe fedylle, and sawtry,
Lute, geteron, and [menstrelcy].   *gittern*
Into the halle knyghtis hem fett.

(lines 595–600)

After the wedding feast, minstrels are rewarded:

The mynstrellis had geftys fre
That they myght the better be
To spende many a day.

(lines 643–5)

The Taill of Rauf Coilyear

Minstrels play before Charlemagne at the Christmas feast in Paris:

Befoir that mirthfull man menstrallis playis;

(line 357)

Titus and Vespasian

Minstrelsy when Vespasian is cured of wasps:

And when he felde hym hool and clene
Men myght mychell joye there seene
Of all manere of mynstracye.

(lines 2545–7)

The Tournament of Tottenham

Trumpeting is among market day entertainment:

Ther trumped Tomkyn

(line 17)

Melody of six men's song at the wedding feast:

> Mekyl myrth was them amang,
> In every corner of the hous
> Was melody delycyous,
> For to here precyus,
> Of six menys sang.

(lines 230–4)

The Weddynge of Sir Gawen and Dame Ragnell

Minstrels from different countries at the wedding feast:

> Ther were mynstralles of diverse contrey.

(line 628)

William of Palerne

Minstrelsy is used to prepare people for battle:

> bugles and bemes men gun blowe fast,   *trumpets*
> and alle maner menstracie there was mad thanne
> for to hardien the hertes of here heigh burnes.   *warriors*

(lines 1154–6)

After battle, the Emperor of Rome and his army relax and are entertained by minstrelsy:

> and holliche thanne with his host hiyede to here tentes   *went; their tents*
> with merthe of alle menstracye, and made hem attese   *at ease*

(lines 1294–5)

When the Emperor of Greece and the wedding contingent ride into Rome, they are greeted with minstrelsy:

> and alle maner menstracie maked him ayens;
> and also daunces disgisi redi dight were,   *?masked; were prepared*
> and selcouth songes to solas here hertes,   *marvellous*

(lines 1619–21)

Minstrelsy for wedding procession to church:

> Alle maner of menstracye maked was sone,
> and alle merthe that any man ever might devise;
> and alle real reveles rinkes rif bigunne,   *royal; men quickly*

(lines 1951–3)

Minstrelsy after William's encouragement speech to his army just before the battle:

> and alle maner menstracie maked was sone
> of tabours and trumpes, non might the number telle.
>
> (lines 3812–13)

Minstrelsy before the triple wedding at the conclusion of the romance – characterized by loud sound:

> To munge of menstracie it might nought be aymed;   *tell; estimated*
> so many maner minstracie at that mariage were,
> that whan thei made here menstracie, eche man wende   *believed*
> that heven hastili and erthe schuld hurtel togader;
> so desgeli it denede, that al therthe quakede.   *extraordinarily; dinned*
>
> (lines 5010–14)

Minstrelsy for the procession from the church to the palace after the triple wedding:

> with al the murthe of menstracye that man might on thenk.
>
> (line 5062)

After the marriage feast the minstrels are richly rewarded:

> Whan bordes were born adoun, and burnes hade waschen,   *tables were dismantled*
> men might have seie to menstrales moche god yif,   *seen many good gifts (given) to minstrels*
> sterne stedes and stef, and ful stoute robes,   *sturdy horses; strong; excellent*
> gret garisun of gold and greithli gode juweles.   *reward; truly*
>
> (lines 5070–3)

When William accompanies the departing Spaniards, his people follow him with minstrelsy:

> his puple him sewed   *people; followed*
> with alle murthe of menstracie that men might on thenk.
>
> (5236–7)

When William and Melior are crowned emperor and empress of Rome, minstrels are rewarded at the fifteen-day feast:

> No tong might telle the twentithe parte
> of the mede to menstrales that mene time was yeve   *reward; given*
> of robes with riche pane and other richesse grete,   *fur lining*
> sterne stedes and strong and other stoute yiftes,   *excellent*
> so that eche man thermide might hold him apaied.   *therewith; satisfied*
>
> (lines 5354–8)

Ywain and Gawain

Minstrelsy when Alundyne welcomes King Arthur to her city:

And damysels danceand ful wele	
With trompes, pipes, and with fristele.	*flute*
The castel and the cete rang	*city*
With mynstralsi and nobil sang.	

(lines 1395–8)

Romances containing no qualifying minstrel reference

The Alliterative Alexander Fragment A or *Alisaunder*
The Alliterative Alexander Fragment B or *Alexander and Dindimus*
Apollonius of Tyre
Arthur
Athelston
The Cambridge Alexander-Cassamus Fragment
The Earl of Toulous
Floris and Blauncheflur
The Grene Knight
Ipomadon A or *Ipomadon*
The Jeaste of Syr Gawayne
Le Morte Arthur (stanzaic)
Roberd of Cisyle
Scottish Troy Fragments
The Sege of Melayne
Sir Amadace
Sir Firumbras (Ashmole)
Sir Perceval of Galles
Sir Triamour
The Song of Roland
The Sowdon of Babyloine
The Turke and Gowin

Appendix B

Medieval Fiddle Tuning and
Implications for Narrative Performance

JOHANNES Tinctoris, probably writing in Naples around 1487, describes two ways of tuning the 'viola' and explains how the instrument can be played:

> ... sive tres ei sint chorde simplices ut in pluribus: per geminam diapentem: sive quinque (ut in aliquibus) sic et per unisonos temperate: inequaliter. Hoc est tumide sunt extente: ut arculus (quom chorda ejus pilis equinis confecta: sit recta) unam tangens: juxta libitum sonitoris: alias relinquat inconcussas.[1]

> (... it has either (1) three simple strings tuned to a pair of fifths, which is the most usual, or (2) five strings tuned unevenly in fifths and unisons. These are stretched in a protuberant manner so that the bow (which is strung with horse-hair) can touch any one string the player wills, leaving the others untouched.)

The first of these approaches, the most common in Italy at the end of the fifteenth century, is precisely the modern violin or viola tuning in fifths, but with three instead of four strings. The 'swollen' ('tumide') arrangement of the strings, probably achieved with an arched bridge, is essential in allowing the player to isolate each string, sounding one string at a time without touching the others.

The second accordatura is less common in Italy this late, and the phrasing is open to several interpretations.[2] Some form of concordant tuning is implied, a structure which would allow the player to sound the five strings or a group of these strings simultaneously. Earlier sources reinforce this understanding. The late-thirteenth-century *Summa Musice*, possibly originating in Paris, uses similar terminology in describing chordophones which, unlike the harp, psaltery and similar instruments, are:

> temperantur ... per consonantias diapason, diatessaron et diapente, et per diversas digitorum interpositiones artifices ipsorum formant sibi tonos et semitonos, et sic de aliis.[3]

> (tuned in the consonances of octave, fourth and fifth; by stopping the strings in various positions with the fingers the players of these produce tones and semitones, and so it is with the rest [of the intervals]).

---

[1] Text and translation from Baines, 'Fifteenth-Century Instruments in Tinctoris's *De Inventione*', pp. 22–3.

[2] See Remnant, *English Bowed Instruments*, p. 66, for two possibilities.

[3] Text and translation from Christopher Page, ed. and trans., *The Summa Musice: A Thirteenth-Century Manual for Singers* (Cambridge: Cambridge University Press, 1991), pp. 87, 169.

The pattern is complicated by a fourteenth-century treatise, probably written by Parisian composer and teacher Jean Vaillant, found in University of California, Berkeley, MS 744. The manuscript contains sketches of instruments with pitches marked on the strings. Christopher Page identifies one of the instruments as a fiddle,[4] though Mary Remnant offers a compelling argument that 'it may have been a plucked instrument of the gittern (citole) family.'[5] The letters marked on the four strings are *c d g c*, which Christopher Page interprets as *c d g c'*.[6] The strings appear to be arranged on a plane, 'with the result that all the strings would have been sounded together'.[7] If this were the case, it would be very difficult to avoid cacophony. As we will see, however, a flat bridge does not necessarily mean that all strings are played at once.

A few decades later, also in Paris, Jerome of Moravia included a fully developed discussion of the fiddle in his *Tractatus de Musica*, probably written in the last two decades of the thirteenth century. Three hands appear in the manuscript: the hand of the main text, 'a hand who supplies material omitted by the first hand', and an annotator convincingly identified by Christopher Page as Pierre de Limoges, who died in 1306.[8] The marginal responses and questions inscribed by Pierre de Limoges give us valuable insight into the assumptions a contemporary reader would have brought to this highly specific text.

Jerome proposes three accordature for the fiddle, specifying that the instrument must have ('habet, et habere debet') five strings.[9] Following medieval convention, I will number the strings from left to right facing the instrument. In modern notation, substituting G for Γ, Jerome's tunings are:

> Tuning 1: *d–G–g–d'–d'*
> Tuning 2: *d–G–g–d'–g'*
> Tuning 3: *G–G–d–c'–c'*

The pitches indicated are best understood in relative relationship with each other rather than equivalent to our modern pitches. Christopher Page provides evidence that 'in the Middle Ages the gamut was an infinitely moveable framework of pitch nomenclature and musicians put it where it was required', and he further observes that the range of two octaves and a fifth of the second tuning renders this the only possible nomenclature.[10] Howard Mayer Brown suggests that the pitch level may have been at least a fourth or a fifth above the pitches

---

[4] Christopher Page, 'Fourteenth-Century Instruments and Tunings: A Treatise by Jean Vaillant? (Berkeley, MS 744)', *The Galpin Society Journal* 33 (1980): 17–35.

[5] Remnant, *English Bowed Instruments*, p. 67.

[6] Page, 'Fourteenth-Century Instruments', p. 27.

[7] Remnant, *English Bowed Instruments*, p. 67.

[8] Christopher Page, 'Jerome of Moravia on the *Rubeba* and *Viella*', *The Galpin Society Journal* 32 (1979): 77–98, at pp. 78–9. All quotations and translation of Jerome of Moravia's *Tractatus* are from this source.

[9] Page, 'Jerome of Moravia', p. 90.

[10] Page, 'Jerome of Moravia', pp. 83–4.

designated by our modern nomenclature.[11] Although Mary Remnant concludes that 'the actual pitch could be set wherever was most suitable for each individual instrument, according to its size',[12] some standardization must have been normal, for otherwise instrumentalists could not have played in consort, as we know they did. The pitch level raises an important question. Since both men and women accompanied solo singing on the fiddle, how would they have accommodated very different pitch relationships with the instrument? For polyphonic music, the octave difference would create inappropriate intervals, but for monophonic music the difference in range would not matter as much. In fact, as I will demonstrate, the fiddle itself is structured to incorporate octave shifts, and Jerome implies as much when he fills in the missing pitches in the first tuning with pitches from a different octave.

I tuned three five-string fiddles to Jerome's accordature. One fiddle has a curved bridge and fingerboard, while two have flat or nearly flat bridges and fingerboards. One is strung in courses and the others have strings evenly spaced. The string spacing varies considerably from one instrument to another, and one has an off-board string. I used three different bows, varying in tension, curvature, and quantity of bow hair. One of the most surprising results was how little difference these features made when I tuned the instruments using Jerome's system, confirming that his approach is robust enough to accommodate a wide range of fiddle types. Jerome does not specify courses. Christopher Page assumes an arrangement in courses, but in practice it does not matter as much as might be expected whether the strings are paired or not, and differences in spacing between strings mattered less than might be imagined. Whatever the curvature of the bridge, and whatever the structure of the instrument and bow, I ended up grouping the lower strings or the upper strings together, though occasionally isolating a string. Timothy McGee makes a strong case that:

> The choice of bridge shape – flat or rounded – that is found in the various iconographic depictions may be simply a design choice related only to artistic preferences of the builder or to inherited construction traditions of the string instrument family, while not carrying any performance implications at all.[13]

I was able to stop two strings at a time with a finger whether they were arranged in courses or not.

One of the great puzzles of Jerome's system is how it can accommodate polyphony. We have evidence that in Paris around 1300 when Jerome was writing, fiddles were participating in complex polyphony,[14] and Jerome and his respondent

---

[11] Brown, 'Trecento Fiddle', p. 325. Brown's solution is ideal for me, and I have tuned my Γ (G) to a modern d♭, 'a range comfortable for women, girls and men singing in falsetto'.

[12] Remnant, *English Bowed Instruments*, p. 66.

[13] McGee, 'Medieval Fiddle'.

[14] Johannes de Grocheio observes that a good fiddle player can play every kind of *cantus* and *cantilena* ('omnem cantum et cantilenam'), and these categories include a number of polyphonic forms, Page, 'Johannes de Grocheio', p. 31. One of the 'instrumental motets' in the Bamberg Codex (*c.* 1300) is

are careful to ensure the instrument can sound every pitch within its range, yet the re-entrant first and second tunings have no advantage unless we assume a fairly consistent presence of a drone. The gap of a seventh in the third tuning similarly seems unmotivated unless we assume some pattern of multiple string use. With a curved bridge, it is possible to isolate pitches on the inner strings and play a polyphonic line using Jerome's tunings, but it is awkward. The most convenient tuning for polyphonic playing is something like Tinctoris's fifteenth-century pattern of fifths. For narrative accompaniment, however, polyphonic playing is not necessary, so I will ignore that aspect of fiddle playing for this discussion.

I decided to explore Jerome's tunings in terms of a narrative passage with an extant notated melody. I selected section 39 of *Aucassin et Nicolete* (see example 4.3) as a focus for experimentation. Although in a Picard dialect, this narrative, like Jerome's and de Grocheio's treatises, dates from the last part of the thirteenth century. The *laisse* is a convenient length, short enough to complete numerous times in a sequence of experiments, but long enough to require a sustain-able approach. It is in couplets consisting of short lines, like most of the French romances, and the melody is clearly notated in the manuscript. The passage, furthermore, describes solo narrative performance with fiddle. Nicolete, having bought a fiddle and learned how to play it, has disguised herself as a jongleur and made her way through Provence playing her fiddle. In Beaucaire, she comes before her beloved Aucassin when he is sitting dejected half way up the steps. As a minstrel, she takes up her fiddle and bow and sings to him the story of their love and the circumstances that have befallen her. In essence, she fiddles while singing to him the whole story that has preceded.

Jerome's first accordatura, *d G g d' d'* with the *d* positioned laterally off the fingerboard, accommodates this melody, though not without two shifts in octave. Jerome specifies that the following pitches can be achieved by placing the fingers on the strings:

d string:	no application of fingers				
G string:	*a*		*b*	*c*	
g string:	*a'*	*bb'*	*b'*	*c'*	
d' strings:	*e'*	*f'*		*g'*	*a"*

The two *b*s on the *g* string are formed by applying the second finger either 'retorti' (bent) or 'cadentis naturaliter' (falling naturally). In the first line of *Aucassin et Nicolete*, the idiomatic drop from the tonal centre *g* to *f♯* a half step below requires an octave shift up to the top string, where it can be played with the second finger. Jerome specifies this solution, observing, 'Unde claves duas quas obmittit, scilicet E et F, quarta et quinta corde in dupla suplebunt' (The two notes which [this tuning structure] omits, namely *e* and *f*, will be supplied by the fourth and fifth strings

labelled 'in seculum viellatoris', possibly indicating that it is intended to include the fiddle, Pierre Aubry, ed., *Cent motets du XIIIe siècle* (New York: Broude Brothers, 1964 [1908]), fol. 63v. Brown, 'Trecento Fiddle', pp. 316–17, demonstrates that the fiddle was involved in polyphonic music in fourteenth-century Italy.

in unison),[15] though he does not mention that the second finger on this string can be applied 'cadentis naturaliter', substituting *f♯* for *f*.[16] When a performer is singing, the instrumental jump to another octave is not as jarring as it would be on its own. It is more convenient, however, to ignore the melodic embellishment on the instrument, substituting an *a* for the three-note ligature *a'–g–f♯*, and this approach keeps the fiddle strictly within the pitches specified by Jerome. In fact, this also provides a way to vary the sung melody, and the same applies to the following ligature *g–a'*, which can occasionally be reduced to *g* for effect.

However, the same solution is not possible for the last line of the *laisse*, in which the tonal centre shifts from *g* to *c*. The only *c* available in this tuning structure is played with the third finger on the second string, but because the first string (*d*) is not positioned over the fingerboard, it is not possible to complete the phrase in this octave, though it is possible to drone on the *c* while singing the melody. The entire melody can be played an octave higher, beginning with *c'* on the third string, possibly stopped together with the second string to create an octave. The melody continues on the top two strings, where the player can choose to isolate the fifth string or incorporate a *d'* drone or stop both strings in unison. None of the possible solutions, however, is practical. Stopping either the *G* string or the *g* string or both with the third finger means depressing the level of the string to the point where it is difficult to sound it in isolation from the neighbouring *d'* or the offboard *d*, creating an infelicitous drone. The difficulties resulting from all solutions made me wonder if de Grocheio, when he observed that the sound of the last line of a *laisse* is 'discordantem', might have meant that it is actually dissonant. My ultimate solution was to stop playing for the last line of the *laisse*, and sing the final phrase *a cappella*. This is not as problematic as it might seem. Most of the passage can be sung with a comfortable fiddle accompaniment, and the change in texture emphasizes the last line, which already stands out because of its shorter length and contrasting melody.

Jerome states that this method of tuning a vielle 'vim modorum omnium comprehendit' (encompasses the material [*or perhaps* the power] of all the modes).[17] *Aucassin et Nicolete*, as Stevens points out, like a number of other *laisse*-type melodies, has 'no clear reciting-note',[18] and it therefore may not be well

---

[15] Page, 'Jerome of Moravia', pp. 90–1.

[16] Clifton Joseph Furness argued that the music for *Aucassin et Nicolete* should be interpreted as written, adhering to the Mixolydian mode, 'The Interpretation and Probable Derivation of the Musical Notation in the 'Aucassin et Nicolette' MS', *The Modern Language Review* 24.2 (1929): 143–52, at p. 147. Nonetheless, I have applied an *f♯* throughout on the grounds that, although principles of *musica ficta* were more pertinent in the fourteenth than the thirteenth century, the cadential raising of the leading tone to create a semitone to the final was common in thirteenth-century secular song; further, the cadential *f* falls between two *g*s; and finally, because of the *b♮* in both the A and B lines of the melody, *f♯* is necessary to avoid a tritone when playing parallel fifths on the fiddle. See Hans Tischler, '"Musica ficta" in the Thirteenth Century', *Music and Letters* 54.1 (1973): 38–56; and Carl Parrish, *The Notation of Medieval Music* (New York: Norton, 1959; reprinted 1978), pp. 199–200.

[17] Page, 'Jerome of Moravia', pp. 90–1.

[18] Stevens, *Words and Music*, p. 226.

suited to this accordatura. It is worth considering, though, what Jerome might mean by relating this tuning structure to the church modes. As Page points out, 'all the modes cannot be played if the instrumentalist restricts himself to the stopping positions which Jerome describes.'[19] The Mixolydian mode can be accommodated with the least difficulty, since it has a final on *g*. By applying the fingers as Jerome specifies, a fiddle player can sound an octave and a whole step in this mode by playing on the middle string (*g*) and then the two high strings (*d'*). The reciting tone in this mode is *d'*, here conveniently supplied by an open string. the first fifth of the plagal mode also falls under the fingers on the *d'* strings, and if just one of these strings is fingered, the other provides an appropriate drone. A fiddle player, looking at this tuning structure, would surely see that it provides a modal framework, with the strings framing the pentachords and tetrachords of the mode and supplying the appropriate drones.

At first the other modes seem problematic. The string where the Dorian mode should begin (*d*) is fixed away from the fingerboard, forcing the player to jump across two strings to sound *e'* and *f'* in the higher octave. The solution may lie in Jerome's final observation regarding the three tunings:

> Finaliter tamen est notandum hoc quod in hac facultate est difficilius et solempnius meliusque, ut scilicet sciatur cum unicuique sono ex quibus unaqueque melodia contexitur cum bordunis primis consonanciis respondere.[20]

> (However, one thing must be finally noted, namely that which is most difficult, serious and excellent in this art: to know how to accord with the *borduni* in the first harmonies any note from which any melody is woven.)

Pierre de Limoges scrawls a note at the bottom of the page interpreting this as follows:

> Quod D bordunus non debet tangi pollice vel arcu nisi cum cetere corde arcu tactu faciunt sonos cum quibus bordunus facit aliquam predictarum consonanciarum scilicet diapente, diapason, diatessaron etc.

> (Because the D *bordunus* must not be touched with the thumb or bow, unless the other strings touched by the bow produce notes with which the *bordunus* makes any of the aforesaid consonances namely fifth, octave and fourth etc.)

But Pierre's interpretation does not fit what Jerome has described. It would not be an advanced technique to memorize which pitches form the prescribed intervals with the *bordunus* and either pluck or bow the *bordunus* at the appropriate moments in a melody. Furthermore, this explanation relates to the pitches on the instrument in general rather than the particular melodies Jerome specifies. Christopher Page suggests that Jerome may be 'describing a playing-style analogous to

---

[19] Page, 'Jerome of Moravia', p. 96.
[20] Page, 'Jerome of Moravia', pp. 92–3.

the contemporary vocal practice of 'fifthing", but the example he provides showing how a fiddler might accompany a singer, while compelling, does not demonstrate how any note from which any melody is woven can be brought into accord with the *bordunus*.[21]

Because the treatises on music are normally geared to vocalists, terminology for discussing modes is structured around a static diatonic framework with two options for *b*. But, as Judy Kadar points out, 'The rules of instrumental and vocal practice are not always the same.'[22] A vocalist can easily shift the tonal centre from one pitch to another, but on the fiddle the tonal centre is anchored on *g* or, to a limited extent, *d'*. An obvious solution can be found in that very stabilization of the final. When the Dorian mode is transposed up a fourth, it fits the framework of the fiddle perfectly, and the same pentachord and tetrachord that applied in the Mixolydian mode apply now in the Dorian mode. The only change in fingering required is to place the second finger close to the first on the *g* string to form *b♭*, an option included by Jerome. In fact, a player can easily improvise in the Dorian mode by placing the first and second fingers close to each other on any string. It is not necessary to work out all the patterns of whole steps and half steps with this simple rule.

This process of transposition could be what Jerome describes when he speaks of the challenging process of bringing each pitch from which each melody is woven into consonance with the *bordunus*. Jerome further advises:

> quod prorsus facile est scita manu secundaria, que scilicet solum provectis adhibetur et eius equante que in fine huius operis habetur.[23]

> (This is certainly known from the suitable second hand, which is only used by advanced players, and from its equivalent which is to be found at the end of this work.)

Christopher Page suggests that this 'second hand' could be 'the Guidonian hand transposed up a fifth',[24] which would simplify the process of 'fifthing'. It could alternatively be a related tool, allowing more flexible transposition, perhaps a hand with the half steps noted or indicating which interval would be required to transpose each mode to accord with the fiddle. However it is accomplished, transposition fits what Jerome describes: it would take an advanced student of music to look at a melody or listen to it, identify the mode, and transpose it to the pitch level of the fiddle; and the process accomplishes exactly the goal Jerome describes.

The remaining modes, however, require a player to move beyond the pitches specified by Jerome. To achieve the authentic Phrygian mode, the player simply 'bends' the first finger, placing it next to the nut on every string. The tonal centre would again be the middle *g* string, and, beginning there, the player simply places the other fingers in ascending whole steps. Jerome has specified that the second

---

[21] Page, *Voices and Instruments*, pp. 69–73.

[22] Kadar, 'Some Practical Hints', p. 128.

[23] Page, 'Jerome of Moravia', pp. 92–3.

[24] Page, *Voices and Instruments*, p. 72.

finger can be applied 'retorti' on the third string, and he implies that the second finger also does this on the fourth and fifth strings (to produce f'). Extending the technique to the first finger seems more reasonable than trying to play this mode beginning on e, which would require a player to begin by substituting $e'f'$ on the top strings, then leap down to the middle g string, from which it would be possible to complete the scale in sequence. Drones would be very difficult to manage. The transposition solution allows the musician to incorporate drones, and it provides the full octave and a step available for the other authentic modes, and the fifth available for the plagal modes. Again, the instrument provides a framework that facilitates improvisation by designating uniform finger placement on every string.

When the less commonly employed Lydian mode is transposed up a step so that the tonal centre falls on g, it requires an extension of the third finger upward toward the bridge on the g string so that the fingers fall in whole steps (as in the Phrygian mode, but a half step higher). Then on the d' string, the second finger falls 'naturaliter' on $f\sharp$, so that the second and third fingers are placed close together. Although the third finger reach is difficult, especially on the G string, it is possible, and it allows this mode, too, to fall comfortably into the grid work of drones established by Jerome's first tuning. Thus, by means of transposition, Jerome's first accordatura 'vim modorum omnium comprehendit', encompasses the power of all of the modes by facilitating improvisation and strengthening structural tones with drones.

In fact the whole purpose of Jerome's tunings is lost without persistent drones. There is otherwise no motive for the re-entrant tuning or the emphasis placed on gs and ds. But the term 'drone' is entirely inadequate in describing the variation in sonic landscape effected by Jerome's approach. Christopher Page perceptively observes that the first tuning 'seems to have been primarily designed to create disjunctions that thread a texture of auxiliary noise through monophonic melody'.[25]

The instrument I used for Jerome's first accordatura was constructed by Timothy McGee, modelled after Andrea di Bonaiuto's fresco "The Church Militant' (1365) in the Spanish Chapel of Santa Maria Novella in Florence, with the pegbox designed after Filippino Lippi's 'Portrait of a Musician' (1486) in the National Gallery of Ireland. One of challenges posed by this instrument was how to incorporate the first string, the lateral *bordunus*, effectively. Jerome states that this string 'quod extra corpus vielle, id est a latere, affixa sit, aplicaciones digitorum evadit' (because it must be fixed outside the body of the *viella*, that is, to the side, escapes the contact of the fingers).[26] Pierre de Limoges, in his attempt at explaining Jerome's advanced approach, states that, except in certain cases, 'D bordunus non debet tangi pollice vel arcu' (the D *bordunus* must not be touched with the thumb or bow). While the primary content of Pierre's marginal comment does not reasonably explicate Jerome's text, as I have discussed above, this offhand

---

[25] Page, *Voices and Instruments*, p. 128.

[26] Page, 'Jerome of Moravia', pp. 90–1.

comment provides evidence of a contemporary assumption that the *bordunus* (in some cases) could be played either with the thumb or with the bow. A number of images show a player's thumb positioned against the *bordunus*.[27] It has generally been assumed this string would be either plucked with the thumb or played with the bow.

Following Timothy McGee's suggestion, I found that I could effectively accent bow changes by plucking the *bordunus* while droning on the top four strings or on the top two, *d'–d'*, or the middle two, *G–g*. It was possible to alternate bowing and plucking, but the stark contrast between the two sounds distracted from the story and required more focused attention to execute. I expected to be able to incorporate pizzicato accents into a bowed melody, but this proved too difficult. In part, the hand position required for fingering is different from that required for plucking with the thumb, though that may be solved by positioning the *bordunus* closer to the other strings. More fundamentally, though, the plucking action affected the other fingers. Pat O'Brien explains the problem in terms of 'physiological aptness', demonstrating that 'tip-flexion of the thumb also has unexpected effects on the surrounding fingers', especially the index and middle fingers.[28]

Many of the eastern bowed chordophones do not have a fingerboard, which gives the player more subtle control over fine shades of pitch, and early crowds were evidently fingered in this way. Thinking of this precedent, I tried stopping the *bordunus* with my thumb while bowing it. To my astonishment, the pitch which resulted most naturally was *g*, the same pitch as the middle string, which is the tonal centre. The iconographic representations of the thumb against the off-board strings, generally thought to represent a plucking action, could equally well be explained by this technique. The effect is striking. In section 39 from *Aucassin et Nicolete*, I used this approach for lines 25–9, when Nicolete describes her sojourn in Carthage. I expressed the exotic character of her original home by droning on the bottom three strings on the pitches *g–G–g*, one bow stroke per line, emphasizing the attack of each stroke by pressing my thumb toward the fingerboard, thus raising the pitch a quarter tone and letting it immediately fall back to *g*. This fits the reference in *Bevis of Hampton* to Princess Josian playing 'garibles gay' on her fiddle, since it creates a kind of warbling sound. (See Chapter 3.)

Fingered embellishments can also create the trilling or twittering sound implied by the term 'garible'. There is support for such ornamentation in medieval advice to singers. Timothy McGee, introducing his cogent assembly of documents on medieval ornamentation and vocal style, observes:

> The sliding sound of a liquescent, the 'abandonment' of the final pitch of a
> pes, the pulsing sounds of the quilisma and oriscus, and use of quarter-tones

---

[27] See, for example, Page, 'Jerome of Moravia', plate 23; and Bachmann, *Origins of Bowing*, plates 71, 72, 74, 75, and 76.

[28] Pat O'Brien, 'Observations on the (Re)creation of Techniques for Historical Harps and their Potential Consequences', in *Historische Harfen: Beiträge zur Theorie und Praxis historischer Harfen*, ed. Heidrun Rosenzweig (Basel: Musik-Akademie, 1991), pp. 101–19, at p. 114.

in trills, vibrato, and filled intervals are all foreign to modern classical Western practices but were in common use during the Middle Ages, and were important basic ingredients in what may be termed 'the medieval vocal sound'.[29]

It seems likely that this characteristic of vocal style would apply to narrative singing and carry over to instrumental playing. It would be natural, for example, to ornament 'soit canter les oisellons' (line 6) with a trill on the top string imitating birdsong. Guillaume de Machaut and other fourteenth- and fifteenth-century composers employ what we might anachronistically call word painting;[30] and Guido d'Arezzo, as we read in Chapter 1, recommends that music should reflect the content of the text:

> Item ut rerum eventus sic cantionis imitetur effectus, ut in tristibus rebus graves sint neumae, in tranquillis iocundae, in prosperis exultantes et reliqua.[31]

> (Likewise, let the affect of the song express what is going on in the text, so that for sad things grave neumes are used, for serene ones they are delightful, and for auspicious texts exultant, and so forth.)

The left hand can supply a melodic line and ornamentation, but one of the most intriguing features is the possibility of stopping two strings at once. When the strings are arranged in close-set courses, the options are more limited. If the courses are set with some distance between the strings, as on the vielle I used, the player can choose to finger just one string of the course or both at once. This works very well on the top course, where a melody can be fingered on two unison strings or just one string while the other supplies a *d'* drone. It is also possible to isolate the top string and play within the interval of a fifth on that string for a very different effect. Kevin James suggests that two different gauges could have been used for the top strings (and, indeed, strings of uniform gauge could hardly have been available). 'The string under high tension will produce a brighter, more projective sound, while the string under comparatively low tension will speak with a more mellow tone.'[32] This effect would provide yet another dimension in the wide range of timbres in shifting combinations supplied the by fiddle in this tuning. On the lower course, the octave *G–g*, the G string can be fingered while droning on the *d* and *g*. Alternatively a player can finger the *g* string while droning either on the lower three strings or the top four, though more bow pressure is required to compensate for the lower position of that string in relation to the others. Because of the significant difference in gauge, when a finger is applied to the two strings together, the octave is never quite in tune. This discrepancy is

---

[29] McGee, *Sound of Medieval Song*, p. 11.

[30] See, for example, Wolf Arlt, 'Musik und Text: Verstellte Perspektiven einer Grundlageneinheit', *Musica* 37 (1983): 497–503.

[31] Quoted and translated in McGee, *Sound of Medieval Song*, pp. 169, 37.

[32] Kevin James, 'The Five-Stringed Fiddle in Medieval Europe', *Continuo* 5.8 (1982): 6–12, at p. 7.

energizing rather than disturbing as long as the divergence is small. Christopher Page notes that the two strings together further 'set up an octave ambiguity leaving the ear uncertain as to where the melody was located, high or low'. [33]

Building on the many drone colours available, the melodic possibilities, the wide range of possible ornamentation, the effects created by double stopping passages, the fiddle became a comfortable and evocative tool for enhancing section 39 of *Aucassin et Nicolete*. A player has no need to play the passage the same way every time, but can draw spontaneously on a wide range of sounds available. Because narrative performance requires a focus on the text, the player benefits substantially from letting the instrument supply the variation as much as possible. It would be natural to associate certain techniques on the instrument with locations, characters, and emotional dimensions in the text. With this approach, the fiddle becomes a connotative tool.

Jerome's second accordatura, *d–G–g–d'–g'*, provides a somewhat different set of available features, but operates on the same principle of heterophony. The only change in pitch is that the top string is set a fourth higher, at *g'*. But another significant modification is made, the repositioning of the *bordunus* over the fingerboard:

> Et tunc necessarium est ut omnes v corde ipsius vielle corpori solido affigantur nullaque a latere, ut aplicacionem digitorum queant recipere. [34]

> (Then it is necessary that all the five strings of this *viella* are fixed to the real body of the instrument, not to the side, so that they may be able to receive the application of the fingers.)

The modal framework of tuning 1, with its open strings tuned to Gs and Ds is here preserved, and the melodic possibilities are extended at the top end by the raised pitch of the string and at the bottom end by the repositioning of the *bordunus* over the fingerboard. With this gain, however, the instrument loses in the low range the possibility of pizzicato with the thumb or ornamentation through off-board stopping, and in the high range the possibility of a ubiquitous *d'* drone through the range of an octave.

For Jerome's second tuning, I used an instrument built by Lyn Elder patterned after the Psalter of Robert de Lisle, *c.* 1330–9, [35] contemporary with the Middle English romances and of a common general provenance. In this tuning it is easy to play every pitch within a range of two octaves and a fifth, precisely matching the pitches of the Guidonian hand. This wide range is, in fact, the characteristic Jerome singles out in introducing this tuning, and he associates it with applications outside the church:

> Alius necessarius est propter laycos et omnes alios cantus, maxime irregulares, qui frequenter per totam manum discurrere volunt. [36]

---

[33] Page, *Voices and Instruments*, p. 128.

[34] Page, 'Jerome of Moravia', pp. 90–1.

[35] See Remnant, *English Bowed Instruments*, plate 87.

[36] Page, 'Jerome of Moravia', pp. 90–1.

(Another [tuning] is necessary for secular songs and for all others – especially irregular ones – which frequently wish to run through the whole hand.)

Extant medieval music, however, sacred or secular, rarely, if ever, runs through the entire range of the Guidonian hand.[37] Christopher Page suggests the possibility of 'rendering material in different registers',[38] and this fits very well with aesthetic of variation fostered by tuning 1. The simple melody of a *chanson de geste* can be played in three different octaves, on the *G*, *g*, or *g'* string; the melody for *Aucassin et Nicolete* can be played readily in three different registers, while only two were available in tuning 1.[39]

The participation of adjacent strings remains vital. While a curved bridge might make it possible to isolate the middle strings as well as the top and bottom strings, Jerome's re-entrant tuning and his insistence on consonant intervals can only be motivated by an expectation that multiple strings would typically sound together. Tuning 2 adds to tuning 1 the option of an eerie *g'* drone, a significant change in landscape.

Timothy McGee makes a compelling case that tuning 2 'was intended for melodic performance by skilled performers, whose repertory included songs, dances, and possibly polyphonic lines', while tuning 1 'was intended for less accomplished performers and its principal repertory was the simple accompaniment of vocal performance'.[40] My experiments corroborate this distinction. Tuning 1 provides a wide range of 'special effects', easily accomplished by a relatively inexperienced player, but with limited flexibility. Tuning 2 offers fewer dramatically divergent sounds, but allows freer use of the left hand fingers, thus demanding a higher skill level. Narrative verse, then, could be effectively performed either by an amateur using tuning 1, or by a 'bonus artifex in viella' using tuning 2.

But what it means to be a skilled player on the fiddle must in this case be construed according to the exigencies of narrative, where the text is much longer than in any other musical form, and where comprehension of the text is vital to appreciation of the performance. Tuning 2 offers a sophisticated palette of options that a trained player might draw on at an intuitive level, simplifying and fragmenting more complex musical techniques so as not to compromise recall and vocal production of the text.

The intervals between strings provide one tool for carefree accompaniment. Sarah Fuller quotes a passage from an early fourteenth-century treatise by Jacques de Liège:

Diaphonia sive discantus multipliciter distinguitur: Uno modo ex consonantiis ex quibus discantus conficiuntur ut, quantum ad hoc, discantans, qui

[37] Page, 'Jerome of Moravia', p. 97.

[38] Page, 'Jerome of Moravia', p. 97.

[39] Some modification of the melody is necessary in the lowest octave of tuning 1 (where *e* is not available) and in the highest octave of tuning 2 (where *e"* is not available).

[40] McGee, 'Medieval Fiddle'.

amplius, frequentius et quasi a domino utitur quintis diapentizare vel quin-
thiare dicatur, vel si amplius quartis utitur, dicatur quartare sive diatesseronare, sic de ceteris.[41]

(Diaphony or discant is classified in many ways. One way is by the conso-
nances from which the discant is produced, so that, according to this, the
discantor who uses fifths predominantly, most frequently, and authorita-
tively is said to *diapentizare* or to fifth, while if he uses the fourth predominantly, he is said to fourth or to *diatesseronare*, and so with the others.)

She goes on to document a practice of 'fifthing', distinct from discant in not
including a rule for contrary motion. She demonstrates that a continuing practice of strict parallel motion is evident in the dismissive language of several of the
standard treatises on discant, and she points out that there would be no need to
notate or discuss 'so simple an improvisational tool'.[42]

Jerome's tuning 2 invites not only parallel fifths, but also parallel fourths and
parallel octaves: fingering the third and fourth strings together (*g* and *d'*) or the
second and first strings (*G* and *d*) automatically produces fifths, fingering the
fourth and fifth strings simultaneously (*d'* and *g'*) automatically produces fourths,
and double stopping the second and third strings (*G* and *g*) produces octaves. Like
the other features of Jerome's fiddle, this technique can only be used in a fragmentary manner, not as a consistent principle (where it would rapidly become tedious).
As soon as the melody moves to another string, the interval of a fifth or a fourth
or an octave is replaced by something else. This feature is most usefully applied to
brief passages, and these passages would not necessarily coincide with melodic or
textual phrasing. The skill of a performer would emerge through strategic choice
of when and how to apply this technique. While it is possible to incorporate some
of the simple principles of 'fifthing' Sarah Fuller discusses, or even more complex
discant, the demands of the text make the simple, automatic parallel intervals
established by the instrument itself a much more practical technique of narrative
accompaniment.[43]

   To illustrate the extensive palette of tool available for accompanying continental narrative, a variety of approaches are included in the following musical
setting of section 39 of *Aucassin et Nicolete* (example B.1); this kaleidoscope
approach to accompaniment is not intended to reflect actual practice. The goal
of narrative self-accompaniment is to strive for simple, intuitive techniques.
One simple approach is to double the sung melody (lines 1–2). Even simpler, are
rhythmic drones, just the open strings with no fingers applied (lines 3–4). By
placing fingers on two strings at the same time, a performer can 'fifth' or 'fourth' in
parallel motion (line 11). Individual words or phrases can be echoed in the music:
when birds are mentioned, a player might imitate birdsong (line 6); when Nicolete

---

[41] Fuller, 'Discant and the Theory of Fifthing', p. 241.

[42] Fuller, 'Discant and the Theory of Fifthing', p. 267.

[43] See Chapter 3 for a discussion of how the reference to 'garibles gay' in *Bevis of Hampton* may relate
to this technique.

Example B.1 Illustration of fiddle accompaniment: *Aucassin et Nicolete*, section 39

continued overleaf

Example B.1 *continued*

Example B.1 *continued*

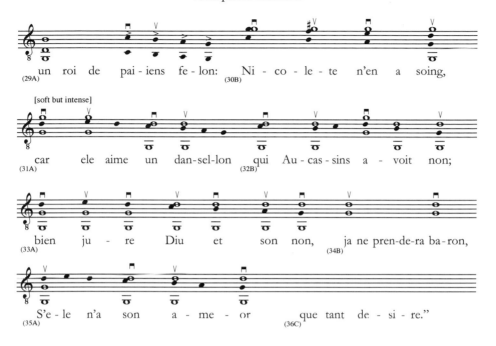

(She took her fiddle and went through the country playing the fiddle until she came to the castle of Beaucaire, where Aucassin was living. At Beaucaire, Aucassin was sitting on a step at the base of the tower, surrounded by his worthy lords. He was looking at the grass and flowers and listening to the birds sing, as he thought about his beloved, Nicolete the valiant, whom he had loved for so many days, for whom he had uttered sighs and shed tears. Then, behold, you, Nicolete, by the step. She took up her fiddle and her bow. Then she spoke, told her story. 'Listen to me, noble lords, whether of low or high station. Would you like to hear a song about worthy Aucassin, and about Nicolete the wise? So long their love endured that he sought her in the deep forest. One day, pagans captured them from the castle at Torelore. I know nothing of Aucassin, but Nicolete the worthy is at the castle in Carthage, for her father, who is lord of that realm, loves her dearly. They want to marry her to a king of the false pagans, but Nicolete wants no part of that because she loves a young gentleman named Aucassin. She vows by God that she will never marry a lord, unless she can have her beloved, whom she so strongly desires.')

comments that some are of low station and some of high, the fiddle music might descend and ascend (line 15). While musicians today strive for a clear, rich tone, other tone qualities were admired in the Middle Ages, and a medieval performer may have varied the timbre, sometime using a harsh tone quality to reflect something unpleasant (lines 25–8), or sometimes a breathy tone, hinting at harmonics (lines 21–2). Then, as now, a musician may have associated a musical pattern with a specific character or location, as here where Nicolete is associated with parallel descending fifths (lines 11, 18, 24, and 30). With a little effort, it is possible to play modified discant on the vielle while singing the primary melody (lines 5–6), and it is very natural to improvise little melodies after phrases (lines 8 and 20).[44]

Jerome's third tuning, G–G–d–c'–c', is the most puzzling.[45] Jerome describes it as the inverse of the other two, but the top two strings, tuned in unison to c', are in no way concordant with the bottom three strings. For this accordatura, I used a curved-bridged instrument, also built by Lyn Elder, designed after a fifteenth-century Aragonese altar painting. I chose a curved bridge, thinking that it might help to isolate pitches, but it was so awkward to fill in the bb' and $b\natural'$ that there were gaps in almost any melody. It worked to play on the bottom three strings or the top two strings, but moving between them created a disjunction that could only be accommodated between phrases. It is possible that the first string, one of two G's, may have been an off-board string, but this would not ameliorate the difficulties presented by the tuning.

Yet why would Jerome have suggested this structure of open pitches if there were not some way of playing that benefited from it? Looking again at Jerome's observation that tuning 3 is the inverse of tuning 1, 'Tertius modus oppositus est primo',[46] suggests the possibility of conceiving of the top two strings as d' (rather than c'), which would make this tuning in some way opposite to the first. By applying the first finger to the top two strings, a player can establish d' as the tonal centre with the middle string (d) as a drone. Following this approach, it is easy to improvise a sung story in Dorian mode within the ambitus of the fifth available while droning on the middle string. This structure has the advantage of incorporating the idiomatic whole step drop below the tonal centre (to the open c'). The approach is easy to sustain and allows some variation.

Werner Bachmann suggests that this tuning 'was originally designed for

---

[44] Example B.1 represents an attempt to notate a specific performance recorded in *Music and Medieval Narrative* (Provo, UT: Chaucer Studio, 2011). The line number of the text and the melodic phrase (see example 4.3) are noted in parentheses before each line of text. Although the text is included, the musical notation indicates the fiddle accompaniment, not the vocal line. Note that bowing does not follow modern conventions and is not regularized, and that the pitch indicated is not necessarily the pitch that sounds because G is not absolute. The tempo is flexible, and fluctuations are not noted. Filled notes indicate melodic components, and hollow notes indicate drones, though it should be noted that the drones are ephemeral. The complex character of the drones is impossible to notate; sometimes an additional drone emerges and fades as more pressure is applied to the bow, and sometimes drones are so soft as to be nearly undetectable.

[45] This accordatura is reminiscent of the Jean Vaillant? tuning, c–d–g–c', and it is likely that the solutions to Jerome's tuning 3 would apply to this tuning as well.

[46] Page, 'Jerome of Moravia', p. 92.

instruments on which only one string – usually the highest – carried the melody', and he adds:

> The c string was perfectly adequate for the vast repertory of archaic four and five-note melodies, and its doubling strengthened the melodic line, while the remaining strings obviously functioned as a drone fifth – G d.[47]

But to what melodies is he referring? Christopher Page infers that this tuning 'aurait pu être idéal pour jouer la musique, très répétitive, des chansons de geste auxquelles la vièle est étroitement associée dans les textes littéraires' (would have been idea for playing the highly repetitive music of the *chansons de geste*, with which the fiddle is closely associated in literary texts).[48] He illustrates with the fragment from *Robin et Marion*, pointing out that this is the only extant *chanson de geste* melody. But, after admiring the heterophony stimulated by Jerome's first two accordature, Page limits the instrumentalist in the third tuning to melodic playing on 'only one string'[49] (the course of two *c'* strings), which significantly reduces the range of sound textures. The melody sounds wonderful the first and second time; with the limited variation available it can be extended to five or possibly ten minutes, but after that some change in sound becomes urgent. Jerome accommodates such a change, specifically stating that notes can be found in this tuning in the same way as in the first, 'Et in hoc quoque modo tercio voces medie inveniuntur modo superius prenotato.'[50] He clearly implies that the second and third strings can be fingered, and possibly the first if it is positioned over the fingerboard, as well as the fourth and fifth *c'* strings. Expanding within this broader framework, the *geste* melody from *Robin et Marion* can alternatively be played on the second and third strings, incorporating a shift in drone structure when the melody moves from the third to the second string. By allowing melodic playing in the lower octave, the player more than doubles options for variation, and the heterophony characteristic of Jerome's other tunings is preserved.

A surprising number of extant narrative melodies can be played in this way with minor modification, leaving out some of the notes or substituting others or droning in various ways while singing the missing notes. The *pastourelle* 'L'autrier par un matinet' from *Robin et Marion*[51] vibrates powerfully in this tuning, requiring only a modification of the *a"* in the ninth and tenth lines to *f'*. In this configuration, the melody no longer seems 'extremely repetitive',[52] especially when it is sometimes played on the bottom strings.

It is also possible to play notes within the range of a fifth with the tonal centre at *c'* by droning on the fourth string while fingering the fifth, just sounding the top two strings. Then the same melody can be played an octave lower with a *G*

[47] Bachmann, *Origins of Bowing*, p. 104.
[48] Page, 'Troisième Accord', p. 91.
[49] Page, *Voices and Instruments*, p. 129.
[50] Page, 'Jerome of Moravia', p. 92.
[51] See Stevens, *Words and Music*, pp. 231–2.
[52] Stevens, *Words and Music*, p. 231.

drone instead of a *c'* drone. Walther von der Vogelweide's 'Under der Linden', for example, has a haunting quality within these parameters.[53]

With a tonal centre of *c*, I found I could play across the instrument, beyond the range of a fifth, as long as I remembered to apply my third finger when I droned on the middle string (sounding *g* instead of open *d*). Since most melodies fall primarily on the *d* string, this does not pose a problem. Some melodies seem designed for this tuning. Though not a narrative melody, Neithart von Reuenthal's 'Winder Wie ist' exactly fits the available pitches.[54] Significantly, Gautier de Coinci's 'Ma viële' is effective in this tuning, more effective than in the other tunings, though the upper end of the range has to be modified.[55] I sang a fairly lengthy section of *Eger and Grime* to the *Gray Steel* melody, playing the melody in two different octaves and droning on various combinations of G, *g* (third finger on the middle string), *c'* or *c* (third finger on the first or second string), focusing around a G–c or g–c' tetrachord.

Turning to the *laisse* from *Aucassin et Nicolete*, a tonal centre of *c* is possible, though the high *a"* in the upper octave is out of range. But the melody sits more comfortably among the drones on the lower three strings with a tonal centre of G. In this setting, however, there is no effective way to incorporate the top strings. It works well to play on the bottom strings, an octave lower than the voice, ignoring the ornamental drop to *f♯*. Some of the variations that can be employed with the first and second tunings are possible, but not as many. It is not until the last line of the *laisse* that the unique advantage of this tuning system appears. The short final line, virtually impossible in the other two tunings, falls under the fingers perfectly on the top string. Admittedly, it is necessary to leap up two octaves, but Jerome has demonstrated that he is not concerned by octave jumps, and the voice can maintain the lower pitch level. In this test case, then, there is a clear advantage to Jerome's third tuning; it facilitates a shift to a different tonal centre.

---

[53] This melody serves well as an example of a French melody used as a contrafactum for a German *Minnesang* which adopts a narrative stance. Both sets of words are provided with the melody by Barbara Thornton and Lawrence Rosenwald, 'The Voice: Poetics as Technique', in *A Performer's Guide to Medieval Music*, ed. Ross W. Duffin (Bloomington: Indiana University Press, 2000), pp. 264–92, at p. 274.

[54] Archibald T. Davison and Willi Apel, *Historical Anthology of Music: Oriental, Medieval and Renaissance Music*, rev. edn (Cambridge, MA: Harvard University Press, 1977), p. 19.

[55] Interestingly, the brief narrative song 'Ce fut en mai', which also includes a reference to a fiddle playing, works best in Jerome's second tuning.

Glossary of Terms

THIS glossary contains musical and literary terms used in the course of the book. Because of the interdisciplinary nature of the discussion, readers focused on literature may find brief definitions of musical terms useful, while readers more conversant with music may benefit from explanation of terms associated with literature. In this list, explanations are highly simplified; fuller discussions are readily available in a variety of sources.

accordatura (pl. *accordature*) The tuning scheme of a stringed instrument.

alliteration (adj. *alliterative*) Repetition of the initial sound in two or more stressed syllables in a group of words.

ambitus The distance between the highest and lowest note in a musical piece; the range.

assonance In francophone poetry, repetition of the sound of the final accented vowel in successive lines of verse.

authentic See under *mode*.

bagpipe A wind instrument with a bag-like reservoir allowing an uninterrupted stream of air. The melody is played on a chanter with a double reed; additional drone pipes have single reeds.

bourdour A storyteller, a mocker, an entertainer, or a jester. Note that medieval terms for narrating do not appear to distinguish between speaking and singing as the modern equivalents do. See also *disour*.

bray pins On a medieval harp, crooked pegs which create a buzz when a string is plucked.

cadence (adj. *cadential*) A formula that marks the end of a musical phrase.

caesura A break in a line of poetry.

chord A simultaneous combination of three or more notes of different pitch.

chordophone A musical instrument that produces sound by means of a stretched, vibrating string or strings.

citole A plucked stringed instrument with a short neck, tentatively distinguished from the gittern and lute by its back, which is not rounded.

clarion A brass instrument, possibly smaller than a trumpet.

concordant Of musical pitches, agreeing in sound, sounding pleasing together.

contrafactum A song in which the original text has been replaced by a new one.

course (*string-course*) On a stringed instrument, two strings set close enough together that they can be fingered together and played as if they were one string.

crowd A bowed stringed instrument characterized by a yoke bridging the two arms which rise from the soundbox; closely related to the later Welsh crwth.

diatonic Pertaining to a scale of eight notes to the octave constructed as a sequence of whole and half steps.

disour A storyteller, entertainer, or jester. Note that medieval terms for narrating do not appear to distinguish between speaking and singing, as the modern equivalents do. See also *bourdour*.

drone A sustained pitch that is not part of the melodic line.

dulcimer A struck stringed instrument; metal strings stretched across a soundbox are struck with small mallet hammers held in each hand.

embellishment Same as *ornamentation*.

fiddle A bowed stringed instrument with a distinct neck and a flat back.

final In music, the tonal centre of a composition. Many compositions end on this pitch.

foot In poetry, the smallest repeating rhythmic unit. See also *mode, rhythmic*.

fytt A section of a poem or song.

garible Probably a melody with second line constructed using parallel intervals.

geste A narrative poem or song. In Middle English, a performed version of a romance, either memorized or improvised.

gittern A plucked stringed instrument with a slender, pear-shaped body, generally smaller and higher pitched than the lute.

gle, gleo, glew, etc. Any music, vocal or instrumental. Also, in a more general sense, any entertainment, including dancing, acrobatics, magic tricks, or juggling, with or without music.

Guidonian hand A mnemonic device, named after the musical theorist Guido of Arezzo, for remembering pitches and their relationships to each other. Each knuckle on the hand is assigned a specific pitch; the pitches ascend from the tip of the thumb in a counterclockwise spiral.

harp A stringed instrument of triangular shape, plucked with a hand on each side of the plane of the strings.

hemiola A rhythmic effect in which two three-beat patterns are replaced by three two-beat patterns.

hemistich A half-line unit of verse.

ictic Characterized by a metrical design based around the *ictus*, the beat or prominent syllable.

instruments Medieval musical instruments are referred to by the names applied, often tentatively, today. Medieval terminology was complex and highly variable.

interval The distance between two notes.

isosyllabic Of a song, consisting of syllables each allotted roughly equal time value.

joglour, jogeler, jugoler, etc. An entertainer. May be a storyteller, an actor, an instrumentalist, a singer, a poet, a jester, a juggler, a tumbler, a dancer, a prestidigitator, a magician, or simply a rascal. Note that several of these functions may be combined.

lai, lay A 'lyrical' *lai* is a complex musical composition in French or Latin; a narrative *lai* tells a story in verse. The spelling *lay* is used to distinguish British usage.

laisse The verse unit of the Old French *chanson de geste*. Each *laisse* consists of an unspecified number of lines linked by assonance (and later by rhyme).

ligature In music, a notational symbol indicating two or more notes connected together.

lute A stringed instrument with a neck and a rounded back, normally plucked or strummed with a quill.

mensural notation In music, written symbols which clearly distinguish between notes of different durations in fixed proportions. Generally there are either two or three *breves* to a *long*, two or three *semibreves* to a *breve*, and two or three *minims* to a *semibreve*.

mode As a melodic or harmonic term, the arrangement of whole and half steps to create a characteristic scale. Each mode has two forms: if the scale (the range of pitches used) begins on the tonal centre, it is *authentic*; if it begins a fourth down, it is *plagal*. The authentic modes are *Dorian, Phrygian, Lydian*, and *Mixolydian*.

mode, rhythmic In music, a repeating metrical pattern of long and short notes. The terminology is drawn from the quantitative metres of classical poetry:

1	*Trochaic*	long–short
2	*Iambic*	short–long
3	*Dactylic*	long–short–short
4	*Anapaestic*	short–short–long
5	*Spondaic*	long–long
6	*Tribrachic*	short–short–short

monophony (adj. *monophonic*) A musical texture consisting of one line of melody.

mouvance A term developed by Paul Zumthor to describe the mobility of a medieval text, the degree to which it varies from one version to another.

nakers Small kettle drums. Normally a pair of different size and pitch were suspended from a belt around the waist.

organistrum See *symphonia*.

organology The study of musical instruments and their classification.

ornamentation The modification of music, variation. Typical resources include adding or eliminating notes, or altering note-value, pitch, timbre, or dynamic. Same as embellishment.

pipe A generic term for any tube-shaped woodwind instrument. May refer to a tabor-pipe, shawm, panpipes, recorder, transverse flute, organ pipe, or small bagpipe.

plagal See under *mode*.

polyphony (adj. *polyphonic*) A musical texture consisting of two or more simultaneous lines of melody.

psaltery A plucked stringed instrument; metal strings stretched across a flat soundbox were generally plucked with two quills.

rebec A pear-shaped bowed stringed instrument with a rounded back, generally higher in pitch than the fiddle.

re-entrant tuning A tuning of a stringed instrument in which there is a break in an otherwise ascending or descending sequence of pitches.

repertoire The body of works performed by a person or consort. (Generally a more restrictive term than *repertory*.)

repertory (*repertoire*) A large body of works in a certain genre or style or geographical area.

rhyme Repetition of the final sound in two or more words, especially at the ends of lines of poetry.

rote A much-disputed stringed instrument, either bowed or plucked.

shawm A double-reed woodwind instrument with a narrow, conical bore and finger holes.

symphonia (or *organistrum*) A stringed instrument. A crank turns a rosined wheel, which produces sound by rubbing against the strings. Melodies are played on a keyboard, which presses small wedges against one or more strings to change their pitch.

tabor A double-headed drum fitted with a snare and played with one stick.

tail-rhyme A stanza form built of units of two or three rhyming lines followed by a line with a different final sound, *aa(a)b*. These concluding *b* lines rhyme throughout the stanza, holding it together, and they are often shorter in length.

timbre Tone quality or colour: the aspects of a musical sound that do not have to do with pitch, volume, or duration.

timbrel A tambourine, a flat frame drum with jingles.

transpose (n. *transposition*) To move a collection of notes up or down in pitch by a constant interval.

troubadour A poet-composer from southern France, the counterpart of the northern *trouvère*.

trouvère A poet-composer from northern France, the counterpart of the southern *troubadour*.

trumpet A brass instrument, normally cylindrical in shape until it flares at the bell. Sound is produced by the lips vibrating against a mouthpiece.

wait A watchman and/or player of a wind instrument.

Bibliography

Editions of Middle English Verse Romances

For ease of reference the editions are listed under the titles given in appendix A and used throughout the discussion.

The Alliterative Alexander Fragment A or *Alisaunder*

Magoun, Francis Peabody Jnr, ed. *The Gests of King Alexander of Macedon*, pp. 121–70. Cambridge, MA: Harvard University Press, 1929.

The Alliterative Alexander Fragment B or *Alexander and Dindimus*

Magoun, Francis Peabody Jnr, ed. *The Gests of King Alexander of Macedon*, pp. 171–216. Cambridge, MA: Harvard University Press, 1929.

The Alliterative Alexander Fragment C or *Wars of Alexander*

Duggan, Hoyt N., and Thorlac Turville-Petre, eds. *The Wars of Alexander*. EETS ss 10. Oxford: Oxford University Press, 1989.

Amis and Amiloun

Leach, MacEdward, ed. *Amis and Amiloun*. EETS os 203. London: Oxford University Press, 1937; reprinted 1960.

Apollonius of Tyre

In *Die alt- und mittelenglischen Apollonius-Bruchstücke*, ed. Joseph Raith, p. 1 facsimile, p. 78 transcript. Studien und Texte zur Englischen Philologie 3. Munich: Max Hueber Verlag, 1956.

Arthour and Merlin

Macrae-Gibson, O. D., ed. *Of Arthour and of Merlin*. 2 vols. EETS os 268, 279. London: Oxford University Press, 1973, 1979.

Arthur

Furnivall, Frederick J., ed. *Arthur: A Short Sketch of his Life and History in English Verse*. EETS os 2. London: Oxford University Press, 1864; reprinted 1998.

Athelston

Trounce, A. McI., ed. *Athelston: A Middle English Romance*. EETS 224. London: Oxford University Press, 1951; reprinted 1957.

The Avowynge of King Arthur

Dahood, Roger, ed. *The Avowing of King Arthur*. New York: Garland Publishing, 1984.

The Awntyrs off Arthure at the Terne Wathelyne

Gates, Robert J., ed. *The Awntyrs off Arthure at the Terne Wathelyne*. Philadelphia: University of Pennsylvania Press, 1969.

Bevis of Hampton

Kölbing, Eugen, ed. *The Romance of Sir Beues of Hamtoun*. EETS ES 46, 48, 65. London: Trübner, 1885–94; reprinted as one volume 1978.

Le Bone Florence of Rome

Heffernan, Carol Falvo, ed. *Le Bone Florence of Rome*. Manchester: Manchester University Press, 1976.

The Cambridge Alexander-Cassamus Fragment

Roßkopf, Karl, ed. *Editio princeps des mittelenglischen Cassamus (Alexanderfragmentes) der Universitätsbibliotek Cambridge*. Inaugural-Dissertation. Erlangen: K. B. Hof- und Universitätsbuchdruckerei von Junge & Sohn, 1911.

Chevalere Assigne

Gibbs, Henry H., ed. *The Romance of the Chevelere Assigne*. EETS ES 6. London: Oxford University Press, 1868.

Duke Roland and Sir Otuel of Spain

Herrtage, Sidney J., ed. *The English Charlemagne Romances Part II*. EETS ES 35. London: Oxford University Press, 1880.

The Earl of Toulous

Hülsmann, Friedrich, ed. *The Erle of Tolous: Eine Paralleledition mit Einleitung und Glossar*. Essen: Verlag Die Blaue Eule, 1987.

Eger and Grime

Caldwell, James Ralston, ed. *Eger and Grime*. Harvard Studies in Comparative Literature 9. Cambridge, MA: Harvard University Press, 1933.

Emare

Rickert, Edith, ed. *The Romance of Emaré*. EETS ES 99. London: Oxford University Press, 1908; reprinted 1958.

Floris and Blauncheflur

McKnight, George H., ed. *King Horn, Floris and Blauncheflur, The Assumption of our Lady*. EETS OS 14. London: Oxford University Press, 1901; reprinted 1990.

Generides (couplet version)

Furnivall, Frederick J., ed. *A Royal Historie of the Excellent Knight Generides*. Roxburghe Club, 1865. Reprint. New York: Burt Franklin, 1971.

Generides (stanza version)

Wright, W. Aldis, ed. *Generydes: A Romance in Seven-Line Stanzas*. EETS 57, 59. London: Trübner, 1878.

Gest Historiale of the Destruction of Troy

Panton, G. A., and D. Donaldson, eds. *The 'Gest Hystoriale' of the Destruction of Troy*. EETS OS 39, 56. London: Oxford University Press, 1869, 1874; reprinted as one volume 1968.

Golagros and Gawane

Hanna, Ralph, ed. *The Knightly Tale of Golagros and Gawane*. Scottish Text Society Fifth Series 7. Woodbridge: Scottish Text Society, 2008.

Bibliography

The Grene Knight

Hahn, Thomas, ed. *Sir Gawain: Eleven Romances and Tales*. Kalamazoo, MI: Medieval Institute Publications, 1995. Available online at <http://www.lib.rochester.edu/camelot/teams/tmsmenu.htm> (13 April 2011).

Guy of Warwick (couplet)

Zupitza, Julius, ed. *The Romance of Guy of Warwick*. EETS ES 42, 49, 59. London: Oxford University Press, 1883–91; reprinted as one volume 1966.

Guy of Warwick (stanzaic)

Wiggins, Alison, ed. *Stanzaic Guy of Warwick*. Kalamazoo, MI: Medieval Institute Publications, 2004. Available online at <http://www.lib.rochester.edu/camelot/teams/tmsmenu.htm> (13 April 2011).

Guy of Warwick (fifteenth-century)

Zupitza, J., ed. *The Romance of Guy of Warwick: The Second or Fifteenth-Century Version*. EETS ES 25, 26. London: Oxford University Press, 1875, 1876; reprinted as one volume 1966.

Havelok

Smithers, G. V., ed. *Havelok*. Oxford: Clarendon Press, 1987.

Horn Child

Mills, Maldwyn, ed. *Horn Childe and Maiden Rimnild*. Heidelberg: Carl Winter Universitätsverlag, 1988.

Ipomadon A or Ipomadon

Purdie, Rhiannon, ed. *Ipomadon* EETS 316. Oxford: Oxford University Press, 2001.

Ipomadon B or The Lyfe of Ipomydon

Kölbing, Eugen, ed. *Ipomedon in drei englischen bearbeitungen*. Breslau: Koebner, 1889.

The Jeaste of Syr Gawayne

Hahn, Thomas, ed. *Sir Gawain: Eleven Romances and Tales*. Kalamazoo, MI: Medieval Institute Publications, 1995. Available online at <http://www.lib.rochester.edu/camelot/teams/tmsmenu.htm> (13 April 2011).

King Horn

McKnight, George H., ed. *King Horn, Floris and Blauncheflur, The Assumption of our Lady*. EETS OS 14. London: Oxford University Press, 1901; reprinted 1990.

The King of Tars

Perryman, Judith, ed. *The King of Tars*. Middle English Texts 12. Heidelberg: Carl Winter Universitätsverlag, 1980.

Lai le Freine

Wattie, Margaret, ed. 'The Middle English *Lai le Freine*'. *Smith College Studies in Modern Languages* 10.3 (1929): i–xxii, 1–27.

Lancelot of the Laik

Lupack, Alan, ed. *Lancelot of the Laik and Sir Tristrem*. Kalamazoo, MI: Medieval Institute Publications, 1994. Available online at <http://www.lib.rochester.edu/camelot/teams/tmsmenu.htm> (13 April 2011).

The Laud Troy-Book

Wülfing, J. Ernst, ed. *The Laud Troy Book: A Romance of about 1400 A.D.* Parts 1 and 2. London: Kegan Paul, 1902, 1903.

Libeaus Desconus

Mills, Maldwyn, ed. *Lybeaus Desconus.* EETS 261. London: Oxford University Press, 1969.

The Lyfe of Alisaunder

Smithers, G. V., ed. *Kyng Alisaunder.* 2 vols. EETS 227, 237. London: Oxford University Press, 1952, 1957.

Le Morte Arthur (stanzaic)

Hissiger, P. F., ed. *Le Morte Arthur: A Critical Edition.* The Hague: Mouton, 1975.

Morte Arthure (alliterative)

Krishna, Valerie, ed. *The Alliterative Morte Arthure: A Critical Edition.* New York: Franklin, 1976.

Octavian (northern version)

McSparran, Frances, ed. *Octovian.* EETS 289. London: Oxford University Press, 1986.

Octavian (southern version)

McSparran, Frances, ed. *Octovian Imperator.* Middle English Texts 11. Heidelberg: Carl Winter, 1979.

Otuel a Knight

Herrtage, Sidney J. H., ed. *The Taill of Rauf Coilyear with the Fragments of Roland and Vernagu and Otuel.* EETS ES 39. London: Trübner, 1882.

Otuel and Roland

O'Sullivan, Mary Isabelle, ed. *Firumbras and Otuel and Roland.* EETS OS 198. London: Oxford University Press, 1935; reprinted 1987.

Partonope of Blois

Bödtker, A. Trampe, ed. *The Middle-English Versions of Partonope of Blois.* EETS ES 109. London: Kegan Paul, Trench, Trübner, 1912.

Reinbrun

Zupitza, Julius, ed. *The Romance of Guy of Warwick.* EETS ES 42, 49, 59. London: Oxford University Press, 1883- 91; reprinted as one volume 1966.

Richard Coer de Lyon

Brunner, Karl, ed. *Der Mittelenglische Versroman über Richard Löwenherz.* Wiener Beiträge zur englischen Philologie 42. Viena and Leipzig: Wilhelm Braumüller, 1913.

Roberd of Cisyle

Foster, Edward E., ed. *Amis and Amiloun, Robert of Cisyle, and Sir Amadace.* Kalamazoo, MI: Medieval Institute Publications, 1997. Available online at <http://www.lib.rochester.edu/camelot/teams/tmsmenu.htm> (13 April 2011).

Roland and Vernagu

Herrtage, Sidney J. H., ed. *The Taill of Rauf Coilyear with the Fragments of Roland and Vernagu and Otuel.* EETS ES 39. London: Trübner, 1882.

Bibliography

The Romauns of Partenay (Lusignan)

Skeat, Walter W., ed. *The Romans of Partenay or of Lusignen: Otherwise Known as The Tale of Melusine.* EETS os 22. London: Trübner, 1866; reprinted 1987.

Scottish Troy Fragments

Horstmann, C., ed. *Barbour's des schottischen Nationaldichters Legendensammlung nebst den Fragmenten seines Trojanerkrieges.* 2 vols. Heilbronn: Henninger, 1881, 1882.

The Seege of Troye

Barnicle, Mary Elizabeth, ed. *The Seege of Batayle of Troye.* EETS os 172. London: Oxford University Press, 1927.

The Sege of Melayne

Lupack, Alan, ed. *Three Middle English Charlemagne Romances.* Kalamazoo, MI: Medieval Institute Publications, 1990. Available online at <http://www.lib.rochester.edu/camelot/teams/tmsmenu.htm> (13 April 2011).

The Siege of Jerusalem

Hanna, Ralph, and David Lawton, eds. *The Siege of Jerusalem.* EETS 320. Oxford: Oxford University Press, 2003.

Sir Amadace

Foster, Edward E., ed. *Amis and Amiloun, Robert of Cisyle, and Sir Amadace.* Kalamazoo, MI: Medieval Institute Publications, 1997. Available online at <http://www.lib.rochester.edu/camelot/teams/tmsmenu.htm> (13 April 2011).

Sir Cleges

Treichel, A. 'Sir Cleges: Eine mittelenglische Romanze'. *Englische Studien* 22 (1896): 345–89.

Sir Degare

Schleich, Gustav, ed. *Sir Degarre.* Englische Textbibliothek 19. Heidelberg: Carl Winter, 1929.

Sir Degrevant

Casson, L. F., ed. *The Romance of Sir Degrevant.* EETS os 221. London: Oxford University Press, 1949; reprinted 1970.

Sir Eglamour of Artois

Richardson, Frances E., ed. *Sir Eglamour of Artois.* EETS 256. London: Oxford University Press, 1965.

Sir Firumbras (Ashmole)

Herrtage, Sidney J., ed. *The English Charlemagne Romances Part I: Sir Ferumbras.* EETS es 34. London: Oxford University Press, 1879 reprinted 1966.

Sir Firumbras (Fillingham)

O'Sullivan, Mary Isabelle, ed. *Firumbras and Otuel and Roland.* EETS os 198. London: Oxford University Press, 1935; reprinted 1987.

Sir Gawain and the Green Knight

Tolkien, J. R. R., and E. V. Gordon, eds. *Sir Gawain and the Green Knight.* 2nd edn. Oxford: Clarendon Press, 1967.

Sir Gowther

Breul, Karl, ed. *Sir Gowther: Eine englische Romanze aus dem XV. Jahrhundert.* Oppeln: E. Franck, 1886.

Sir Isumbras

Schleich, Gustav, ed. *Sir Ysumbras: Eine englische Romanze des 14. Jahrhunderts.* Berlin: Mayer und Müller, 1901.

Sir Landeval

Kittredge, George Lyman, ed. 'Launfal (Rawlinson Version)'. *American Journal of Philology* 10.1 (1889): 1–33.

Sir Launfal

Chestre, Thomas. *Sir Launfal*, ed. A. J. Bliss. London: Thomas Nelson, 1960.

Sir Orfeo

Bliss, A. J., ed. *Sir Orfeo.* 2nd edn. Oxford: Clarendon Press, 1966.

Sir Perceval of Galles

Braswell, Mary Flowers, ed. *Sir Perceval of Galles and Ywain and Gawain.* Kalamazoo, MI: Medieval Institute Publications, 1995. Available online at <http://www.lib.rochester.edu/camelot/teams/tmsmenu.htm> (13 April 2011).

Sir Torrent of Portyngale

Adam, E., ed. *Torrent of Portyngale.* EETS ES 51. London: Trübner, 1887; reprinted 1973.

Sir Triamour

Hudson, Harriet, ed. *Four Middle English Romances.* Kalamazoo, MI: Medieval Institute Publications, 1997; 2nd edn 2006. Available online at <http://www.lib.rochester.edu/camelot/teams/tmsmenu.htm> (13 April 2011).

Sir Tristrem

Lupack, Alan, ed. *Lancelot of the Laik and Sir Tristrem.* Kalamazoo, MI: Medieval Institute Publications, 1994. Available online at <http://www.lib.rochester.edu/camelot/teams/tmsmenu.htm> (13 April 2011).

The Song of Roland

Herrtage, Sidney J., ed. *The Sege of Melayne and The Romance of Duke Rowland and Sir Otuell of Spayne.* EETS ES 35. London: Trübner, 1880.

The Sowdon of Babylon

Lupack, Alan, ed. *Three Middle English Charlemagne Romances.* Kalamazoo, MI: Medieval Institute Publications, 1990. Available online at <http://www.lib.rochester.edu/camelot/teams/tmsmenu.htm> (13 April 2011).

The Squyr of Lowe Degre

Kooper, Erik, ed. *Sentimental and Humorous Romances.* Kalamazoo, MI: Medieval Institute Publications, 2006. Available online at <http://www.lib.rochester.edu/camelot/teams/tmsmenu.htm> (13 April 2011).

Bibliography

Syre Gawene and the Carle of Carelyle

Hahn, Thomas, ed. *Sir Gawain: Eleven Romances and Tales*. Kalamazoo, MI: Medieval Institute Publications, 1995. Available online at <http://www.lib.rochester.edu/camelot/teams/tmsmenu.htm> (13 April 2011).

The Taill of Rauf Coilyear

Herrtage, Sidney J. H., ed. *The Taill of Rauf Coilyear with the Fragments of Roland and Vernagu and Otuel*. EETS ES 39. London: Trübner, 1882.

Titus and Vespasian

Herbert, J. A., ed. *Titus and Vespasian or The Destruction of Jerusalem*. Roxburghe Club 146. London, 1905.

The Tournament of Tottenham

Kooper, Erik, ed. *Sentimental and Humorous Romances*. Kalamazoo, MI: Medieval Institute Publications, 2006. Available online at <http://www.lib.rochester.edu/camelot/teams/tmsmenu.htm> (13 April 2011).

The Turke and Gowin

Hahn, Thomas, ed. *Sir Gawain: Eleven Romances and Tales*. Kalamazoo, MI: Medieval Institute Publications, 1995. Available online at <http://www.lib.rochester.edu/camelot/teams/tmsmenu.htm> (13 April 2011).

The Weddynge of Sir Gawen and Dame Ragnell

Hahn, Thomas, ed. *Sir Gawain: Eleven Romances and Tales*. Kalamazoo, MI: Medieval Institute Publications, 1995. Available online at <http://www.lib.rochester.edu/camelot/teams/tmsmenu.htm> (13 April 2011).

William of Palerne

Bunt, G. H. V., ed. *William of Palerne: An Alliterative Romance*. Groningen: Bouma's Boekhuis, 1985.

Ywain and Gawain

Friedman, Albert B., and Norman T. Harrington, eds. *Ywain and Gawain*. EETS 254. London: Oxford University Press, 1964.

Other Primary Sources

Adam de la Halle, *Le Jeu de Robin et Marion*, ed. and trans. Shira I. Schwam-Baird. New York: Garland Publishing, 1994.

Andrew, Malcolm, and Ronald Waldron, eds. *The Poems of the Pearl Manuscript: Pearl, Cleanness, Patience, Sir Gawain and the Green Knight*. 2nd edn. Exeter: University of Exeter Press, 1987.

Anglés, Higinio, ed. *La Música de las Cantigas de Santa María des Rey Alfonso el Sabio: Facsímil, Transcripción y Estudio Crítico*. 2 vols. Barcelona: Diputación Provincial de Barcelona, 1943.

Aubry, Pierre, ed. *Cent motets du XIIIe siècle*. New York: Broude Brothers, 1964 [1908].

Blodgett, E. D., ed. and trans. *The Romance of Flamenca*. New York: Garland Publishing, 1995.

Boor, Helmut de, ed. *Das Nibelungenlied*. Wiesbaden: F. A. Brockhaus, 1979.

Bourdillon, F. W., ed. *Aucassin et Nicolete.* Manchester: Manchester University Press, 1970.

Brewer, D. S., and A. E. B. Owen, eds. *The Thornton Manuscript (Lincoln Cathedral MS.91).* London: Scolar Press, 1975.

Buffum, D. L., ed. *Le Roman de la Violette ou de Gerart de Nevers.* Paris: SATF, 1928.

Cloetta, Wilhelm, ed. *Les Deux Rédactions en vers du Moniage Guillaume: chansons de geste du XIIe siècle.* 2 vols. Paris: Firmin-Didot, 1906.

Davison, Archibald T., and Willi Apel. *Historical Anthology of Music: Oriental, Medieval and Renaissance Music.* Rev. edn. Cambridge, MA: Harvard University Press, 1977.

Dickson, Thomas, *et al.*, eds. *Compota Thesauriorum Regum Scotorum.* 13 vols. Edinburgh: HM General Register House/Her Majesty's Stationery Office, 1877–1978.

Dobson, E. J., and F. Ll. Harrison, eds. *Medieval English Songs.* London: Faber & Faber, 1979.

Geoffrey of Vinsauf. *Documentum de modo et arte dictandi et versificandi*, trans. Roger P. Parr. Milwaukee, WI: Marquette University Press, 1968.

—— *Poetria nova of Geoffrey of Vinsauf*, trans. Margaret F. Nims. Toronto: Pontifical Institute of Mediaeval Studies, 1967.

Gottfried von Strassburg. *Tristan*, ed. Rüdiger Krohn. 3 vols. Stuttgart: Reclam, 1980.

——.*Tristan*, trans. A. T. Hatto. Harmondsworth: Penguin, 1960.

Greene, Richard Leighton, ed. *The Early English Carols.* 2nd edn. Oxford: Clarendon Press, 1977.

Hanna, Ralph, ed. *Speculum vitae: A Reading Edition.* 2 vols. EETS 331, 332. Oxford: Oxford University Press, 2008.

Heldris de Cornuälle. *Silence: A Thirteenth-Century French Romance*, ed. and trans. Sarah Roche-Mahdi. East Lansing, MI: Colleagues Press, 1992.

Ingram, R. W., ed. *REED: Coventry.* Toronto: University of Toronto Press, 1981.

Kane, George, ed. *Piers Plowman: The A Version.* London: Athlone Press/ Berkeley: University of California Press, 1988.

Kimmel, A. S., ed. *A Critical Edition of the Old Provençal Epic Daurel et Beton.* Chapel Hill: University of North Carolina Press, 1971.

Liber Usualis. Tournai and New York: Desclée, 1961.

Marie de France. *The Lais of Marie de France*, trans. Robert Hanning and Joan Ferrante. Durham, NC: Labyrinth Press, 1982.

—— *Les Lais de Marie de France,* ed. Jean Rychner. Paris: Honoré Champion, 1983.

Panayotova, Stella, ed. *The Macclesfield Psalter.* New York: Thames & Hudson, 2008.

Pearsall, Derek, and I. C. Cunningham, eds. *The Auchinleck Manuscript: National Library of Scotland Advocates' MS. 19.2.1.* London: Scolar Press, 1977.

Pope, Mildred, ed. *The Romance of Horn by Thomas.* 2 vols. ANTS IX–X, XII–XIII. Oxford: Basil Blackwell, 1955–1964.

Renart, Jean. *Galeran de Bretagne: roman du XIIIe siècle*, ed. Lucien Foulet. Paris: Champion, 1975.

Robert Mannyng of Brunne. *The Chronicle*, ed. Idelle Sullens. Medieval and Renaissance Texts and Studies 153. Binghamton, NY: Center for Medieval and Early Renaissance Studies, 1996.

Roque, Mario, ed. *Aucassin et Nicolette.* Paris: Honoré Champion, 1982.

Rosenberg, Samuel N., and Hans Tischler, ed. *Chanter m'estuet: Songs of the Trouvères.* London: Faber Music, 1981.

Ruiz, Juan. *Libro de Buen Amor*, ed. Raymond S. Willis. Princeton, NJ: Princeton University Press, 1972.

Russell, George, and George Kane, eds. *Piers Plowman: The C Version*. Berkeley: University of California Press, 1997.

Stevens, Martin, and A. C. Cawley, eds. *The Towneley Plays*. 2 vols. EETS ss 13, 14. Oxford: Oxford University Press, 1994.

Stimming, Albert, ed. *Der festländische Bueve de Hantone*. 3 vols. Dresden: M. Niemeyer, 1911–20.

Wailly, Natalis de, ed. *Récits d'un ménestrel de Reims au treizième siècle*. Paris: Librairie Renouard, 1876.

Wasson, John M., ed. *REED: Devon*. Toronto: University of Toronto Press, 1986.

Wolfram von Eschenbach. *Titurel*, ed. Helmut Brackert and Stephan Fuchs-Jolie. Berlin: Walter de Gruyter, 2002.

Wright, Thomas, ed. *St Brandan: A Medieval Legend of the Sea*. London: T. Richards, 1844.

Zeydel, Edwin H., ed. and trans. *Ruodlieb: The Earliest Courtly Novel (after 1050)*. University of North Carolina Studies in the Germanic Languages and Literatures 23. Chapel Hill: University of North Carolina Press, 1959.

Secondary Sources

Alburger, Mary Anne. 'The "Fydill in Fist": Bowed String Instruments from the *Mary Rose*.' *The Galpin Society Journal* 53 (2000): 12–24.

Amodio, Mark, ed. *Oral Poetics in Middle English Poetry*. New York: Garland Publishing, 1994.

Arlt, Wolf. 'Musik und Text: Verstellte Perspektiven einer Grundlageneinheit'. *Musica* 37 (1983): 497–503.

Attridge, Derek. *The Rhythms of English Poetry*. London: Longman, 1982.

Aubrey, Elizabeth. 'Non-Liturgical Monophony: Introduction'. In *A Performer's Guide to Medieval Music*, ed. Ross W. Duffin, pp. 105–14. Bloomington: Indiana University Press, 2000.

Bachmann, Werner. *The Origins of Bowing and the Development of Bowed Instrument up to the Thirteenth Century*. London: Oxford University Press, 1969.

Baines, Anthony. 'Fifteenth-Century Instruments in Tinctoris's *De Inventione et Usu Musicae*'. *The Galpin Society Journal* 3 (1950): 19–26.

Bec, Pierre. *Vièles ou violes? Variations philologiques et musicales autour des instruments à archet du moyen âge*. Paris: Editions Klincksieck, 1992.

Bernhard, B. 'Recherches sur l'histoire de la corporation des ménétriers ou joueurs d'instruments de la ville de Paris'. *BEC* 3 (1841–2): 377–404.

Bertau, Karl H., and Rudolf Stephan. 'Zum sanglichen Vortrag mittelhochdeutscher strophischer Epen'. *Zeitschrift für deutsches Altertum und deutsche Literatur* 87 (1957): 253–70.

Blades, James. *Percussion Instruments and their History*. New York: Frederick A. Praeger, 1970.

Blades, James, and Jeremy Montagu. *Early Percussion Instruments from the Middle Ages to the Baroque*. Early Music Series 2. London: Oxford University Press, 1976.

Blanchfield, Lynne. 'The Romances in MS Ashmole 61: An Idiosyncratic Scribe'. In *Romance in Medieval England*, ed. Maldwyn Mills, Jennifer Fellows, and Carol M. Meale, pp. 65–88. Cambridge: D. S. Brewer, 1991.

Boulton, Maureen. *The Song in the Story: Lyric Insertions in French Narrative Fiction, 1200–1400*. Philadelphia: University of Pennsylvania Press, 1993.

Bowles, Edmund. 'Haut and Bas: The Groupings of Musical Instruments in the Middle Ages' (1954). In *Instruments and their Music in the Middle Ages*, ed. Timothy J. McGee, pp. 3–28. Farnham: Ashgate, 2009.

Bradbury, Nancy Mason. *Writing Aloud: Storytelling in Late Medieval England*. Urbana: University of Illinois Press, 1998.

Bracken, Paul. '*Halt sunt li Pui*: Toward a Performance of the *Chanson de Roland*'. *Nottingham Medieval Studies* 47 (2003): 73–106.

Brown, Howard Mayer. 'The Trecento Fiddle and its Bridges' (1989). In *Instruments and their Music in the Middle Ages*, ed. Timothy J. McGee, pp. 293–313. Farnham: Ashgate, 2009.

—— 'The Trecento Harp'. In *Studies in the Performance of Late Mediaeval Music*, ed. Stanley Boorman, pp. 35–73. Cambridge: Cambridge University Press, 1983.

Bullock-Davies, Constance. *Menestrellorum Multitudo: Minstrels at a Royal Feast*. Cardiff: University of Wales Press, 1978.

—— *Register of Royal and Baronial Domestic Minstrels, 1272–1327*. Woodbridge: Boydell Press, 1986.

Butterfield, Ardis. *Poetry and Music in Medieval France: From Jean Renart to Guillaume de Machaut*. Cambridge: Cambridge University Press, 2002.

Cable, Thomas. *The Meter and Melody of Beowulf*. Urbana: University of Illinois Press, 1974.

Carter, Henry Holland. *A Dictionary of Middle English Musical Terms*. Bloomington: Indiana University Press, 1968.

Chambers, E. K. *The Mediaeval Stage*. 2 vols. Oxford: Clarendon Press, 1903.

Chesnutt, Michael. 'Minstrel Poetry in an English Manuscript of the Sixteenth Century: Richard Sheale and MS. Ashmole 48'. In *The Entertainer in Medieval and Traditional Culture: A Symposium*, ed. Flemming G. Andersen, Thomas Pettitt and Reinhold Schröder, pp. 73–100. Odense: Odense University Press, 1997.

—— 'Minstrel Reciters and the Enigma of the Middle English Romance'. *Culture and History* 2 (1987): 48–67.

Coelho, Victor. 'Raffaello Cavalcanti's Lute Book (1590) and the Ideal of Singing and Playing'. In *Le Concert des voix et des instruments à la Renaissance*, ed. Jean-Michel Vaccaro, pp. 423–42. Paris: Centre National de la Recherche Scientifique, 1995.

Coldwell, Maria V. '*Jougleresses* and *Trobairitz*: Secular Musicians in Medieval France'. In *Women Making Music: The Western Art Tradition, 1150–1950*, ed. Jane Bowers and Judith Tick, pp. 39–61. Urbana: University of Illinois Press, 1986.

Coleman, Joyce. *Public Reading and the Reading Public in Late Medieval England and France*. Cambridge: Cambridge University Press, 1996.

Cook, Ron. 'The Presence and Use of Brays on the Gut-Strung Harp through the 17th Century: A Survey and Consideration of the Evidence'. *Historical Harp Society Bulletin* (1998): 2–39.

Cooke, William G. '*The Tournament of Tottenham*: An Alliterative Poem and an Exeter Performance'. *Records of Early English Drama* 11.2 (1986): 2–3.

Cooper, Helen. *The English Romance in Time: Transforming Motifs from Geoffrey of Monmouth to the Death of Shakespeare*. Oxford: Oxford University Press, 2004.

Crane, Frederick. *Extant Medieval Musical Instruments: A Provisional Catalogue by Types.* Iowa City: University of Iowa Press, 1972.

Cummins, Fred. 'Interval Timing in Spoken Lists of Words'. *Music Perception: An Interdisciplinary Journal* 22.3 (2005): 497–508.

Cureton, Richard D. ' A Disciplinary Map for Verse Study'. *Versification* 1 (1997). <http://www.arsversificandi.net/backissues/vol1/essays/cureton.html> (8 January 2011).

Doane, Alger Nicolaus, and Carol Braun Pasternack, eds. *Vox intexta: Orality and Textuality in the Middle Ages.* Madison: University of Wisconsin Press, 1991.

Dobozy, Maria. *Re-Membering the Present: The Medieval German Poet-Minstrel in Cultural Context.* Turnhout: Brepols, 2005.

Duffell, Martin. *A New History of English Metre.* London: Modern Humanities Research Association and Maney Publishing, 2008.

Duggan, Hoyt N. 'Extended A-Verses in Middle English Alliterative Poetry'. *Parergon* 18.1 (2000): 53–76.

—— 'The Shape of the B-Verse in Middle English Alliterative Poetry'. *Speculum* 61.3 (1986): 564–92.

Duggan, Joseph. 'Oral Performance of Romance in Medieval France'. In *Continuations: Essays on Medieval French Literature and Language in Honor of John L. Grigsby*, ed. Norris J. Lacy and Gloria Torrini-Roblin, pp. 51–61. Birmingham, AL: Summa Publications, 1989.

Dutka, JoAnna. *Music in the English Mystery Plays.* Kalamazoo, MI: Medieval Institute Publications, 1980.

Edwards, J. Michele. 'Women in Music to ca. 1450'. In *Women and Music: A History*, ed. Karin Pendle, pp. 8–28. Bloomington: Indiana University Press, 1991.

Erbes, Roslyn Rensch. 'The Development of the Medieval Harp: A Re-Examination of the Evidence of the Utrecht Psalter and its Progeny'. *Gesta* 11.2 (1972): 27–36.

Evans, Murray J. *Rereading Middle English Romance: Manuscript Layout, Decoration, and the Rhetoric of Composite Structure* (Montreal: McGill-Queen's University Press, 1995).

Faral, Edmond, ed. *Les Arts poétiques du XIIe et du XIIIe siècle: recherches et documents sur la technique littéraire du moyen âge.* Paris: Honoré Champion, 1962.

Fassler, Margot E. 'Accent, Meter, and Rhythm in Medieval Treatises "De rithmis"'. *The Journal of Musicology* 5.2 (1987): 164–90

Fellows, Jennifer. 'Editing Middle English Romances'. In *Romance in Medieval England*, ed. Maldwyn Mills, Jennifer Fellows, and Carol Meale, pp. 5–16. Cambridge: D. S. Brewer, 1991.

Fellows, Jennifer, and Ivana Djordjevic, eds, *Sir Bevis of Hampton in Literary Tradition.* Cambridge: D. S. Brewer, 2008.

Finlay, Ian F. 'Musical Instruments in Gotfrid von Strassburg's "Tristan und Isolde"'. *Galpin Society Journal* 5 (1952): 39–43.

Foley, John Miles. *The Singer of Tales in Performance.* Bloomington: Indiana University Press, 1995.

Fowler, David C. *A Literary History of the Popular Ballad.* Durham, NC: Duke University Press, 1968.

Fuller, Sarah. 'Discant and the Theory of Fifthing'. *Acta Musicologica* 50 (1978): 241–75.

Furness, Clifton Joseph. 'The Interpretation and Probable Derivation of the Musical Notation in the "Aucassin et Nicolette" MS'. *The Modern Language Review* 24.2 (1929): 143–52.

Gasparov, M. L. *A History of European Versification*. Trans. G. S. Smith and Marina Tarlinskaja. Oxford: Clarendon Press, 1996.

Giacchetti, André, ed. *Roman arthurien du moyen âge tardif*. Publications de l'Université de Rouen 142. Rouen, Université de Rouen, 1989.

Glowka, Arthur. 'The Function of Meter According to Ancient and Medieval Theory'. *Allegorica* 7 (1982): 100–9.

Guddat-Figge, Gisela. *Catalogue of Manuscripts Containing Middle English Romances*. Münchener Universitätschriften 4. Munich: Wilhelm Fink, 1976.

Guthrie, Steven. 'Meter and Performance in Machaut and Chaucer'. In *The Union of Words and Music in Medieval Poetry*, ed. Rebecca A. Baltzer, Thomas Cable, and James I. Wimsatt, pp. 72–100. Austin: University of Texas Press, 1991.

Hanham, Alison. 'The Musical Studies of a Fifteenth-Century Wool Merchant'. *The Review of English Studies*, New Series 8 (1957): 270–4.

Hanna, Ralph. 'Reconsidering the Auchinleck Manuscript'. In *New Directions in Later Medieval Manuscript Studies: Essays from the 1998 Harvard Conference*, ed. Derek Pearsall, pp. 91–102. Woodbridge: York Medieval Press, 2000.

Hayes, Bruce P., and Margaret MacEachern. 'Quatrain Form in English Folk Verse'. *Language* 74.3 (1998): 473–507.

Haynes, Bruce. *The End of Early Music: A Period Performer's History of Music for the Twenty-First Century*. Oxford: Oxford University Press, 2007.

Hindley, Alan, Frederick W. Langley, and Brian J. Levy. *Old French–English Dictionary*. Cambridge: Cambridge University Press, 2000.

Hoppin, Richard H. *Medieval Music*. New York: Norton, 1978.

Hughes, Andrew. *Style and Symbol: Medieval Music, 800–1453*. Ottawa: Institute of Mediaeval Music, 1989.

Ivanoff, Vladimir, 'An Invitation to the Fifteenth-Century Plectrum Lute: The Pesaro Manuscript'. In *Performance on Lute, Guitar, and Vihuela: Historical Practice and Modern Interpretation*, ed. Victor Anand Coelho, pp. 1–15. Cambridge: Cambridge University Press, 1997.

James, Kevin. 'The Five-Stringed Fiddle in Medieval Europe'. *Continuo* 5.8 (1982): 6–12.

Jammers, Ewald. *Ausgewälte Melodien des Minnesangs*. Tübingen: Max Niemeyer Verlag, 1963.

Jefferson, Judith, and Ad Putter, eds. *Approaches to the Metres of Alliterative Verse*. Leeds Texts and Monographs New Series 17. Leeds: University of Leeds School of English, 2009.

Jeffries, Helen Marsh. 'Job Descriptions, Nepotism, and Part-Time Work: The Minstrels and Trumpeters of the Court of Edward IV of England (1461–83)'. *Plainsong and Medieval Music* 12.2 (2003): 165–77.

Johnston, R. C. 'On Scanning Anglo-Norman Verse'. *Anglo-Norman Studies* 5 (1983): 153–64.

Kadar, Judy. 'Some Practical Hints for Playing Fourteenth and Fifteenth Century Music'. In *Historische Harfen: Beiträge zur Theorie und Praxis historischer Harfen*, pp. 120–32. Dornach: Eigenverlag der Musik-Akademie der Stadt Basel, 1991.

Kelly, Douglas. *Medieval French Romance*. New York: Twayne Publishers, 1993.

Kennedy, Ruth. 'New Theories of Constraint in the Metricality of the Strong-Stress Long Line as Applied to the Rhymed Corpus of Late Middle English Alliterative Verse'. In *Métriques du moyen age et de la renaissance: actes du colloque international du Centre d'Études Métriques*, ed. Dominique Billy. Paris: L'Harmattan, 1999. pp. 131–44.

Kramer, Jonathan D. *The Time of Music*. New York: Schirmer, 1988.

Lawrence, Marilyn. 'Minstrel Disguise in Medieval French Narrative: Identity, Performance, Authorship'. PhD diss., New York University, 2001.

—— 'Oral Performance in *Ysaÿe le Triste*'. In *Performing Medieval Narrative*, ed. Evelyn Birge Vitz, Nancy Freeman Regalado, and Marilyn Lawrence, pp. 89–102. Cambridge: D. S. Brewer, 2005.

Leech-Wilkinson, Daniel. *The Modern Invention of Medieval Music: Scholarship, Ideology, Performance*. Cambridge: Cambridge University Press, 2002.

Legge, M. Dominica. *Anglo-Norman Literature and its Background*. Oxford: Clarendon Press, 1963.

Lerdahl, Fred, and Ray Jackendoff. *A Generative Theory of Tonal Music*. Cambridge, MA: MIT Press, 1983.

Liu, Yin. 'Middle English Romance as Prototype Genre'. *The Chaucer Review* 40.4 (2006): 335–53.

Liuzza, Roy Michael. '*Sir Orfeo*: Sources, Traditions, and the Poetics of Performance'. *Journal of Medieval and Renaissance Studies* 21 (1991): 169–84.

Looper, Jennifer. 'L'épisode de la Harpe et de la Rote dans la légende de Tristan: Étude sur le symbolisme de deux instruments de musique', *Cahiers de civilisation médiévale* 38.4 (1995): 345–52.

Lord, Albert. *The Singer of Tales*. Cambridge, MA: Harvard University Press, 1960.

Machan, Tim William. 'Editing, Orality, and Late Middle English Texts'. In *Vox intexta: Orality and Textuality in the Middle Ages*, ed. Alger Nicolaus Doane and Carol Braun Pasternack, pp. 229–45. Madison: University of Wisconsin Press, 1991.

Macklin, Christopher. 'Approaches to the Use of Iconography in Historical Reconstruction, and the Curious Case of Renaissance Welsh Harp Technique'. *Early Music* 35.2 (2007): 213–23.

Maw, David. 'Accent and Metre in Later Old French Verse: The Case of the Polyphonic *Rondel*'. *Medium Aevum* 75.1 (2006): 46–83.

McDonald, Nicola, ed. *Pulp Fictions of Medieval England: Essays in Popular Romance*. Manchester: Manchester University Press, 2004.

McGee, Timothy J. *The Ceremonial Musicians of Late Medieval Florence*. Bloomington: Indiana University Press, 2009.

—— *Improvisation in the Arts*. Kalamazoo, MI: Medieval Institute Publications, 2003.

—— 'The Medieval Fiddle: Tuning Technique and Repertory'. In *Instruments, Ensembles, and Repertory, 1300–1600: Essays in Honor of Keith Polk*, ed. Timothy McGee and Stewart Carter. Forthcoming.

—— *The Sound of Medieval Song: Ornamentation and Vocal Style according to the Treatises*. Oxford: Clarendon Press, 1998.

McGillivray, Murray. *Memorization in the Transmission of the Middle English Romances*. New York: Garland Publishing, 1990.

Mehl, Dieter. *The Middle English Romances of the Thirteenth and Fourteenth Centuries*. London: Routledge & Kegan Paul, 1968.

Menegaldo, Silvère. *Le Jongleur dans la littérature narrative des XIIe et XIIIe siècles: du personnage au masque*. Paris: Honoré Champion, 2005.

Meyer, Leonard B. *Emotion and Meaning in Music*. Chicago: University of Chicago Press, 1956.

—— *Explaining Music: Essays and Explorations*. Berkeley: University of California Press, 1973.

Montagu, Jeremy. 'Musical Instruments in the Macclesfield Psalter'. *Early Music* 34.2 (2006): 189–204.

Nicolaisen, W. F. H., ed. *Oral Tradition in the Middle Ages*. Medieval and Renaissance Texts and Studies 112. Binghamton, NY: Medieval and Renaissance Texts and Studies, 1995.

O'Brien, Pat. 'Observations on the (Re)creation of Techniques for Historical Harps and their Potential Consequences'. In *Historische Harfen: Beiträge zur Theorie und Praxis historischer Harfen*, ed. Heidrun Rosenzweig, pp. 101–19. Basel: Musik-Akademie, 1991.

Olson, Clair. 'The Minstrels at the Court of Edward III'. *PMLA* 56.3 (1941): 601–12.

Page, Christopher. 'An Aspect of Medieval Fiddle Construction'. *Early Music* 2 (1974): 166–7.

—— 'Fourteenth-Century Instruments and Tunings: A Treatise by Jean Vaillant? (Berkeley, MS 744)'. *The Galpin Society Journal* 33 (1980): 17–35.

—— 'Jerome of Moravia on the *Rubeba* and *Viella*'. *The Galpin Society Journal* 32 (1979): 77–98.

—— 'Johannes de Grocheio on Secular Music: A Corrected Text and a New Translation'. *Plainsong and Medieval Music* 2.1 (1993): 17–41.

—— ed. and trans. *The Summa Musice: A Thirteenth-Century Manual for Singers*. Cambridge: Cambridge University Press, 1991.

—— 'Le Troisième Accord pour vièle de Jérôme de Moravie: Jongleurs et "anciens Pères de France"'. In *Jérôme de Moravie: un théoricien de la musique dans le milieu intellectuel parisien du XIIIe siècle*, ed. Michel Huglo and Marcel Peres, pp. 83–96. Paris: Editions Créaphis, 1992.

—— *Voices and Instruments of the Middle Ages: Instrumental Practice and Songs in France, 1100–1300*. London: Dent, 1987.

Parrish, Carl. *The Notation of Medieval Music*. New York: Norton, 1959; reprinted 1978.

Parry, Milman. *The Making of Homeric Verse: The Collected Papers of Milman Parry*, ed. Adam Parry. Oxford: Clarendon Press, 1982.

Pearsall, Derek. 'The Development of the Middle English Romance', *Mediaeval Studies* 27 (1965): 91–116.

Pensom, Roger. *Accent and Metre in French: A Theory of the Relation between Linguistic Accent and Metrical Practice in French, 1100–1900*. Bern: Peter Lang, 1998.

—— 'Performing the Medieval Lyric: A Metrical-Accentual Approach'. *Performance Practice Review* 10.2 (1997): 212–23.

Percy, Thomas. *Reliques of Ancient English Poetry*. 3 vols. Dublin: P. Wilson and E. Watts, 1766.

Popławska, Dorota, and Tadeusz Czechak. 'The Tuning and Playing of a Medieval Gittern and Fiddle from Elblag, Poland'. *The Consort* 58 (2002): 3–12.

Purdie, Rhiannon. *Anglicising Romance: Tail-Rhyme and Genre in Medieval English Literature*. Cambridge: D. S. Brewer, 2008.

Purdie, Rhiannon, and Michael Cichon, eds. *Medieval Romance, Medieval Contexts*. Cambridge: D. S. Brewer, 2011.

Purser, John. 'Greysteil'. In *Stewart Style, 1513–1542: Essays on the Court of James V.*, ed. Janet Hadley Williams, pp. 142–52. East Linton: Tuckwell Press, 1996.

Putter, Ad. 'Metre and the Editing of Middle English Verse: Prospects for Tail-Rhyme Romance, Alliterative Poetry, and Chaucer'. *Poetica* 71 (2009): 29–47.

Putter, Ad, and Jane Gilbert, eds. *The Spirit of Medieval English Popular Romance*. Harlow: Pearson Education, 2000.

Putter, Ad, Judith Jefferson, and Myra Stokes. *Studies in the Metre of Alliterative Verse*. Medium Aevum Monographs New Series 25. Oxford: Society for the Study of Medieval Languages and Literature, 2007.

Quinn, William A., and Audley S. Hall. *Jongleur: A Modified Theory of Oral Improvisation and its Effects on the Performance and Transmission of Middle English Romance*. Washington, DC: University Press of America, 1982.

Ramey, Lynn Tarte. 'Minstrels and Other Itinerant Performers as Travelers'. In *Trade, Travel, and Exploration in the Middle Ages: An Encyclopedia*, ed. John Block Friedman, Kristen Mossler Figg, *et al.*, pp. 401–2. New York: Garland Publishing, 2000.

Rastall, Richard. 'The Minstrel Court in Medieval England'. *Proceedings of the Leeds Philosophical and Literary Society* 18.1 (1982): 96–105.

—— 'Minstrelsy, Church and Clergy in Medieval England'. *Proceedings of the Royal Musical Association* 97 (1970–71): 83–98.

—— 'The Minstrels of the English Royal Households, 25 Edward I–1 Henry VIII: An Inventory'. *Royal Musical Association Research Chronicle* 4 (1967): 1–41.

—— 'Some English Consort-Groupings of the Late Middle Ages'. *Music & Letters* 55.2 (1974): 179–202.

Reaney, Gilbert. 'Concerning the Origins of the Medieval Lai'. *Music & Letters* 39.4 (1958): 343–46.

Reichl, Karl. 'Comparative Notes on the Performance of Middle English Popular Romance'. *Western Folklore* 62.1 (2003): 63–81.

Remnant, Mary. *English Bowed Instruments from Anglo-Saxon to Tudor Times*. Oxford: Clarendon Press, 1986.

—— 'Musical Instruments in Early English Drama'. In *Material Culture and Medieval Drama*, ed. Clifford Davidson, pp. 141–94. Kalamazoo, MI: Medieval Institute Publications, 1999.

Rensch, Roslyn. *The Harp: Its History, Technique and Repertoire*. New York: Praeger Publishers, 1969.

—— *Harps and Harpists*. Bloomington: Indiana University Press, 1989.

Rice, Joanne A. *Middle English Romance: An Annotated Bibliography, 1955–85*. New York and London: Garland Publishing, 1987.

Ritson, Joseph. *Ancient Songs from the Time of Henry the Third to the Revolution*. London: J. Johnson, 1790.

Rokseth, Yvonne. 'Les Femmes musiciennes du XIIe au XIVe siècle'. *Romania* 61 (1935): 464–80.

Sager, Alexander. *Minne von Mæren: On Wolfram's 'Titurel'*. Transatlantic Studies on Medieval and Early Modern Literature and Culture 2. Göttingen: Vandenhoek and Ruprecht Unipress, 2006.

Salas, Susan Reit de. 'Thumb-Under Technique on Gothic Harps'. In *Historische Harfen: Beiträge zur Theorie und Praxis historischer Harfen*, ed. Heidrun Rosenzweig, pp. 120–32. Dornach: Eigenverlag der Musik-Akademie der Stadt Basel, 1991.

Segerman, E., and D. Abbott. 'Jerome of Moravia and Bridge Curvature in the Medieval Fiddle'. *Fellowship of Makers and Restorers of Historical Instruments Quarterly* 6 (1977): 34–6.

Severs, J. Burke, ed. *A Manual of the Writings in Middle English, 1050–1500, 1: Romances*. New Haven, CT: Connecticut Academy of Arts and Sciences, 1967.

Shire, Helena M. 'Music for "Goddis Glore and the Kingis"'. In *Stewart Style, 1513–1542: Essays on the Court of James V*, ed. Janet Hadley Williams, pp. 118–41. East Linton: Tuckwell Press, 1996.

Shuffelton, George. 'Is There a Minstrel in the House?: Domestic Entertainment in Late Medieval England'. *Philological Quarterly* 87.1–2 (2008): 51–76.

Smith, Douglas Alton. *A History of the Lute from Antiquity to the Renaissance*. Fort Worth, TX: The Lute Society of America, 2002.

Smith, Jeremy. '"The Metre Which Does Not Measure": The Function of Alliteration in Middle English Alliterative Poetry'. In *Approaches to the Metres of Alliterative Verse*, ed. Judith Jefferson and Ad Putter, pp. 11–23. Leeds Texts and Monographs, New Series 17. Leeds: University of Leeds School of English, 2009.

Southworth, John. *The English Medieval Minstrel*. Woodbridge: Boydell Press, 1989.

Spring, Matthew. *The Lute in Britain: A History of the Instrument and its Music*. Oxford Early Music Series. Oxford: Oxford University Press, 2001.

Springfels, Mary. 'The Vielle after 1300'. In *A Performer's Guide to Medieval Music*, ed. Ross W. Duffin, pp. 302–16. Bloomington: Indiana University Press, 2000.

Stevens, John. *Music and Poetry in the Early Tudor Court*. Cambridge: Cambridge University Press, 1961.

—— 'Reflections on the Music of Medieval Narrative Poetry'. In *The Oral Epic: Performance and Music*, ed. Karl Reichl, pp. 233–48. Intercultural Music Studies 12. Berlin: Verlag für Wissenschaft und Bildung, 2000.

—— *Words and Music in the Middle Ages: Song, Narrative, Dance and Drama, 1050–1350*. Cambridge: Cambridge University Press, 1986.

Symes, Carol. *A Common Stage: Theater and Public Life in Medieval Arras*. Ithaca, NY: Cornell University Press, 2007.

Taylor, Andrew. 'Fragmentation, Corruption, and Minstrel Narration: The Question of the Middle English Romances'. *The Yearbook of English Studies* 22 (1992): 38–62.

—— 'Was there a *Song of Roland*?' *Speculum* 76 (2001): 28–65.

—— 'Songs of Praise and Blame and the Repertoire of the *Gestour*'. In *The Entertainer in Medieval and Traditional Culture: A Symposium*, ed. Flemming Andersen, Thomas Pettitt, and Reinhold Schröder, pp. 47–72. Odense: Odense University Press, 1997.

Thompson, John J. *Robert Thornton and the London Thornton Manuscript: British Library MS 31042*. Cambridge: D. S. Brewer, 1987.

Thornton, Barbara, and Lawrence Rosenwald. 'The Voice: Poetics as Technique'. In *A Performer's Guide to Medieval Music*, ed. Ross W. Duffin, pp. 264–92. Bloomington: Indiana University Press, 2000.

Tiella, Marco. 'The Violeta of S. Caterina de' Vigri'. *The Galpin Society Journal* 28 (1975): 60–70.

Tischler, Hans. '"Musica ficta" in the Thirteenth Century'. *Music and Letters* 54.1 (1973): 38–56.

Tsur, Reuven. *Poetic Rhythm: Structure and Performance*. Berne: Peter Lang, 1998.

van Deusen, Nancy. *The Harp and the Soul: Essays in Medieval Music*. Lewiston, NY: Edwin Mellen Press, 1989.

van Schaik, Martin. *The Harp in the Middle Ages: The Symbolism of a Musical Instrument*. Amsterdam: Rodopi Editions, 1992.

Vitz, Evelyn Birge. *Orality and Performance in Early French Romance*. Cambridge: D. S. Brewer, 1999.

Bibliography

Vitz, Evelyn Birge, Nancy Freeman Regalado, and Marilyn Lawrence, eds. *Performing Medieval Narrative*. Cambridge: D. S. Brewer, 2005.

Waldron, Ronald. 'Measured Discourse: The Fourteenth-Century Alliterative Long Line as a Two-Tier System'. In *Approaches to the Metres of Alliterative Verse*, ed. Judith Jefferson and Ad Putter, pp. 235–54. Leeds Texts and Monographs, New Series 17. Leeds: University of Leeds School of English, 2009.

Warton, Thomas. *The History of English Poetry from the Close of the Eleventh to the Commencement of the Eighteenth Century*. 3 vols. London, 1774–81.

Wiggins, Alison, and Rosalind Field. *Guy of Warwick: Icon and Ancestor*. Woodbridge: D. S. Brewer, 2007.

Wilkins, Nigel. 'Music and Poetry at Court: England and France in the Late Middle Ages'. In *English Court Culture in the Later Middle Ages*, ed. V. J. Scattergood and J. W. Sherborne, pp. 183–204. London: Duckworth, 1983.

Wright, Craig. *Music at the Court of Burgundy, 1364–1419: A Documentary History*. Musicological Studies 28. Henryville, PA: Institute of Medieval Music, 1979.

Wright, L. M. 'More on the Meanings of Jongleur and Menestrel'. *Romance Studies: A Journal of the University of Wales* 17 (1990): 7–19.

Wright, Laurence. 'The Role of the Musicians at Court in Twelfth-Century Britain'. *Art and Patronage in the English Romanesque* 8 (1986): 97–106.

Young, Abigail Ann. 'Minstrels and Minstrelsy: Household Retainers or Instrumentalists?'. *Records of Early English Drama* 20.1 (1995): 11–17.

Zaerr, Linda Marie. 'Meter Change as a Relic of Performance in the Middle English Romance *Sir Beves*'. *Quidditas* 21 (2000): 105–26.

—— 'Songs of Love and Love of Songs: Music and Magic in Medieval Romance'. In *Words of Love and Love of Words in the Middle Ages and the Renaissance*, ed. Albrecht Classen, pp. 291–317. Tempe: Arizona Center for Medieval and Renaissance Studies, 2008.

Zaerr, Linda Marie, and Mary Ellen Ryder. 'Psycholinguistic Theory and Modern Performance: Memory as a Key to Variants in Medieval Texts'. *Mosaic* 26.3 (1993): 21–35.

Ziolkowski, Jan. *Nota Bene: Reading Classics and Writing Melodies in the Early Middle Ages*. Publications of the Journal of Medieval Latin 7. Turnhout: Brepols, 2007.

Zumthor, Paul. 'Body and Performance'. In *Materialities of Communication*, ed. Hans Ulrich Gumbrecht and K. Ludwig Pfeiffer, trans. William Whobrey, pp. 217–26. Stanford, CA: Stanford University Press, 1994.

—— 'Intertextualité et mouvance'. *Littérature* 41 (1981): 8–16.

—— 'Les Traditions poétiques'. In *Jeux de mémoire: Aspects de la mnémotechnie médiévale*, ed. Bruno Roy and Paul Zumthor, pp. 11–21. Montréal: Les Presses de l'Université de Montréal, 1985.

—— 'The Vocalization of the Text: The Medieval "Poetic Effect"'. *Viator* 19 (1988): 273–82

Recordings of Middle English Verse Romances

Audio and video recordings are listed by primary reader/reciter/singer.

Baker, Alison, *et al. King Arthur's Death: Selections from the Middle English Stanzaic Morte Arthur and Alliterative Morte Arthure*. CD/Download. Provo, UT: The Chaucer Studio, 2002–7.

Havely, Nicholas R., *et al. Sir Orfeo*. CD. Provo, UT: The Chaucer Studio, 1996.

Hunter, Andy, and William Taylor. *Graysteil* (excerpts with clarsach). CD. New York: Dorian Discovery, 1997.

Mills, Maldwyn. *Horn Childe*. Audiocassette. Provo, UT: The Chaucer Studio, 1990.

Rendall, Thomas, *et al*. *Sir Gawain and the Green Knight*. CD/Download. Provo, UT: The Chaucer Studio, 1990.

Zaerr, Linda Marie. *Music and Medieval Narrative* (includes *The Tournament of Tottenham* with fiddle self-accompaniment) DVD. Provo, UT: The Chaucer Studio, 2011.

Zaerr, Linda Marie, and Joseph A. Baldassarre. *Three Medieval Romances* (includes *The Tournament of Tottenham* with medieval lute). Audiocassette. Boise, ID: Silver Quill, 1992.

Zaerr, Linda Marie, Shira Kammen and Laura Zaerr. *Sir Gawain and the Green Knight* (excerpts with fiddle and harp). DVD and VHS. Provo, UT: TEAMS and The Chaucer Studio, 2002.

Zaerr, Linda Marie, and Laura Zaerr. *Sentimental and Humorous Romances* (includes *The Tournament of Tottenham* and *Floris and Blauncheflur* with gothic harp). CD. Provo, UT: The Chaucer Studio, 2007.

—— *The Weddynge of Sir Gawen and Dame Ragnell* (with gothic harp). DVD and VHS. Provo, UT: TEAMS and The Chaucer Studio, 1999.

Index

Studies in Medieval Romance